HARRY FISCHEL
Pioneer of Jewish Philanthropy

*Forty Years of Struggle for a Principle
and the Years Beyond*

Augmented Edition

HARRY FISCHEL
Pioneer of Jewish Philanthropy

Forty Years of Struggle for a Principle and the Years Beyond

Augmented Edition

Forty Years of Struggle for a Principle (through 1928)
Edited by Rabbi Herbert S. Goldstein

Continuation (1928–1941)
Written by Harry Fischel

Preface to Augmented Edition
By Chief Rabbi Emeritus Shear-Yashuv Cohen
Chairman of the Board of the Harry and Jane Fischel Foundation;
President of Machon Harry Fischel;
Founder of the Ariel United Israel Institutes for Training of Rabbis

Augmented Edition (through 1948 and beyond)
Edited by Rabbi Aaron I. Reichel, Esq.

KTAV Publishing House, Inc.

Jersey City, New Jersey

About the cover photographs:
Top: original building of Yeshiva College in New York. Bottom: original building of Harry Fischel Institute for Research in Jewish Law (Machon Harry Fischel) in Jerusalem. Center: Harry Fischel as he appeared at cornerstone laying ceremony of Yeshiva College in 1927.

About the photograph in the back flap:
The official Jerusalem street sign named for Yisrael Aharon (Harry) Fischel includes a description, in Hebrew, which can be translated as follows: "philanthropist, founded Institute for Talmudic Research in Jerusalem, 5625-5708 (1865-1948)."

Manufactured in the United States of America

KTAV Publishing House, Inc.
888 Newark Avenue
Jersey City, NJ 07306
Tel. (201) 963-9524
Fax. (201) 963-0102
www.ktav.com
bernie@ktav.com

ISBN 978-1-60280-221-6 (pbk.)
ISBN 978-1-60280-222-3 (hard cover)

Library of Congress Cataloging-in-Publication Data

Forty years of struggle for a principle.
  Harry Fischel, pioneer of Jewish philanthropy : forty years of struggle for a principle and the years beyond. -- Augmented ed.
       p. cm.
  Original title: Forty years of struggle for a principle (through 1928), edited by Herbert S. Goldstein; continuation (1928-1941), written by Harry Fischel; augmented edition (through 1948 and beyond), edited by Aaron I. Reichel.
  ISBN 978-1-60280-221-6 (pbk.) -- ISBN 978-1-60280-222-3 (hard cover)
1. Fischel, Harry, 1865-1948. 2. Jewish philanthropists--United States--Biography. I. Fischel, Harry, 1865-1948. II. Goldstein, Herbert S. (Herbert Samuel), 1890-1970. III. Reichel, Aaron I. IV. Title.
  CT275.F558A3 2012
  361.7ʹ4092--dc23
  [B]

Comprehensive Table of Contents

Table of Contents of
Forty Years of Struggle for a Principle

5a

CONTENTS OF CONTINUATION OF BIOGRAPHY OF
FORTY YEARS OF STRUGGLE FOR A PRINCIPLE

ILLUSTRATIONS TO CONTINUATION

Introduction to the Augmented Edition

When Harry Fischel wrote the text that became his biography, *Forty Years of Struggle for a Principle*, he was sixty-three years old and had accomplished more in general, and especially in philanthropy, than most people can even fantasize about accomplishing in a lifetime. He could not have known then, in 1928, that he was destined to live another twenty years, and that in those twenty years he would do more to perpetuate his name and legacy, by creating new Jewish institutions bearing his name, than he had in the prior sixty-three years, during which he had focused on creating, supporting, and strengthening myriads of other Jewish institutions! Incredibly, it was not until after his official biography was published—the only edition actually published in his lifetime—that he founded the Harry Fischel Institute (known as the Machon Harry Fischel) in Jerusalem, the Harry Fischel School for Higher Jewish Studies at the Bernard Revel Graduate School of Yeshiva University, and the Harry Fischel Foundation (later renamed the Harry and Jane Fischel Foundation) in New York, the latter of which continues to initiate projects as it has done for the past eighty years. Nor could he have known that during the Great Depression, which began in 1929, a year after his biography was initially published, he would almost single-handedly save Yeshiva College from bankruptcy and dissolution. He surely could not have anticipated actually becoming the Acting President of the College at one point, even if for a limited period of time, as memorialized in a plaque in the lobby of the main building of the campus he had conceived in his capacity as a very active Chairman of the Building Committee.

The story of the creation of Machon Harry Fischel is really the story of two visionaries. After the Great Depression set in, Fischel consulted Rabbi Abraham Isaac Hacohen Kook, the Chief Rabbi of Palestine, as to ideas for a unique school for higher rabbinic studies. Rabbi Kook suggested recruiting the best young Talmudic

14a

scholars in the country for a yeshiva that would stand out not just for the scholarship of its students but for their research as well. The two visionaries founded such a school, and about two decades later, when it became apparent that there was a need for judges to staff the new religious courts being set up to serve the religious community in the new State of Israel, a nucleus of the best and the brightest was already at hand. The next Chief Rabbi of Israel, Isaac Herzog, established a rigorous program in the Machon to train these seasoned scholars to serve as judges in the new courts. A majority of the openings on the religious courts have for decades been filled by graduates of the Machon Fischel, which has also continued to maintain its preeminent reputation in the yeshiva world and beyond for its research projects from original sources and its publications on a high level, as well as its services for the local community. (The reader will find more about the Machon beginning on page 410 and on page 475.) For decades, the Chief Rabbi of Israel served as president of the Machon and delivered lectures there.

The Harry Fischel School for Higher Jewish Studies at the Bernard Revel Graduate School of Yeshiva University is discussed beginning on page 478. The text of the agreement signed by Harry Fischel, the president of the Rabbi Isaac Elchanan Theological Seminary and Yeshiva College (together known as Yeshiva University when subsequently reorganized), and the chairman of the board begins on page 481. Under the terms of the agreement, the Fischel Foundation agreed to pay an annual sum (which it has since increased unilaterally) "in order to induce the 'Yeshiva' [and its successor, the university] to found, maintain, and bear the expenses of said Harry Fischel School for Higher Jewish Studies . . . [which sum] shall be used exclusively for the instruction only," except that up to 20 percent may be spent for publications, "and all other expenses [are to] be paid by the 'Yeshiva' in running the said School. . . . it is also mutually agreed that the said 'Harry Fischel

School for Higher Jewish Studies' shall always be conducted in accordance with the law and spirit of Orthodox Judaism."

The Harry and Jane Fischel Foundation (originally, the Harry Fischel Foundation) is discussed primarily on pages 424–425 of the Continuation, and on the web site at fischelfoundation.org, which describes how the primary purpose of the Foundation remains to support the Harry Fischel Institute in Israel, but the Foundation's scope has been broadened to also contribute to the support of the Harry Fischel School for Higher Jewish Studies, affiliated with the Bernard Revel Graduate School at Yeshiva University, and other particular institutions, as well as many creative projects that the Foundation has initiated in the United States.

Beit Harav Kook, the residence and *beit midrash* (house of study) built for the first Chief Rabbi of what was then known as Palestine— and is now Israel proper, of course— was discussed in detail in *Forty Years of Struggle for a Principle*, reproduced in this volume on pages 238–241 and 287–303. What is *not* mentioned there, however, and what could not have been known at the time, is that, as a byproduct of the original concept of being a residence for the Chief Rabbi, the structure that Harry Fischel built and subsidized at his own expense served from 1924 to 1964 as the venue of the religious Zionist flagship yeshiva, HaYeshiva HaMercazit HaOlamit, which came to be known as Yeshivat Merkaz HaRav—a historic venue for forty years of study for a principle. The full significance of this yeshiva, along with its official English name, is discussed in the Preface.

The Yeshivat Merkaz HaRav was relocated to an independent structure in the Kiryat Moshe neighborhood of Jerusalem in 1964. Beit Harav has been preserved ever since as a resource center and a living museum under the leadership of Rabbi Yochanan Fried, with audiovisual presentations, and ongoing study sessions and seminars conducted by Rabbi Itzchak Marmorstein and others. It is a landmark to this day, situated at Rechov Rav Kook 9, and is part of the tours of the city of Jerusalem conducted by professional tour guides to the gratification of all people who wish to see the inspirational sights of this most inspirational city.

This supplemented edition of the biography of Harry Fischel came about for several reasons, each of which would alone have justified the republication of the book. (1) The original biography, as published in 1928, could no longer possibly do justice to its founder in light of all that he accomplished in the years afterward. (2) Harry Fischel had written a Continuation taking him into the 1940s, but it had never been circulated and published beyond his family and close friends and associates. (3) Not only is the original biography out of print, but its publisher has been out of business for many years. (4) At the time the republication was approved, the original biography was barely available for purchase even on the Internet. (5) It is now being made available to be downloaded with some of the currently most popular technologies. (6) As time progresses, the pressures of economics and technology will discourage the hard-copy publication of more and more books, so the window of opportunity for publishing books in traditional hard copy is gradually closing. (7) The Fischel Foundation wants the biography to be available in as many forms as possible, hardcover and paperback, traditional, digitized for the present, and available for the future via technologies not yet invented. (8) The publication of the supplemented edition makes the book available for the present generation, and also for future generations. (9) The supplementary portions correct, for the record, certain mistakes in articles about Harry Fischel and his achievements in encyclopedias and other publications. (10) Above all, the goal is greater than to merely tell the life story of an individual, for it is designed to recount what a single person who came to America penniless could do for himself and for humanity in general, and for traditional Judaism in particular, in the hope that readers will be inspired by his example to stand steadfastly for their principles and to dream dreams just as ambitious as his and then to implement them.

In every era, many people who fail to achieve their potential blame it on their environment or on their lack of opportunities in life. Many fall into a state of despair, and never rise out of it. This book and the life of its protagonist, should provide them with hope. Many people feel that even if they have good credentials and work hard, they are no longer guaranteed a rewarding job, and the situation is even bleaker for people who were not fortunate enough to have been born in surroundings conducive to success in the workplace. They would do well to examine the life of Harry Fischel, as described in this book. He came to this country as an immigrant without any money to speak of, without any English to speak in, and without any of today's commonly available social benefits to avail himself of. To make matters tougher, he came without any other family members to support him, and in fact shared his meager initial earnings with his elderly parents in Europe, to whom he sent money when he was still living on bread and coffee.

To make matters even more difficult for him, Harry Fischel was a Sabbath observer. His religion forbade him to work on Saturdays, this in an era when the six-day work week was the norm. In consequence, he was unwilling and unable to work on a day that for others was a normal working day. Employers and potential employers were not willing to make exceptions for Sabbath-observing employees. Thus, even when Fischel managed to find a job, he was routinely fired on the first Monday of his employment, and sometimes without even being paid for the hard work that he had performed in good faith.

Nevertheless, Harry Fischel persevered; he did odd jobs at first; he worked very hard; eventually he was hired for full-time employment; at some point he became an employer himself; and eventually he made it into the top tier of that coveted top 1 percent of Americans. Clearly, when Fischel came to this country, he was poorer than most poor Americans today; his early years were more difficult and challenging; his American education was lower; his knowledge of English was worse; there were no bilingual programs on the federal, state, or local level; welfare benefits and food stamps did not exist; there was no safety net for the poor. Yet with a work ethic, a creative mind, and a belief in G-d, he accomplished more than most people with a far more auspicious upbringing. So almost every reader of this book will begin life, or did begin life, with a head start on him, and can dream of going as far as he did, or further, knowing that such dreams can turn into realities.

Rags do not necessarily turn into riches, however. Many people work as hard as Harry Fischel did and never even rise into, let alone past, the middle class. Those who have analyzed the charmed life of Harry Fischel often come to the conclusion that the almost supernatural challenges he faced and overcame, and the almost superhuman sacrifices he made, in observing the Sabbath, and in caring for and following the guidance of his elderly parents half a world away, may have been rewarded by his corresponding subsequent seemingly almost supernatural successes.

Fischel's road to riches was not an easy one, but in fact was a rather unconventional one. He figured out how to develop irregularly shaped lots of land that were not being utilized, bought them at bargain prices, developed them far beyond their apparent potential, and before long, "the story of the next few years reads like a fairy tale." Harry Fischel, the poor immigrant, overcame the restrictions of his religion to develop not just land into buildings, and buildings into institutions, but also uneducated students into scholars with unlimited repositories of Jewish culture, tradition, and scholarship, via a combination of educational, spiritual, and charitable organizations.

Fischel was described in a scholarly journal as "perhaps the richest Orthodox Jew in New York" in his prime (see Ophir, in References). Whether or not this was actually true, what is far more significant is the way he spent his money and his time after rising to financial and social prominence. He has also been described as a visionary and a pioneer on behalf of the growth of American Judaism as we know it, as well as of Judaism in Israel. He was instrumental in the creation and maintenance of more national and nationally known Jewish institutions, and most especially of Orthodox Jewish institutions, than virtually anyone else in history before or since, and certainly in the first half of the twentieth century.

Perhaps no less remarkable, in an era when Orthodox Jews were virtually unable to find employment if they followed Jewish law and their consciences by refusing to work on the Jewish Sabbath, Harry Fischel, upon becoming a successful independent employer, became an icon in the Jewish world by giving his employees both Saturday and Sunday as paid days off at a time when the six-day work week was universal.

This expanded book incorporates the original biography, *Forty Years of Struggle for a Principle*, exactly as it was originally produced in 1928, and adds the Continuation that takes the reader into the 1940s, along with a Preface entitled "The Founder," by a most illustrious Chief Rabbi (now emeritus) whose own achievements are legendary. It also includes a brief description of the Harry Fischel Institute for Research in Jewish Law (the Machon Harry Fischel) as it has developed over the years; a brief description of the Harry Fischel School for Higher Jewish Studies (HFSfHJS) at the Bernard Revel Graduate School of Yeshiva University, written by the dean of those schools; an Appendix consisting of the original agreement for the creation of the HFSfHJS, as signed by Harry Fischel plus the president of Yeshiva University and the chairman of its board of directors; an Epilogue taking the reader through Harry Fischel's final years; a brief listing of significant references to him in print; and a supplementary index of all the new material that appears in this now completed biography.

May the augmented edition inspire a new generation and generations to come to apply the values and dynamic, creative, and optimistic spirit of Harry Fischel to the future of Judaism in Israel, America, and throughout the world.

Aaron I. Reichel
Administrator
Harry and Jane Fischel Foundation

ר' ישראל אהרן פישל ז"ל—Harry Fischel of blessed memory—was one of the most famous Jewish philanthropists in Eretz Yisrael and the United States, known all over the world as a leading founder and supporter of תורת ארץ ישראל, Religious Zionism, and modern Orthodoxy. He was not merely a most generous donor who supported many institutions as well as many needy individuals and families. His way was not only to be benevolent to worthy people and institutions. He involved himself personally in the projects and worthy causes to which he contributed large sums, and he tried to make sure that they would continue to exist in perpetuity. His name is attached to many of the most important institutions of Orthodoxy, that were founded during his lifetime and serve as a legacy to his family, recalling his seminal contribution to the destiny of the Jewish people in the Holy Land, in the United States, and the world over.

Harry Fischel's success in business enabled him to initiate projects that he regarded as vital for the development of Torah Study and Religious Zionism in the modern world. He was part of the founding group that created Yeshiva College, and he helped Rabbi Dr. Bernard Revel זצ"ל enlarge it into Yeshiva University. He led the effort to build a new campus for it in Washington Heights in New York City and served as the chairman of its building committee for many years. He himself gave very sizeable contributions to Yeshiva and was also one of its leading fund-raisers.

In recognition of his efforts, the Beth Midrash—the synagogue and main lecture hall in the main building of Yeshiva University—was named in perpetuity The Harry Fischel Study Hall. This recognized Harry Fischel's part in the founding and furthering of the university's *Torah u-Madda* heritage, which has become the hallmark of American Jewry and is connected with such illustrious names as Rabbi Bernard Revel, Rabbi Samuel Belkin, and last but not least, the great Rabbi Joseph B. Soloveitchik זצ"ל.

*

On his first visit to Palestine, Harry Fischel was the guest of the British High Commissioner of Palestine, Sir Herbert Samuel, who was himself Jewish. Sir Herbert convinced him to build Beit Harav, which served as the home, office, and yeshiva of the founder of the Chief Rabbinate in the Holy Land, who was also its first Chief Rabbi, Rabbi Abraham Isaac Kook o.b.m. (זצ"ל מרן הראי"ה קוק). When Harry Fischel met the great Rabbi Kook, he was deeply impressed with his views and personality, and the two men became life-long partners in the work for *Klal Yisrael*.

Out of this partnership many great institutions were established under the umbrella of the Central World Yeshiva, better known today as Yeshivat Mercaz Harav, the alma mater of all Bnei Akiva yeshivot and the *yeshivot hesder*, whose students combine Torah study with sharing the burden of defense, serving side by side with the rest of the country's youth in the Israel Defense Forces. Its students and graduates serve in many elite security positions as well as in positions of rabbinic leadership, and they are admired both by Israel's leaders and by the rank-and-file of the people of Israel.

In 5692/1932 Harav Kook זצ"ל and Harry Fischel זצ"ל together established Machon Harry Fischel, the world-renowned postgraduate Institute for the Research and Study of Talmud and Jewish Law. A committee of renowned *Gedolei Hatorah* (recognized Torah authorities) of the Holy Land interviewed the many candidates and chose eighteen outstanding graduates of the leading yeshivot in Jerusalem to be the first Fellows of the Institute (known as the Machon). Over the years, hundreds of outstanding young scholars—עילויים—have become Fellows. Almost all of them eventually went on to become important rabbis, rabbinic judges, educators, and other leaders of the Jewish world. To this day the graduates of "Harry Fischel," as it is popularly called, are regarded as the elite, not only of the Israeli rabbinate but also of the spiritual leadership of Jewry the world over. Finally, the publications of the Machon are regarded as outstanding in the fields of classic Jewish law and Talmudic research.

*

Rabbi Herbert S. Goldstein ז"ל, my late father-in-law, convinced Harry Fischel ז"ל, his father-in-law, to write his autobiography, with the idea that Fischel could serve as an exemplar for other Orthodox business people and leaders. The result was the book *Forty Years of Struggle for a Principle*, which was edited by Rabbi Goldstein and published in 1928 by Bloch Publishing Company. Impressive as the book is, however, it does not cover Harry Fischel's life and manifold activities and contributions, during the pivotal years of Jewish growth worldwide, culminating with the events that brought about the establishment of the State of Israel. His deeds and great achievements in the last twenty years of his life are certainly part of Jewish history.

We are indeed very lucky that Harry Fischel and his son-in-law wrote a further account of his life. Several copies of this account, which we refer to as the Continuation, survived in a typed manuscript that remained in the hands of the Goldstein children. Reading that part of the biography is a most fascinating experience.

Harry Fischel passed away in Jerusalem in Tevet 5708 at the age of eighty-three, and was buried in the impressive mausoleum he had prepared for himself, just as the fighting of the Israel War of Independence commenced. He was the last Jew to be buried on the Mount of Olives, until it was reconquered in 1967.

The Harry and Jane Fischel Foundation has now taken the initiative to prepare and publish a complete biography of Harry Fischel ז"ל that includes both the first, already published volume, and the Continuation, which until now was only available in manuscript form. We are very grateful to the Almighty and are proud to make this work available to the public using the good and professional offices of the KTAV Publishing House.

Our Rabbis tell us that עיקר תולדותיהם של צדיקים תורה ומעשים טובים. This is certainly true when we speak about Harry Fischel's life. May we all acquire merit in his זכות.

יהי זכרו ברוך וזכותו תגן עלינו ועל כל ישראל. אמן

Chief Rabbi Emeritus Shear-Yashuv Cohen, Haifa
President, Machon Harry Fischel, and
Founder, Ariel: United Israel Institutes

כנפש המברך באהבה

הכותב וחותם לכבוד התורה

לומדיה ועושיה,

הרב שאר ישוב כהן

החופעיה"ק חיפה ת"ו

Acknowledgments

The Board members of the Harry and Jane Fischel Foundation deserve commendation for not just approving the project of republishing and augmenting the Fischel biography, but also for reviewing the new material and debating various issues. This Board also benefits from the wise and useful advice of the respective spouses of some of its members, most notably Dr. Naomi Goldstein Cohen (a granddaughter of Harry Fischel and the wife of Chief Rabbi Emeritus Shear-Yashuv Cohen) and Deborah "Debby" Jane Stepelman (a great-granddaughter of Harry Fischel, the wife of the Foundation Board member Jay Stepelman, and mother of the Foundation 2nd Vice-President Chaim Stepelman, Esq.).

The augmented edition is greatly enhanced and placed in perspective by the eloquent Preface entitled "The Founder," written by the Chairman of the Board of the Foundation, Haifa Chief Rabbi Emeritus Shear-Yashuv Cohen.

The presidents and other leaders of the Foundation who have made all its activities possible—from the Founder until the current President, Seth Michael Goldstein, Esq.—and spanned by the Founder's protégé and grandson Simeon H. F. Goldstein as the long-time executive director—are duly noted on page 29a, below.

I deeply appreciate the opportunity I was given to implement the Foundation's resolution to publish an augmented version of the biography by writing an Introduction and an Epilogue, by writing some preliminary notes about the Continuation, augmenting the Index as described below, and compiling an expanded list of references, placing Fischel's activities and the organizations he supported in further perspective.

Appreciation is also accorded to Rabbi Hillel M. Reichel, Director of the Machon and 1st Vice-President of the Foundation, for updating the Continuation as to the works of the Harry Fischel Institute (the Machon) and putting the Machon into a contemporary context. Similarly, appreciation is accorded to Dean David

Berger, of the Bernard Revel Graduate School, and therefore also of the Harry Fischel School for Higher Jewish Studies. He explained most succinctly, compellingly, and persuasively the ongoing value of the latter school. Finally, Fischel Board member Donald Moses chaired a committee to advise the publisher's staff in designing the cover of this book, with remarkable professionalism, creativity, and sensitivity.

The publisher, Bernie Scharfstein, not only approved the project but also oversaw every aspect of it with the enthusiasm, energy, and creativity of two men half his age combined. He also edited all the new material, along with the experienced and proactive copy editor he selected, Robert Milch. The original biography had been written in the third person and edited by Rabbi Dr. Herbert S. Goldstein. The Continuation was written by Harry Fischel himself, in the first person, and was edited by Rabbi Goldstein in Fischel's lifetime and then was lightly edited again by yours truly twice, once before and once after submitting the manuscript to KTAV, as discussed above. Adam Bengal was also very much involved in the production of the book.

The designing of the book was led by Lori Martinsek, President of Adept Content Solutions. Her credits read like a *Who's Who* of the most elite publishers in the world, from Britannica to Merriam-Webster, Microsoft Press, and MIT Press. She instantly internalizes concepts, understands challenges, and comes up with perfectly targeted options and solutions. Working cooperatively with her were Jason Pankoke, who developed the cover and text design, and Raymond Stoia, who coordinated the editorial efforts and indexed the new content to closely parallel the style of the original title.

I am particularly grateful to the Foundation for giving me the opportunity to insert into the Supplemental Index many key words from the original book that had been omitted from the original index or that had not been cited by more than one version or cross-referenced. Some entries in the original index have taken on new nuances with the passage of time. Thus, the Supplemental Index is of significant assistance to readers and potential readers seeking to know whether and to what extent key topics and personalities are covered. The original classic work was on assigned reading lists in American Jewish history when it was originally available and can now be restored to such lists, more useful, comprehensive, and accessible than ever before.

Shirley Weisberger and Rochelle Ackerman, of the Foundation office, were also tremendously helpful in a variety of ways.

May G-d bless all those who have implemented the values of Harry Fischel, and may G-d bless this book and the institutions that continue to carry on his good deeds the way G-d blessed these institutions in his lifetime.

AIR

Harry And Jane Fischel Foundation

Past Presidents
Harry Fischel, of blessed memory
Rabbi Herbert S. Goldstein, of blessed memory
Albert Wald, Esq., of blessed memory
Dr. Gabriel Goldstein, of blessed memory
Rabbi Dr. O. Asher Reichel, of blessed memory

Past Chairman of the Board
Rabbi Dr. O. Asher Reichel, of blessed memory

Past Executive Directors
Simeon H. F. Goldstein, of blessed memory
Michael Jaspan, Esq.

Present Officers, Board of Directors
Chief Rabbi Emeritus Shear-Yashuv Cohen, Chairman of the
  Board (spouse of descendant)
Seth M. Goldstein, Esq., President (descendant)
Rabbi Hillel M. Reichel, 1st Vice-President (descendant)
Chaim Stepelman, Esq., 2nd Vice-President (descendant)
Menachem David, CPA, Treasurer (independent)
David Locker (independent)
Donald Moses (descendant)
Jay Stepelman (spouse of descendant)

Rabbi Aaron I. Reichel, Esq. Administrator, and Board Secretary
  (descendant)

Associate Board Members
Benjamin Bronner (descendant)
Avishai Kraus, Esq. (descendant)
Rabbi Yonatan Kraus (descendant)

MR. FISCHEL AS HE IS TODAY AT THE AGE OF
SIXTY-THREE.

FORTY YEARS OF STRUGGLE FOR A PRINCIPLE

THE BIOGRAPHY OF HARRY FISCHEL

Edited by

RABBI HERBERT S. GOLDSTEIN

Compiled from Mr. Fischel's daily
diary, newspaper clippings, editorials,
and addresses delivered by him
during his forty years of service
to the Jewish Community.

NEW YORK
BLOCH PUBLISHING COMPANY
"The Jewish Book Concern"
1928

Printed in the U. S. A. by
BARNES PRINTING CO., NEW YORK

PREFACE

By Rabbi Herbert S. Goldstein

It is both a delicate and grateful task that has been entrusted to me by my dear father-in-law, Mr. Harry Fischel, that of editing his biography. Were I not tied to him by a close bond of family relationship, as well as by strong ties of affection and respect, this history might never have been compiled.

Despite the many significant achievements in diverse fields which have given to Mr. Fischel an international reputation and have caused him to be loved and admired by Jewry throughout the world, it is the human element which is the dominating note in Mr. Fischel's career.

It is this personal side of Mr. Fischel, quite as much as his public side, that has gained for him the lasting gratitude of his co-religionists of Russian birth, and early earned him the respect of the most powerful figures in American Jewry, with whom he met as an equal and whose gifts to philanthropy he matched, or exceeded, although his wealth was infinitesimal as compared to theirs.

By his example, indeed, he set an entirely new standard of giving for the Jew of Russian birth and not undeservedly has been hailed in many quarters as the Russian Jacob H. Schiff. Not only his money contributions to religious and philanthropic causes, but his life-time of service to these causes, has resulted in the name of Harry Fischel being almost as well known in Europe and in Palestine as in America, for he has never geographically limited his interest or his aid, and his service has been universal where Jewry and Israel were concerned.

Mr. Fischel's life, surrounded by even greater privations, hardships and temptations than fall to the lot of the average man, has been directed by a singleness of purpose, amounting to a passion, which has had as its sole objective, the perpetuation of orthodox Judaism, both in precept and in practice. It will be only possible for the reader to understand Mr. Fischel's passion for a life of service to humanity when he grasps the conditions of his early environment and the parental influences that moulded his character, a character that is, indeed, unusual, as his life has been unusual, possibly unique, among those who have contributed to the world's good and whose deeds have secured general recognition.

The title of this biography is expressive of the mainspring actuating Mr. Fischel's whole life, for his single thought and purpose has been to advance the cause of Orthodox Judaism in America and throughout the world, no matter at what sacrifice to himself.

Since the Jewish religion teaches us charity as one of its most important principles, it has followed, as a matter of course, that Mr. Fischel's life should have been largely devoted to philanthropy.

It is noteworthy that Mr. Fischel has been a pioneer in almost every phase of his life's activities, a pioneer, first among those Jews who emigrated to this country from their native Russia, and made America the land of their adoption and fealty; second, a pioneer in showing how the traditions of Judaism might be transplanted to alien soil and still be made to flourish; third, a pioneer in pointing the way and making it possible for thousands of Jewish working men and women to maintain their religious principles, live up to the dietary laws of their faith, and observe the sacredness of the Sabbath day, despite economic pressure; fourth, a pioneer in leading the cause of Jewish education and religious training for the young; fifth, a pioneer in Jewish philanthropy, setting an example to the Jews of Russian birth by his unusual contributions to Jewish charities; six, a pioneer in business method and practice in his chosen field of building, which not alone enabled him to be of distinct service to the community in these activities but to earn the comfortable fortune which has made possible the devotion of his time and of his means to the manifold religious, educational and philanthropic movements with which his entire life has been identified.

The first chapters of this biography have been evolved entirely from Mr. Fischel's personal recollections of his boyhood and youth which he has related to the writer solely from the storehouse of his memory. These chapters bring his career up to the year 1900, and may be said to represent the first phase of a life that, from this period on, was to be marked by undertakings in the world of charity and business that brought him into the closest relations with men of affairs, leaders in finance, in communal endeavor, in religion, scholarship and learning, and in public and private citizenship, including several Presidents of the United States and others in high office.

Fortunately for this record, the principal events in these later years are kept green by public addresses, manuscripts, letters, newspaper articles, editorials and other documents which form a complete history, not alone of Mr. Fischel's connection with the many occurrences of historic importance to Judaism, but of the events themselves.

It is my hope and prayer that, in later years, I may have the opportunity of editing Mr. Fischel's biography from the point where this chronicle leaves off and that this book, together with succeeding chapters that may be written, will be the means of giving a new impetus to the religious faith and teachings of our fathers, to the unification of Israel, to the education of our children in the holy law of the Talmud and the Bible and, finally, to the perpetuation for all time of those ideals and standards of religious conviction which comprise our faith and which it is our duty to preserve in all their original beauty, truth and sanctity, not alone for our children, but for the generations yet unborn.

May God bless this work.

CONTENTS

ILLUSTRATIONS

FOREWORD

I HAVE been urged by many persons to set down the details of what they have been good enough to interpret as a varied, interesting and useful life, largely spent in the fields of religious, educational and philanthropic endeavor.

The requests of these kindly disposed individuals would not have prevailed had I not wished primarily to preserve the record of my early struggles, and what I may have since been enabled to accomplish, for the benefit and instruction of my children and grandchildren and, in turn, for their children, in the hope that they may derive from this history some measure of inspiration, namely to be true to the ideals of their religious heritage and to serve their fellowmen.

My first thought was to write an autobiography, but as I can lay no claim to sufficient literary ability, on account of lack of opportunity in my early youth to acquire an extensive education, I have sought to do the next best thing, namely to prepare the story in my own simple way. This I have given to another to set forth in a manner that I trust will interest and appeal to the reader.

I have entrusted this work to my son-in-law, Rabbi Herbert S. Goldstein, who is far better qualified than I in the art of putting pen to paper and whose life and labors in the Rabbinate and in the fields of Jewish education and communal activities are so entirely in keeping with my own sympathies and efforts.

Rabbi Goldstein has assumed the task as a labor of love, eager and anxious to perform what we both hope will be a service to those causes which shall best advance the future of Judaism and shall help preserve our traditional faith for the generations to come after us.

The Almighty has vouchsafed to me the means, the time and the opportunity to devote a large part of my energies to the cause of Jewish education, to the religious training of the orphans and other young people, and to many philanthropic objects throughout the world designed to extend aid to the afflicted or distressed.

I have always believed that one should not shirk an obligation or shift it to other shoulders and so, in order that this biography might have the merit of a true history and in order that I might see it when completed and have the privilege of giving to others the lessons I have learned, I have personally prepared the facts.

Up to the year 1900, when my activities began to attract public notice, I have relied entirely upon my memory to relate to Rabbi Goldstein the account of my boyhood and the first fifteen years of my struggles and early undertakings in America. From that point on, my personal recollection has been reinforced by newspaper articles, editorials, speeches and reports which I have preserved and value highly.

I am now at that period in life when I can peacefully contemplate those youthful experiences which, at the time, were fraught with difficulties and anxieties and I look forward to the future years with the hope of being spared, to use the blessings that have been vouchsafed me, in the interests of those religious and philanthropic movements which lie closest to my heart.

It is my desire in the coming years, not only to devote the major portion of my time to labors that shall advance the cause of Israel, but also to expend, while living, a portion of the wealth with which I have been endowed, in support of those objects which are most likely to preserve our Orthodox faith and to be of the largest benefit to mankind.

It is my belief that philanthropy's gain is largest where personal service goes hand in hand with giving and that the giver derives from this system the keenest satisfaction and contributes most to the causes he would assist. For this reason, I have no desire to accumulate a fortune merely with the idea of bequeathing it to charity at my death. It is rather my intention to give while I am living and while I may have the opportunity of exercising a controlling influence over my gifts, to the end that they may most fully accomplish their purpose.

I feel it my duty to give credit for the inspiration which has guided my life and made possible whatever I have accomplished, to my sainted father and mother of Blessed Memory, from whom I gained those religious precepts and the example of righteous living which they set forth in their daily lives. To their teaching was due entirely my determination to consecrate my life to acts of service to others.

I also owe a debt of gratitude to my children who have given me the great joy of inclining from their earliest years toward lives of piety and charitable deeds and who have required no urging to prompt them to follow the example I have tried to give them. The Almighty in His Wisdom saw fit to take away four sons in their infancy, but He has blessed us with four daughters who have been afforded the opportunities for education denied me in my youth. I am also thankful to the Almighty that each of my daughters is happily married to a worthy man and blessed with lovely children. It is a source of still further thankfulness to me that each of my sons-in-law is imbued with the same inherent love of religion and charity as are my daughters.

It is to my wife and daughters, to my sons-in-law and my grandchildren that this biography is dedicated, and I shall here take the liberty of naming them.

There is first my beloved wife, whose maiden name was Jane Brass, and to whom I have been happily joined in bonds of holy matrimony for over forty years, a loyal wife, a devoted mother and a true companion.

My daughters are, first, Sadie Gertrude, who graduated from Public School as valedictorian of her class, is a graduate Bachelor of Arts of Hunter College, and holds the degree of Master of Arts from Columbia University.

On November 26th, 1914, she became the wife of David Kass, a son of A. L. Kass, for a generation respected by his fellowmen in the field of banking, in which business his son is now engaged for himself. They had grown up together from childhood, both families having been friends for years, and having neighboring country homes, where they spent their summers. Their union has been blessed with two daughters, Helen Joy, ten years of age, who is named after my sainted Mother, and Babette who is seven years old. These two children are receiving a thorough Jewish religious education and the knowledge of Hebrew as a living language is set down for them as a necessary part of their studies, as is their study of English and French.

My daughter Rebecca, a graduate of Barnard College, on March 7, 1915, married Rabbi Herbert S. Goldstein, then Rabbi of the Congregation Kehillath Jeshurun, 121 E. 85th Street, New York City, where I came to form a fond attachment for him.

I first knew him as a boy of ten when he attended the Congregation Beth Hamedrash Hagadol in Norfolk Street, where I was Vice-President. It was in this capacity that I attended his Bar Mitzvah little dreaming at that time that he would one day be my son-in-law. Rabbi Goldstein is now Rabbi of the Institutional Synagogue, 37 West 116th Street, which he himself organized in 1917. He is assistant professor of Homiletics in the Yeshiva Rabbi Isaac Elchanan Theological Seminary. He is also President of the Union of Orthodox Jewish Congregations of America. Their union has been blessed with two sons and a daughter, Simeon Hai, age twelve, Gedalia, age ten, and Josephine Hannah, one month old.

My daughter Bertha is a graduate of Barnard College. On April 10, 1921, she married Dr. Henry A. Rafsky, a noted stomach specialist of high standing in his profession. Among his affiliations are the Lenox Hill and Beth Israel Hospitals and the Hospital of the Home of the Daughters of Jacob. At the latter institution he has been President of the Medical Board since its organization.

Dr. Rafsky has written extensively on the subject of gastroenterology and was formerly instructor of medicine at the N. Y. Post Graduate Hospital. He is associated with the noted stomach specialist, Dr. Max Einhorn. Dr. Rafsky is a strict observer of traditional Orthodox Judaism. Their union has been blessed with two daughters, Ann Esther, five years old, and Jean Carol, two years old.

My youngest daughter Rose, a graduate of Barnard College was married to Albert Wald on February 18, 1923. Mr. Wald is a lawyer and has been practising in New York for some time. He comes of a family descended from a long line of Rabbis renowned for their piety and learning. Like my other sons-in-law he is a strict observer of our traditional Judaism. This union has been blessed with two children, Judith, three years old, and Nachman (Nathaniel), two years old, who was named after my revered father.

It is my prayer to the Almighty that together with all the members of my family, I may be spared for many years to extend my assistance to those educational and philanthropic projects in which I am now engaged, so that it may be possible for me at a future date to add many interesting and significant chapters to this biography, chapters that will be filled with a record of important achievements for the preservation of traditional Judaism and for the benefit of mankind generally.

In conclusion, I will say that when I left my home town at the age of twenty years, the last words uttered by my parents were, "You are going to America, the land of gold. 'DON'T EXCHANGE YOUR RELIGION FOR GOLD.'" These words have always been ringing in my ears. The command of my parents, I think, has been faithfully carried out by me. In fact, I have sought to do more, that is, to use my gold for the purpose of beautifying and strengthening our religion.

FORTY YEARS OF STRUGGLE
FOR A PRINCIPLE

CHAPTER I

BOYHOOD

HARRY FISCHEL retains a vivid memory of his birthplace and boyhood. The little Russian town of Meretz where he first saw the light of day in the middle of the last century was as bleak, drab and uninviting a place as one can well imagine. The town was composed of a motley collection of ill assorted, ramshackle frame dwellings, one and two stories high, with here and there an unsightly factory; stores, where the barest necessities of life might be purchased; unpaved streets, either buried in the snow during the winter or running rivers of mud during the spring and summer.

Such was the outward appearance of Meretz in the middle of the last century. Such is its appearance today. The world has moved on, but Meretz, for hundreds of years, has remained the same.

Add to its external aspects the fact that Meretz is situated nearly fifty miles away from the nearest cities of appreciable size, Grodno, Kovno, and Vilna; that, at the time of which we write, the only means of communication with these cities was by horse and wagon, or by foot—in the long cold winters by sleigh—and one gets a partial idea of the remoteness and inaccessibility of this Russian town.

Meretz was virtually incommunicado with the outside world. Seldom did a newspaper reach its environs. Its population of about fifteen hundred families, for the most part, was born, lived, worked and died without ever setting foot outside its precincts, except those who left for America.

But one problem was presented by life in Meretz. This consisted of the necessity of eking out an existence and it was a problem which faced practically every resident of the town, man, woman and child, from the day of their births until it was finally settled by their departure for a better world.

About two-thirds of the population of the town was Jewish. The Jews did not fare either better or worse than their Gentile neighbors and lived with them, on the whole, in a state of amity and peace. This was before the days of Russian pogroms and of the persecutions that began with the knout and ended with the grave.

Most of the population existed by supplying each others' needs. They were artisans, mechanics, storekeepers, doing little or no business outside the limits of the town. All were struggling for existence.

It was in this community and under such conditions that Harry Fischel was born on July 19, 1865, the 17th day of Tammuz, 5625.

If his parents, like most of the families in Meretz, were poor, they enjoyed in unusual degree the respect of the community and did their utmost to rear and educate their six children to be God-fearing, self-respecting men and women. Until their son, in later years, sent them money, it is doubtful if the elder Fischel ever had the equivalent of twenty-five American dollars at a single time. Thrift, then, in the Fischel family ceased to be a virtue and became a habit, so that, despite his generous gifts in later years to many causes, Harry Fischel early had instilled into his consciousness the value of every rouble and later of every dollar that he earned, a knowledge quite as valuable from the viewpoint of helpfulness to those charities he was to assist as of practical use to himself.

Despite the poverty against which his parents had ever to combat, there was a distinction about Nachman Fischel, Harry's father, that set him apart and above his neighbors. By trade a cabinet maker, on which vocation he relied for his daily bread, he was yet a man of unusual and marked attainments, although he lived and died without ever going beyond the town limits.

He was noted among his neighbors not alone for his deep piety, but for his unusual store of practical knowledge of the world, coupled with a native store of wit and keenness of perception that caused him to be much in demand as a local arbiter of disputes and made him a venerated and conspicuous figure in the life of the community.

It was, however, the religious and spiritual side of his father's character that left its deepest impress upon the boy.

Thus, while yet in his teens and before he had come to form any but the most rudimentary outlook on life, the boy received many hours of instruction in the Torah and, as he grew older, gradually came to put the spiritual significance of life above its material side, forming a deep interest in and an abiding attachment for the teachings of traditional Judaism, an interest and devotion that was later to cause him many hours of bitter mental and spiritual conflict, when he was to be put to the test of remaining true to his father's teachings or deserting them to secure monetary advantage.

The instruction and example of his father, the respect in which Nachman was held by his neighbors and men of prominence in the town and beyond it, and the calm, capable, unworried life he led, exercised a remarkable influence upon the boy.

His mother, Hannah Fischel, was a fitting helpmate for her husband. A sturdy, loyal and competent wife, she shared unflinchingly and without complaint the vicissitudes which fell to her lot and maintained withal that nobility of character and demeanor which caused her to be endeared quite as strongly by the people of Meretz as was her husband. She was, moreover, a woman of the deepest piety and helped on every occasion to impart religious instruction and training to her children.

Without the worldly means to indulge in many gifts to the needy she was, nevertheless, charitable in the broadest sense of the term, and continually gave, not alone of her broad and understanding sympathies to the afflicted, but of her time and physical resources, so that it became commonly known in the town that no one had ever appealed to her for aid and been denied.

The marriage of young Fischel's parents was one of those rare human and spiritual relationships contemplated by Holy Writ but seldom in these days met with in real life. It endured for sixty-two years until the death of Nachman in 1897 and, during the whole of these sixty-two years, the husband was never separated from his wife for a longer period than was made necessary on the Sabbath and holidays when they went to the Synagogue.

Never, in all these years that were lived side by side together, amid conditions of strain, anxiety and stress, was a single angry or unkind word spoken by the husband to his wife, or the wife to her husband, a married existence that ran its course from the altar to the grave without a real quarrel or dispute.

What a lesson is here to be found, especially for many Americans of the present generation, who, without fear or reverence for God in their souls, pursue their selfish ways leading to the divorce courts. Divorce was a thing unknown to the pious souls of Meretz with all their lack of modern culture.

Thus it was, in truth, the teachings and example of his parents that caused the boy early to turn his steps toward a life of service to his people and in appreciation of whose influence, Mr. Fischel, at the outset of the talks that finally led to the writing of this biography, remarked:

"Of all the influences which have guided my life, the noble example of goodness and charity which every day was set before me by my father and mother, formed the one outstanding factor in moulding my character and exerted the greatest force in directing all my steps. My strivings for the perpetuation of Orthodox Judaism were inculcated through the teachings of my parents that have ever remained indelibly imprinted on my heart and mind."

It was thus, through his early years, the boy's mind, like the highly sensitized plate of a camera, absorbed the impressions created through his home life and he turned his thoughts in a direction unusual in one so young.

This is possibly best illustrated by the fact that, at the age of

MR. FISCHEL'S PARENTS.

only ten years, he spent some weeks in modelling from wood, with a lowly pen-knife, a miniature replica of the Tabernacle, so accurately designed according to the description in the Scriptures, and so carefully executed, as to excite the wonderment and surprise of the dwellers in the town and to be exhibited in the Synagogue where it drew forth the praise, not alone of the patriarchs of Meretz, but even of the Rabbi.

Through this bit of work, done on his own initiative, the boy developed a taste for the profession he was later to adopt and that was ultimately to bring him success in the business world of the Metropolis of a far off land.

From his tenth to his fifteenth year, Harry Fischel, with other boys of his age, attended the local school, imbibing such limited general knowledge as was contained in the curriculum of the schoolmaster. Needless to say, he supplemented the religious instruction received at home with attendance at the Talmud Torah, but he was always prevented from securing a higher secular education, not alone by reason of his parents' poverty, but because the higher institutions of secular learning required attendance on the Sabbath.

When, in his fifteenth year, it became necessary for him to consider preparation for the future so that he might lend help at home, he hit upon the architect's profession as the one that most interested him. Accordingly, at the age of eighteen, he had mastered the rudiments of this calling.

But now that he had acquired some architectural knowledge, what was he to do with it? The nearest cities, Grodno, Kovno and Vilna, were all many miles away and there was little employment in the town of Meretz where the construction of a new building was of rare occurrence indeed.

The fame of America, its welcome to those from other lands, its equal opportunities held out to all, irrespective of race or creed and the brilliant future it promised to those with determination and character, had even then begun to penetrate to this remote and obscure Russian town. A few of the more hardy and daring young men of this and surrounding communities had already packed their scanty belongings and, with a few roubles in their pockets, had set forth for this land of hope.

These pioneers had written letters to their relatives and these letters had been handed around for others to read and to marvel at, for they told of fabulous earnings to be made, of a prosperity and freedom wholly foreign to this little town, and of a mode of living that could only be regarded as luxurious, compared with anything they had known before.

These letters gave rise to wholly unexpected thoughts and ambitions in the mind of young Fischel, and he came to feel that by emigrating to America he would find a solution to all the problems which beset him, as contrasted with the dreary outlook presented in Meretz. He did not seriously contemplate the step at this time, however, as he could not bear the thought of separation from his beloved parents.

But destiny has a queer way of making its purposes felt, and of giving expression to its will. While the youth had definitely put aside the longing to emigrate to America, he was suddenly confronted with the early prospect of military service, from which no able bodied Russian youth was exempt, and which meant he would be compelled to spend five years in the army as soon as he reached the age of twenty-one.

Young Fischel did not object to serving his country, even at the cost of a sacrifice to his ambitions, but he did strenuously object to the fact that in the army he would be forced to violate many of the religious principles which had become a sacred necessity to his very being, even to desecrate the Sabbath and partake of forbidden food.

In addition, the pittance in the way of salary he would receive would make it impossible for him to be of any assistance to his parents.

He was the youngest child, his parents expected him to be with them for the remainder of their days. What should he do?

He went to his father and put the situation clearly before

him. He could not, he told him, be false to the teachings which had been instilled in him. There was but one way out, this was for him to seek his future in America. If God blessed him, he would prosper and would be enabled to live in conformity with his religious principles, and, at the same time would be in a position where he could extend assistance to his family.

After much persuasion the youth prevailed, and his father's consent was won. Next, it became necessary to break the news to his mother and this, for all concerned, was an ordeal never to be forgotten. But the aged woman bore the blow with the fortitude that was to be expected of her and, finally, with her eyes full of tears and her hands trembling with emotion, she, too, gave her consent.

It is one thing to reach a determination and another to execute it. America was thousands of miles away by sea and land. It cost money to get there, all of two hundred roubles—in those days about one hundred dollars in American money—and this sum was not to be found. Two hundred roubles, indeed, when an entire family could subsist for a full month on ten roubles!

It seemed as though leaving for America were to be only a chimera of youth's fancy, that, instead would come his dreaded induction into the army and with it an end to all his hopes and his forced abandonment of the tenets of his faith.

But here Divine Providence, the Loving Kindness of the Almighty, intervened and a ray of hope pierced the blackness that enshrouded him.

A terrific fire enveloped the city of Grodno, hundreds of dwellings were razed by the flames, scores of business houses and public dwellings were destroyed or damaged by the blaze, and the virtual rebuilding of the city was required. This was known throughout Russia as the great fire of Grodno and occurred in the year 1883.

Here, at last, was an opportunity for the youthful architect and embryo builder. Hundreds of mechanics were required for the work of reconstruction and these had to be supervised by men of training in the building crafts, who, likewise, could do their share of manual labor if called upon.

Young Fischel, on learning of the demand for workers, lost no time in setting out for Grodno, determined to turn this trick of fortune to his advantage. Many of the wearisome miles intervening between Grodno and Meretz he was compelled to walk, for others he managed to obtain lifts in farmers' wagons or other vehicles. At night he lay down by the wayside and covered himself with straw.

So well did he represent himself that he at once obtained employment in Grodno as an architect and foreman of construction, a most responsible position for one of his tender years and lack of experience. He gave such satisfaction, however, that he remained in Grodno a year and a half steadily employed, during which time he managed, in addition to maintaining himself and sending money to his parents, to save the tremendous sum of two hundred and fifty roubles.

He returned to his parents' home but a few months before his summons to military service was expected.

The next two weeks were devoted to preparations for the epochal journey which was to change the whole complexion of his life and which, though he could not then foresee it, was to open the way for blessings to himself and others which were even to exceed his parents' fondest hopes. Most of the time during these days, which sped with amazing quickness, was spent with his mother whom he tried to comfort as best he could over the imminence of the separation that was to come.

Of the two hundred and fifty roubles he had saved, the dutiful son gave fifty roubles to his parents, a sum sufficient to insure them against want for many weeks to come or, until he felt confident, he should be able to send them further funds from his earnings in America.

At last the day for parting came and the young man, true to his teachings, went to the good Rabbi of Meretz to receive his blessing, which was gladly and fervently bestowed. He then took a sorrowful farewell of his parents and, in turn, received their blessing and advice, together with their final words of admonition which were:

"When you reach the golden land, do not exchange your religion for gold,"—words which to this day he has never forgotten and which, sooner than he expected, he was to be called upon to put into practice.

Thus, with only the clothes upon his back and bearing his prayer shawl and phylacteries under his arm, this youth of twenty set out to conquer in a strange land.

Yet, so sincere was his belief that he would be befriended by the God of his Fathers, whose watchfulness would ever be exerted over him, that he set forth proud and unafraid, with a mighty resolution not only to succeed, but to be true to that faith and to those precepts which he had been taught from his cradle were indispensable to a life of virtue and honor.

CHAPTER II

AMERICA

THE America to which this youth of twenty journeyed by slow and laborious stages, husbanding his every penny, carrying with him bread and a bit of herring to sustain himself on shipboard, lest he partake of food that was not kosher, was not the America of today. Young Fischel made the journey by land to Hamburg and there embarked on the now forgotten, but then mighty steamship, Raitia, using almost the last of his resources to pay his passage in the steerage. The voyage consumed many days and was a wearisome one, confined as he was in close and uncomfortable quarters with others not less poor and forlorn than himself.

Jewish immigration had only just set in in large volume, for there were then no restrictive immigration laws to stem the tide or to deny opportunity to all who sought the hospitality of America's shores, here to find new courage and new hope.

Had the restrictive immigration laws of the present day been then in force, Harry Fischel would not have been the only man from his immediate native environment to be denied admittance, but a host of men who have contributed much in the way of good citizenship to the land of their adoption would also have been barred. From the little town of Meretz, alone, came then and in after years, a score of men who have won prominence and have made their contribution to America's greatness in many fields.

A few of these men, some of whom were classmates of Harry Fischel as a boy, may here be mentioned as illustrating the valuable human material which immigration laws, founded upon arbitrary quotas or geographical and racial considerations, inevitably must bar.

Some of the landsmen of Harry Fischel who, like himself, were transmuted into true and stalwart Americans, are: Professor Max

Margolis of Dropsey College: Judge David Lourie, of the Superior
Court of the State of Massachusetts: Messrs. Frank and Cedar,
owners of the great Pittsburgh department store that bears their
name: Isidore Ruby, Boston Councilman: Bernard Ratkovsky,
the New York furrier: and, finally, the venerable Rabbi M. S.
Margolies, dean of Orthodox Rabbis in New York, who was a close
friend of Mr. Fischel's father and at one time Rabbi of Meretz.
There are also many others who have won distinction as Supreme
Court Judges, Congressmen, State Legislators, in business and in
the professions in many parts of the United States, but whom it
is difficult for Mr. Fischel to identify for the reason that they
have changed the names by which they were known to him in
Russia, for names that have been Americanized to be more easily
remembered and pronounced.

On a bitter cold day, late in December of 1885, a day on which
the rigors of the elements reminded him of his native Russia,
Harry Fischel found himself at Castle Garden, the Battery, where
immigrants were then landed. There were few formalities to be
gone through at the hands of the immigration authorities, it
being necessary only to show a clean bill of health. There was no
literacy test to be undergone and no need even to examine his
baggage, for he had none.

The youth had but sixty cents remaining of the two hundred
roubles with which he had set out from Meretz, plus the clothes
upon his back, but if he was short of cash, he was long on vigorous
health and an abundance of determination.

In the voyage across the ocean he had not neglected, with his
accustomed studious habits, to utilize his time to advantage.
Understanding no word of English when he got on shipboard,
he realized this deficiency would have to be overcome as speedily
as possible, if he were to procure work without delay, and, accordingly, he contrived to borrow an English and German dictionary
which he pored over for hours at a time, with the result that,
when he landed he had mastered enough of the language to inquire his way and to make his simple wants known.

He had with him the address of a Landsman at 77 Essex Street, in that part of the lower East Side where already the Jews from the old world had congregated and by one means or another contrived to earn a livelihood. Approaching a policeman for directions, he was told to take the elevated railroad to Canal and Allen Streets. There, at the foot of the elevated stairs, he received the first shock of his career in his new found home when he was addressed in his own tongue by a perfect stranger. The man evidently had no difficulty in sensing from the boy's garb and demeanor that he had only lately landed. Why the stranger should take the trouble to address him, the youth could not understand, but it was with all the feeling of delight with which a person greets one of his own race in a strange land, that he prepared to engage in friendly conversation with him.

What was his consternation and surprise when the stranger, without indulging in preliminaries, turned to him and said:

"Young man, you have just landed in the great city of New York, where all the opportunities are opened to you, but if you want to succeed, you must forget about God and your religion and especially about the Sabbath and dietary laws. You must work every day including the Sabbath and eat what you can get, for God has been left on the other side of the ocean."

So great was the shock which these words produced in the mind of Harry Fischel, that he could only conclude that one who would utter such blasphemies must be a lunatic and he fled precipitately from him. Nor did he ever set eyes upon this man again or learn of his fate.

"How could a man be a Jew and not be struck down by the Almighty for his wickedness, if he did not observe the Sabbath and keep the dietary laws?" he pondered. For Harry Fischel knew but one kind of Jew, the kind his parents exemplified.

The mental and moral gymnastics by which Jews have of late years divided themselves, in America and to some extent abroad, into the three classifications of Orthodox, Conservative and Reform were then and still are, inexplicable to Harry Fischel. He

MR. FISCHEL AT THE AGE OF TWENTY WHEN
HE CAME TO AMERICA.

cannot conceive of a man professing a religion and not following
its teachings to the letter. To him, such a course of action is
like inviting down the direct wrath of the Almighty.

In the little town of Meretz, he knew only Jews and Christians,
each was faithful to the religion in which he was born or else was
regarded as a heretic. There was no middle road, no acceptance
or rejection of this or that ritual or dogma because it was either
pleasing or distasteful to the individual, no possible modification
of the laws for Sabbath observance that did not constitute desecration, no ignoring of the equally stringent laws of diet for the
reason that they were difficult to follow or because other food was
more readily available. If one could not secure Kosher food, he
went without eating; if it were necessary to labor on the Sabbath
to obtain employment, then one remained jobless.

Had he, indeed, come all these thousands of miles with the chief
object of enjoying the liberty of worshiping God in his own way,
only, as this stranger had said, to find himself denied this right:
to find America, instead a land where there was no God, a land
ruled by Mammon alone? His mind failed to conceive such a
condition, the stranger must indeed be crazed.

It was only in after years that he learned such men were employed to wean away the Jew from his religious heritage, to sub-
vert or destroy his faith in the interests of wordly gain or in the
mistaken belief that any other religion can supplant in the true
Jewish soul that which has been handed down to him by his
fathers. Of the effects of such proselyting, Harry Fischel declares:

"The good Jew will not sell his religious heritage and a bad
Jew will always make a bad Christian."

CHAPTER III

EARLY STRUGGLES

HARRY FISCHEL was at once confronted with the task of finding work. The pleasant distractions he might have enjoyed in looking about the great city were not to be experienced with but sixty cents in his pockets. Enjoying the temporary hospitality of comparative strangers and, above all, with his aged parents waiting anxiously at home to receive news of his progress and his financial aid, his entire thoughts were centered upon obtaining employment.

For the next several days, until his few remaining pennies were exhausted, he utilized his time in making inquiries as to where it was most likely his services would be in demand and then set forth in search of work. Even with the confidence he possessed in his own abilities, he found the task a difficult one.

His greatest handicap was lack of knowledge of the language, for there were at this time no Jewish architects, or at least he knew of none, and he was compelled to seek employment in the offices of Gentiles. Even this proved unavailing, for after walking the streets for several days, making countless applications, he found no one who was willing to give him the opportunity for which he so earnestly prayed. What architect, indeed, had use for a greenhorn immigrant boy of twenty who could not even understand the instructions that might be given him? Why, furthermore, should a Jew from Russia be given the chance of such an apprenticeship when there were many native American youths to be had? It was such arguments as these with which he was rebuffed. It was, in fact, during his first week in America that he made application for citizenship papers.

Finding that his expectations of at once securing an opening with an architect were to be denied him, he did not permit his disappointment to prevent his continuing the search for any work that might bring him a living, and finally was successful in securing a job with a boss carpenter, as assistant to the foreman, a place that paid the munificent wage of three dollars a week. It had, however, the advantage of permitting young Fischel to use his training as an architect to some extent, for the foreman had had no such training and was only too glad to take advantage of the knowledge of blue prints and plans possessed by his youthful assistant.

The entire sum of his first week's wages, the young man sent to his parents from whom he had now been separated for many weeks and whom, he felt sure, were in need of even this slight assistance. In order that he might be enabled to do this, he arranged with the family with whom he lived to extend him credit for his board and lodging until a later date. From this time on, the young man never failed to send his mother and father a monthly remittance of at least ten roubles, or about five dollars in American money, so budgetting his expenses and living on such fare as to make this possible, no matter how small his earnings were.

While he worked steadily at his job, which occupied twelve of his waking hours, the youth was far from satisfied with the progress he was making and kept his mind steadily fixed on the main incentive of his life at that time, namely to eventually procure work with an architect, so that he might be able to advance in his profession. The carpenter by whom he was employed, was engaged solely in alterations and jobbing, and it was not this sort of occupation, but the opportunity to create, to engage in the construction of new buildings, that fired the young man's imagination and to do which he was more than ever determined he would find the way.

In spite of his long hours he decided that the only course by which he could hope to better his prospects was to attend night school, where, besides achieving a greater mastery of the English language, he might also broaden his architectural knowledge. For the next six months, therefore, his hours of labor were sixteen a day, twelve hours with his employer, two spent in the night school and two preparing his work for the following day.

At the expiration of these six months, it seemed at last his diligence was to be rewarded, for he finally came upon a firm of architects that was ready to engage him at ten dollars a week, a figure that sounded princely indeed.

But once again his hopes were to be blasted for, in connection with this position he learned it would be necessary for him to work on the Sabbath and he was instantly reminded of the words of the stranger to whom he had spoken on his arrival in New York, and who told him that, in order to succeed in America, he must forget God and forget his religion.

What then was he to do? There was set before him the opportunity for which he had so long searched and had striven so hard, the opportunity to take up seriously and with every prospect of success, the architectural profession; there was also presented to him the opportunity of making his financial status secure, for what would not this increase in pay from three to ten dollars a week mean both to him and to his aged parents?

How was he to resist this offer, how remain true to all that he had been taught? As he pondered over the problem, there suddenly resounded in his ears, as though the words were again spoken directly to him, the parting injunction of his parents: "Do not exchange your religion for money," and with this recollection, all the strength of his early resolutions returned to him. Peace came to his soul as he decided to refuse the proffered employment and continue in his present place.

It was not long after reaching this decision, that the young man was called to face what came in the nature of a calamity.

Arriving one day in the middle of the month of July at his employer's place of business, he found the establishment closed, a notice of bankruptcy posted upon the door and he, in consequence, without employment. He was also practically without funds for he had been able to save but little from his wages except the sum he had sent monthly to his parents. His own plight caused him but trifling worry or concern, compared with the thought of his father and mother cut off from his help on which they chiefly relied.

How was this tragedy to be averted?

For many days and nights he walked the streets communing with himself and uttering prayers to the Almighty that he might receive the strength to resist temptation. Meanwhile, he sought by every means which he could think of to obtain employment. His every effort proved fruitless until,—purposely omitting mention of the Sabbath—he succeeded in obtaining a position with a firm of architects, trusting to the hope that after he had been with them a few days and had made himself as useful as possible, he might obtain the privilege of working five days a week for much less pay than he was promised for six days.

He went to work one Monday morning for his new employers, Schneider and Herter, whose offices, by some strange coincidence, were situated in the Bible House. Never had he found work more congenial, more to his liking, having in it the possibilities for promotion and service opening to him a new vista of long deferred hopes.

So happy was he in his work that Friday came on wings, almost before he could believe it. Early Friday afternoon he approached his employer with the request that he might be absent on the next day, Saturday, making the proposition that a portion of his pay be deducted in view of the arrangement.

His request was immediately and firmly denied, his employer flatly declaring: "If you don't come tomorrow, you need not come on Monday." It seemed as though God had decided to give him another test of his devotion to his religious principles and his ability to withstand temptation.

Again Harry Fischel's world went crashing about his ears. "Never," so he declares, "shall I forget that Friday night!"

Was he to give up this position, the first he had been able to secure that offered him the slightest prospect of advancement in his profession: were all his hopes to be dashed, the comfort of his parents jeopardized, or was he not justified in succumbing to the tempter's voice and returning the following day to his work?

He spent a sleepless night considering these questions and, finally, as morning dawned, he reached a compromise with his conscience. He would not give up his position, but, before going to work he would attend services in the synagogue of the Congregation Scharey Torah, Hester and Orchard Streets, to which he was in the habit of going every Saturday.

Accordingly he arose at five o'clock, carefully attired himself in his Sabbath clothes, intending later to change them for his every day apparel, and set forth for the early services.

Once in the Synagogue, the sight of the several hundred worshipers; his conviction that, despite their poverty, none of these could be prevailed upon to desecrate the Sabbath for profit; the thought of generations of his forebears who had remained true to their faith; the realization that he would be the first of his family to break God's law, all these thoughts crowded into his consciousness while, at the same time, he was unable to force from his mind his fears as to what should become of his parents deprived of his support.

At the conclusion of the services, still confused and undecided, the young man went to the Ark and there silently prayed for God's guidance. Even his fervent supplication remained unanswered and he stumbled into the street, weak from the ordeal through which he was passing; intending to return to his lodgings, change to his work clothes and proceed to the office of the architect.

On his way and when he had arrived at the corner of Hester and Essex Streets, at that time the busiest corner on the entire East Side, he was forcibly struck with the observation that, as far as his eye could reach there was not a single store open, not even a solitary push cart to be seen. On the other hand, the street was filled with men, women and children in their Sabbath dress, none having thoughts of business, each spending the day in harmony with its holiness. Again he asked himself, would not his parents die of shock could they but know the step he contemplated?

Suddenly, although the day was in mid-August and the heat was stifling, he trembled as with the ague. A chill went through every fibre of his being, as though he were confronted with the biting winds of January. At the same time a strange sensation attacked his heart and he was unable to move. It seemed as though he were paralyzed and he would have fallen, had not his body been supported by a friendly wall.

When with difficulty he recovered himself, his decision had been reached. The terrible temptation of the past few hours had been thrown off, and he knew that neither then nor later would it ever be possible for him to desecrate the Sabbath. His prayer to the Almighty in the synagogue had been answered by a mysterious manifestation of the Divine Power.

Finally, he returned to his abode with slow and faltering steps but with a strange and perfect peace and happiness in his heart, as though he had been born anew or some horrible spectre which had haunted him had been forever removed. The doubts which had assailed him were gone. His way was made clear and for the remainder of that memorable Sabbath, he forgot all his temporal troubles and gave himself over to the gratification of having resisted the greatest temptation he had ever known.

The following day he dispatched a letter to his parents informing them of the spiritual conflict through which he had passed and asking them if, in view of their poverty, he had decided aright.

Only a month passed before he had their answer which read: "Not only are we satisfied even to suffer hunger, but we are also willing to sell the pillows from under our old heads to send you money to pull you through to the time when you will succeed in getting a position that will not compel you to desecrate the Sabbath."

On the next day, Monday, young Fischel went again to the

offices of Schneider and Herter to renew his plea that he be permitted to work five days a week, even at one half the salary they had agreed to pay him. Not only was his request again refused, but payment was withheld for the labor he had already performed.

It is difficult to picture the trials and deprivations the young man was compelled to undergo in the next three months. It is impossible for the American of today to conceive of a human being existing in such manner as this youth existed and, through it all, losing neither courage nor high resolve.

When the young man was turned away from the doors of Schneider and Herter to renew his ceaseless search for work, his entire possessions consisted of two dollars and a half. The frugality he had practiced in the past he at once foresaw must now be doubled and, accordingly, he sought to reduce his living expenses to a point that almost reached the dimensions of a cipher.

The Landsman with whom he lodged and who possessed a true Jewish heart, took pity on the boy and out of his almost next to nothing of this world's goods, managed to give young Fischel a place to sleep and three cups of coffee a day, this charity being augmented on Friday evenings with a plate of soup.

But life cannot be sustained on a single plate of soup a week and to supplement what his kindly benefactor contributed, young Fischel purchased daily, for three cents, a loaf of bread which he broke into three pieces, each piece, with the cup of coffee he received, constituting a meal.

On a few occasions he purchased either a cent's worth of cheese or a cent's worth of herring, and this expenditure he regarded in the nature of a real extravagance, only justified because it reduced to some extent the pangs of hunger from which he was never wholly free.

By thus arranging his fare and thanks to the goodness of the man who sheltered him, the youth's expenditures for three months, from August to October, when he again found work, did not go above twenty-five cents or at the utmost thirty cents a week.

During these months, when not walking the streets seeking work, the young man attended Cooper Union Institute, continuing to satisfy his thirst for a greater knowledge of architecture and gradually acquiring more proficiency in the English language.

It was in mid October of 1886 that the first rift in the clouds appeared. It was at this time that early one morning the youth received word from a carpenter and builder named Feldman, asking him to call at his shop at 31 Orchard Street. Feldmar offered him a position as foreman, carrying with it the responsibility of superintending the work of a number of men. So overwhelmed with joy was he at the prospect of work that he did not even think to inquire what pay he was to receive, and it was only at the end of his first week that he was told he was to receive seven dollars, and was promised an increase later, should he give satisfaction to Mr. Feldman and his wife, whom he also was to assist in her domestic duties.

Let us for a moment consider the conditions of employment the young man was called upon to meet and contrast them with conditions as they exist today.

His day's labor began at six in the morning when he was expected to be at the Feldman home to bring up coal and wood from the cellar and to start the fire. At seven he had to be on whatever building job he was engaged upon to start the men at their several tasks and there he remained until nightfall when Mr. Feldman would come around to note the day's progress and to say, "Boys, you may go home." Sometimes this was at seven in the evening and at other times it was as late as ten o'clock, but no matter how late the hour, no one thought of stirring from the job or of ceasing his labors until released by the "Boss".

But young Fischel's labor was not ended with this release for the others, he had still to return to his employer's home, make a report of the day's work and arrange the assignments of the men for the following day, and when all of this was accomplished he yet had to bank the fire for the night. Only then could he gratify himself with the thought that "he had nothing to do till tomorrow."

And he remained in this position for more than a year, that is from October 1886 to November 1887, winning, during this period, increases in salary that finally brought his pay to eleven dollars a week instead of the seven at which he had begun.

These days, as he recalls them were among the happiest of his life and neither the long hours nor the heavy tasks he was called upon to perform, could diminish his satisfaction that he was able to increase the sum sent monthly to his parents, allowing them for the first time to live in comparative comfort; that he was permitted to keep the Sabbath holy and that all the time he was gaining valuable experience that he would be able later to use with profit and advantage.

MR. FISCHEL AS A BRIDEGROOM AT THE AGE OF
TWENTY-TWO WITH MRS. FISCHEL.

CHAPTER IV

ROMANCE

IT was quite natural that Harry Fischel, who had by this time been in the country for a year and a half and had attained his majority, his twenty-second birthday not being far off, should, on occasions have been affected by a poignant feeling of lonesomeness. While his duties, occupying as they did most of his waking hours on five days of the week, left him little time for introspection, yet there were many hours during the long and bitter struggle he had experienced, when he yearned for human sympathy and companionship.

It is true that from time to time the young man met a Landsman from his own town or province, and sometimes had brought to him direct word of how his beloved parents were faring, with a message of blessing from them. But this only accentuated his loneliness and intensified his desire to unburden his heart to a kind and compassionate listener.

It was about this time, in May of the year 1887 to be exact, that, at the home of a mutual friend, he was introduced to Miss Jane Brass. Aside from the quiet dignity of the girl and her kindly disposition, an immediate bond of sympathy was developed between the young man and woman by reason of the fact that she hailed from the town of Eishishock, not far from Meretz and that, while they had never met in their native land, there was much in common between them.

It was, therefore, not to be wondered at that they were at once drawn to each other by a strong mutual attraction, for the young woman could not help but admire the youth who had gone through so much, who revealed to her his ambitions and whose kindliness and courtesy were only matched by the fire of his indomitable purpose.

She, too, was lonely, although she had about her in New York, many members of her immediate family, a family of distinction, learning and piety.   She possessed, furthermore, that same religious zeal and love for her faith that was the all consuming trait of the youth at her side and, with him, her hopes for the future were to be of service to mankind and to advance the cause of Judaism in the land of her adoption.

Miss Brass' father was noted for his learning and devoutness and had committed to memory one half of the entire Talmud. Her grandfather was the celebrated Rabbi Alexander Sisskind, author of several books read throughout the world and held in high esteem and reverence as a man and a Rabbi.   Her brother, Rubin Brass, is now a Rabbi in Wisokedvah, Vilna, and the famous Hebrew writer, Joseph Klausner, is her cousin.

Thus, the young woman possessed in both her antecedents and upbringing all those qualities most likely to appeal to the young man and to strengthen and encourage all that was best in his own character.

It is by no means remarkable, therefore, that after a few meetings the respect and admiration each had for the other ripened into a stronger sentiment and within the space of several weeks developed into a love that has endured through forty years of married life.   They met in May, 1887, and on July Fourth, became engaged.

Miss Brass had emigrated to America two years earlier than her fiancee.   Like him, she had been compelled to earn her living and had worked as a dressmaker, managing to accumulate the sum of two hundred and fifty dollars, whereas, up to this time, young Fischel had only been able to set aside forty-seven dollars in savings.

Miss Brass was not above certain vanities of her sex and she desired for a betrothal gift a gold watch and chain, the cost of which proved to be fifty dollars.   Toward this, young Fischel contributed his entire fortune of forty-seven dollars, his fiancee making up the remaining three dollars needed for the purchase from her own money. To this day, the watch and chain is in her possession and is being jealously guarded by her to be passed on in future years as a priceless family heirloom.

The courtship and betrothal days of these two bore little resemblance to this period in the lives of our young people of the present day. There was neither time nor money for entertainment and amusements, there were no theatres, dances, flowers or confections, but these things were neither desired or missed. Despite their respective labors and duties they contrived, as young people in love will ever contrive, to be much in each others' company and in the mere fact of being together they found an enjoyment and happiness neither had ever known before.

At last the young man had some one in whom he could confide, always assured of sympathy, interest and the understanding helpfulness a good woman is ever able to impart to the man she loves. Their hours together were mainly spent in planning with the Almighty's aid for the future. They decided that, in after years and as soon as there was no longer occasion for anxiety as to how they were to procure the necessaries of life, they would devote themselves to communal work and to activities that should more strongly entrench the principles of Orthodox Judaism in this new land.

By late fall, the two felt they had enough money to set the wedding day and November 26, which fell on Thanksgiving Day that year, was chosen for this momentous event in their lives. It was decided to hold the nuptials in the American Star Hall at 165 East Broadway, which was forthwith engaged for the purpose at the then considerable sum of twenty-five dollars. This figure included also the cost of refreshments, comprising tongue sandwiches, fruit and lastly a barrel of beer, which beverage was regarded in those days as an indispensable adjunct to a wedding celebration.

When these arrangements had been perfected, however, and when even the invitations for the ceremony had been extended to the friends and relatives of both bride and groom, Mr. Fischel's mind began to be filled with misgivings as to how he might be able to discharge the new responsibilities he was about to assume.

A good part of the savings of both young people had been invested in furnishings for their home, consisting of three rooms on the top floor of number five Chrystie Street, the rental of which was eleven dollars a month. The young man worried greatly as to the contingency of losing his position and how he would then manage to care for his aged parents abroad, and still support his home, for he realized he could not ask his young wife to live as he had lived when misfortune overtook him.

Would he again be confronted with the old problem of being called upon to desecrate the Sabbath if he would fulfill his obligations to those he loved? These thoughts weighed heavily upon him and caused him to wonder if, after all, he had done right to ask this girl to face the prospect of poverty which he gloomily conjured up in his mind as none too certain not to be realized. His entire future, he felt, hung on the very slight thread by which he was attached to his present position and which he knew could be easily broken by the first breath of hard times or a slack season.

This worry, which he kept to himself, was nevertheless reflected in his face and put a decided damper on the happiness he would otherwise have been permitted to enjoy. It was not long before Miss Brass perceived that something was wrong. It was impossible for him to conceal from his betrothed his thoughts and fears, for the slightest shadow which crossed his mind was intuitively apparent to her.

Finally she frankly told him of her suspicion that he was withholding something and urged that he make known to her what it was that was distressing him. When he had complied, glad of the opportunity to unburden his heart, she took his head in her hands and with the utmost tenderness and sympathy, replied:

"My dear, don't worry. Should misfortune come to us through the loss of your position, I will gladly live on three dollars a week and pay our rent of eleven dollars by taking in a boarder, if need be. But my heart tells me that we are to be blessed by the Almighty and that He will show us the way to carry out our plans for the sake of our religion, for which you have already made such sacrifices."

While he was greatly comforted by these words and by the knowledge they conveyed that his beloved would stand by him in the face of adversity, he was not completely reassured. He decided he must not rely on miracles from Above for aid but upon himself and must so plan his future as to insure himself against loss of his employment and which he still could not help but feel was a possibility by no means remote.

After many sleepless nights spent in consideration of the problem, the idea finally occurred to him that he might approach Mr. Feldman, tell of his approaching marriage and suggest that his employer give him a year's contract at nine dollars a week, instead of the eleven he was receiving, in return for which reduction in pay he would be guaranteed steady work for this period. His employer unhesitatingly consented to these terms.

The youth was overjoyed at the prompt acceptance of his proposal and his pleasure was heightened when Feldman remarked that, inasmuch as business was slow, he might take two weeks' vacation with pay as his wedding present. With this good news he hurried to his fiancee's side, and a day or two later the wedding was solemnized with the Feldmans among the guests at the happy event.

Now the young man's cup was filled to overflowing, never had he or his bride known such bliss as in the days immediately following their marriage, and the two weeks' vacation given the husband was largely devoted to helping his wife arrange their home. They felt indeed they were the happiest couple in all America, if not in the world, and it seemed no cloud could come to mar their perfect joy.

But in this they were mistaken, for their honeymoon was not yet at an end when the direst forebodings of the husband were realized and when not only was he once more put to the severest test of his devotion to his religious principles, but his young wife was called upon to share this test with him.

His two weeks' vacation over, he returned to Feldman to report for work. What was his amazement and chagrin when he was informed by his employer there was no work and he had better seek another position.

This information came to him with the effect of a thunderbolt. When he finally realized that he was dismissed, he felt as though every prop had been removed from under him. It was a rude shattering of all his hopes and ambitions. The bright new world into which he had so lately been ushered came tumbling in havoc about him. All his doubts and fears returned. How could he have been so rash as to enter into marriage when he could not even support himself and with his parents still dependent upon him?

With slow and dejected steps and crestfallen coutenance he re-returned to his home to be greeted at the threshold by his wife. It was not necessary for him to tell her what had happened. She read the news at a glance and immediately exclaimed: "You have been discharged!"

In a voice of deepest tenderness, love and sympathy, a voice that at the same time betokened her resolution and courage, she added, "My dear, don't worry, everything is for the best. You will now have the opportunity to start in business for yourself and I will help you in every way that lies in my power. I will keep my promise. We will live on three dollars a week and take in a boarder to help us pay the rent."

With these words ringing in his ears, and the note of strength and confidence, sacrifice and affection they sounded, the young man could not help but steel himself to meet the future, whatever it might bring, with a spirit of determination equal to that of his loyal help-meet, who, though married only two weeks, would not allow discouragement to overwhelm her, despite the ominous outlook with which the couple was confronted.

The winter of 1887-1888 which they now faced, with but little saved and without employment, was one of the severest on record.

It was the winter of the great blizzard of March 12, 1888, still vividly remembered by all who were living at that time and which, coming at the end of a long siege of bitter cold and hard times, laid the city paralyzed and inert beneath its mountains of snow.

It was a winter that tried men's souls yet through it all, the shipwrecked bride and groom managed to live and to be content in the love and peace each contributed to the other. From December until July, Harry Fischel fruitlessly tramped the streets, in search of work, until finally their money gave out and they were compelled to pawn, not only the watch and chain that had constituted the betrothal present, but the watch the husband carried and every other article of value they possessed.

Through all these long and weary months that contained not a single ray of sunshine, the young man held firm to his resolve to seek no work that should cause him to violate the Sabbath and in this resolution he was supported by his wife who repeatedly expressed her faith that this was the last great test of fidelity to his religious principles to which her husband would be put and that, should he triumph over his present temptation, the turning point would be reached, their needs would be supplied and peace would come to them. As she predicted, so it came to pass.

CHAPTER V

FIRST BUSINESS SUCCESSES

DURING the months when Mr. Fischel hunted in vain for work and when the future seemed the darkest, his wife had never ceased to urge that he go in business for himself. Several times contracts had been offered to him but always his lack of capital with which to purchase needed material had served as an insurmountable obstacle.

Finally on a pleasant morning in July the tide turned and he was asked by the late Mr. Newman Cowen, a glass dealer, who had been a customer of his former employer, Feldman, to estimate on the cost of a large job, namely raising the roof of the building occupied by Cowen at Canal and Mulberry Streets. Many contractors, including Feldman, regarded the work so difficult that they had refused to figure on it.

Mr. Fischel informed Cowen that he had no capital with which to engage in such an undertaking, but the manufacturer replied that if his price was right, he would arrange a credit for him. Mr. Fischel spent that entire day in working out an estimate. The next morning, considerably to his surprise, this was accepted by Cowen, who, giving him his check for two hundred and fifty dollars, took him to the Mechanics and Traders' Bank, then at the Bowery and Broome Street, where Mr. Cowen opened an account in young Fischel's name, his first bank account, at the same time arranging a further credit of two hundred and fifty dollars for him.

With this sum at his command, Mr. Fischel entered upon the work which took nearly five months to complete. So well had he computed the cost that he not only made a comfortable living during this period but was able to redeem all the articles he had pledged in the pawn shop and also to save two hundred and fifty dollars in cash, besides providing with greater liberality for his parents.

Even more valuable to him than these considerations was the fact that he succeeded in establishing such a good name that he no longer had difficulty in obtaining credit from those in the building material line, so that he was enabled to undertake many additional contracts of considerable size and importance and in less than a year he had managed to save the sum of two thousand five hundred dollars. He was now fairly launched in business and his mind turned to bigger things and he determined to engage in building on his own account. The story of the next few years reads like a fairy tale.

The lower East Side of those days harbored most of the city's Jewish population which, however, probably did not exceed 200,-000 in all. The families were huddled together each occupying at most a few rooms in four and five story tenement buildings, erected on plots 25 x 100, some of them ancient structures, others hurriedly put up to meet the need for housing which this influx of aliens had created. Virtually all of these buildings were the same as to type and plan and number of rooms to a floor, and all lacked every semblance of modern convenience and sanitary safeguards, with a minimum of light and air, as at this time there were no laws regulating tenement house construction. The few families that could afford to do so lived in private houses.

Harry Fischel, with his knowledge of architecture, gained both through his studies and practical experience, decided that he could improve on these factory fashioned tenements, all restricted to the same sized plots of ground. There were at this time many irregularly shaped lots on the East Side which had gone begging because of the inability of the builders of that day to see how they could be utilized, plots 40 by 100, or 30 by 70, and even plots of odder dimensions. These Mr. Fischel learned he could purchase cheaply and with his ability to draw plans, an ability possessed by few builders of those days, he found he could use these little desired pieces of ground to advantage.

Thus, he was the first builder in New York to depart from the stereotyped ideas of tenement construction, from stock plans. Besides showing how irregularly shaped plots could be utilized, he was able to introduce many novel features in his buildings of benefit to those who were to live in them. These conveniences procured their ready sale when completed.

But he went to further lengths than this in his efforts to be of benefit to the community, for he was largely instrumental in getting the city to adopt its first sanitary code related to tenements and insuring the dwellers therein greater convenience and safeguards to their health, not alone in the matter of light and air, but in relation to plumbing, fire escapes, stairways and cellars, matters that, up to this time, had received little consideration from the authorities. In order to accomplish these things he sought out the then Tammany leader of the East Side, the late John F. Ahearn, whom he convinced of the desirability of these reforms and whose aid toward securing their enactment into law he was able to enlist.

With the two thousand five hundred dollars he had saved, his first operation was the purchase of a parcel of land at 168 Clinton Street on which, in five months, he completed a building that he was able to sell at a profit of five thousand dollars. But his establishment as the first successful Jewish builder on the East Side was fraught with much larger significance than the individual rewards for his enterprise and energy that he, himself, obtained.

His lead which, of course, was soon followed by others, resulted in opening an entirely new field for Jewish labor and almost immediately there was developed a demand for Jewish mechanics and artisans in every branch of the building industry. With this demand there followed at once the organization of Jewish trades unions, for there were, unfortunately, many employers who demanded half a day's work on the Sabbath.

Mr. Fischel's principles as to Sabbath observance went far deeper than merely refusing to work himself on that day, his religious code held it equally wicked to cause others to work and he at once met the problem, not only by closing down the operations on his own buildings, but by setting an example for others by paying hundreds of men the wage they would have obtained by working the half day Saturday, in order that they might resist the temptation to desecrate the day.

Not only then, but in later years, when he came to build on a very extensive scale, it is Mr. Fischel's pride that not a single Jew has ever worked on the Sabbath on any operation on which he has been engaged or in which he has been interested.

The three years following his first building enterprise were marked by unusual success. He built and sold in this period fifteen large tenement houses on the East Side, having the foresight, however, to dispose of all his holdings prior to the financial panic of 1891 which found him with only one building in his possession, a structure at Jefferson and Madison Streets, and that was free and clear of mortgages, principally for the reason that in those troublous financial times, it was difficult to borrow money on the security of real estate.

With the panic at an end, Mr. Fischel sold this remaining building for seventy-five thousand dollars cash and with this money at once renewed his building operations on a still larger scale, so that by 1900 he owned a number of tenements that brought him a large annual income.

This rise, in a little more than thirteen years, from a condition of direst poverty to one of affluence, caused Mr. Fischel and his wife to raise their voices in thankfulness to the Almighty. They were both firmly convinced that the blessings thus showered upon them were directly due to their loyalty to Orthodox Jewish tradition, and to the manner in which the young man had resisted the manifold temptations placed before him, in order, both believed, to test his courage and strength of character.

CHAPTER VI

EARLY COMMUNAL ACTIVITIES

INURED as Mr. Fischel had been to privation and even want, accustomed to the most rigorous self-denial, the sudden, almost miraculous, acquirement of what for those days was considerable wealth, might easily have been expected to turn the young man's head. It might either have caused him to seek a soft and easy life, given over to the enjoyment of material pleasures or, as is frequently the case, acted as an incentive to greater efforts toward the accumulation of a still larger fortune to the exclusion of the higher purposes of life.

In the case of Mr. Fischel, however, he regarded the prosperity which had come to him as a direct answer to his prayers and considered that it imposed a definite obligation upon him to express his gratitude in good deeds.

While he was not unmindful of the desirability of this world's goods and while he continued to strive to increase his holdings and to make more secure his fortune, it was mainly with the desire to place himself in a position where he might devote himself with greater zeal to his religion and might have more time to be of service to others.

Thus, long before he had acquired even a modest competence and while he still was compelled to labor both with his hands and with his head to earn a livelihood for his family, his thoughts were concentrated upon the needs of the community. While yet a poor man and with his most bitter struggles still fresh in his memory, Mr. Fischel began upon a career of communal activity that was destined to closely connect him with virtually every important Jewish religious, educational and philanthropic movement to be initiated in New York in the ensuing years.

True to the courtship understanding and pact of the young couple, that, once blessed by the Almighty with the means of a livelihood, they would immediately devote a goodly portion of both their time and money for the benefit of the community at large, the Fischels lost no time in so doing.

A year following their marriage, they moved from their first home at 5 Chrystie Street to 55 Norfolk Street, which was directly opposite the Congregation Beth Hamaedrash Hagodol, the building of which had only just been purchased from a Methodist Church. Mr. Fischel joined this congregation and here secured his first opportunity to be of service by assisting in the work of reconstruction of the building for synagogue purposes, giving voluntarily and without charge of his time and experience.

So highly appreciated by the members of the Congregation were Mr. Fischel's labors, that at the first meeting he was elected to the Board of Trustees and a year later was chosen Vice President which office he continued to hold until 1902 when he moved to Yorkville and when he was succeeded as Vice President by Mr. Morris Goldstein of Blessed Memory, the father of this editor. Mr. Fischel continued, however, to serve as a member of the Board of Trustees.

Mr. Fischel at this time, as later in life, was possessed of an insatiable desire to live up to the precepts that had been impressed upon his conscience by his parents and he was continually searching for opportunities whereby he might serve his fellows, devoting to this ideal the same energy and resourcefulness that he had previously shown in overcoming the obstacles and trials that had confronted him in the effort to earn a living.

In 1903, two years after his first connection with the Congregation Beth Hamaedrash Hagodol and just at the beginning of his early business success, he took advantage of a further opportunity for service, when he became a director of the Hebrew Sheltering and Immigrant Aid Society, then known as the Hachnosas Orchim and destined in later years to exercise a powerful influence in the life of world Jewry. In 1890, he was chosen treasurer of that Society, in the work of which, as a one-time immigrant boy himself, he has always taken the keenest interest. In recognition of his continuous efforts in behalf of this Society, he has for thirty-six years been annually re-elected as treasurer, still holding the office up to the present day.

In 1889, Mr. Fischel became a director of the Yeshiva Etz Chaim, whose building at number One Canal Street had been condemned by the city for the use of Seward Park. Once more Mr. Fischel's experience and ability were employed to advantage. To him was delegated the task of securing a building in place of the one the Yeshiva was compelled to vacate.

Mr. Fischel succeeded in locating new quarters at 85 Henry Street and purchased the building, giving as the initial payment thereon his own check for five hundred dollars, an act that filled his heart with joy for it was the first considerable contribution to charity that he had been enabled to make.

The purchase of this property was followed by Mr. Fischel's appointment as chairman of the Building Committee, a place that once again was more than an honorary one for he took upon his own shoulders the work of reconstructing the house for the needs of the Yeshiva. Shortly thereafter he was elected Vice President.

There were in these early days of Mr. Fischel's first religious and charitable activities, few great names in Jewish philanthropy. When unemployment, sickness or death were encountered, these immigrant Jews were frequently hard put to make ends meet, but at such times the pledge and promise of the Jew, ever to take care of his own, and the large part that charity plays in the Jewish religion, were brought to the fore and from their meager means one helped the other as best he could.

There was little or nothing of organized Jewish charity as it is known today, great institutions for the care of the orphaned, the aged and the sick and campaigns for the raising of vast sums for the support of these institutions. The charity of those days was private charity, help extended by the poor to those poorer than themselves, the making of neighborhood collections to save the destitute from eviction, to put food into the mouths of the famished, to bring medical aid to the sick, to bury the dead. Great individual contributions to charity, made possible in later years by the amassing of huge fortunes, were then unknown.

CHAPTER VII

FIRST RELIGIOUS CLASSES FOR YOUNG GIRLS—
FOUNDING OF THE HEBREW FREE LOAN

IT was not long after the purchase of the building for the Yeshiva Etz Chaim and, despite his preoccupation in this work, that Mr. Fischel introduced an innovation in the religious training of the young that was attended by far reaching consequences.

Up to this time, all of the large Jewish institutions provided classes in religious instruction for boys and young men and there were many Talmud Torahs on the Lower East Side for this purpose but none had thought it desirable or necessary to provide similar instruction for girls. Mr. Fischel held that this was both illogical and wrong and that the future mothers of Jewish youth should be accorded the same opportunity for absorbing the teachings of Juadism as their brothers. He had long privately held this opinion, inspired as he had been by the religious training given to him by his own mother, but it was not until 1892 when he became a director of the Machzikay Talmud Torah at 225-227 East Broadway, the oldest Talmud Torah in the city, that he had the opportunity of putting his thoughts into action.

Shortly after becoming interested in this institution, of which in 1894 he became vice president, he proposed to the late Moses Butkowsky and several other of the directors that the Talmud Torah open a school for girls to be under the direction of a young woman teacher who had lately come to this country from Palestine.

The idea was at first bitterly opposed. No one had previously conceived of religious classes except for boys. In spite of the opposition to his plan, Mr. Fischel finally prevailed upon the directors to permit him to make the experiment, with the result that within a year, the applications from parents for admission

38

of their daughters ranging in age from ten to twelve years, far exceeded the school's accommodations.

This was the first time in the history of American Jewish institutions that a religious school for girls had been organized, although later every Jewish institution was to adopt the principle and furnish such instruction to both sexes. In order to make his experiment possible, Mr. Fischel personally engaged and personally paid the teacher.

At about this time one of the most imporant Jewish institutions of the present day was organized, one that has since its inception, enabled hundreds of thousands of men and women to overcome misfortune and to become independent, self-respectful and useful citizens. This institution, founded upon one of the basic tenets of the Jewish religion, is the Gemiluth Chasodim (Hebrew Free Loan Society). This Society now more than one-third of a century old, the president of which for many years has been Julius J. Dukas, was started with a capital of about $200, contributed by poor men, who sought by making loans without interest to others poorer than themselves, to enable these needy to overcome temporary misfortune and to be placed in a position to earn a livelihood.

These loans frequently afforded the beneficiaries the opportunity of establishing themselves in a business, which in those days required only a few dollars. Since that time the Society has loaned many millions of dollars without impairment of its original capital which has been increased by donations and bequests on the part of such men as the late Jacob H. Schiff, The Baron and Baroness DeHirsch, Adolph Lewisohn and many other leading figures in Jewish philanthropy.

The New York Hebrew Free Loan Society has, furthermore, been the pattern for many other similar institutions established throughout the United States and all over the world. These have extended the most useful and practical form of assistance, namely, helping others to help themselves. The Society has further proved that most men, even when poor, are honest, and will, if afforded the opportunity, repay their obligations.   The formation of the Hebrew Free Loan Society was, of course, the outgrowth of the constantly multiplying needs of the Jewish community of New York, and Mr. Fischel was one of the first men to become interested in it and to assist in its development.

In 1897 he turned over the basement of his home, at this time located at 215 East Broadway, to this institution which occupied it rent free for several years.   Mr. Fischel had the privilege of being one of the first directors of the Free Loan Society and its vice president.   He has always maintained his interest and pride in the fine work accomplished by this society, of which he is still a director.

The dominant trait of Mr. Fischel's character, his religious fervor, which had merely become intensified by his early hardships and experiences and even more by the prosperity which followed, was now again expressed in a unique way.   The ritual and the external attributes employed in the Orthodox observance of his faith, had exercised a potent influence on Mr. Fischel from the days of his boyhood.   These things had appealed deeply to his imagination and to his love of the beautiful.   He had for a number of years wished to make more sacred and impressive the religious observances in his own home and it was with this thought in mind that he purchased at this time, a small private house at 14 Jefferson Street.   Here he was enabled to carry out a long cherished desire to have his own succah (tabernacle).   This was one of the first private succahs of an elaborate character in New York and soon became a center of interest for the Jews of the entire neighborhood in which his home was situated.   In this house, the family occupied the parlor floor and basement, as was then the fashion for those who had attained some means.

The Fischels remained in this house but two years, however, as his wife gave birth to two sons, whom the Almighty saw fit to take away in their infancy.   As a result of these bereavements and in accordance with Talmudic injuction, they decided to change their abode in order to change their fortunes.

They then moved to a house at 235 Madison Street, where Mr. Fischel built a new succah, still finer than the one in his previous home. Here again the Fischel family was to be visited by sorrow, for two more sons were born whom the Lord, in His Wisdom, again saw fit to take from this life.

In 1896, four years after taking up their home in the Madison Street house, they moved to 215 East Broadway where they occupied the parlor and first floor, the basement being given over to the Free Loan Society. Here Mr. Fischel erected a more beautiful succah than he had enjoyed hitherto, and here, in 1897, the Fischels celebrated the tenth anniversary of their wedding, the occasion being observed as a formal housewarming as well. The family remained in this house until 1903 when they moved their residence uptown to 118 East 93rd Street.

CHAPTER VIII

EARLY CONNECTION WITH THE BETH ISRAEL HOSPITAL

IT was in 1889 that Mr. Fischel's attention was strongly directed to the need for an adequate Jewish Hospital on the lower East Side. He then decided to devote as much of his time as possible to the work of the Beth Israel Hospital which had only just been organized. By this time, his ability, sincerity and generosity in connection with communal endeavors were beginning to become widely known and in 1891 he was invited to serve as a director of the Hospital. Nine years later, in 1900, he became Vice-President, and still occupies that post, having the distinction of being in point of service, the oldest member of the Board of Directors.

During the ten years that ensued from 1889 to 1899, Mr. Fischel devoted himself largely to the needs of the hospital, although at the same time he was active in a number of other religious and philanthropic movements.

The hospital's first home of its own was at 206 East Broadway, in a very dilapidated building and one entirely inadequate to the many demands made upon it by the population of this greatly congested neighborhood. Due to the high quality of its service, however, and the efficiency of its medical staff, the hospital attracted to its Board many prosperous merchants of the neighborhood who were eager to see it progress to the point where it might fill its obligations to the community.

At the meetings of the directors, Mr. Fischel continually urged that a new building be erected, but he failed to convince his associates that they were in a position to embark upon the project, as the hospital faced a considerable yearly deficit, there was practically no money in the treasury and it was only with difficulty the current expenses could be met.

He had continuously in his mind, nevertheless, a picture of Beth Israel occupying a building fully adapted to its requirements. One day he noticed a piece of property at Jefferson and Cherry Streets which was advertised for sale at auction. Thoroughly familiar with East Side real estate values Mr. Fischel conceived this to be an unusual opportunity to purchase a site for Beth Israel at a low figure and went at once to the residence of the late Harris Cohen, of Blessed Memory, at that time president of the institution and who resided at 236 Madison Street. Mr. Fischel proposed that a committee be named to attend the auction sale and to buy the property if it could be purchased at a reasonable figure.

The idea struck Mr. Cohen as preposterous in view of the institution's financial condition at that time and he declared Mr. Fischel must be a dreamer to think of such an undertaking under the circumstances. This opposition did not, however, serve to lessen Mr. Fischel's enthusiasm or his belief that the plan was feasible. He proceeded to visit a number of the other directors with the final result that a special meeting was called to consider the proposal.

In extenuation of Mr. Cohen's attitude, it must be remembered that the communal activities of those days were conducted in a very different way from the manner in which they are carried out at the present time. Most men of that day, even those who were in comfortable circumstances, had but lately risen from conditions of poverty and were not so ready as is now the case to contribute of their cash or to lend their names to enterprises requiring large sums.

When, therefore, Mr. Fischel arose at a meeting of the Directors and expressed himself as willing to lend the institution one thousand dollars with which to bid in the property, provided four others were willing to do likewise, his suggestion was considered revolutionary.

It was, in fact, an unheard of idea at the time, but from this thought, implanted in the minds of the few men present at this meeting, it may be said the entire course of financing charitable undertakings was changed and the way was opened for philanthropic enterprises of far greater scope and magnitude than had ever before been attempted.

Upon the system of pledging financial support to the accomplishment of a philanthropic project as yet in its embryonic state and without financial resources, may be given the credit for the building in later years of virtually every large charitable and educational institution irrespective of the creed sponsoring it.

This same principle applied to giving, has, indeed, formed the basis for the conduct of every great philanthropic drive in the years which have followed and has resulted in the raising of countless millions of dollars that never could or would has been raised had any other method been followed. By the plan of first enlisting a man's interest in a cause and then securing his pledge to give to that cause from his income or according to his future ability to do so, the foundation was laid for the raising of funds that it would be utterly impossible to raise were an individual compelled to give only from his cash reserve of the moment.

Furthermore, by this plan it has been made possible to enlist a much broader and wider interest in such undertakings and to secure the aid and cooperation not only of individuals of wealth but of those of smaller means who have the desire and will to contribute but who have not always at their command the sum they are qualified and prepared to give over an extended period and under conditions made convenient for them.

Mr. Fischel furthermore suggested at the meeting where his revolutionary proposal was put forth that, if after two months, it was found impossible to raise the balance needed to take title to the property, the contract be sold and the profit applied to the institution. Should, however, the necessary sum be raised, the five-thousand dollars represented by his loan and that of the four others, should remain in the treasury as a permanent donation.

After a great deal of discussion, the late Nathan Hutkoff declared himself ready to follow Mr. Fischel's example. Next was Mr. Louis L. Richman and then the president, Mr. Cohen, who had at first been against any such plan, also agreed to lend one thousand dollars to the institution. The late Supreme Court Justice David Leventritt, who at the time was the attorney for Mr. Hutkoff, then drew up an agreement setting forth the terms Mr. Fischel had proposed and a committee of five was named to attend the auction and to bid on the property.

When the day of the auction arrived, it was learned that the property was to be sold in five separate parcels, and Mr. Fischel suggested that, in order that the auctioneer might not become aware of this philanthropic conspiracy, each of the five members of the purchasing committee, including himself, bid on a separate parcel. So well were his plans laid and so carefully was the program staged that the property was purchased for a total of $46,000 regarded by experts as about one-third of its true value.

Mr. Fischel was then named as the chairman of the Building Committee to prepare plans for a new Beth Israel Hospital and for the next few months devoted himself assiduously to the task, marking as it did, the first large constructive work he had been privileged to carry into execution. The entire Jewish population of the lower East Side joined in the rejoicing that followed announcement of the plans for the new hospital, with the result that in December, 1899, the Jewish Herald, at that time a very influential newspaper, printed the following editorial, accompanied by the architect's drawing of the proposed structure and which article gave voice to the general rejoicing:

"The persecutions of the Jews in Russia have brought to our shores many men who have made their mark in the community, and who have contributed their talents to the development of Greater New York. Conspicious among this number is Harry Fischel. Mr. Fischel is a director of the Beth Israel Hospital, and one great desire that always seemed to possess him was to build a new hospital. How was this to be brought about. The hospital was in a bad way—could not pay its rent, was very much in debt, and seemed to be in the very throes of despair. At one of their meetings, when the directors were cudgelling their brains how to meet current expenses, Mr. Fischel entered and went to work at once on the business of the evening. He told them that there was to be a partition sale of five lots, corner Jefferson and Cherry Streets at the Real Estate Exchange on the following Wednesday, and if they did not buy these lots they would lose the opportunity of their lives. He offered to loan the hospital $1000, if $5000 could be raised by the directors. Messrs. Nathan Hutkoff, Louis L. Richman and Harris Cohen, each volunteered to loan the hospital $1000. They borrowed another $1000 and with this money they went to the Real Estate Exchange. They there conferred with prospective bidders and told them not to bid as they intended these five lots for hospital purposes. They purchased these lots for $46,000 and twenty-four hours afterwards were offered $10,000 profit by one of the prospective bidders, since which time Mr. Fischel has been untiring in his energies to raise money in order to build on this ground. He has been very successful. The money was raised, sufficient to start with, and the Beth Israel Hospital will soon put up a handsome structure which is sorely needed on the East Side, and which happy event was brought about through the efforts and energy of one man—Mr. Fischel."

In the early part of 1900, arrangements were made for laying the cornerstone of the new Hospital, that was to be in every way a modern and sanitary building, thoroughly equipped to care for the needs of the poor people who flocked to the institution for treatment. The cornerstone was finally laid by Mr. Fischel on Sunday, April 1, an event in celebration of which the entire population of the lower East Side joined.

MR. FISCHEL AT THE AGE OF THIRTY-FIVE.

CHAPTER IX

A VISIT TO HIS MOTHER

The enduring affection Mr. Fischel held for his parents through all the years which had elapsed since his departure from Meretz and although separated from them by many leagues of land and water, forms an insight into the very human qualities he possesses.

At no time in all these years and no matter how scanty his resources, had he ever failed to send to his aged mother and father every penny that he could afford until not only were their wants fully supplied but until his father was moved to write him that the care of so much money as his son sent him was becoming a burden and asked him to desist in his beneficence. Nor did Mr. Fischel confine his monetary help to his own relatives. He gave with equal liberality to his wife's family.

The mere knowledge that his parents were no longer in want, were, indeed, in possession of every luxury that money could provide in their primitive home, did not serve to appease the son's longing once more to clasp them in his arms. This desire became overwhelming and caused him to decide to return to the place of his birth while his father and mother were yet alive and which he feared, because of their advanced age, could not be for long.

His expectations were, however, never to be wholly realized for the reason that on April 10, 1897, Adar the second, in the leap year 5657, he received a cable message that his father had passed away. This, of course, only intensified his eagerness to see his mother and caused him at once to make plans for the journey abroad, plans which did not materalize until three years later, due to a variety of causes.

It was on May 1, 1900, that, with his wife and the four little daughters with whom they had been blessed, Mr. Fischel finally embarked on the liner Deutschland, bound for Hamburg, occupying a first class cabin. What a contrast was here presented to his earlier voyage, when he had been confined in quarters worse than the steerage of this later day, and had lain with hundreds of others in a large compartment with hammocks three deep, one above the other and without ventilation of any kind.

As he entered the spacious and magnificent dining saloon, its tables loaded with delicacies, he could not but think what his fare had consisted of on that first ocean voyage, when in cramped quarters he subsisted on dry bread, a bit of herring and tea. Before boarding the Deutschland, Mr. Fischel had arranged with the chief steward to secure new dishes and cooking utensils in order that the food for his family, the preparation of which he himself supervised, might be cooked and served strictly in accordance with the dietary laws. It was probably the first time any passenger traveling in this class had made such arrangements.

On arriving at Hamburg, the Fischels proceeded at once to Koenigsburg, only a day's journey removed from Meretz. What joy and happiness here filled his heart at the prospect of so soon feeling his mother's embraces after an absence of nearly fifteen years! With what pride and satisfaction would he not introduce his wife and four little ones! He could scarcely wait for the hours to pass before the reunion should occur.

At Yatkunin, the Russian frontier, however, his eyes gazed upon a sight that filled him with dread, lest, in some manner, this reunion should never take place. This spectacle was the view of a Russian soldier pacing forbiddingly up and down, a bayonet over his shoulder. Although Mr. Fischel carried his American citizen's passport he could not but fear that he might be seized by the authorities and forced into the military service, without ever having the opportunity of again meeting his mother, a contemplation which caused him to grow cold with apprehension and terror.

But his good wife at his side, then, as on other occasions in his life, solved the difficulty by suggesting that he remain in Germany and that she would cross the border and bring his mother to him. Despite his mother's age, she was now almost 80, he could see no other way out of the dilemma and consented to the plan.

It was decided that the reunion of mother and son should take place at Insterburg, the nearest town on the frontier to Meretz, and here the aged woman and her daughter-in-law repaired.

It would be impossible to convey adequately the picture of this meeting between Mr. Fischel and his venerable parent, to whom he was now, with the death of her husband, the chief solace and comfort. Leaning heavily upon her daughter-in-law's arm she entered the hotel room where her son awaited her. With her age-dimmed eyes, however, she did not at once see him, but sensing his presence, exclaimed at the top of her voice: "Ahrzik!" —the term of endearment by which she had always addressed him, "Where are you? Come to my arms that I may kiss you."

They held each other in a close embrace for many moments after which she said:

"Since the Almighty has given me the blessing of again holding you in my arms, I am now ready to die and join your father in the better world."

After a short lapse in which both were too overcome with emotion to talk, she then uttered, in the words of Jacob, this sentence:

"To see you again I never expected, and now the Almighty has given me the privilege not alone to see you, but also to see your children."

Together with his mother, Mrs. Fischel also brought to this frontier town Mr. Fischel's two sisters and their children. Three days in all were spent in this family reunion, during which Mr. Fischel recounted to his mother and sisters all his experiences in America, a story that was, of course, of absorbing interest to them. He then heard, in turn, an account of what, during the years, had befallen them, heard the details concerning his father's death and was the confidant of his sisters who related their troubles to him, troubles for which, happily however, he had the solution.

For, after listening to these difficulties, he purchased a supply of pocketbooks, changed a large sum of American money into twenty rouble gold pieces and filled each pocketbook in accordance with the needs of the recipient. So swiftly did the time fly that before anyone realized it, the hour for a new separation had arrived.

Instantly all the joy and gladness of the hour was changed to sadness and the thought that he would, in all probability, never see his mother again caused Mr. Fischel the deepest anguish. With tears filling his eyes, he escorted his mother and sisters to the train and kissing them fondly, bid them all farewell. It was Mr. Fischel's final leave taking of his mother, for despite all the care that was lavished upon her and the ample means at her command, she lived but two years longer. On January 29, 1902 (the 21st day of Schvat, in the year 5662) this noble woman, the mother of six children, three sons and three daughters, passed away at the ripe age of eighty-two. Not Mr. Fischel alone, but all who were acquainted with her many sacrifices, devout life and kindly deeds, are certain that she joined her husband in Heaven. May both their souls rest in peace!

While Mrs. Fischel remained with her children for four weeks at the home of her youth, Mr. Fischel awaited her in Berlin where most of all he was impressed with the mode of living practiced by the Germans in contrast to the bustle and hustle of America. Here, he saw everyone apparently taking life easy and yet enjoying prosperity and happiness, there was no rush, no nervous strain, no excitement. Business men took two hours in the middle of the day, from twelve to two, for lunch, called Mittag Stunde, and everyone seemed to have the leisure to seek and find enjoyment. His thoughts then strayed to New York, where very few took the time for a lunch hour, where everyone raced at top speed from early morning till late at night, wearing them-

selves out and seemingly accomplishing no more by such strenuous living than these slow-moving, contented Germans.

When he was rejoined by his wife, the couple went to Paris,
where they remained two weeks, during which time they had
the opportunity to visit the great world's exposition of that year
and finally at Hamburg, boarded the then Leviathan of the seas,
the Kaiser Wilhelm der Grosser, for the journey back to the
United States, the beloved country of their adoption.

With these chapters is concluded that part of Mr. Fischel's
life which he has recounted from memory and which comprises
the first fifteen years of his career in America. The rest of this
biography will be compiled largely from records Mr. Fischel has
preserved regarding his activities in many fields of endeavor.
These consist of speeches and reports he has made on numerous
occasions and which are a part of the history of the principal
Jewish movements initiated during his life. Many of the facts
also are taken from thousands of items in the press, both news
articles and editorial comment upon the activities with which
Mr. Fischel has been identified and his participation in them.

CHAPTER X

FIRST MEETING WITH JACOB H. SCHIFF

THE late Jacob H. Schiff, of Blessed Memory, was the outstanding leader of his people at this period as, indeed, he was up to the time of his death. Mr. Schiff's advice and aid were sought in every matter affecting the welfare and needs of the city's Jewish population. He had achieved wide fame as a philanthropist and, of course, was recognized as among the leading financiers of the world. Not only were his personal benefactions large and numerous, establishing what was then unquestionably the record for individual giving but he was actively interested in a great number of institutions.

Mr. Schiff was to a large degree Mr. Fischel's ideal of a public benefactor, so that his first meeting with the great man, who was later to be his friend and supporter in many controversies connected with the conduct of the city's Jewish institutions, stands out among the most important of his recollections.

Mr. Fischel returned from Europe with his family toward the end of September, just prior to the High Holidays, his mind filled with plans as to how he should employ his future time. He had been greatly impressed as has been noted, with what he had seen while abroad, particularly the quiet life in Germany, and he determined to alter his own mode of living to conform somewhat with what he believed to be the saner methods of the German people.

This he could not very well do, however, if he was also to return to his business undertakings with his former energy, and at the same time comply with all the demands made upon his time by the large number of religious and philanthropic causes with which he was by now connected. Accordingly, he decided that, for a year, he would take a rest from business and devote his entire time to communal work.

His reputation in philanthropy grew rapidly and his services came to be in great demand on all sides. Before long he was invited to serve on the Board of Directors of most of the important religious, educational and philanthropic institutions in New York and soon earned the name of being the leading figure among Orthodox Jews in these fields of public endeavor.

This prominence enabled him to be of much greater usefulness than in former years, for it widened the circle of his acquaintances and largely increased his influence, so that, in the course of time, his advice on many matters affecting Orthodox Jewry came to be sought by those who represented other factions of Jewish religious thought.

Thus it was that his first meeting with Mr. Schiff was brought about. This occurred in the year 1901 at the annual meeting of the Hebrew Free Loan Society, when Mr. Fischel was invited to address the directors on the subject of "Philanthropy and Religion—The Basic Principles of Life."

At the close of his remarks, Mr. Schiff walked over to Mr. Fischel, then about thirty-five years of age, and warmly congratulated him on the views he had expressed in his address at the same time extending to him the invitation to become a member of the Advisory Board of the Montefiore Home, of which Mr. Schiff was then President. Thus began the friendship between the two men which lasted until Mr. Schiff's death. Mr. Fischel, of course, gladly accepted the invitation to become associated with the Montefiore Home, representing as it did a new phase of philanthropic work with which he had not previously been identified.

Shortly after this meeting, Mr. Schiff visited Japan and was decorated by the Japanese Government for the financial assistance his banking firm, Kuhn, Loeb and Company, had extended to that country. On his return to the United States, the directors of the Montefiore Home arranged a large reception for

Mr. Schiff at Sherry's, at which Mr. Fischel, as a member of the Advisory Board of the Home, was present.

After the formal reception, the guests were ushered into a private dining room where a buffet lunch was to be served. What was Mr. Fischel's consternation when he observed that one of the courses on the menu was lobster.

So great was Mr. Fischel's indignation and resentment at the thought that this biblically forbidden article of food was to be served to Jews at a function of this character that, despite his being the newest member of the Advisory Board of the Home, he at once addressed himself to the Chairman, who was a Supreme Court Justice, and voiced his feelings in the following words:

"Judge, if you will not consider me in contempt of court, I wish to express my indignation at the arrangements of your committee."

Mr. Schiff, who was standing close by and overheard this remark, exclaimed: "Go ahead, Mr. Fischel, and say what is in your mind. If the Judge has you arrested, I will furnish bail."

Mr. Fischel then again turned to the Judge and said:

"We have assembled here to honor Mr. Schiff as the president of Montefiore Home. I have had the great privilege of reading the life of Sir Montefiore, for whom this institution was named and in his biography it is shown that he lived a strictly Orthodox Jewish life. I am, therefore, of the opinion that, if the late Sir Montefiore had been asked to lend the use of his name to an institution serving lobsters for luncheon, he would unquestionably have refused his consent."

Before the Judge had even the opportunity to reply to Mr. Fischel's protest, Mr. Schiff at once broke into the conversation saying:

"Mr. Fischel is right. I am positive Sir Montefiore would not have allowed the use of his name for our institution had he thought that it was to be desecrated by such an act."

The Judge then apologized profusely, ordered the lobster

course removed and promised that, should he again be the chairman of such an affair, the offense would not be repeated.

Mr. Fischel felt that by this victory he had accomplished a great deal in making clear to those Jewish leaders of the community, who were not Orthodox, the necessity of observing the laws of the Jewish faith, especially in the institutions they conducted. From that time on, he never failed, whenever the opportunity presented itself, to stand up and fight for his convictions and for the enforcement of every provision of Jewish religious injunction.

CHAPTER XI

BUILDS FIRST MODERN JEWISH THEATER

THE great influx of Jewish immigration of the early nineties brought forth many new problems for solution.

Having so lately arrived from their native lands, chiefly Russia and Poland, many of the new settlers could speak little if any English and there was a real need for supplying the rapidly increasing Jewish population with the opportunity for mental relaxation and diversion of the type to which the people were accustomed and which they could understand.

Such places of amusement as then existed on the Lower East Side for the Hebrew and Yiddish speaking population, were antiquated structures that had long out-grown their usefulness and many of which were regarded as fire traps.

They were totally inadequate to the needs of the public which they were called upon to serve and failed to give the opportunity for full expression of that literary, artistic and dramatic genius the Jew has always possessed.

It was about this time, in 1902, that Mr. Fischel was approached by that great actor of the Yiddish stage, the late Jacob P. Adler, who suggested to him a project which was neither strictly business nor strictly philanthropic, but one in which both elements were in a degree combined.

Mr. Adler asked Mr. Fischel to build a new theater which should be entirely devoted to plays acted in Yiddish. This, as Mr. Adler pointed out, was a pressing necessity of the moment.

Although Mr. Fischel believed that business and philanthropy can rarely be successfully joined, the idea appealed to him and he accordingly purchased the old Lord and Taylor property at

NEW YORK'S FIRST MODERN YIDDISH THEATRE.

Erected by Mr. Fischel in 1904 at the suggestion of the great Jewish actor, the late Jacob P. Adler, at Grand and Chrystie Streets.

Grand and Chrystie Streets, on which site he constructed the Grand Theatre, the first modern Yiddish theatre in New York.

The building, which was strictly fireproof, contained every known improvement in playhouse construction up to that time, and when it was formally opened on February 4, 1904, was regarded as one of the finest theatres in the city. The opening exercises were attended by the then Mayor of New York, the Hon. Seth Low and many other public officials of both city and state. These officials highly commended Mr. Fischel for the time, energy and money he had put into this project, which really meant the safeguarding of human lives.

So heavy was the Jewish immigration in the year 1903 that the Lower East Side, previously congested to the point of saturation, became seriously overcrowded. Many of the people who had come to America in earlier years and who had prospered, consequently began to move their residences to the section of the city known as Yorkville and to the lower West Side. Mr. Fischel decided to move with the tide.

He accordingly purchased a plot of land at 118 East 93rd Street, where he erected a handsome and commodious private residence, having in mind the provision of rooms where the directors of the many institutions with which he was affiliated might meet, and also where his four daughters, rapidly growing into young womanhood, might have a place to entertain. In this home Mr. Fischel, true to his ideals, also built a very beautiful tabernacle, by far the finest he had had in any of his homes. Most of the furnishings for the new residence were purchased at the St. Louis World's Fair which he and Mrs. Fischel attended in the summer of 1904.

Although the Ninety-third Street house was occupied by the Fischels in 1905, the housewarming was not held until March 10, 1907.

This celebration was attended by the most prominent leaders in New York Jewry of that day, including the directors of nearly every Jewish institution in the city.

It had been Mr. Fischel's custom while he lived downtown to be easily accessible to all who might wish to see him and he there had maintained an office in his parlor where hundreds who required assistance of one kind or another, who desired financial aid or who wished to obtain admission to a hospital, orphan asylum, home for the aged or other institution, were in the habit of visiting him. Much of Mr. Fischel's time was occupied with these matters and he would either give these poor people a letter of introduction to the proper institution or would personally visit in their behalf the various philanthropies to which he contributed.

When Mr. Fischel moved to Yorkville, he was not long in discovering that it was exceedingly difficult for these needy ones to see him. For a year after moving uptown, Mr. Fischel arranged office hours in the evenings in which these people might visit him and made it a practice to defray their carfare. Even this arrangement, however, proved unsatisfactory because it was inconvenient to Mr. Fischel's visitors and also served to disturb his hours with his family. Accordingly he leased an office in the World Building on Park Row where he spent every afternoon and where he was able to renew close contact with the unfortunate ones.

In 1904, Mr. Fischel was honored by the President of the Borough of Manhattan, Jacob A. Cantor, with an appointment as a member of the Local School Board of the Board of Education. At the first meeting of the Board which he attended he was elected secretary.

It so happened that at this time the Superintendent of Schools had plans in view to raise the height of new school buildings from five to six stories and to install elevators in them. The architect of the Board of Education, knowing of Mr. Fischel's practical knowledge of architecture and building construction requested him to give his opinion regarding the experiment, and Mr. Fischel at once and unhesitatingly expressed his entire disapproval of the proposal on the ground that a six story building, especially with elevators, constituted a menace to the safety of the children who, at opening and closing time, might easily be injured in rushing to and from their classes.

Despite Mr. Fischel's objections, however, Public School 62, occupying the block on Hester Street, from Essex to Norfolk Streets, was constructed with elevators and, as a matter of record, proved a failure from a practical viewpoint, from the day it was opened.

CHAPTER XII

ERECTING A SYNAGOGUE IN THE CATSKILLS

IN the years following the first considerable influx of Jews from Europe to the United States many had achieved prosperity by dint of hard work, ability and sacrifice and as a result of the opportunities afforded them in the new land.

These, like Mr. Fischel, employed their good fortune to give their families comforts and advantages that had been denied to them in their youth and so it was that many had provided themselves with summer homes to which they repaired with their families for their vacations.

One of the most favored of the localities for summer Jewish colonies was the Catskill Mountains and shortly after moving to Yorkville, Mr. Fischel purchased a plot of ground at Hunter, Greene County, New York, where he proceeded to build a summer residence which he first occupied in 1904.

In the summer of 1905, Mr. Fischel was approached by a large number of the Jewish residents of Hunter who told him of the difficulty they experienced in finding a place in which to hold Sabbath services.

Mr. Fischel at once decided to remedy the situation and, with the late Morris Levinsky, approached each one of the Jewish people in the town asking them to contribute to the building of a synagogue.

The effort was unavailing, as sufficient interest could not be aroused nor could funds be obtained. This did not deter Mr. Fischel. He decided that a synagogue was necessary for the town's welfare, and determined to build it himself. Through the generosity of Dr. Samuel Friedman, who owned a large plot of

SYNAGOGUE ERECTED IN 1906 AT HUNTER, N. Y.

The first orthodox Jewish House of Worship in the Catskill Mountains, erected by Mr. Fischel and still maintained by him.

ground in the center of the village, a site was secured, together with considerable lumber which Dr. Friedman also contributed.

One Saturday night in the beginning of August, Mr. Fischel commenced work on the plans for the synagogue and before the summer ended, a beautiful structure accommodating 250 persons, was completed. Mr. Fischel donated the necessary scrolls of the law, Talmudic and other books, pews and such further equipment as was needed for the services and he has since maintained the synagogue at his own expense during every summer from 1904 to the present day, thus affording thousands of Jewish people the opportunity of worshipping while on their vacations, amid suitable surroundings.

In its issue of June 22, 1906, the Hebrew Standard took formal notice of this opportunity for religious service afforded to the summer residents of the Catskills, by printing on its first page a picture of the synagogue at Hunter, with the following comment.

"The evergrowing number of Jewish residents in Greene County, Catskill Mountains, has made a permanent place of worship an absolute necessity. It took the effort of Mr. Harry Fischel assisted by Dr. Samuel Friedman, to supply this need. Mr. Fischel has erected a synagogue on a site furnished by Dr. Friedman. The sacred edifice, is not only used for divine worship, but has Hebrew and religious classes therein as well. An official teacher has been engaged by Mr. Fischel for this purpose. Regular money offering is not permitted at the Sabbath services. The expense incurred in engaging of the Chozan, Shochet, Teacher and Sexton are defrayed by the summer residents, and at the close of the season, the deficit and all other expenses in connection with the synagogue are borne by Mr. Fischel personally."

CHAPTER XIII

FORMATION OF AMERICAN JEWISH COMMITTEE

IMMEDIATELY after the frightful pogroms in Kishinev, Russia, in the year 1905, steps were taken by the leading Jews of the United States to collect a fund for the victims and to safeguard the right of the Jewish people throughout the world to worship God according to their faith. This movement resulted in the formation by seventy representative Jews (of whom Mr. Fischel had the honor to be chosen as one) of the American Jewish Committee. The first annual meeting took place at the Hotel Astor, New York City, on November 14, 1906, lasting from 10 A.M. until 6 P.M. with a luncheon dividing the sessions. The meeting was presided over by the late Judge Meyer Sulzberger, in that year President of the Committee.

When the hour for luncheon arrived, Mr. Fischel arose and asked the privilege of the floor and when it was accorded him, he said:

"Mr. President and Members of the Committee. We have assembled here for the purpose of discussing problems affecting all Jews. Many of the members of this Committee are members of some of the largest philanthropic institutions of America, which are proud to boast that they are conducted in a non-sectarian manner, which is as it should be.

"However, when it comes to serving luncheon to our own people this is a different matter and the luncheon served here is nothing but sectarian, whereas it should be strictly non-sectarian."

The Chairman here interrupted Mr. Fischel's remarks by saying:

"I believe I am thoroughly conversant with the English language and I have never heard the term non-sectarian as applied to a luncheon. Will you please explain what you mean by that?"

Mr. Fischel then replied:

"A non-sectarian luncheon means that the Orthodox Jew can eat it, the Conservative Jew will not spoil his stomach by it and even the Reform Jew will not die from it.

"Instead of such a repast you are serving here a strictly sectarian meal, of which only the Reform Jew can partake and you are depriving all those who believe in observance of the Jewish dietary laws from eating the food served, compelling them to go home and, in many cases, preventing them from returning, which I believe is most unjust."

Judge Sulzberger and the other members of the Committee expressed themselves as in accord with the views presented by Mr. Fischel with the result that he was asked to act as chairman of the luncheon for the following year, and to provide what, in his judgment, should be a meal of which every faction of Jewry might partake without injury to their religious sensibilities.

Mr. Fischel accepted the assignment and shortly before the time for the next annual meeting, arranged for the serving of a genuinely Kosher luncheon.

On the day of the meeting and just prior to the hour for luncheon, Judge Sulzberger, who again was chairman, announced:

"Gentlemen of the Committee—it gives me great pleasure to inform you that today we are to have a non-sectarian luncheon under the chairmanship of Mr. Harry Fischel."

As chairman of the luncheon, it was Mr. Fischel's privilege to have the late Jacob H. Schiff seated on his right and that other great philanthropist, Julius Rosenwald, of Chicago on his left. Upon entering the dining room, Mr. Rosenwald expressed his pleasure and surprise at finding that a strictly Kosher luncheon could be prepared with such appetizing attractiveness. Before the meal was concluded, he gave further expression to his enjoyment and his thanks to Mr. Fischel, exclaiming that if the dietary laws could be so well and beautifully observed, then he would like to have them followed in his own home.

The occasion proved to Mr. Fischel's satisfaction that where one insists upon that which he thinks is right, especially where the question is one of principle, he invariably wins respect even from those who differ with him.

In 1906, the Home for the Daughters of Jacob, now one of the largest institutions in the city, was organized in Mr. Fischel's home. Mrs. Fischel, was one of the organizers and first vice-president from the time of the Home's inception up to 1925. The institution soon found its first quarters at 40 Gouverneur Street entirely too small for its use and purchased the property at 301-302-303 East Broadway. Due to Mrs. Fischel's importunities, Mr. Fischel was prevailed upon to accept the appointment as chairman of the Building Committee and spent a great deal of time on this work. Mr. Fischel laid the cornerstone of this building on October 6, 1907.

Shortly after he had finished this undertaking for the Daughters of Jacob, the Hebrew Sheltering House amalgamated with the Hebrew Immigrant Society, forming the institution known as the Hebrew Sheltering Immigrant Aid Society of America, of which Mr. Fischel was the treasurer. This institution required a new building to be used as a home for immigrants and Mr. Fischel took advantage of his friendship with Mr. Schiff to appeal to him for assistance in financing the project.

Mr. Schiff, who was greatly interested throughout his life in immigration work, agreed to loan the Society the sum of $35,000 in the form of a mortgage on property to be purchased at 229-231 East Broadway, comprising two old houses, which were to be reconstructed for the purpose in view. Mr. Schiff agreed, furthermore, that, should the work prove successful within a period of ten years, he would cancel the mortgage without any payment.

Mr. Fischel was again drafted as chairman of the Building Committee and successfully carried out the work of remodelling these two houses into an immigrant home. The building was completed in February 1907, and on March 15 of that year, the formal opening of the structure by the Hebrew Sheltering Immigrant Aid Society of America took place, the institution continuing to be housed there until it moved in later years to its new building at 425 Lafayette Street.

From the time of his completion of the Grand Theatre project in 1903 until 1911, Mr. Fischel did practically no work of a commercial character. Between these years there occurred the panic of 1907, which caused thousands of persons to lose their fortunes and which particularly affected those engaged in the real estate and building lines, as well as practically all financial institutions. Except for the fact that his income was temporarily depleted and that he was called upon to meet large demands upon his purse by reason of the general poverty which ensued, Mr. Fischel was in no way affected by this panic, as he was virtually out of business at the time, a stroke of good fortune for which he gave fervent thanks to the Almighty as it enabled him to continue, without curtailment, his work for and contributions to charitable causes.

CHAPTER XIV

MR. FISCHEL AND THE JEWISH ORPHAN PROBLEM

IT was in February 1909 that Mr. Fischel's thoughts and efforts were directed into an entirely new channel, namely the problem of the Jewish child in this great city, particularly the orphans. In this connection the first step was the organization in his home, with Mrs. Fischel as one of the guiding spirits, of the Hebrew Day Nursery, whose function it was to care for the children of mothers who were compelled to go out to work by the day. Mrs. Fischel, who was elected treasurer of this institution, which office she still holds, requested her husband to look for a home for the nursery and he succeeded in buying the house at 262 Henry Street, for which as a deposit, he gave his own check of $500. He then altered the building, which the institution still occupies. In addition to the original building, a branch was later added at 63 East 107th Street.

A still greater problem than that which the Day Nursery was designed to solve was that of the Jewish children in the orphan asylums, who in those days were left entirely without religious instruction or training. These children, who were to become a part of the future generation of Jewish men and women, were taught nothing about Judaism and its history, were ignorant of the meaning of the Sabbath, and of the Jewish dietary laws and were even without the knowledge of Jewish prayers. Aside from an occasional sermon, the meaning of which they little understood, no effort was made to care for anything but their physical well-being and of course their secular instruction.

This problem had for years been a sore point with many Orthodox Jews, who had striven ineffectually to convince the heads of the institutions, particularly the Hebrew Orphan Asylum and the Hebrew Sheltering Guardian Society, that they were derelict in their duty toward their wards in failing to give them religious instruction.

The brunt of the effort had fallen upon the Union of Orthodox Jewish Congregations of America, of which Dr. H. Pereira Mendes, emminent Rabbi, was the president and who had used his wide acquaintance and considerable influence with the leaders of all shades of religion, in the effort to make them realize the seriousness of this omission in its effect on the future lives of these children. Despite the efforts of Dr. Mendes and many other Rabbis, however, no progress had been made.

The two institutions together cared for more than 1800 children. Many had gone from the institutions to take positions of importance in business and the professions with no conception of the sacredness of the religion to which they were by birth attached.

Mr. Fischel had many times given earnest consideration to this question and to its ultimate effect upon the Judaism of the future and had hoped for the opportunity to do something that might alter these conditions.

Thus it seemed almost like an answer to his prayers, when a real estate broker came to his office in October 1909, and offered for sale the property of an old infant asylum situated at 161st Street and Eagle Avenue.

Mr. Fischel at once went to look at the property, which consisted of about ten city lots, on which were several good buildings with accommodations for about 200 children. The minute he saw it, the thought occurred to him that here was the opportunity to start an orphan asylum to be conducted under strictly orthodox methods. With the germ of this idea firmly implanted in his mind, he returned to his office and at once called a conference of several of his friends at which he laid the plan before them.

The idea met with enthusiastic response and before the meeting adjourned, Mr. Fischel had raised pledges for a fund of $3000 to make a deposit on the property, provided a suitable purchase price could be arranged. He then entered into negotiations with the broker, finally agreeing to pay $35,000 for the property, which was much less than its real value.

When he again called his friends together to collect the $3,000 they had volunteered to contribute, he found, however, they had undergone a change of heart and all were agreed that the proposition was entirely too large to undertake, especially in view of the existing institutions, with millions of dollars behind them, and the opposition to the undertaking that might be expected to develop from this source.

Mr. Fischel did not permit this bogey to frighten him and when he found he could not expect to receive help from these men, he decided to conclude the purchase in his own name. As soon as he had closed the contract, Mr. Fischel took steps to obtain a charter for an orphan asylum as required by law, but, on consulting with counsel, found that, in order to secure such a charter, he would first have to secure the consent of the then Council of Communal Institutions, which consisted of the presidents of all the large charitable institutions of the City.

Judge Samuel Greenbaum was the president of this Council and Mr. Fischel turned to him to put his case and to obtain his approval. He was considerably surprised on being informed by Judge Greenbaum that he had no power to give such approval but that he would call a meeting of the Council members and that Mr. Fischel would be later advised of the decision reached.

Then followed a long and bitter struggle on Mr. Fischel's part to win consent for the undertaking or else to change conditions in the existing institutions, a struggle in which he was compelled to surmount great opposition on the part of the most influential men in the community.

Mr. Fischel waited in vain for several weeks after his visit to Judge Greenbaum for word of what had transpired and failing to hear anything, again went to the Judge with the demand that he receive an answer one way or the other. After waiting again some little time he was informed that the Council had met and had refused its approval of the proposed asylum on the ground that it would interfere with the two large existing institutions for the care of orphans.

This discouragement only served to strengthen Mr. Fischel's determination to launch the new orphanage and he, accordingly, notified Judge Greenbaum that he intended retaining a lawyer and that he would demand a charter without the consent of the Council, if that body did not afford him a hearing in the presence of its full membership. After a number of pleadings before Judge Greenbaum, the latter promised that he would call such a meeting and do what was within his power to assist him.

Shortly thereafter, a hearing on the project was arranged for, in the office of Adolph Lewisohn at 42 Broadway. This meeting was attended by the heads of many institutions and, besides Mr. Lewisohn, those who were present included the late Jacob H. Schiff, president of Montefiore Hospital; Mr. George Blumenthal, president of Mt. Sinai Hospital; Judge Joseph Newberger, president of the Hebrew Orphan Asylum; Judge Greenbaum, president of the Educational Alliance and the late Edward Lauterbach, who was present as the attorney for the Council.

Mr. Fischel went fully into his plans, explaining how he had come to purchase the property and how he felt that an orphan asylum where Jewish children would be brought up under strictly Orthodox auspices would fill a long felt want in the community. But Mr. Fischel went further than this, he attacked the existing institutions as being not, in fact, Jewish, although they were represented as such.

After fully two hours of discussion the members of the Council at first flatly refused to entertain the idea, but before the meeting finally adjourned changed their minds to the extent of agreeing to another hearing on the matter the following week.

In order to more fully fortify himself with facts to overcome the opposition he now knew he could expect, he decided to take with him to this second meeting as spokesmen, other than himself, a Rabbi, a lawyer and a business man. The three men he chose to accompany him were Dr. H. Pereira Mendes, as the Rabbi; the late Adolph Cohen, then a prominent member of the bar, a native American and strictly Orthodox in his principles and observance, as the lawyer, and the late Samuel I. Hyman, a very successful merchant who strictly adhered to Orthodox observances, as the business man. Mr. Hyman was also selected for the reason that he had been brought up in an orphan asylum.

Upon arriving at the meeting, Mr. Fischel learned that Jacob H. Schiff was to preside. He found the same men present, (with one or two additions,) who had attended the previous meeting. Mr. Fischel made the demand that a stenographer take down every word which should be uttered, his argument being that, should the Council again refuse to give its approval to the project, he desired the stenographic minutes of the meeting for the purpose of starting legal proceedings by which to compel the granting of a charter and also that he might preserve the record to leave to his children in after years, that he might show them how he had fought to perpetuate the ideals of Judaism in America. Mr. Schiff granted Mr. Fischel's request and a stenographer was called in.

Mr. Fischel asked the privilege of speaking last and first introduced Dr. Mendes who made a strong plea for preserving Judaism in America. He next called upon Mr. Cohen, who pleaded the case from its legal aspects, and finally asked Mr. Hyman to give his views. The latter declared that, had it not been for the religious training he had received in his youth in the orphan asylum, he would not have been able to face life as he had and that, had he been brought up in either of the two institutions represented in the Council, both he and the generations of Hymans to come after him would have been lost to Judaism entirely.

Despite the eloquence and strong logic of these pleas, Mr. Fischel saw the Council was not yet convinced of the necessity of the new asylum and that stronger arguments still would have to be used if the plan was not to suffer defeat.

Accordingly, he arose and using language that was probably the strongest which had ever been addressed in such circumstances to leaders of Jewry of this importance, he denounced them as be-

ing false to the trust imposed in them by the Jewish people and
delinquent in the duty they owed to Judaism.   He further declared that, if the institutions they directed were not to be conducted in a Jewish manner and in accordance with the teachings
of the Jewish religion, the necessity for separate Jewish institutions was then made manifest.   He also pointed out that the
parents of these children entrusted to their care had no other hope
than that their offspring might be brought up as good Jews and
perpetuate the principles of their faith after they had gone.

Mr. Fischel was moved to an exhibition of intense feeling during this discourse, gaining courage from the righteousness of his
cause, that of the preservation of his religion.   At the conclusion
of his remarks, Mr. Lauterbach arose and said:

"Mr. Fischel is perfectly right.   I had the privilege of drawing
the charter for our orphan asylum myself and it provides for a
strictly religious institution, with religious instruction."

This intention of the organizers, Mr. Lauterbach added, had
never been carried out.

This stand so bravely taken by the attorney for these institutions entirely changed the complexion of the meeting and Mr.
Fischel at once noticed by the expression of those present that
they began to see justice in the claims he had set forth.

He then made them the following proposition: "If they would
agree to install (kashruth), observance of the Jewish dietary laws,
in their two institutions and give the children a religious education, he would abandon his proposed institution and give them
the profit he had been offered upon the property toward the expense of purchasing new cooking utensils and dishes."

Immediately after this offer, the committee adjourned to another room to confer alone and in a few minutes returned, much
in the manner of a jury rendering its verdict, with Mr. Lauterbach as their foreman. Addressing himself to Mr. Fischel, Mr.
Lauterbach, said:

"Mr. Fischel, we have discussed your proposition from every
point of view and after due consideration have decided that, since

your action in this matter is for the interest and welfare of the Jewish children and since you have so clearly shown your sincerity and personal disinterestedness, we will grant your request.

"We agree to install kashruth and religious education in such a manner as will be satisfactory to a Rabbi of your selection. As to your kind offer to turn over to us the profit on the property you bought for this purpose of establishing an orphan asylum, we cannot accept this for the reason that we do not wish to be paid for performing our duty. We certainly appreciate the sacrifice you are willing to make in giving away such a large sum of money and we suggest, since you have decided not to profit in any way from this transaction, that you turn the property back to the original owner, the Hebrew Infant Asylum, and let them have the profit which they can use toward the construction of a new building."

Mr. Fischel accepted this suggestion and turned the property back to the president of the Hebrew Infant Asylum, Mr. Beno Newberger, together with his check for $500 as a personal contribution to the building fund. The institution shortly thereafter disposed of the property for a much larger price than that at which it had been sold to Mr. Fischel.

The radical change in attitude toward observance of the dietary laws and toward religious training for the children in the institutions, embodied in the far reaching surrender by their directors, naturally filled Mr. Fischel's heart with joy. He was not satisfied merely to have the decision spread upon the minutes, however, but insisted that it be reduced to a formal agreement in writing, stating just how and when the change in the system of management of the institutions was to be effected.

Judge Newberger, president of the Hebrew Orphan Asylum, suggested that, as the Passover Holidays were approaching, kashruth be installed in his institution at that time. Adolph Lewisohn, speaking in behalf of the Hebrew Sheltering Guardian Society, of which he was president, proposed that it be installed in the latter institution on the completion of the new cottages at

Pleasantville, New York, then under course of construction and which were expected to be occupied in about two months, pointing out that this would save the expense of installing new kitchens and providing new dishes in the building about to be vacated.

Mr. Fischel was satisfied to accept both suggestions and an agreement was accordingly drawn up and signed by Judge Newburger, for the Hebrew Orphan Asylum, and by Mr. Lewisohn for the Hebrew Sheltering Guardian Society. This agreement, still held by Mr. Fischel, is one of his most prized possessions. It is worthy of record here that the Hebrew Orphan Asylum has carried out the agreement to the letter. While the Hebrew Sheltering Guardian Society has lived up to the terms, insofar as religious instruction for its wards is concerned, the dietary laws have never been carried out in the same manner and spirit as has been true of the Hebrew Orphan Asylum.

Credit for the results obtained in the Hebrew Orphan Asylum is largely due to Dr. Solomon Lowenstein, then its superintendent and now the executive head of the Jewish Federation. Dr. Lowenstein, almost overnight, it may be said, changed the Asylum from an institution in which religion was practically unknown to a strictly Orthodox one.

In accomplishing this, a large room was at once converted into a separate kitchen, so that the preparation of meat and dairy products should be kept entirely apart. Additional ice boxes were also constructed for the storage of meats, in order that supplies need not be purchased on the Sabbath or holidays and a similar ice box was built in that part of the institution where dairy products were stored.

A supervisor, recommended by Rabbi M. S. Margolies, was engaged and on frequent occasions when the institution was subsequently visited by Rabbi Margolies and Mr. Fischel it was found that the dietary laws were faithfully and carefully observed. More than this and true to the terms of the agreement, immediately following the Passover Holidays, a principal and teachers were employed and a thorough system of religious and

Hebrew instruction was permanently adopted, a step which has resulted in instilling a love for their faith in the hearts of thousands of children, who have since gone out into the world as good Jews, ready to adhere to the religion of their fathers and to battle for its preservation.

Immediately prior to the first Feast of the Tabernacle following these changes, a large Succah was erected. As it was not large enough to accommodate all the children at one time, they took turns in attendance, and nearly every child partook of at least one meal therein.

This victory, won by Mr. Fischel practically single handed and over the opposition of the then most prominent and powerful leaders of New York Jewry, who completely changed their views as a result of his representations, is regarded by him as one of the most significant and important accomplishments of his career.

It is difficult to estimate the effect upon thousands of lives of the way that was thus opened to them to acquire religious knowledge and instruction, nor is it possible to measure the influence exerted in behalf of traditional observance by this recognition of its importance, on the part of those at first hostile to the thought of converting these institutions to Orthodox Jewish principles.

But Mr. Fischel was not alone in deriving pleasure and satisfaction from the success with which his efforts were crowned. The great Jewish public of New York was quick to recognize and approve the new order of conduct of the institutions. This approval was voiced by the many editorial comments in the New York Jewish and English press. Typical of these is an editorial which appeared in the Hebrew Standard.

"WITH A MIGHTY HAND"

We are glad to know that there are some right-thinking Jews still left in this community. For years the effort has been made to have our Jewish communal institutions observe the dietary laws, maintain a Jewish ritual and religious instruction for their charges and, in short, be thoroughly Jewish in fact, not merely in name.

It remained, however, for Mr. Harry Fischel in the movement recently initiated for a third Jewish orphanage in this City, to bring order out of chaos. Year after year, appeal after appeal had been made to the Hebrew Orphan Asylum and the Hebrew Sheltering Guardian Society to convert their institutions into real Jewish organizations. Children coming to these institutions at a tender age leave them in the formative period of their lives, neither Jews nor Gentiles. They, the charges of a Jewish institution, know nothing of the Jewish religion and the dietary laws. Such procedure, as we have often pointed out, is criminally neglectful on the part of the directors.

Fortunately, the matter wears a different aspect now. At a meeting of a committee of the Council of Jewish Communal Institutions in this city on the 17th, a hearing was had on the question of approving the proposed formation of a new Jewish Orphans' Home. All the talk about duplication of existing institutions was then heard. But this time, the Orthodox communal workers succeeded in no uncertain way with their cause.

Mr. Edward Lauterbach, a director of the Hebrew Orphan Asylum, pointed out that his institution is historically committed to maintain the Jewish ritual and dietary laws. In an election held in 1864, the bone of contention was the observance of the laws of Kashruth. Mr. Joseph Seligman was elected president of the Orphan Asylum and its constitution was made to read that the institution was obliged to observe the Jewish dietary laws, as these were then maintained at the Mt. Sinai Hospital. This requirement must still be enforced today, and it will be, we are glad to say, now that the gentlemen associated with the movement for a third orphanage have brought the situation squarely and fairly before those who are charged with the execution of this duty.

And Mr. Fischel has succeeded even beyond their own expectations. Their proposed institution will not be erected. The need for it vanishes as soon as the existing institutions do their bounden duty by this community. The Hebrew Orphan Asylum has pledged itself to install a kosher kitchen and to instruct its wards in the Jewish ritual and religion. The Hebrew Sheltering Guardian Society, claiming not to be financially able to incur these expenses, will be aided with the money pledged to the new proposed institution to carry out its duty. When Mr. Joachimson was defeated in 1864 for the office of president of the Orphan Asylum, he organized the Sheltering Guardian Society, apparently in order to create a truly Jewish Instiution. After the lapse of years since then, this institution will become what it has hiherto only purported to be: A Jewish institution in the real sense of the word.

We congratulate Mr. Fischel on the complete success which has attended his effort to achieve this much needed reform. As Rabbi Margolies pointed out to Superintendent Bernstein of the Guardian Society: Kosher is kosher! There are no degrees in kosher.

Our final word on this subject is: let the Mt. Sinai Hospital directors be made to see the light!

CHAPTER XV

FIRST VISIT TO PALESTINE

PALESTINE, both because of its holy traditions and the increasing importance attaching to the country by reason of its potentialities as a Jewish homeland, had for a long period exerted a powerful attraction for Mr. Fischel.

In 1909, years before the Balfour Declaration, which was fraught with such mighty import for the Jews of the whole world, conditions in Russia were intolerable and the Jewish population of that country found it all but impossible to earn a livelihood. Not all, of course, were in a position to emigrate to America, though the restrictive immigration laws of the present day were not then in force.

In pondering over the plight of his own and his wife's relatives still in Russia and whom he had sought to assist but who had found it impossible to become self-supporting even with his aid, the idea suddenly came to Mr. Fischel to have them settle in Palestine. This inspiration indirectly led to Mr. Fischel's first visit to the Holy Land.

It was, of course, first necessary that he learn what their attitude might be and to determine this, Mr. Fischel sent each a letter in which he outlined his plans and asked that they advise him as to their decision.

Mr. Fischel's proposal was that he would purchase sufficient land in Palestine to support several families and when this land had been cultivated by them, the other families would follow, until in the end, all would be made self-supporting. By this plan he would accomplish a dual purpose, first he would solve the problem affecting the lives of his relatives by taking them out of Russia, and second, he would be performing a considerable service for the upbuilding of Palestine.

Within a month, Mr. Fischel had received replies from all of his own and his wife's relatives in which they joyfully acceded to the proposal, even going so far as to declare that they would prefer to live on bread and water in the Holy Land than to remain in Russia, no matter how favorable their financial condition in the latter country might be.

Mr. Fischel accordingly decided to send an emissary to Palestine to select suitable land for the purpose he contemplated, and chose as his representative his wife's brother, Mr. Wolf Brass. Mr. Brass sailed for Palestine in October 1909, his instructions being to spend six months there in studying conditions and in formulating his recommendations, it being arranged that Mr. Fischel would join him in July of the following year.

When it became known to Mr. Fischel's friends that he had engaged passage for Palestine and was to leave on June 29, 1910, on the steamship Kaiser Wilhelm, the directors of a number of institutions arranged to tender Mr. Fischel a testimonial on the eve of his departure.

This function took the form of a dinner which was held at the Hotel Astor on the evening of June 27, 1910, and was attended by several hundred men and women representing many important New York institutions with which Mr. Fischel was affiliated. Among them were the Beth Israel Hospital, Hebrew Sheltering and Immigrant Aid Society, Hebrew Free Loan Society, Jewish Maternity Hospital, Jewish Community of New York (the Kehilla), Home of the Daughters of Jacob, the Uptown Talmud Torah, Congregation Kehilath Jeshurun, Union of Orthodox Jewish Congregations of America and numerous others.

Judge Leon Sanders was chairman of the dinner committee and toastmaster of the evening, and among those who made addresses were Rabbi M. S. Margolies, Rabbi H. Periera Mendes, Judge Abram I. Elkus, later Ambassador to Turkey, Judge Otto A. Rosalsky, Supreme Court Justice Nathan Bijur, Congressman Henry M. Goldfogle, A. E. Rothstein and the late Edward Lauterbach. The last speaker presented Mr. Fischel with an engrossed resolution in a gold frame signed by all the representatives of the institutions responsible for the testimonial. This resolution read as follows:

WHEREAS, Mr. Harry Fischel by his inherent and faithful devotion to the cause of charity and philanthropy has endeared himself to the People of the City of New York—

WHEREAS, his liberal generosity and unerring judgment in the distribution of aid to the poor and needy has had a tendency to make them self-supporting and useful members of our country and

WHEREAS during a period of almost a quarter of a century he has given to the various Jewish Institutions of our City the benefit of his wise counsel and cooperation and liberal contributions, thereby rendering himself useful to all those interested in the material welfare of our Jewish race and

WHEREAS he is about to leave this country on a tour through the Holy Land for the purpose of giving a fresh and lasting stimulus to the efforts of Israel's pioneers in the land of their fathers, therefore

BE IT RESOLVED that we, the undersigned representatives of Jewish Institutions, express our love and appreciation for Mr. Harry Fischel, by extending to him in the name of the Jewish Community of the City of New York, our best wishes for a bon voyage and safe and happy return, and

BE IT FURTHER RESOLVED that a copy of this resolution be engrossed and presented to Mr. Harry Fischel before his departure for Palestine.

In making the presentation of the resolutions, Mr. Lauterbach, in a feeling and eloquent address, referred to Mr. Fischel's services to the community in the fields of religion and philanthropy, placing special emphasis on what he had been enabled to accomplish in introducing observance of the dietary laws and religious training in those two great institutions, the Hebrew Orphan Asylum and the Hebrew Sheltering Guardian Society.

Mr. Fischel was so overcome with emotion by the tributes paid him by Mr. Lauterbach and other speakers, that his own remarks in response were brief. He contented himself with voicing his appreciation of this testimonial on the part of his friends, the number of whom he said, he had not previously realized.

Mr. Fischel left for Palestine the following day. Up to the last moment, Mrs. Fischel had intended to accompany him, but she finally decided otherwise, and, in her place, sent their eldest daughter, Sadie, who had only just graduated from Hunter College and whose education, it was felt, would be properly supplemented by this opportunity to visit the Holy Land and to see a considerable part of the rest of the world. The Kaiser Wilhelm took the two to Hamburg, whence they went by train to Marseilles and from there by boat to Alexandria. At that time there was no train connection between Alexandria and Jerusalem as there is today. Therefore, they concluded their trip by boat to Jaffe.

On this last stage of their journey occurred one of the most affecting and unusual experiences in Mr. Fischel's entire career. Boarding the boat at Alexandria, his attention was directed to what appeared to be an aged Rabbi, with flowing beard, accompanied to the pier by a large number of Roman Catholic priests who bid him an ostentatious bon voyage. Mr. Fischel could not understand what relation such a man might bear to these priests and, so soon as the boat had left its moorings, could not restrain his impulse to approach the seeming Rabbi and question him.

He replied to Mr. Fischel's interrogations by saying: "I am a Catholic Jew."

Never having heard of such a religious combination in all his years and travelings, Mr. Fischel asked the man to define what might be meant by this term. The old fellow replied that he had been converted to Roman Catholicism and that he made his living by doing Christian proselyting in Palestine, which, he added with enthusiasm, was a great field in which to capture Jewish souls at exceedingly small cost.

While Mr. Fischel was astounded by this confession, he found the old man a most interesting character and determined to engage him in conversation with the idea, if possible, of causing him to return to his own faith. He found him possessed of great Talmudic as well as worldly knowledge, and in their discussion, which lasted most of the night, each tried to convert the other to his way of thinking. Finally Mr. Fischel told the aged man that, at his time of life it was his duty to repent and return to Judaism before it was too late and he should be called to go to another world, where his soul would be denied rest throughout eternity. Mr. Fischel further told the aged man he was positive that, before his end came, he would repent and would send for a Jewish Rabbi to administer to him the last rites.

Before the man left the steamer, his farewell words to Mr. Fischel were:

"I am convinced that you are not to be converted to Christianity, but please do not try to convert me back to Judaism as I am too old to start life over again."

Shortly thereafter on his arrival in Jerusalem, Mr. Fischel was informed that a Christian Missionary, a Jew by birth, was dangerously ill and had sent for a Jewish Rabbi to say Vidooy (the Jewish confessional) with him. Curious to learn who the man was, Mr. Fischel went to his house and what was his surprise and gratification to learn it was the man he had met on the steamer.

On seeing Mr. Fischel, the ill man, his last breath almost spent, turned to him and said: "You won. Your prophecy has been realized. I regret that I have spent thirty years of my life simply for the purpose of exchanging my religion for gold. Now I have neither gold nor religion. I am dying a poor man. This should be an example for others who are tempted to do as I have done."

Arriving with his daughter at Jaffe early in the morning and realizing that he was about to enter Palestine, the one place to which the Jews of all the world pray to the Almighty they may have the privilege of going, Mr. Fischel's heart was filled with gladness and the hardships he had endured in the past dwindled into insignificance compared with the joy he now experienced.

His first thought was to fulfill the mission which had brought him all these miles, namely that of providing for his relatives who were anxiously awaiting word from him in Russia.   Mr. Brass had selected the colony known as Petach Tikvah for the settlement and Mr. Fischel went at once to this place.   He found the land chosen so completely satisfactory for the purpose that, within an hour, he had concluded its purchase.   Within two months, two families had migrated from Russia to Palestine and the settlement had been started.

Mr. Fischel's hopes to found a large colony were never to be fully realized, however, for just when the land had been made productive and when it was ready to provide for four additional families, the World War broke out and his expectations were frustrated.

During his stay in Palestine, Mr. Fischel not only visited all of the institutions there, but with his daughter endeavored to view the principal spots of historic and scriptural interest.

On one occasion they went to the city of Hebron.   Here are located the tombs of the patriarchs of old, Abraham, Isaac and Jacob, who are interred there with their wives Sarah, Rebecca and Leah, in addition to Adam and Eve who are also buried there. Upon reaching the steps of this holy place they attempted to ascend, only to find their way barred by an Arab bearing a great sword in his hands and refusing to allow them to mount more than the first six steps.

Mr. Fischel was not greatly exercised by this interception as he knew most of the sacred places of the Holy Land were in Moslem control, but to his daughter, born in America and thoroughly imbued with American ideas of religious free-dom, it seemed a wholly unnatural and unwarranted assumption of power on the part of the Moslems to deny Jews admittance to a spot which is the Jews' rightful heritage.

While Mr. Fischel had intended to remain in Palestine for some time, he limited his stay to two weeks, as Miss Fischel urged him to leave, saying: "Let us go back to America, where we can do what we wish, see what we wish and take advantage of every opportunity."

Acceding to his daughter's request, Mr. Fischel returned by way of Italy, visiting Naples, Venice, Milan, Florence and Rome. It so happened that they arrived in Rome just before the ninth day of the month of Ab, the day on which the Jews mourn for the destruction of the Temple in Jerusalem. In the evening they attended the services in the synagogue, probably the largest and most beautiful in Europe, and were greatly impressed. In a room on one side of the synagogue set apart especially for this occasion, with no light other than candles which are held in the hands of the worshippers, the members of the Congregation sit on small stools reading from the Book of Lamentations. The candles, it is their belief, originate from those used in the Temple before its destruction.

The next day, following lamentation services in the morning, they went to the Arch of Titus, erected by the Romans in commemoration of their victory over the Jews at the time of the destruction of the Temple. It seemed to them most appropriate that they should visit this scene on the anniversary of this historic Jewish event, and should take the occasion not only to pray but to shed some tears over the loss of the great temple in Jerusalem.

Leaving Rome, Mr. Fischel and his daughter journeyed again to Hamburg, from which port they set sail for their beloved America.

XVI

A CONFERENCE WITH PRESIDENT TAFT

RETURNING to the United States during the month of September, Mr. Fischel found the various activities in which he was interested again ready to make large demands, not only upon his time but upon his purse.

He was, furthermore, shortly to be engaged in a new work which was to exert a potent influence on the future of American Jewry, in that it was to make possible the admission to this land of many Jews who had previously been excluded under the rulings of the Immigration authorities but who nevertheless constituted the most desirable element for future citizenship. These additional labors were also to mark his first meeting with a President of the United States.

Before being called to enter upon his new tasks, however, Mr. Fischel employed the respite to set his own affairs in order. He had not been engaged in business for some years and while the panic of 1907 had spared him from the unhappy consequences affecting nearly all those who had extensive realty investments, his income had not increased but had, on the contrary, undergone some depletion.

In order to continue his communal and charitable activities as in the past, he decided once again to engage in building operations. With the exception of the building of the Grand Theater Mr. Fischel, up to this time, had almost exclusively been engaged in the construction of tenement houses on the Lower East Side. He had not only profited largely in this field but had earned the gratitude of the community for the type of buildings he had erected and which had greatly altered the character of the neighborhood and had set a new standard for sanitary conditions and for living accommodations for the poor generally. These tene-

ments, it may be said, were the forerunner of future movements
to improve housing conditions in the congested quarters of the
city which even at this day constitutes one of the most important
matters in the public eye.

Mr. Fischel had no desire at this time, however, to resume the
construction of tenements but looked for new fields to conquer
and finally decided upon adventuring into the construction of
mercantile buildings in which he was later to have considerable
success.

He purchased a plot of ground on Broadway facing Bond
Street, on which he erected a twelve story, fireproof office building, modern in all its appointments and containing every known
improvement in that type of structure. The venture was not
as successful as he had anticipated, for no sooner was the building completed, than the trend of business moved uptown and
the neighborhood suffered in consequence.

This experience, while it ended for the time being Mr. Fischel's
resumption of building, proved to the advantage of the Jewish
public for it caused him once more to devote his time exclusively
to communal matters.

It was at this period, early in 1911, that the question of immigration and the problems connected with it imposed a heavy
burden upon the Hebrew Sheltering and Immigrant Aid Society,
of which Mr. Fischel was treasurer.

The immigration from Russia, Poland and Lithuania was exceedingly heavy that year and hundreds of immigrants on arriving
here were ordered deported to their native lands because of their
failure to pass the physical or other requirements the government
insisted upon.

While the Society succeeded, through its representations made
directly to Washington, in securing the admission of many immigrants who were at first rejected there was one class among
those seeking entrance in whose behalf such individual appeals
proved futile. Those in this class were merely tagged with a
ticket on which were the letters "L.O.P.D." signifiying Lack of

Physical Development and their case had up to now been hopeless. Pale and suffering from lack of nourishment, these unfortunates were rejected as they passed before the examiners.

Of special concern to the Society and to Mr. Fischel was the fact that in this class was to be found the most valuable material for the future preservation of Judaism in America as, for the most part, the rejected ones comprised the intellectuals, students, teachers, Rabbis and members of other professions. Their lives having been spent almost entirely indoors, the long journey to America, occupying in those days about two weeks, with the privations they endured on the way, had sapped their scant physical resources to the utmost.

Most of these immigrants were scrupulous as to their religious practices and observance of the Dietary Laws and the last straw which had served to undermine their constitutions and make them appear wan and ill, was the fact that on their journey to America they had eaten little or no food.

On his frequent visits to Ellis Island, Mr. Fischel had especially sympathized with these immigrants and had been much moved by the pitiable stories they recounted to him concerning the dark future they must, of necessity, face if not permitted to remain here.

After a great deal of consideration given to the problem, Mr. Fischel saw, as he believed, a solution. This was that if these immigrants could be afforded the opportunity to rest for several weeks after reaching these shores, meanwhile receiving an abundance of strictly kosher food, and then he re-examined, they would be able to pass the government's requirements, as they would be restored to a normal condition of health and strength.

Having come to this conclusion, Mr. Fischel lost little time in broaching it to the Board of Directors of the Hias. He proposed that the attempt be made to secure permission from the Government to install a kosher kitchen at Ellis Island and also to be granted the privilege of having these immigrants held over for several weeks in order to be re-examined. Mr. Fischel explained to the directors that, while it would mean a considerable expense to the Society if this permission were granted, the plan would, nevertheless, be well worth while if it was successful in securing even for only a few of those previously barred, the right to remain here.

So forcefully did Mr. Fischel paint the situation to the Board of Directors that they at once agreed to his proposal and a committee was named to go to Washington and seek permission from the government, first to install a kosher kitchen at Ellis Island and, second, to allow the rejected immigrants to remain there two weeks on probation, subject to a re-examination at the expiration of that period.

On February 4, 1911, the Committee, consisting of Leon Kamaiky, Isidore Hirschfield and Mr. Fischel went to Washington and were received in the White House by President William Howard Taft, who met them in the company of Secretary of Commerce and Labor Nagel, under whose jurisdiction Ellis Island then came. Both President Taft and Secretary Nagel were greatly moved by the facts as they were placed before them, admitting the justice and humanity of the demands that were made. Finally, President Taft, turning to Secretary Nagel, requested that the latter do all in his power to work out a plan whereby the suggestions might be carried into effect.

As a result, Secretary Nagel invited the members of the Committee to have lunch with him at the Hotel Willard for the purpose of further discussing the arrangements. At this luncheon Mr. Thompson, Mr. Nagel's secretary, was seated next to Mr. Fischel. True to his practice throughout his life of complying with the Jewish dietary laws, whether at home or abroad, Mr. Fischel found that he could not partake of the repast served on this occasion and contented himself with eating only some fruit.

Mr. Thompson noticing this remarked, "Did you have luncheon before coming here, Mr. Fischel?"

"No," replied Mr. Fischel, proceeding further to utilize this splendid opportunity of explaining to Mr. Thompson more fully the reasons which had prompted the Committee to visit the President and the Secretary of Commerce and Labor. He stated that he had only just returned from Europe and, as an American and having sufficient means at his disposal, he had been able to travel first class. Even so, he declared, he had been unable to procure the food to which he was accustomed and had lost in weight and vigor in consequence.

Had he been compelled to travel in the steerage and to pass an examination at Ellis Island he, too, Mr. Fischel said, would no doubt have been excluded as were the poor immigrants whose cause he pleaded and who, throughout their long voyage, had to undergo hardships because they had not the means with which to provide themselves with the food their religion prescribes. He continued to describe the hardships confronting these poor people, how they disposed of all their belongings to make the journey, which took months before they ultimately reached America, and finally asked Mr. Thompson how, under the circumstances, the immigrants could be expected to appear vigorous and robust.

The conversation Mr. Fischel had carried on with Mr. Thompson had been overheard by Secretary Nagel, who finally brought the discussion to a conclusion by saying:

"Gentlemen, you have my approval and support in helping to carry out your plan."

Secretary Nagel then made inquiries, before the Committee had left Washington, as to how many such cases were held at Ellis Island at the time and on being informed by telegraph there were forty-seven immigrants awaiting deportation, he issued instructions that they be detained until the kosher kitchen had been installed and they had been given the opportunity to be re-examined.

In less than two weeks after the installation of the Kosher kitchen at Ellis Island, which, by the way, is still maintained at the expense of the Hebrew Sheltering and Immigrant Aid Society, Mr. Fischel had the great satisfaction of seeing many of these immigrants, restored to strength and health by the food supplied them by the Society, admitted to the United States.

Since that time, thousands of immigrants of this same and highly desirable type have been admitted to the country, largely as a result of this instrumentality and due to the large heartedness and spirit of justice which animated President Taft in consenting to this epochal experiment. In all the history of the United States there has never been a better friend of the Jewish people than President Taft proved himself to be on this and on many other occasions.

CHAPTER XVII

A BATTLE FOR EDUCATIONAL PROGRESS

MR. FISCHEL had shown by his success in enforcing recognition of Orthodox principles in the orphan asylums his courage and ability in the face of opposition, no matter how powerful. Now, quite unwittingly, he was to become engaged in another struggle in behalf of his convictions as to the proper education of the Jewish young, that for the next several years, was to utilize every ounce of energy and all the fighting qualities he possessed.

Always intensely interested in the rising generation, Mr. Fischel, despite all his many other activities, decided to give a larger share of his time to the problems connected with Jewish religious education. He was then the vice-president of the Uptown Talmud Torah as well as a director of many other Talmud Torahs throughout the city. From a small institution, occupying an old building with few classrooms, the Uptown Talmud Torah had but lately completed the construction of a fine new structure, costing upwards of $200,000 and situated at 132-134 East One Hundred and Eleventh Street. This building was practically the first structure to be erected in New York solely for the purpose of a Talmud Torah and was in every sense, a modern and adequately equipped religious school.

The expenses of the institution had naturally increased with its expansion from about $10,000 to $30,000 annually. The Board of Directors had experienced a great deal of difficulty in raising funds to meet the increased expenses and had found their individual efforts insufficient to meet the institution's needs.

They reached the conclusion that it would be necessary to enlist the cooperation of someone who should give his entire time to the undertaking in order that the income might square with the

budget required if the Uptown Talmud Torah was to function in
a manner befitting its new home and enlarged facilities.

In this emergency they turned to Mr. Fischel, the only member
of the Board who was not actively engaged in business. Through
a committee which waited upon him they offered him the Presidency of the institution, pointing out that it was the belief of the
directors that he would not only be able to solve its financial
problems but would be in a position to greatly advance its educational standards, its prestige and service to the community.

Mr. Fischel, loath though he was to accept the tremendous
additional responsibilities involved in assuming the leadership of
so great an enterprise, nevertheless felt it his duty to do so, especially since the directors were unable to secure any other man
who was in a position to give to the work the time and effort it
demanded.

He, accordingly proposed to the Committee that if the directors would make up the deficiency outstanding at that time,
amounting to about $17,000, he would accept the presidency.
The Committee at once agreed to this proposal and Mr. Fischel
was elected president of the Uptown Talmud Torah, then the
most important Jewish educational institution in America.

His first step on assuming office was to make a thorough investigation of every department and every phase of the work, not
alone the institution's financial situation but its educational program, teaching staff and even the management of the building.
It soon became apparent that the burden he had taken on his
shoulders was an even heavier one than he had anticipated.

On every side he found that chaotic conditions prevailed, conditions that required industry, patience and diplomacy to
straighten out before order was restored, involving an effort that
consumed much more of his time than he had supposed might
reasonably be required. If, however, he was to succeed in causing
the institution to occupy the commanding position he pictured
for it, there was nothing to be done but to exert his every energy
to that end and, accordingly, he at once established regular office

hours in the building from nine until eleven in the morning, although he often remained much later than this hour in order to see all those whom he wished to consult or who wished to consult him.

In addition to interesting all those persons he could personally influence to become members, he engaged and himself paid several solicitors to interest the general public. As a result of this concentrated effort, Mr. Fischel was able to report on March 17, 1912, at the first annual meeting following his election to the presidency, that the annual income had been raised from $22,000 at the time he took office, to more than $30,000 an increase of $8,000 in a single year, a remarkable gain for those times, when it is considered that the appeal had been for funds for maintenance only.

During this period, the school had grown from thirty-eight classes, accommodating 1275 children, to forty-eight classes, with an enrollment of 1707 pupils.

At the annual meeting of that year more than 2,000 persons were present, including such outstanding leaders as the late Jacob H. Schiff, Judge Samuel Greenbaum and others. In his report, Mr. Fischel dwelt upon the necessity for improving the standards of Jewish education in New York, constituting the largest Jewish community in America and advanced the desirability of attracting to the Uptown Talmud Torah, the children of the wealthier class families to whom a modern educational program in conformity with the spirit of the times might reasonably be expected to make a strong appeal.

At the conclusion of his report, Mr. Schiff arose and declared that, while he had attended previous annual meetings of the institution, he had never before heard such a wonderful record of achievement and progress as had been attained in a single year.

Having succeeded during the first year of his presidency in greatly improving the institution's finances, Mr. Fischel decided to devote his second year to its educational curriculum and facilities. It so happened at this time, that Mr. Schiff, who was keenly interested in all matters pertaining to Jewish education in the City of New York, had just donated the sum of $50,000 for the purpose of establishing a Bureau of Education connected with the Kehillah. The work of this Bureau was to formulate a standard curriculum to be used in all Jewish institutions.

To accomplish this, Mr. Schiff secured the services of the well-known educator, Dr. S. Benderly, who had been notably successful in carrying out a similar program in the city of Baltimore. Mr. Fischel immediately offered Dr. Benderly the use of the Uptown Talmud Torah as the laboratory for installing the new system. This arrangement brought so much public notice to the institution that the applications from parents who wished to enroll their children as pupils many times exceeded the ordinary capacity of the school.

In order, however, that no applicant should be turned away, Mr. Fischel accepted Dr. Benderly's suggestion that a course be provided, with classes meeting two or three times a week in the auditorium. Thus nearly a thousand additional children were accommodated. This was a preparatory course for the younger children and Dr. Benderly felt that it would be made much more interesting and attractive if a stereopticon machine were provided with slides illustrating some of the outstanding events in Jewish history, together with Jewish customs and religious rites.

Since this constituted a decided innovation in the system of education then prevailing and, as Mr. Fischel did not care to invest the Talmud Torah's funds in what was in the nature of an experiment, he purchased the stereopticon machine himself and presented it to the institution. The innovation was immediately successful, the children being enabled to better visualize and understand the lessons which were imparted to them.

They gained, furthermore, a much more graphic realization of Jewish historial facts than was possible through oral instruction alone. Mr. Fischel derived from this comparatively small expenditure a great deal of pleasure and satisfaction in the appreciation the children themselves expressed and in the benefit they unquestionably obtained through what, at that time, was regarded as a most radical step in religious teaching.

Another notable accomplishment of the second year of Mr. Fischel's presidency was the institution of a children's synagogue, the congregation of which was made up of more than four hundred boys and girls, and which has since grown to much larger proportions. The boys, proud of the opportunity to display their ability in directing the congregation, established strictly Orthodox services with American methods of order and decorum. At first the services were held only on the Sabbath but later daily services were held, attended each morning by a large number of boys. In order that these boys might get to Public School on time, a few individuals defrayed the cost of serving them breakfast. This practice is in operation up to the present day.

The progress made by Mr. Fischel in adding to the attractiveness of the courses and in providing many other improvements in the institution, called forth expressions of praise not alone from the members and Board of Directors, but from the pupils themselves. The latter voiced their sentiments in the publication "Hope," edited by the boys of the institution. In the December 1912 issue of the publication the following article, expressive of the youthful enthusiasm of the editors, appeared:

Many men have come and many men have gone, during the still short career of our Talmud Torah, but there are not many whose memory will linger longer in the minds of our children, than that of Mr. Harry Fischel. There are few, if any, who have done as much for us as has the energetic President of the Uptown Talmud Torah.

Every child and student that attends our school loves and reveres his name. He has done more for them than possibly any other individual. In times of need it is always he who has stepped to the front and turned the tide. He takes special interest in all our activities and has been the cause of many needed reforms. It is through his unceasing and untiring efforts, our school has become so popular in the house of our people. Seeking to do some good for our school and the Jewish community as a whole, he donated to us a stereopticon machine. With the help of this machine, lecturing has been added to the list of our Talmud Torah's activities and many instructive illustrated lectures are now given in our auditorium.

It is chiefly through him that many additional Harlem children will soon be enabled to get a true Jewish education by the plan to partition our gymnasium into more classrooms. Besides always being ready to listen to the appeals of our young folk, he has furthered the work of many of our Jewish societies by granting them a meeting room.

While, during the second year of his stewardship, Mr. Fischel mainly concerned himself with the educational side of the institution, this did not prevent his finding time to continue to improve its financial condition, so that at the annual meeting held on February 10, 1913, he was able to report a $4,000 surplus, in spite of the fact that expenses had been increased to $38,000 annually. The income of $42,000 for the year represented a gain of $12,000 over the preceding year. At the same time, the number of classes had been increased from 48 to 52, with an enrollment of more than 1800 children, exclusive of the nearly 1000 additional pupils who attended the special classes.

So greatly had the Uptown Talmud Torah risen in public esteem by this time that this second annual meeting, under Mr. Fischel's regime, was by far the most largely attended one in its history.

Once again Jacob H. Schiff graced the meeting by his presence and as usual made a notable address in which he praised anew the achievements recounted, especially stressing the valuable cooperation his Bureau of Education had received and the importance of so teaching the principles of Judaism that they would most strongly appeal to the Jewish child in America. Mr. Schiff's address was as follows:

ADDRESS OF MR. JACOB H. SCHIFF AT ANNUAL MEETING OF THE
UPTOWN TALMUD TORAH

March 17, 1912

I thank you, ladies and gentlemen, for your kind and generous
consideration of me.   I have, perhaps proven my friendship to
you, but I am only one amongst you who is trying to do his duty,
and nothing more.   I have not come here to make an address;
I do not make addresses.

You have referred, Mr. Chairman, to my promotion of the
Bureau of Education of the Kehillah.   Perhaps nothing that I
have done in recent years gives me more satisfaction or has made
me more proud than the work of the Bureau.

Last night I happened to be invited to a reception to Marconi,
the inventor.   I listened to addresses on the progress that has
been made during recent years from the telegraph to the telephone, and from the telephone to the wireless telegraph, which
now sends messages in ten minutes from one point of the world
to another, far outrivalling the cable, and anything else that has
been invented.

Thus, Mr. President, it is with Jewish education.   Just think,
a few years ago, perhaps not more than twenty or twenty-five,
even less, what condition Jewish education was in, in this city,
and see the progress it has made from disorderly to orderly conditions, from inefficiency to efficiency.

We often hear people speak of Reform and Orthodox forms
of instruction in Judaism.   That does not mean that there is a
different method of instruction in the traditions of our law which
was given to us on Mount Sinai.

As I have said, order, method, decorum, does not mean the
destruction of orthodoxy.   It means just the reverse.   It means
the promotion of the love for our Jewish religion and that, as I
understand it, is what the Bureau of Education means.   I am
mortified, more than I can express, to see how the unselfish work
of these men, of Dr. Magnes, of Dr. Benderly, of Prof. Friedlander, who are giving their days and their nights to it, is attacked in certain sections as being destructive of good Orthodox
Judaism.   If we want our children, under American conditions,
to retain that love and that attraction which we have for the

faith of our fathers and forefathers, we must practice such methods as those in which you have been the pioneers.

And because of this, my interest is so warm in your work. Because of this, I saw that you meant not alone to remain attached to the traditions of the Jewish religion as it has come down to us from our forefathers; not alone that you would honor it, but that you would teach it in such a manner that the American Jewish child would love it and remain in the religious school and the Synagogue, instead of losing himself in Atheism. Because of this, I was glad to give you my support.

Mr. President, I have listened with great interest to your report. You really, you personally, did establish the connecting link; you have so efficiently and courageously forged one of the steels that merge American conditions with Jewish conditions and yet enable us to remain good Jews. You have personally accomplished this in our community and you have set a noble and splendid example.

Mr. Fischel, in his report delivered at this meeting, laid special emphasis on the necessity of enlarging the Talmud Torah in order to provide for a special school for girls of high school age whom he deemed it desirable to be taught in classrooms separate from the boys.

A still more important recommendation was that urging the establishment of a branch of the Uptown Talmud Torah in a location which should be more accessible to the homes of the better-off Jewish families. In this connection Mr. Fischel pointed out that it was most necessary for the future of Judaism that children of the well-to-do class, receive a sound religious education as it was from among this class that the future generations of leaders of Jewish philanthropy and directors of Jewish institutions would have to be mainly recruited.

These future leaders, Mr. Fischel went on, must have a thorough knowledge and love of Jewish traditions which could only be obtained through a proper religious education. It was not to be expected that the youth in poor circumstances who was compelled to work his way through school and college in order to get an education, should at once take up the reins of Jewish institutional life or devote his time to communal work.

On the other hand, the young men of the wealthier class, with their greater means and leisure, Mr. Fischel pointed out, might, if properly trained, be expected to develop into leaders of the community and proper guardians of the communal institutions. He regarded it as of the utmost importance, for this reason, that the opportunity for a true Jewish education be extended into the neighborhood where the wealthier Jews resided and suggested the Lenox Avenue section as the locality best suited to the purpose of expansion of the Talmud Torah's activities.

In view of the fact that these recommendations met with the general approval of the entire gathering and were repeatedly seconded in the addresses of the speakers who followed, Mr. Fischel was much surprised later to find an undercurrent of opposition to the plans among the members of the Board of Directors.

This resulted in a certain amount of ill-feeling on the part of several of the older directors who were unaccustomed to the methods which had resulted in such a speedy growth for the institution. From this time on, Mr. Fischel was unable to secure a unanimous vote by the directors on the various matters he placed before them.

Always a firm believer in the rights of the minority, Mr. Fischel had long held to the custom that where he could not get the approval of everyone present at a Board meeting, no resolution should be allowed to pass. In order, however, that the progress of the institution might not be impeded he was compelled to alter this practice in connection with the Talmud Torah, and to rely upon a majority vote. The majority continued to staunchly support him in his program.

Shortly after the second annual meeting, Mr. Fischel received convincing proof that his recommendations were strongly approved by the outstanding leaders of New York Jewry.

This proof came in the form of a letter from Jacob H. Schiff, who was departing for Europe and who enclosed a check for $25,000 to Mr. Fischel's order, at the same time expressing his warmest endorsement of Mr. Fischel's plan to establish a branch of the Uptown Talmud Torah for the children of the wealthier Jewish families. Mr. Schiff, in his letter, stated that if Mr. Fischel could raise an additional $25,000 he might make use of the check for the purpose of establishing a branch of the institution on the west side.

Mr. Fischel lost no time in calling a meeting of the directors to place Mr. Schiff's proposal before them. This meeting was held on April 3, 1913. After reading Mr. Schiff's letter, which was received with every evidence of enthusiasm, Mr. Fischel declared it to be incumbent upon the directors to carry out their part of the bargain and to raise the additional $25,000 which was a condition of Mr. Schiff's gift. He realized, however, that it would be a difficult task to raise so large a sum among them and had come prepared for this emergency.

In the interim between the receipt of Mr. Schiff's letter and the meeting, Mr. Fischel had held a conference with the members of his family and had decided, with them, to build an annex adjoining the existing institution for which he was prepared to defray the entire cost. Mr. Fischel had, indeed, gone so far as to prepare a set of plans for the proposed building, arranged to meet the requirements of the increased activities of the school.

With this purpose in view, Mr. Fischel made the proposition to the Board that he would erect this building at his own expense contributing for the purpose the sum of $10,000 or whatever might be required, but that, in order to meet the terms of Mr. Schiff's gift, the balance of $15,000 toward the required $25,000 was to be raised by them. Mr. Fischel's offer was enthusiastically accepted and $12,000 was immediately subscribed by the directors as they sat around the table.

With the assurance of this sum and the check of $25,000 from Mr. Schiff in his possession, Mr. Fischel began to envisage the realization of both his dreams, that of the annex to the Talmud

Torah and the erection of a West Side Branch.   It was determined at the meeting of the Board that news of Mr. Schiff's
munificence and the plans the institution had made for the use
of the gift, were of sufficient importance to give to the public
with the result that once more the Uptown Talmud Torah received many columns of space in the press of the entire country.

The Hebrew Standard issue of April 18, 1913, commented edi-
torially upon the announcement as follows:

"The subscriptions to the work of the Uptown Talmud Torah,
which we duly chronicled in our last issue, call for a word or two
of comment.   All possible credit is due and extended to each of
the generous donors: Jacob H. Schiff's donation of $25,000 is,
as customary, a princely gift.   Without wishing in the slightest
degree to be invidious, we deem it appropriate, however, to call
special attention to the gift of $10,000 by Harry Fischel.   The
latter gentleman will gladly concede we take it, that his fortune
is not as large, as say, Mr. Schiff's.   Therefore, when Harry
Fischel gives $10,000 to a communal institution, it means so
much more to him and should signify much more to the organization benefited.   However, this gift of Mr. Fischel's shows
that the Russian Jews and the representatives of the more recent
immigrant section among our co-religionists are endeavoring to
do their full share in the cause of Jewish education in this city.
That Russian Jews like Harry Fischel do their duty is no more
than one anticipates and expects from men who have the means,
and above all who have the heart. Zedakah, for such it truly is,
is a living force for them!"

Mr. Fischel at once set to work to begin construction of the
annex as well as to prepare for the erection of the West Side
Branch and appointed a committee, with Mr. Leon Tuchman as
chairman, which was charged with the duty of carrying out the
latter undertaking.   Property was purchased at 42-44-46 West
115th Street, as a site for the branch, and Mr. Fischel personally
prepared the plans for it.   These provided for a school to accommodate more than 600 children, club rooms, a gymnasium

and a children's synagogue, which also was to be used as an auditorium.

Construction of the Annex began immediately after the Passover Holidays and Mr. Adolph Lewisohn laid the cornerstone on June 15, with appropriate and impressive ceremonies in the presence of a large number of invited guests. Addresses were made by Rabbi M. S. Margolies, president of the school's board of education, Dr. H. Periera Mendes, Isidore Herschfield, Honorary Secretary of the institution and others.

In his remarks, Mr. Lewisohn said, in part:

"I have watched the growth of this institution very carefully and I am very proud to have the honor of laying the cornerstone for this important annex. The president and donor of this new building, my personal friend, Mr. Harry Fischel, has set an example to all Jewish leaders, illustrating that when one gives of his entire time and energy to an institution it becomes a part and parcel of himself, and he is even giving above his means in order to extend the accommodations of this institution.

"Let us hope that this example set by the president of the Uptown Talmud Torah will serve as a lesson and incentive to others among our Jewish brethren, that they may do likewise for the cause of Jewish education, which, without a doubt, is today the most vital problem confronting the American Jew."

It had been Mr. Fischel's custom to take his vacation during the summer months but so engrossed was he with the project he had in hand, that he dispensed with his annual rest and remained in the city most of the summer giving his attention solely to the task of completing the new annex and Branch. By October, he was able to view with satisfaction the two buildings finished and to appoint a committee to arrange for a double celebration. This celebration took place on November 2, 1913.

In the morning of that day, the West Side Branch was opened to the people of the neighborhood in order that they might be acquainted with the facilities the building was to offer in the way of filling a long felt want in that part of the city. In the afternoon, the Board of Directors marched in a body from the main building to the Branch where, after a prayer and a short address

by the venerable Rabbi Margolies, Mr. Fischel delivered the key
of the building to Jacob H. Schiff, who had returned from his
vacation in time to take part in the ceremony. Entering the
auditorium, Mr. Fischel also unveiled a tablet which had been
erected in Mr. Schiff's honor and in connection with this unveiling
delivered the following address:

"I welcome you all to this new building which is a branch of
that well-known institution, the Uptown Talmud Torah.

"We are indeed making history today. We are not merely
dedicating a Talmud Torah,—a school house for Jewish learning—
but we are on the threshold of a new era in Jewish education.
Today, for the first time in our communal life, we are making
provisions for children whose parents God has endowed with
material gifts, to receive a systematic and, above all, a thorough
Jewish education.

"At present, the children of the poor have far more opportunities for getting a thoroughly Jewish training than their wealthier brethren. Their parents make every effort to place their
children in a Talmud Torah, even though same be located at a
great distance from them. We have children at our main building on 111th Street who come as far as 25 blocks for the purpose
of imbibing Jewish learning. This, however, is not the case with
the children of the rich. They do not send their children to a
Talmud Torah because they are obsessed with the idea that a
Talmud Torah is made only for the poor. Some parents are more
broad-minded and do send the children, but only when they live
near the Talmud Torah. Some parents send the children to a
Chedar, located usually in a basement or some other unsanitary
place, which does not meet with the desire of the parents and is
not to the satisfaction of the children. For such reasons, then, a
vast majority of the children of the rich are brought up without
any Jewish moral and religious training.

"We, the Board of Directors of the Uptown Talmud Torah,
after much deliberation, came to the conclusion that the only
way to solve this problem would be to erect a building especially
adapted for this class of children of whom there are at least 25,-
000 within 10 square blocks of this spot.

"We were powerless, however, to realize our desire as we did not have the necessary funds to construct such a building, until our friend—the friend of Jewish education, the well-known philanthropist,—Mr. Jacob H. Schiff, became interested in our work and came to our assistance with a donation of $25,000. Our Board of Directors succeeded in raising a like sum of $25,000 and then it was possible to realize our dream and to construct this building, well ventilated, strictly fireproof, with all sanitary improvements and a large playground.

"The School is well equipped with a competent principal and staff of teachers, who will give Jewish instruction by the most up-to-date methods to about 800 boys and girls, whose parents are well able to pay a minimum sum of $3.00 per month for the instruction of their children, thus making this school self-supporting.

"My friends, the success of this, our new venture, rests with you. You will either eagerly grasp the God-given opportunity and crown our work with your interest, or you will reject it by failing to send your children here. I trust you will do the former and thus comply with the wishes of our sages, who commanded us in the following phrase: 'Be careful, that the Torah shall not come forth from the poor only!'

"My friends: I have a duty to perform which I consider a great honor and privilege. I have to report to you that at a special meeting of the Board of Directors, it was unanimously resolved that, whereas the erection of this building was made possible through the generosity of Mr. Jacob H. Schiff, that in appreciation thereof a tablet be placed on the walls of this auditorium, which I herewith unveil, and which reads as follows: 'A tribute to the services and devotion of Jacob H. Schiff, to the cause of Jewish education.'

"Mr. Schiff, as a further token of our esteem and appreciation, I take great pride in delivering to you a key to this building as you always held the key to the situation confronting Jewish education, and I am sure that those who are here assembled, as well as the thousands of children who will derive the benefit of your generosity, join me in wishing that you may hold the key for many, many years to come."

Following this celebration, most of those present adjourned to take part in the dedication of the Annex which occurred immediately afterward. These exercises were followed by a dinner tendered to Mr. and Mrs. Fischel by members of the Board of Directors. So complete was the building in every respect that the dinner was held in the new structure.

At this function Mr. Fischel was honored in a manner that came as a complete surprise to him. The lights were suddenly extinguished and when they were flashed on again he saw on the wall opposite his place at the table, a life size portrait of himself done in oil. The thought that, despite the differences he had had with some members of the Board, his work for the institution had nevertheless been appreciated to the extent that he should be thus honored, caused him intense gratification and he was so affected that he had great difficulty in replying to the address of presentation.

Mr. Fischel then delivered the deed of the building and the double celebration that focused the eyes of the entire Jewish population of the city upon the Uptown Talmud Torah, was brought to an end.

THE FISCHEL ANNEX TO THE UPTOWN TALMUD TORAH,
140 *East* 111*th Street, New York City, completed in* 1913.

CHAPTER XVIII

MEETING A CRISIS

THE apparently happy conclusion of the many months of arduous effort put forth in behalf of the Uptown Talmud Torah with Mr. Fischel again overcoming the opposition to his program voiced by some of the directors, gave promise that the institution would realize his fondest hopes for its future usefulness.

The two new buildings commenced to function at once and filled a long felt want in both localities. The Fischel Annex was in use twelve of the twenty-four hours of the day and the West Side Branch, with the exception of the school itself, was likewise taken advantage of to its capacity by the young people of that part of the city.

There were still difficulties to be overcome, however, before the school on the West Side was to justify its existence. These difficulties mainly arose from the fact that the part of the public which the school was especially designed to serve, was not accustomed to sending its children to religious classes or paying for religious education and it became necessary to educate the parents as well as the children, before the new branch was to become entirely successful.

In order to accomplish this and to provide every possible advantage that might be expected by persons of wealth for their children, Mr. Fischel appointed a special Board of Education for the Branch, with instructions to work out a curriculum that should not alone contain every educational facility provided in the main building of the Talmud Torah, but a number of additional subjects and improvements intended to appeal to the richer element in the community. In this connection, Mr. Fischel was able to secure the valuable cooperation and assistance of Dr. S.

Benderly, who not alone gave personal advice, but recommended Mr. A. Duschkind for the position of principal of the school.

By Mr. Fischel's close study of the problem and the changes in policy, which he effected, more than three hundred children were within a short time enrolled in the school, paying from three to ten dollars a month for their tuition. This revenue not alone put the Branch upon a paying basis but resulted in the accumulation of a considerable surplus which, it was planned, should go to help support the work carried on in the main building.

This success was, however, to be short lived and Mr. Fischel was once more compelled to engage in a struggle to uphold the principles he believed to be right, a struggle which taxed his energies to the utmost, seriously undermined his hitherto vigorous constitution and left him sick at heart and wearied in body and mind.

In spite of the tremendous strides which had been made by the Uptown Talmud Torah during the years of Mr. Fischel's administration, the fact that its finances were sound, its membership greatly increased and its accomplishments recognized by all sections of the community, the dissension which had first made itself apparent some months before, was now revived.

Some of the older directors saw in every step which Mr. Fischel had taken to broaden the curriculum and to introduce improvements in the systems of education, a blow at their conception of what was proper. They failed even to be satisfied with the knowledge that Mr. Fischel had made no move without first obtaining the consent and hearty approval of Rabbi M. S. Margolies, the dean of the Orthodox Jewish Rabbinate of America, who was the chairman of the Talmud Torah's Board of Education.

Mr. Fischel at a meeting of the Board of Directors held on February 15, 1914 indulged in a heart to heart talk with them. He carefully went into everything he had done since assuming the office of President three years before, explaining how his first year had been devoted almost solely to placing the institution on a sound financial footing and how, at the conclusion of this period, he had enjoyed the appreciation, support and confidence of every member of the Board.

This, he said, had also been true of his second year in office when, besides further strengthening the finances of the institution, he had devoted much effort to working out a suitable program of instruction. The confidence then imposed in him, he declared, had been the incentive which had caused him to work still harder toward the realization of even larger usefulness for the institution and, at a time when he was already worn out by his labors and had not expected to continue in office.

He then explained how the offer of Mr. Schiff to contribute $25,000, provided an equal sum was raised by the directors, had filled him with new hope and ambition for the attainment of the objects in view and how he had decided to continue to serve as President. He reminded the Board that, not only had he contributed a large sum of money for the building of the Annex, but that he had sacrificed his summer vacation in order that this building and the West Side Branch might be completed by the Fall. He had not, he stated, expected or looked for any thanks for this labor of love, undertaken to achieve the fulfillment of a holy purpose, but, on the other hand, he certanly had not anticipated being subjected to such obstructive measures as those with which he had been rewarded.

Mr. Fischel then made clear to the Board that he would refuse the presidency for another term.

This plain declaration created a tremendous commotion among the members of the Board, causing the meeting to be prolonged until nearly two A. M. Those directors constituting the majority of the Board pleaded with Mr. Fischel to remain in office and gave him their assurance that they would do everything possible to help him in the performance of his duty.

Mr. Fischel, however, was convinced, despite these earnest pleas on the part of his supporters, that complete harmony could not again he expected to prevail and therefore decided that he would resign at the annual meeting scheduled to be held a week later, on February 22, 1914.

At this meeting were, Mr. Jacob H. Schiff, Mr. Adolph Lewisohn, Judge Samuel Greenbaum, Judge Otto A. Rosalsky and Dr. Judah L. Magnes among many others of prominence in communal and institutional work.

After reading his annual report, showing the progress of the institution in the year just ended, Mr. Fischel made the following statement:

"My friends, from the bottom of my heart I thank you for your kind attention in listening to the lengthy report of our activities during the past year, and I would ask your indulgence for a few minutes more as I have an additional statement to make.

"After mature deliberation, I have fully decided to retire from the high office of President of this institution, which I have occupied for the last three years. During that period, the Uptown Talmud Torah has progressed marvelously in transmitting to thousands of our young, the traditions, culture and history of our people. It has built up a healthy Jewish environment through its social work. It has made history in establishing a Talmud Torah on a self-supporting basis for the children of those parents who cannot afford to pay for their tuition. It has acquired an annex to this building which gives a thorough Jewish and moral education to nearly 500 girls. It has also placed the administrative work on a business-like and systematic basis. The membership income has increased from $6,486 per annum to $14,712. The number of pupils has increased from 1000 to over 2100, besides the 900 in the extension school, which is conducted by the Bureau of Education. I have also succeeded in inducing the Council of Jewish Communal institutions to take the Uptown Talmud Torah as one of its members and this is the only educational institution that the Council has ever admitted.

"With the aid of the Bureau of Education of the Kehillah, I am happy to say that I was also able to elevate our institution to the position which it now occupies among educational institutions. Nevertheless, there is still a great deal of room for progress and advancement.

"However, in order to maintain this high standard of efficiency and to carry on the work on this basis, a president must have the cooperation and undivided support of the entire Board of Directors, a Board of Directors who are open to conviction, fair in their views and liberal in their ideas and principles, who are able to be convinced that an institution like ours can be conducted under the best and most modern methods, without sacrificing any religious principles whatsoever, and who will not allow some of their colleagues to condemn a system of education which was introduced by a man who has devoted all his life to that purpose and who has been largely misunderstood and unappreciated.

"In view of the impossibility of obtaining the cooperation of the entire Board of Directors I have, therefore, finally decided to retire. I hope that my successor in the Presidency will be firm enough to withstand unfounded prejudices against the efficient methods now in force in our institution, so that those of the Board of Directors who as yet have failed to recognize the progress which has been made by this new system, will eventually realize their mistake and will gladly embrace and continue the standard of education which I have labored unceasingly to uphold and maintain."

No sooner had Mr. Fischel finished the announcement of his resignation than Mr. Schiff asked for the floor and said:

"Ladies and Gentlemen:

"We are old friends and your president was good enough to say that I have been with you now many a time each year at the annual meetings. I have spoken always to you from a full heart because of the pleasure I have had in seeing the progress of this institution. It has grown from little beginnings to this great civilizing and educational center.

"I must say that I am very much taken back by this announcement which has just been sprung upon us.

"I have not known of any intention of Mr. Fischel to retire from the leadership of this institution. I only knew it since he announced it a few minutes ago. I cannot imagine this Talmud Torah without Mr. Fischel at the head of it. I do not understand the motives that have induced him to retire, but a few words which he said in making the announcement indicated that there is a difference in the Board of Directors as to the methods by which this institution shall be conducted. I do not propose to pronounce judgment upon anything I do not know both sides of, but if, as your president has just said, some of your directors are not in accord with the new methods,—and by this I suppose is meant the methods, such as have been brought about by the Bureau of Education—perhaps I am mistaken—that these methods have not the approval of the entire Board of Directors of this institution, I should consider this nothing less than a calamity to the Jews of this city. For the standing of the Jew of this city rests now and hereafter, more than anything else, upon the quality, not the quantity of the religious education he is going to give his children.

"We cannot take any step backwards. Evolutions and revolutions never work backwards, and I will say to these directors, I do not care who they are, I do not know how many of them there are, I will say to these directors, if they stand in the way of modern Orthodox Jewish education, that the community will sweep over them like the ocean over a little islet in its midst. (Applause)

"If this institution has progressed and is obtaining the confidence of those who are not entirely in accord (because they know nothing of it) with Jewish education as it is given here, I mean the confidence of the German Jews, who have largely supported it, it is to a great extent due to the fact that they knew that Mr. Fischel is Orthodox, and that his immediate supporters are Orthodox Jews—they are Americans, progressive Americans and they want to have a Jew a good Jew—a good Jew, and a good American as head of this institution (applause) and you cannot be good Americans if you do not educate your children in the way of Judaism.

"Now, Mr. Fischel, don't be discouraged in your great and noble work. Possibly you are not appreciated by some of the Directors, but the people are with you. I do not know how many Directors or what Directors are opposing you, but I will say to them that, if they are standing in the way of Modern Jewish Education, as I said before, the Community will sweep over them, like the ocean sweeps over a little island. If this association has increased, progressed and spread its influence among the Jews, it is in the greatest part due to Mr. Fischel, whom I know is

trusted by thousands as a good Jew and a good American.   I
will say frankly that I should consider it nothing less than a
calamity if unprogressive ideas within the Board of Directors
were to force Mr. Fischel's retirement."

No sooner had Mr. Schiff concluded his remarks than he was
followed in due order by Judge Rosalsky, Judge Greenbaum and
Dr. Magnes, who not only echoed Mr. Schiff's plea that Mr.
Fischel should not resign but, if anything, couched their views in
stronger language even than Mr. Schiff had used.

Some small idea of the consternation which prevailed in Jewish circles over Mr. Fischel's unexpected action is given by the
newspaper accounts of the meeting which appeared the following
day and which were supplemented by no end of editorial comment
in New York and in other cities to which the reports were carried
by the Associated Press wires.

Several of the headlines in the principal New York dailies are
here reproduced together with the full and very accurate account
published by the New York Times.

NEW YORK HERALD
Harry Fischel, President of Harlem Institute, resigns as protest
against all prejudice.   Jacob H. Schiff urges his retention.

NEW YORK AMERICAN
Harry Fischel resigns after clash in Hebrew Institute.   Mr.
Jacob H. Schiff and Judge Rosalsky deplore his action.

NEW YORK TELEGRAM
Sensation in Hebrew Institute when Harry Fischel president
of Harlem Institute, resigns.   Progressive members urge him to
reconsider.

The article from the New York Times was as follows:

Fischel to Resign From Talmud Torah
Tells Annual Meeting Directors are Not in Favor
of His Progressive Ideas

Jacob H. Schiff Protests
Banker Asserts that Fischel's Retirement would be a Calamity to the
Jews of the City.

Harry Fischel, President of the Uptown Talmud Torah Association, announced at its annual meeting yesterday at 132-142 East 111th Street, that he intended to resign his office because of prejudices within the organization against what he termed as progressive ideas and up-to-date methods. The announcement was a surprise to the members of the association. Jacob H. Schiff and Judge Otto A. Rosalsky both expressed regret that a condition had arisen within the board of Directors that could provoke Mr. Fischel's retirement. Mr. Schiff said that, if the association lost the services of its president it would be a calamity to the Jews of this city, and Judge Rosalsky offered a motion placing the audience on record as opposed to the acceptance of Mr. Fischel's resignation.

Mr. Fischel's announcement was made after he had read his annual report showing the steady growth of the association.

Mr. Schiff followed Mr. Fischel and began at once upon the President's resignation. (Here follow excerpts from Mr. Schiff's remarks).

Before he attempted to introduce his motion opposing Mr. Fischel's resignation, Judge Rosalsky said:

"I want to say to the members of the Board of Directors of the Talmud Torah that there should be no differences among them. It will be a serious mistake upon your part if you do not insist upon Mr. Fischel's continuing as President of this association. The Russian Jews were deprived by his coming to America twenty-nine years ago and American Jewdom is the richer therefore, I beg this audience not to let this man go."

The Rev. Dr. Judah L. Magnes spoke of the need for a larger view of Judaism without petty differences disturbing the great work before the association. He said:

"If it be true that there is a dissension in your midst, I am sure, and I know that Mr. Schiff is sure, that the differences are honest and upheld with the best of intentions; but your disputes over methods should be dropped in the knowledge that Jews all over this country are modelling their institutions after this Talmud Torah. In view of this it would be well that any controversy you may have be stilled at once.

"If the Board of Directors are fighting about a method, if they are disputing over a dollar, if they disagree because they do not like the looks of a certain teacher or his accent, they should remember that, while they are airing their petty differences, 185,000 Jewish boys and girls are running around the streets of this city as little pagans and infidels without the opportunity for Jewish teaching and training."

Other speakers were Rabbi M. S. Margolies, Harold Debrest, the Rev. H. Masliansky and Rabbi B. Pearl.

Two editorials from the English-Jewish Press, one from the American Hebrew and one from the Hebrew Standard, are here given:

American Hebrew

Mr. Harry Fischel should not allow himself to feel discouraged because he does not at once secure the cooperation of all his associates in the progressive work of the Uptown Talmud Torah. This organization, under his presidency, has grown from strength to strength in the development of modern educational standards and general good work. It was, we believe, the first to cooperate with the Kehillah's Bureau of Education and to put in effect the standardized methods which the Bureau advised. Any backward slip now would be most deplorable and we earnestly hope that the Board of Directors will not only decline to accept Mr. Fischel's resignation, but that they will sustain his policies in every way.

Hebrew Standard

Mr. Fischel's Resignation

What is the trouble that Mr. Fischel has had with some of the directors of the Harlem Institute? Is it something like the story of Sysiphus, who was perpetually laboring in pushing a stone up-

hill but which always rolled down again to the botton just when
he was trying to place it on the top of the hill? Or, will the
differences between Mr. Fischel and some of the directors be
settled amicably? No details were forthcoming at last Sunday's
meeting as to the causes of the trouble, but it was gathered from
the speeches of Mr. Schiff, Dr. Magnes and others that some of
the ignorant zealots of the Old Brigade—the Sanhedrin of
Mount Morris Park—object to the Uptown Talmud Torah being
made a "social centre" as well as a school for the teaching of
Hebrew. Mr. Fischel himself said that his resignation was actuated by the fact that he found it impossible to convince the full
Board of Directors that an institution like the Harlem Talmud
Torah "can be conducted with the best and most up-to-date
methods without sacrificing in the least any religious principles
whatsoever." In a general way, Mr. Fischel indicated that the
clash with the Board of Directors had come over his attempts
in the capacity of President, "to combine ideas of Judaism and
Americanism in the management of the Association, and his efforts
to extend its activities in other than purely religious fields." The
public, however, would like to know something more concerning
the trouble with the directors. Unquestionably as Mr. Schiff, who
was taken aback with the announcement of Mr. Fischel's resignation, said.—"It is nothing less than a calamity if unprogressive
ideas within the Board were to force Mr. Fischel's retirement," as
it was difficult to imagine the Uptown Talmud Torah without Mr.
Fischel at the head of it.

Let us, therefore, hope that the prophecy of Mr. Schiff to the
effect that, if the directors of the Uptown Talmud Torah "are
standing in the way of modern Orthodox Jewish education, the
community will sweep over them like the ocean sometimes sweeps
over a little island in a storm," will have the effect of changing
the minds of the directors so that Judge Rosalsky, may succeed
in keeping Mr. Fischel at the head of the institution.

The day after the meeting, Mr. Fischel received the following
letter from the Bureau of Education.

BUREAU OF EDUCATION

Mr. Harry Fischel,   February 23, 1914.

118 East 93rd Street,

My dear Mr. Fischel:

I am writing this letter to you in order to give you my view of the main incident at the Annual Meeting yesterday—your resignation in public. At first, I was of the opinion that it might have been wiser for you not to do so publicly, but merely to state to the Board that, in view of the fact that some members of the Board disagree with you on account of your progressive ideas about Jewish education, you do not see your way clear to serve as President any longer. This, of course, would have permitted the Annual meeting to proceed in the usual way and none of the public present would have had an inkling about the difference of opinion in the Board. After reconsidering the matter, however, I feel that you were probably justified in doing the thing the way you did.

I have no doubt that you strengthened the cause of Jewish education considerably yesterday afternoon. Instead of permitting all those petty things to go on in the dark, you forced a flood of light on the subject and you have once for all made the issue clear—whether in this country we are to raise a Jewish generation that will be loyal to Judaism and at the same time fully equipped to take part in the upbuilding of this great Republic, or whether we must continue a system of education that may have rendered good service four hundred or five hundred years ago, when we were locked up in Ghettos, but has proven powerless in this country, as may be proved by the lamentable failure of Jewish education in the past twenty-five years.

I could see yesterday that the public was with you. The people demanded progress, for they have learned to their sorrow that the old way has never gotten their children to remain loyal to Judaism. I hope that you will forget these petty things which wasted so much of your energy during the past three years. I have no doubt that time will demonstrate to those gentlemen who are opposed to you that, in opposing you, they have opposed the progress of Jewish education.

I want to assure you, Mr. Fischel, that the great cause of Jewish education in this country needs you. I trust that you will be able to come forward and help the Bureau of Education in its larger plans. The field that we can offer you is one that will involve the education of tens of thousands of our children. A man with your energy, heart and willingness will be able to render a great service to the cause of Jewish education in this country. This is not only my sentiment, but also that of Dr. Magnes and Dr. Friedlander who feel that a great task awaits you in the Jewish educational field.

Very truly yours,

S. BENDERLY.

It was the custom of the Board of Directors to hold its election of officers shortly after the annual meeting and they gathered for this purpose on March 7, 1914.

It is difficult to describe the tenseness of feeling which prevailed on this occasion so that the very atmosphere seemed to be electrically charged. Those few directors who had before been pronounced in their opposition to Mr. Fischel, were more than ever enraged by the realization that they constituted a small minority, and that the entire Jewish public was, in fact, solidly behind Mr. Fischel and gave its entire approval to the steps he had taken for the advancement of Jewish education.

Knowing they were beaten, these few men maintained, with added bitterness, their previous position.

The large majority, however, stood with Mr. Fischel and exerted every appeal and every pressure to cause him to reconsider his decision to resign and expressed their readiness to tender him an almost unanimous nomination for a fourth term as president.

Deeply appreciative of this confidence, Mr. Fischel might have reconsidered his decision were it not for the fact that his health had been seriously impaired as a result of the practically continuous concentration he had given to the affairs of the institution and the strain that had attended the long conflict of opinion with some of the directors, culminating in the excitement and turmoil attending his resignation which had left him both physically worn out and mentally exhausted.

Proof of the great change which had taken place in the minds of most of the directors was further afforded by the selection of Mr. Henry Glass to succeed Mr. Fischel in the office of president. A business man of wide prominence, Mr. Glass was a firm believer in the policies Mr. Fischel had inaugurated and at once committed himself to a continuance of them, requesting Mr. Fischel to give him his support and counsel in executing the duties of his office, which Mr. Fischel promised to do as soon as his health was restored.

Under Mr. Glass' administration the work of the institution went forward without interruption along the same lines Mr. Fischel had laid down and it continued as a model in the field of Jewish education.

CHAPTER XIX

FIRST COMMERCIAL BUILDING ON UPPER BROADWAY

A BUSINESS enterprise that was to change the character of the improvements on Broadway in the upper Thirties and was to largely determine the future of this section of that famous thoroughfare in a commercial sense, engaged, quite accidentally, Mr. Fischel's attention while he was still president of the Uptown Talmud Torah.

During most of his incumbency of that office he had devoted himself exclusively to the interests of the institution, but in 1912, when it seemed desirable and necessary, he again turned his mind to his own affairs, particularly in view of the steady drain upon his financial resources. It was just at this time that the opportunity for the most important building operation on which he had yet been engaged was opened to him. He managed, by securing competent assistance, to take advantage of this opportunity without interfering with what he held to be his first responsibility, namely towards the institution of which he was the head.

He was approached by the brokerage firm of Horace S. Ely and Company with a proposition to lease a large plot of ground at the corner of Broadway and thirty-seventh street, which was owned by a Western client of theirs, a Mr. McCutcheon, who had had few, if any, business dealings with Jewish people.

This man on, being introduced to Mr. Fischel, took him in from head to foot, and it was quite clear from the expression on his face, that he preferred not to have anything to do with him. Mr. Fischel suggested that it might be well if Mr. McCutcheon obtain some references as to his financial and personal standing before proceeding to business and among many other names suggested that he might make inquiries of Mr. Jacob H. Schiff and Mr. Adolph Lewisohn.

Mr. Fischel suggested that, should the references obtained from these gentlemen be satisfactory, another meeting could be arranged at which the matter of the lease might be more fully discussed.

A few days later, Mr. Fischel was advised by the brokers that Mr. McCutcheon was ready to talk business and at this meeting the latter's demeanor, had completely changed. Mr. McCutcheon declared that the references he had received were more than satisfactory and that he was quite ready to proceed to the affair in hand. In a very short time after this conference, the transaction was closed to the satisfaction of both parties.

At this time, the neighborhood of Broadway and Thirty-seventh Street constituted the heart of the theatre district and Mr. Fischel prepared plans for a theatre with offices on the upper floors which promised to prove a profitable undertaking. It so happened, however, that his plans underwent a change.

In connection with his many communal activities, Mr. Fischel had, as a matter of course, formed acquaintances and friendships with a large number of prominent men in all walks of life and in virtually every business, whose confidence and respect he had gained. Many of these men regarded Mr. Fischel's financial responsibility as even greater than it was, for they judged his means by the large sums of money he contributed to philanthropic causes and by the fact that he gave virtually all of his time to these activities.

It was such an indirect benefit as resulted from these contacts which caused Mr. Fischel to change his mind regarding the construction of a theatre on the Broadway site. While attending a directors' meeting of the Beth Israel Hospital, with which many prominent merchants were connected, he was approached by four men who had learned of the transaction and who persuaded him to abandon the theatre project and to erect on the property a strictly mercantile building instead.

The proposal was very tempting and practically insured the

success of the undertaking, as Mr. Reuben Sadowsky agreed to lease five floors of the projected building, Blauner Brothers, two floors, Zelenko and Moskowitz, two floors and David Harris, one floor.

Aside from the financial aspects of the undertaking, this venture appealed strongly to Mr. Fischel because it once again permitted him to be a pioneer, as this was the first large mercantile building to be erected on that part of Broadway, which today is a center of both retail and wholesale trade.

When Mr. Fischel was ready to proceed with this large building operation he decided to secure an associate whom he might entrust with actual supervision of the work, in order that his time might not be too largely taken away from the Talmud Torah. His choice fell upon Mr. Joseph Ravitch. Mr. Ravitch not only ably carried out this trust but has ever since that time remained as Mr. Fischel's associate, enabling the latter to continue to devote a major portion of his own labors to the community.

The enterprise was in every way successful and Mr. Fischel's business foresight and acumen were vindicated anew by the fact that, within a short time, this neighborhood was transformed into its present importance as one of the most active business sections of the city. A few years after completion of the structure, Mr. Fischel sold it at a handsome margin of profit to Mr. Sadowsky.

CHAPTER XX

HELPS FORM RELIGIOUS PROGRAMME FOR Y. M. H. A.

THE programme Mr. Fischel had carried out while President of the Uptown Talmud Torah and which had led to his difficulties with some of the directors, had in no sense lessened his influence in the field of Jewish education but had, as a matter of fact, served to strengthen his position not only with the public but with the important Jewish leaders who had closely followed the progress he had made.

The Talmud Torah, which was also known as the Harlem Jewish Institute, during his regime as President became much more than merely a school for religious instruction. The building was also in reality a Young Men's and Young Women's Hebrew Association, with all the many physical and social facilities to be expected in such an institution.

These included a number of well appointed club rooms, lectures on a wide variety of subjects of general interest and a finely equipped gymnasium, with a trained physical instructor in attendance. Mr. Fischel placed a great deal of importance upon the physical training of the children and was instrumental in having adopted a system of regular calisthenics.

His interest in this work was so well known and his experience regarded as so valuable that at the time of the formation of the Council of Young Men's Hebrew and Kindred Associations, Mr. Fischel was very naturally asked to serve as one of fifteen members of the Board of Managers, the New York members of which were comprised of the heads of the Young Men's Hebrew Associations of the Metropolitan District, with Judge Irving Lehman as president.

So it was that once more Mr. Fischel was to be given the opportunity of impressing his ideas of what constituted proper conduct of Jewish institutions for the young upon the conscience of the community. He again insisted upon adherence to a religious programme in the administration of the Y.M.H.A.'s although, as seemed invariably the rule when this subject was broached, he at first met with considerable opposition.

On April 7, 1914, Mr. Fischel received from Mr. Felix M. Warburg the following invitation to attend a dinner of the charter members of the Council to be held at his residence:

Mr. Harry Fischel,   April 7th, 1914.
World Building,
Manhattan.

Dear Mr. Fischel:

Inasmuch as the bills for the incorporation of the Council and of the Trustees of the Council of Young Men's Hebrew and Kindred Associations, have through the kind efforts of Mr. Marshall, been signed by the Governor, and we are now incorporated, it is important that we officially take cognizance of our duties and hold a meeting for the purpose of accepting the respective acts of incorporation (hereafter to be known as Chapters 74 and 75 of the Laws of 1914) and of organizing and adopting a constitution and by-laws.

You are therefore cordially invited to attend a dinner and meeting at my home, 1109 Fifth Avenue, on Wednesday evening, April 22nd, at eight o'clock.

Sincerely yours,

FELIX M. WARBURG

Secretary, Board of Managers,

Council of Y.M.H. & Kindred Ass'ns.

At this dinner, held in Mr. Warburg's residence, the following fifteen charter members of the Board of Managers were present: I. W. Bernheim, Louisville, Kentucky; Alfred M. Cohen, Cincinnati, Ohio; David A. Ellis, Boston, Massachusetts; Harry Fischel, New York; Judge Samuel Greenbaum, first vice president, New York; Isaac Hassler, Philadelphia, Pennsylvania;

Judge Irving Lehman, treasurer, New York; Jacob M. Loeb, Chicago, Illinois; Judge Julian W. Mack, president, Chicago; Louis Marshall, New York; Jacob Newman, second vice-president, New Orleans, Louisiana; M. C. Sloss, San Francisco, California; Mrs. Israel Unterberg, New York; A. Leo Weil, Pittsburgh, Pennsylvania and Felix M. Warburg, Secretary, New York.

Following the reading by Mr. Warburg of the charter, which outlined the general plan of activities to be inaugurated in all Young Men's Hebrew and Kindred Associations, Mr. Fischel embraced the opportunity to make the same plea he had made years before in relation to the conduct of the orphan asylums, namely that the Young Men's Hebrew Associations must be conducted in accordance with the traditional principles of the Jewish faith.

Otherwise, and if physical and social activities were to be the only benefits derived at a Y.M.H.A. there was no necessity of separate institutions for the Jewish youth, he asserted. They might just as well be members of the Young Men's Christian Association or other similar organizations.

Louis Marshall immediately supported Mr. Fischel in his demand that religion be introduced into the work of the institutions, insisting that it should not only be a part of the programme to be adopted but should form a considerable part of such programme.

As a result of his plea, seconded so eloquently by Mr. Marshall, Mr. Fischel was appointed chairman of a Religious Committee and was entrusted with the task of helping to prepare a suitable plan whereby the associations' activities should combine consideration of the spiritual with the physical needs of those who should come to them.

When, in later years, the Council of Y.M.H.A. and Kindred Associations was merged with the Jewish Welfare Board Mr. Fischel continued to serve as a member of the Board and still does.

CHAPTER XXI

JEWRY'S WORLD CALL IN THE GREAT WAR

THE outbreak of the Great War in 1914, coming with cataclysmic suddenness and fury upon the world, was destined to impose hitherto unprecedented obligations and burdens upon American Jewish philanthropy and, for the next ten years, to occupy a very large place in the attention and activities of Jewish leaders.

At the commencement of the titanic struggle, even after all the great powers except the United States, were involved, few persons either in Europe or America anticipated that the conflict, because of its very hugeness, could be of long duration. While, from bitter experience, it was appreciated that the Jews must suffer most from a war in which all of Europe was embroiled, it was not for some months that any organized effort was made to meet the situation which was inevitable.

Even at the outset of the war, however, business in Europe came to a complete standstill and the Jews, largely engaged in small trade or artisans and mechanics and with few exceptions having investments from which they derived an income, found themselves placed in a critical situation. For a few weeks they were enabled to live upon their small savings or to borrow from those more fortunately situated, but the Jewish institutions, the Yeshivas, Talmud Torahs and the charitable organizations generally, at once felt the effects of the changed economic conditions.

The people, themselves, their employment endangered or cut off, their business forced to suspend, had first to care for their own needs and were unable to continue to give support to their institutions. These, faced with the danger of being compelled to close or else to greatly limit their activities, had no recourse but to appeal to their brethren in America, the only country thus far not drawn into the war.

But even these first appeals which reached America did not begin to convey a true picture of the situation as it affected millions of Jews throughout Europe whose sufferings were already becoming intense and whose institutions and traditions were threatened with extinction if help were not extended them.

It is, therefore, a notable historic fact that the first steps taken to meet the situation were at the instance of the Union of Orthodox Jewish Congregations of America which, on September 28, 1914, addressed a telegram to its constituent congregations setting forth the needs and calling a conference of prominent Orthodox Jews to consider them.

This conference, held on October 1, 1914 at the residence of the late Rev. Dr. Philip Klein, Rabbi of the First Hungarian Congregation Ohab Zedek, resulted in the decision to form a relief committee, with the primary purpose of extending assistance to the Jewish institutions of Europe and Palestine, but which later came to embody the scope of individual aid as well.

This committee was organized on October 4, 1914 at the office of the Jewish Daily News, under the name of the Central Committee for the Relief of Jews Suffering through the War and the following officers were chosen: Leon Kamaiky, chairman; Harry Fischel, Treasurer; the late Albert Lucas and Morris Engelman, Secretaries.

Shortly after this another historic event took place when the Central Committee issued the first formal appeal to be made to the Jews of America in behalf of their suffering co-religionists abroad, an appeal which was the forerunner of countless others to be issued during the ensuing years and by which millions of dollars were raised and successfully distributed.

This appeal, which constitutes a document of extraordinary interest and significance to Jewry the world over, was as follows:

FIRST CALL OF CENTRAL COMMITTEE

FOR THE RELIEF OF

JEWS SUFFERING THROUGH THE WAR

TO THE JEWS OF AMERICA:

Our brethren are dying. Widows and orphans are wandering homeless, naked and hungry. Women, old and young, with their little ones and the aged find no refuge. In every land that we or our fathers once called home, bloody war with all its unspeakable horrors stalks abroad. Thousands of villages have been ravaged and great cities laid waste. Mourning, they lift up their eyes. Whence shall come their help!

More than half of the Jews of the world are overwhelmed in the present conflict. The condition of our brethren in Palestine, also, is past description. Its institutions can no longer be supported by the generosity of our brethren in Europe, as today the Jews of Europe are themselves sore beset.

Another most serious condition brought about by the war must not be overlooked. Thousands among us have regularly sent money to our families and friends "at home" to help our less fortunate kinsmen.

All the world is looking to us for aid and direction. We will surely not be deaf to their prayers.

We have therefore formed in New York a committee of representative rabbis and laymen to help our co-religionists in Europe and Palestine.

This committee is extending its organization throughout the United States and appeals to you to join it. It asks you either to call a meeting in your synagogue, or to join with others to call a meeting in your city, at which contributions shall be collected, local officers elected and representatives chosen to be added to our Central Committee in New York. We want at least two representatives in each city of the United States to be in constant communication with us in order to organize the Jews of America into one compact body, ready and willing to raise a large

RELIEF FUND FOR JEWS SUFFERING THROUGH
THE WAR.

REMEMBER—This war has ruined hundreds of thousands of our brethren.

REMEMBER—No one can tell, today, whether his own relatives are not refugees far from their own home.

REMEMBER—That the assistance of this Committee may save the lives of those who are near and dear to you. You cannot know where your own father or mother, sister or brother is. Your help through us, may help them.

AND REMEMBER—that this war will cause an amount of suffering unprecedented in history. Ways and means must be devised to raise an enormous amount of money at once, and to continue the effort throughout the weeks and months, aye, possibly even through the next few years to come.

This Committee is preparing plans which will enable every one to help daily, weekly and monthly, without taxing the resources of anyone beyond his means.

Join us at once. Send in your names and the names of those associated with you to the secretary of the committee. The Union of Orthodox Jewish Congregations of America, the Agudas Harabonim, the Mizrachi and the Central Committee of Palestine Institutions are all represented on this committee. A large number of collections have already been made in response to their appeals. All amounts should be remitted as soon as possible to the financial secretary of this committee; and checks drawn made payable to the order of the treasurer.

Five thousand dollars has been sent to a committee of Palestinian Jews comprising Guedalia N. Broder, Isaac Chagis, Joseph Eliaschar, Behr Epstein, Saul Isaac Freund, Dr. Isaac Levy, Solomon Perlman, Alter Rivlin, Dr. Arthur Ruppin, Solomon Rubin, Wolf Schechter, Salmon Soloweitchik, Aaron Vallero, David Yellin.

Five thousand dollars has been sent to the Israelitische Alliance, Vienna, for the relief of Galician Jews and one thousand dollars for the Yeshibath.

In securing the services of Mr. Harry Fischel as Treasurer, the Committee has obtained the advantage of his wide acquaintance throughout the United States. All moneys received by him are deposited in the Guaranty Trust Company of America. Arrangements will be made through the accredited representatives of the U. S. Government to forward money to our stricken brethren as soon as we can get in touch with responsible people in all the war zones who will distribute it without favor for the immediate relief of the Jewish widows and orphans, sick and wounded, aged and infirm; in short, to all those who will die of hunger and cold, unless you promptly help.

> Leon Kamaiky, *Chairman*
> Harry Fischel, *Treasurer*
> World Bldg., 63 Park Row, New York.
> J. J. Bernstein, *Recording Secretary*
> Morris Engelman, *Financial Secretary.*
> Albert Lucas, *Corresponding Secretary.*

It is the intention of this Committee to cooperate with the Committee of 100, as soon as it is formed.

Committee

Rabbi M. S. Margolies, President, Agudas Harabonim, Rabbi Congregation Kehillath Jeshurun.

Rabbi Wolf Margolies, Adath Israel.

Rabbi Philip Klein, President, Mizrachi.   Congregation Ohab Zedek.

Rabbi Solomon E. Jaffe, Congregation Beth Hamedrash Hagadol.

Rabbi J. H. Leventhal, Agudas Harabonim (Philadelphia).

Rev. Dr. H. Pereira Mendes, Spanish and Portugese Congregation.

Rev. Dr. Bernard Drachman, President, Union of Orthodox Jewish Congregations of America.   Congregation Ohab Zedek.

Rev. Dr. Moses Hyamson, Congregation Orach Chaim.

Rabbi Herbert S. Goldstein, Congregation Kehillath Jeshurun.

Rabbi Benj. B. Guth, Congregation Chassam Sofer.

Rabbi Samuel Glick, Secretary Agudas Harabonim.

Rabbi Israel Rosenberg, Agudas Harabonim (Paterson, N. J.)

Rabbi M. Peikes.

Rev. Harris Masliansky.

Rev. Phillip Jaches.

Mr. Bernard Bernstein   Mr. Geudalia Bubelik
Mr. David Blutreich   Mr. Moses Davis
Mr. Louis Borgenicht   Mr. Julius J. Dukas

Mr. E. W. Lewin Epstein
Mr. William Fischman
Mr. Aaron Garfunkel
Mr. Henry Glass
Mr. Jacob Hecht
Mr. Albert Herskowitz
Mr. Samuel I. Hyman
Mr. Nathan Hutkoff
Mr. Lewis J. Kapit
Mr. David Kass
Mr. Edwin I. Kaufman
Mr. Arnold Kohn
Mr. Nathan Lamport
Mr. Samuel Mason
Mr. Max Meyerson

Mr. Morris Neuman
Mr. Moses H. Phillips
Hon. N. Taylor Phillips
Mr. Nathan Roggen
Mr. J. Rokeach
Mr. Nathan Rosenzweig
Mr. G. S. Roth
Mr. Jacob Rubin
Hon. Leon Sanders
Mr. Ezekiel Sarasohn
Mr. Bernard Semel
Dr. P. A. Siegelstein
Mr. Elias Surut
Mr. Leon Tuchman
Mr. Jonas Weil

Mr. P. A. Wiernik

Make Checks payable to HARRY FISCHEL, Treasurer, and mail to

CENTRAL COMMITTEE FOR THE RELIEF
OF JEWS SUFFERING THROUGH THE WAR
1103 World Building, New York.

Upon Mr. Fischel's shoulders fell the task of receiving the moneys that were to come in response to this appeal and in order to save expense he volunteered to have the Committee's campaign conducted from his offices in the World Building at 61 Park Row where contributors were asked to send their donations to him as Treasurer.

No sooner had the appeal been issued through the newspapers of the country than checks began to pour in, in a very torrent. The appeal had struck a responsive chord in the heart of American Jewry and even in the first mail to be received after the publication of the Committee's letter thousands of checks in small amounts reached Mr. Fischel's office, so that he and his limited office force, totally unprepared for any such response, found themselves unable to cope with the situation.

It was still the general opinion, however, that the war would be of but a few weeks longer duration at most and it was deemed inadvisable under the circumstances to introduce elaborate machinery to handle the remittances, with all the cost of clerks and bookkeepers this would involve. For the next two weeks, therefore, Mr. Fischel, working night and day with his assistants, endeavored to keep up with the flood of checks that continued to arrive with every mail.

As reports of conditions in Europe continued to grow steadily worse and it became apparent the need was not to be so short lived as had been hoped, Mr. Fischel finally engaged an accountant and a number of bookkeepers and installed a card system by which every contribution was tabulated.

The system devised by Mr. Fischel called for the alphabetical tabulation by name, city and state of every contributor, so that it was possible to determine at a glance what any individual in a given community had given to the relief fund. This system proved a model not only for the needs of the Central Relief Committee but for many others, Jewish and Gentile, that were later formed.

Shortly after the system was installed, an official of the government who was ordered to look into the work the various relief organizations were doing, examined the Central Committee's accounts and on completing his examination issued a statement to the press in which, among other things, he stated:

"If all relief committees would do the same work in the same manner, with the same system as the Central Committee for the Relief of Jews Suffering Through the War, a great deal of money and effort could be saved, which could be used for the benefit of war sufferers."

Some idea of the magnitude of the work of the Central Committee may be gained from the fact that there passed through Mr. Fischel's hands as Treasurer the enormous sum of more than $20,000,000 received in amounts ranging from five cents to $10,000.

In these early days of the Committee the number of subscribers mounted into the thousands but the individual contributions were comparatively small and the total sum did not begin to meet the constantly growing need. The first plan put into operation by the Committee was to forward the money, after a certain total was collected, to the cities then most largely affected by the war and where it was apportioned among the institutions, Yeshivas and Talmud Torahs, according to their needs.

It was not long, however, before a still greater call for assistance reached over the seas to America. The war had not stopped, as was anticipated. Instead it was daily reaching over a wider area and thousands of individuals in every land had been deprived of their homes, and had been made refugees without food or clothing. In the number were the aged and infirm, women and children, many of the latter rendered orphans.

The Jewish people of Europe would perish, would be blotted out of existence unless much greater aid from America was forthcoming at once. The situation, at first but little understood or realized, had by now, less than a month after the work was started by the Central Committee, come to be partially appreciated by the Jewish leaders of America, with the result that it was determined to make an effort to reach the wealthier class of Jews to whom the Central Committee's appeal had not directly been made.

In accordance with this determination, Mr. Louis Marshall, President of the American Jewish Committee, on October 24, 1914, issued a call for a conference at the Temple Emanue-El for the purpose of organizing a larger committee whose object it should be to reach all the Jews throughout the United States and bring home to them the dire plight of their brethren in Europe.

At this meeting it was decided to appoint a Committee of Five, whose duty it should be to select a national committee of One Hundred to comprise the American Jewish Relief Committee.

On this Committee of Five were named United States Supreme Court Justice Louis B. Brandeis, the late Congressman Meyer London, Judge Julian W. Mack, the late Secretary of Commerce, Oscar S. Straus and Mr. Fischel.

Little time was lost by the Committee of Five, in getting down to the task of selecting one hundred men from among the most prominent and representative Jews in America to comprise the American Jewish Relief Committee. Within a very few days after the meeting called at Temple Emanu-El, Justice Brandeis, as chairman, summoned the members to meet at the Bar Association Building on West Forty-fourth Street, New York City.

Practically the entire night was spent in carefully going over the names of leading Jews throughout the United States with the purpose of selecting not only the most prominent but those most likely to take effective leadership in this great cause.

On November 15, or as soon after this meeting as it was practicable to get them together from distant points, the Committee of One Hundred, representing as many national Jewish organizations, was formally summoned to meet at the offices of the United Hebrew Charities, now the Jewish Social Service, with the object of completing its organization, electing officers and selecting an Executive Committee of twenty-five, upon whom the chief burdens of the actual work were to be imposed. Louis Marshall was chosen chairman, Felix M. Warburg, treasurer and A. H. Fromenson, secretary.

A week after this meeting, Mr. Fischel received the following letter from Chairman Marshall, notifying him of his appointment to the Executive Committee.

MEMBERS OF THE JOINT DISTRIBUTION COMMITTEE
*For the Relief of Jews Suffering Through the War,
of which Mr. Fischel was One of the Founders.*

Mr. Harry Fischel,
61 Park Row,
New York City.

Dear Sir:

I beg to inform you that at the meeting of the Committee of One Hundred, you were elected a member of the Executive Committee of Twenty-Five and I have called a meeting of the said Executive Committee for Tuesday evening, November 24th, at 8 o'clock at the United Hebrew Charities Building, 358 Second Avenue and another meeting to be held at the same address on Sunday morning, November 29th at 10:30 o'clock. Since you have been one of the five who have organized the American Jewish Relief Committee, your presence at these meetings is of the utmost importance.

Very sincerely yours,

LOUIS MARSHALL

CHAPTER XXII

WEDDING OF HIS FIRST DAUGHTER

BETWEEN the dates of these two meetings of the Executive Committee, November 24th and November 29th, 1914, a momentous event in Mr. Fischel's life, on its personal side, took place. This was the marriage of his eldest daughter, Sadie, to Mr. David Kass by Rabbi M. S. Margolies and the editor of this work, marking the realization of Mr. Fischel's hope to see his first daughter happily married to a worthy man who should live up to the ideals of religion and charity which he held and which he had imparted to his children. So well has Mr. Kass realized these ideals, that he has recently been elected President of the Congregation Kehillath Jeshurun, and is the youngest man ever to have held that office in one of the foremost Orthodox Synagogues in the United States, numbering among its members and trustees leaders in every communal endeavor, religious and charitable.

As for Sadie Fischel Kass, she is walking directly in the footsteps of her father, and Mr. Fischel points with justifiable pride to a partial list of her communal activities as follows:— She has been Recording Secretary of the Women's Auxiliary of the Central Jewish Institute since its organization ten years ago. She is Treasurer of the Jewish Students' House on the Columbia Campus. She is a member of the Executive Committee of the National Women's League and has been Treasurer of the Women's League, New York City Branch, since its inception and is a directress of the Home of the Daughters of Jacob. With an inherited tendency to build, directly communicated to her from her father, she had been instrumental in the erection of two synagogues. One is the Welfare Island Synagogue, erected under the auspices of the Council of Jewish Women, of which she is Corresponding Secretary of the Welfare Island Synagogue Committee, and the other, now in process of construction, is the Jerusalem Synagogue and Center of which Mrs. Kass is Honorary National Treasurer.

MR. FISCHEL'S FIRST SON-IN-LAW,
Mr. and Mrs. David Kass and their children.

CHAPTER XXIII

ORGANIZATION OF AMERICAN JEWISH
RELIEF COMMITTEE

At the meeting of the Executive Committee of Twenty-five of the American Jewish Relief Committee, attended by Mr. Fischel on November 29, it was decided to issue a general appeal for large contributions, the purpose being to concentrate the attention of American Jewry as a whole upon the pressing necessities of the situation confronting European Jewry and the Jews in Palestine, as a result of the great war which was being waged with ever increasing bitterness.

This first appeal of the American Jewish Relief Committee is herewith reproduced:

First American Jewish Relief Committee Appeal

The American Jewish Relief Committee, called into being at a conference of over 100 National Jewish organizations, which was held at Temple Emanu-El, New York City, on October 25th to consider the plight of over six million Jews who live within the war zone, has issued the following appeal:

The American Jewish Relief Committee for Sufferers from the War appeals to you to aid, with the utmost generosity and self-sacrifice, the fund now being gathered to provide relief for the families of the Jewish people in various parts of Europe and Asia who have been deprived of their means of sustenance either through the killing or wounding of their breadwinners, through the destruction of the towns in which they live, or through the resulting economic distress.

Our co-religionists, in common with their fellow-citizens of other creeds, are contributing with their usual liberality to the

135

several national and international relief funds.   Neither these contributions nor those for local charities should be lessened by reason of the necessity which impels us to make this SPECIAL APPEAL to their generosity.

The disaster, in which the whole world shares, falls with disproportionate weight upon the Jewish people, more than nine millions of whom live in the countries at war, and over six million of those in the actual war zones in Poland, Galicia and the whole European frontier.   Throughout this section the horrors of war and the devastation due to conflict have come upon a population already so oppressed and impoverished by persecution as to leave no reserve for this new calamity.   Hunger, disease, destitution in its extremest form confront a Jewish population as numerous as the population of Belgium.

These exceptional circumstances have impelled the formation of the American Jewish Relief Committee, with a view of uniting all sections of Jewry in the United States in this supreme effort in the greatest crisis that has faced the Jewish people in modern times.   Representatives from all parts of the United States and of every shade of opinion have participated in the deliberations which brought about the formation of this Committee, in the hope that united, concerted action would produce the most effective results.

In Poland and Galicia, where great contending armies are now engaged, it would not be so wise to entrust a committee or people who have instituted a religious and racial boycott against Jews with the duty of aiding or distributing funds among the large Jewish population in those countries.   The sad conditions in Russia are well-known.   Palestine, whose main source of subsistence is cut off and whose economic life has been paralyzed, is likewise in urgent need.

In view of these conditions and the exceptional severity of the conditions, we appeal to the Jews of America to come without stint to the rescue of their afflicted brethren.   It is the purpose of this Committee, should it be found that no other relief funds are available in those districts, that this fund shall be applied to the relief of the most urgent distress, without regard to race or creed.

At the time of the Russian Pogroms the Jews of this country contributed nearly $1,500,000 for the relief of the victims.   The

A SESSION OF THE JOINT DISTRIBUTION COMMITTEE.

present calamity is vastly greater and requires accordingly greater measures of relief.

In cities which have already established associate relief committees we ask you to make your donations and pledges to your local treasurer, or, if you are a member of a national organization acting in co-operation with this Committee, to the treasurer of your organization or to send your check and pledges direct to the treasurer of the American Jewish Relief Committee, Felix M. Warburg, 52 William Street, New York City.

THE AMERICAN JEWISH RELIEF COMMITTEE

BY THE EXECUTIVE COMMITTEE

Cyrus Adler, Philadelphia; Isaac Adler, Rochester; Louis D. Brandeis, Boston; Caeser Cope, Greensboro, N. C.; Samuel Dorf, New York; Harry Fischel, New York; J. Walter Freiberg, Cincinnati; Harry Friedenwald, Baltimore; Moses Gries, Cleveland; Louis E. Kirstein, Boston; Abr. G. Becker, Chicago; E. W. Lewin Epstein, New York; Meyer London, New York; Julian W. Mack, Chicago; J. L. Magnes, New York; M. S. Margolies, New York; Louis Marshall, New York; Leon Sanders, New York; Moses Schoenberg, St. Louis; Jacob H. Schiff, New York; Oscar S. Straus, New York; Mayer Sulzberger, Philadelphia; Cyrus L. Sulzberger, New York; Isaac N. Ullman, New Haven; Felix M. Warburg, New York; A. Leo Weil, Pittsburgh; Harris Weinstock, San Francisco.

As was to have been expected the response to this call, issued by the leading Jews of America, was both generous and enthusiastic. American Jewry was at last thoroughly aroused to the gravity of the situation and ready to exert itself to the umost in its alleviation. Contributions in large amounts at once began to flow from every section of the country into the office of the treasurer, Felix M. Warburg, so that by late November a sufficient sum had been collected to make possible the holding of the first meeting of the Executive Committee to consider the problem of the distribution of the funds in hand.

CHAPTER XXIV

THE JOINT DISTRIBUTION COMMITTEE

A Significant Chapter in Jewish History

IT soon became apparent to those engaged in war relief work that the problem of distribution was to be quite as important and equally as difficult as that of collecting funds, for there came from every part of Europe appeals from the stricken Jewish population, one more tragic and heart rending than another. It was therefore essential that such sums as were collected should not only be used in those places where they were most needed but for those particular objects that would accomplish most in relieving the acutest forms of distress.

Accordingly, at a meeting of the Executive Committee of the American Jewish Relief Committee held late in November, it was decided to keep separate and distinct the work of collection and distribution and at about this time there came into being the Joint Distribution Committee of the American Funds for Jewish War Sufferers, with Felix M. Warburg as chairman, which was organized as the result of the initiative of the American Jewish Relief Committee and the Central Committee for the Relief of Jews Suffering through the War, of which Mr. Fischel was treasurer.

Immediately after this meeting, Mr. Fischel was appointed as a member of the Executive Committee of the Joint Distribution Committee, which, during the war and subsequent to the Armistice, distributed nearly $100,000,000 of relief moneys collected through its subsidiary committees, the American, Central and People's Relief Committees, continuing its activities down to the present time.

The letter notifying Mr. Fischel of his appointment as a member of this Committee was as follows:

138

Mr. Harry Fischel,   November 25, 1914.
61 Park Row,
New York City.
Dear Sir:

The executive committee of the American Jewish Relief Committee has appointed you a member of its committee on distribution, of which Mr. Felix M. Warburg is Chairman. Since you are the Treasurer of the Central Relief Committee, it is of the utmost importance for you to accept this designation. A meeting of this committee will be called shortly by the Chairman.

Very truly yours,
A. H. FROMENSON
Secretary of the Executive Committee.

The first meeting of this committee, organized for distribution of the vast sums collected and to be collected for the aid of the suffering Jewish populations of Europe and Palestine, marked an epoch in the history of American Jewry as it was the first time that every section of Jewry, the Orthodox and Reform elements, as well as the element represented by the workers through their labor unions, was to be united for the fulfillment of a common purpose.

At the meetings of the Joint Distribution Committee were gathered round a single council table, the rich and the poor, the aristocrat and the middle class, the banker and the toiler, the professional man and scholar, all with the single object in view of securing a maximum of efficiency and a maximum amount of good from the disbursement of the moneys collected from the public for relief.

It is unnecessary at this time to record exactly how much and to what places the first funds were distributed but it is a matter of historic record and a cause for pride on the part of Mr. Fischel that the first money to reach Europe from America came from the Central Relief Committee, the first of the relief organizations to be formed and through whose instrumentality many Jewish institutions were saved from destruction.

The Central Committee collected its funds chiefly through appeals made in the Orthodox synagogues and from Orthodox Jewish institutions, lodges and societies and its money was used principally for direct aid to the institutions, Talmud Torahs and Yeshivas in Europe and Palestine.

The American Committee sought its funds for general relief from the wealthier class of Jews throughout the United States, while the contributions to the Peoples' Committee, the last to be organized, came from the working classes through the unions.

Each committee conducted its own separate campaigns but but the funds of all were turned over to the Joint Distribution Committee, comprised of the leading members of the three committees, whose sole task it was to designate the amounts to be sent to the several parts of Europe and the purpose for which they were to be expended. Later on and following the Armistice the Joint Distribution Committee had its own representatives scattered throughout Europe for the purpose of making recommendations direct to the New York headquarters.

Despite the fact that the American and Central committees were functioning and were putting forth every effort to collect as large amounts as possible, the demand for aid from the sufferers in the constantly widening war zones, with their scenes of indescribable devastation, continued to grow and to far exceed the total of the contributions to date. It was, furthermore, by this time, late in 1914, clearly apparent that the end of the war was not in sight and that the longer it should last the greater would be the calls upon American Jewry for aid.

Accordingly and to increase both the number and volume of contributions a meeting of all those engaged in war relief collections in every part of the country, was arranged to be held in Carnegie Hall, New York, on December 21. Prior to this meeting Mr. Jacob H. Schiff invited the members of the Executive Committee of the American Jewish Relief Committee and the speakers at this conference to be his guests at dinner, to which, on December 14, Mr. Fischel received the following invitation.

My dear Mr. Fischel:

I am inviting the speakers at the Carnegie Hall meeting next Tuesday to dine at my residence, 965 Fifth Avenue, at 7 o'clock to meet the executive committee and a few others. I shall be pleased if you will honor me with your company. We will proceed after dinner to Carnegie Hall in a body.

Respectfully yours,

Jacob H. Schiff

It is doubtful if ever before or since in the history of American Jewry such a scene has been witnessed as the demonstration that took place at this Carnegie Hall meeting. After hearing a description of the appalling conditions confronting the Jews of Europe and listening to the eloquent appeals made in their behalf by Jacob H. Schiff, Dr. Judah L. Magnes, Nathan Straus, the late Bishop David H. Greer of the Episcopal Church, Rabbi M. S. Margolies, the late Congressman Meyer London and the Rev. Dr. Leon Harrison of St. Louis, the audience responded in a manner that showed how deeply their hearts had been touched.

As the result of a collection made during the meeting more than $700,000 was realized in cash, pledges and checks and many of the women in the audience took off their jewels and dropped them in the contribution baskets as their donation to the cause.

As the outcome of this meeting and the tremendous amount of attention it received from the press of the entire country contributions were for a while largely stimulated and the American Jewish Relief Committee received a number of individual donations that were the largest amounts to be given for a Jewish charitable cause ever recorded up to that time.

The Central Relief Committee, however, had a much more difficult task than that which confronted the American Committee, for its field, comprised of the Orthodox congregations and the institutions and societies, was limited and already had been pretty thoroughly canvassed.

Following the Carnegie Hall meeting, Mr. Fischel again concentrated his attention on finding some way in which the Central Relief Committee might reach individual Orthodox Jews, who, while not able to give the large contributions the American Jewish Relief Committee was receiving, could afford to give sums in proportion to their means.

In order to reach every such home in the United States the Committee decided, in connection with its appeal, to issue certificates in sums ranging from $5 to $100 which should be given to contributors in these amounts. It was felt that people would give much more willingly and freely if they received some recognition of their gifts which might be preserved to posterity. This idea proved a good one and resulted in thousands of dollars in additional contributions being secured which might otherwise not have been donated.

MEETING OF THE DIRECTORS OF THE CENTRAL JEWISH
RELIEF COMMITTEE

*For which Mr. Fischel as Treasurer Handled More
Than Twenty Million Dollars.*

CHAPTER XXV

WEDDING OF HIS SECOND DAUGHTER

ANOTHER happy event occurred in Mr. Fischel's family on March 7, 1915, when his daughter Rebecca was married to Rabbi Herbert S. Goldstein. The marriage ceremony was performed in the Congregation Kehillath Jeshurun, where the bridegroom was the Junior Rabbi, with the following noted Rabbis officiating: Rabbi M. S. Margolies, senior Rabbi of the Congregation; Dr. H. Pereira Mendes, President of the Union of Orthodox Jewish Congregations of America and the late Solomon Schechter, President of the Jewish Theological Seminary.

The wedding dinner was held in Mr. Fischel's home. A souvenir of the occasion was given to the guests in the form of a book entitled "Praise for Righteousness," by Moses Haym Luzatto, translated by the bride and bridegroom. This marked the first Hebrew play to be translated into English. It is an Epithalameum (written by Luzatto in honor of his friend's wedding) which made it a most fitting memento of the marriage ceremony.

"Who's Who in American Jewry" for 1926 contains, among other references to Rabbi Goldstein, the following:

"Received B.A. and M.A. degrees from Columbia University; Smicha (Right to Decide Religious Questions) conferred by Rabbi S. E. Jaffe; graduate Jewish Theological Seminary of America; Founder and Rabbi Institutional Synagogue, New York City; Assistant Professor of Homiletics, Rabbi Isaac Elchanan Theological Seminary; President Union of Orthodox Jewish Congregations of America; Author of 'Comments on the Ethics of the Fathers,' 'Extracts from the Paths of Righteousness' (translation); compiler, 'Home Service Prayers'."

The same book of Jewish reference gives the following record of Mrs. Goldstein's chief activities:

"Received B.A. degree from Barnard College, Columbia University; graduate of Teachers' Institute of the Jewish Theological Seminary of America; Member of Board, New York Section Council of Jewish Women; President Women's Branch Union of Orthodox Jewish Congregations of America and founder of the Union's Collegiate Branch; Vice Chairman Women's Committee Yeshiva College Dormitory Fund; Chairman Committee on Religion, Council of Jewish Women; directress, Home of Daughters of Jacob and Hebrew Day Nursery."

In 1917, Rabbi Goldstein, actuated by the purpose of broadening his activities in the direction of the religous training of the Jewish youth, founded the Institutional Synagogue. Mr. Fischel, in furtherance of the undertaking, purchased the institution's first building at 112 West 116th Street. This building formed the nucleus for the present structure of the Institutional Synagogue at 37-43 West 116th Street, constituting one of the largest and most important Orthodox Synagogues and Talmud Torahs in the country.

As was to have been expected of her, Mrs. Goldstein has been most active not only in aiding her husband in this work but in the work of the Union of Orthodox Jewish Congregations of America, of which she is the president of the Women's Branch. She also founded a Collegiate Branch of the Union which has spread the message of Orthodox Judaism among countless college students.

MR. FISCHEL'S SECOND SON-IN-LAW

Rabbi and Mrs. Herbert S. Goldstein and their children.

CHAPTER XXVI

PRESIDENT WILSON'S PROCLAMATION
IN AID OF THE WAR SUFFERERS

WITH all of the means that had thus far been used to stimulate contributions to the various Jewish war relief committees the sums collected still fell far short of the needs and Mr. Fischel spent a great deal of thought in trying to devise some method by which the attention of the entire country might be concentrated upon this cause.

Mr. Morris Engelman, the Financial Secretary of the Central Relief Committee, hit upon the idea that if the President of the United States could be interested in issuing a proclamation setting aside a certain day to be designated as Jewish War Relief Day, this would accomplish the purpose and would at one stroke acquaint the entire people of the country with the full gravity of the situation and result in a very large sum being collected on the day fixed.

Acting upon this idea, which was communicated to the other executives of the Central Relief Committee, an attempt was immediately made to find an individual who could best place the matter before the President and enlist his sympathy and cooperation. Upon inquiry it was learned that Senator Martine, of New Jersey, of which state President Woodrow Wilson had been governor, was the right man to approach and Mr. Fischel accordingly entered into correspondence with Senator Martine explaining the object it was sought to achieve. Senator Martine was at once interested and promised to do everything in his power to induce the President to issue such a proclamation as was suggested.

First, however, the Senator procured the passage of a resolution in the United States Senate calling attention to the pitiable condition of the nine million Jews in the war zones and to their cry to America for aid. The resolution requested the President to take notice of the situation by designating a day on which the citizens of this country might give expression to their sympathy by contributing to the funds for relief of these Jewish war sufferers.

Finally, on January 11, 1916, the Committee was formally advised by Senator Martine that the President had acceded to its request and had set aside January 27, as Jewish War Relief Day, issuing a proclamation to that effect. This news was received with great joy and satisfaction by the members of the Central Relief Committee as it was felt that, more than any other single measure that had thus far been taken, this would focus the attention of all Americans on the tragic necessity which impelled such a nation-wide appeal for help.

The President's proclamation, issued on January 11, 1916, was as follows:

BY THE PRESIDENT OF THE UNITED STATES OF AMERICA—A PROCLAMATION

WHEREAS, I have received from the Senate of the United States a Resolution, passed January 6, 1916, reading as follows:

"WHEREAS, in the various countries now engaged in war there are nine millions of Jews, the great majority of whom are destitute of food, shelter and clothing; and

"WHEREAS, millions of them have been driven from their homes without warning, deprived of an opportunity to make provision for their most elementary wants, causing starvation, disease and untold suffering; and

"WHEREAS, the people of the United States of America have learned with sorrow of this terrible plight of millions of human beings and have most generously responded to the cry for help whenever such an appeal has reached them; Therefore be it

"RESOLVED, That, in view of this misery, wretchedness, and hardships which these nine millions of Jews are suffering, the President of the United States be respectfully asked to designate a day on which the citizens of this country may give expression to their sympathy by contributing to the funds now being raised for the relief of the Jews in the war zones."

AND WHEREAS, I feel confident that the people of the United States will be moved to aid the war-stricken people of a race which has given to the United States so many worthy citizens;

NOW THEREFORE, I, Woodrow Wilson, President of the United States, in compliance with the suggestion of the Senate thereof, do appoint and proclaim January 27, 1916, as a day upon which the people of the United States may make such contribution as they feel disposed for the aid of the stricken Jewish people.

Contributions may be addressed to the American Red Cross, Washington, D. C., which will care for their proper distribution.

IN WITNESS WHEREOF, I have hereunto set my hand and caused the seal of the United States to be affixed.

SEAL OF
THE UNITED STATES
OF AMERICA

Done at the city of Washington this eleventh day of January, in the year of our Lord, one thousand nine hundred and sixteen, and of the Independence of the United States the one hundred and fortieth.

WOODROW WILSON

By the President:
    ROBERT LANSING
        Secretary of State.

The original of President Wilson's proclamation was received by the Central Relief Committee on January 14 and steps were immediately taken by the Committee to insure the largest possible response to the President's message, $3,000,000 being fixed as the smallest sum that should be contributed by American Jewry on the day set apart as Jewish Relief Day.

The Committee at once arranged for a lithographed certificate bearing an exact copy of the President's proclamation, with a beautiful illuminated border which, it was announced, would be issued with every contribution of from one dollar to one hundred dollars. Reproductions of these certificates, of which several thousands were made ready, appeared in practically every daily newspaper in the United States, with the result that the demand for them was so large that it was difficult to meet it and the certificates brought a large sum of money into the Committee.

To make the facts relating to Jewish War Relief Day as widely known as possible the Committee also sought to bring about meetings to be held in every city on that day for the purpose of making collections and issued the following statement which appeared in the press of the country and was also sent to the Committee's branches:

To the Jews of America

The President of the United States has issued a special proclamation designating Thursday, January 27, as the day upon which every man, woman and child in America, without regard to race or creed, has been officially requested to assist the nine million Jews that are suffering unspeakable outrages—all the horrors of expulsion from their homes—starvation and nakedness, in all the lands that are now engaged in the war. Unlike the Belgians, the Armenians, the Serbians and other people who have a flag to which they can rally, our brethren are landless, and though they are fighting under every flag, no one of the nations for which they offer their life's blood offers them any protection as Jews. The greatest misfortune through which our people have lived is now presented to us.

The intention of the President is that Thursday, January 27, shall be a day that shall have historic importance for the Jews residing in this country. Every one, both Jew and those that are not of our faith, is requested by him to contribute to the fund. Surely such a request addressed by him to the citizens of the United States, without regard to race or creed, should have a special significance to us, we the brothers and sisters, the sons and daughters of the nine million Jews that are suffering in the war zones.

It must be remembered that the resolution passed by the Senate, through which the President issued this proclamation, was introduced by Senator Martine at the urgent request of Mr. Harry Fischel, treasurer of the Central Jewish Relief Committee.

It, therefore, becomes the bounden duty of every Jew to do all in his power, both in honor of the President of the United States and in honor of his own race and creed. It is surely not too much to ask from the three million Jews in America that on the Jewish Relief Day proclaimed by the President of the United States there shall be collected from the Jews alone a sum equal to at least one dollar per head, that is to say, it is the earnest wish of the Central Jewish Relief Committee that the Jews of the United States shall respond to the President's proclamation by contributing on the 27th of January at least $3,000,000. Doubtless many among us can give much more than one dollar. But in asking the Jews to contribute $3,000,000 for the Jewish Relief Fund to be collected on the special Jewish Relief Day, it must be remembered that a number of children and a large number of poor, will not be able to contribute at all. It is, therefore, the duty of all those whom fortune has favored, to contribute to the very best of his ability and as large a sum as possible, to make up for those who will not be able to contribute anything at all.

The Central Committee has prepared a copy of the President's proclamation and is also issuing certificates representing contributions of $1, $5, $10, $25, $50 and $100. One copy of the President's proclamation will be issued with each certificate.

Doubtless many of those who are not of our faith will also be willing to purchase one of these historic documents and all that we now need to do is to prepare for the Great Day. Every one who is able should volunteer to place his or her services at the disposal of the local Branch of the Central Committee or of some other representative Jewish body in every village, town and city in the country. Every rabbi should feel it his duty to preach a special sermon on Sabbath, January 22. Doubtless many Christian ministers will also take advantage of the following Sunday to appeal to their congregations. Meetings should be organized and every effort should at once be made. Let us hear from you at once telling us how many certificates we many send you and of what denominations. Checks should be made payable to the order of Mr. Harry Fischel, Treasurer.

There will be a large meeting in every city of the United States on the Jewish Relief Day, January 27. Everything must be done in advance so that everything shall be in order. Work must go on smoothly, punctually in every city and town of the United States.

The sooner you send us your orders the sooner we shall be able to fill them. All committees are requested from now until midnight of January 27th to telegraph to this office, the details of the work they are doing. Let us know what mass meetings they have arranged and the amounts which have so far been collected and what pledges are already in hand.

The effect of the President's Proclamation and the interest aroused by the Jewish Relief Day was immediate and far reaching, so that the campaign to raise hitherto unheard of sums for a Jewish charitable purpose was given new life and branch committees were formed in every town in the country where even a few Jews had their residence.

At a meeting of the Central Committee held just after the National Jewish Relief Day, Mr. Fischel proposed that a suitable resolution of appreciation be prepared by the Committee and presented to the President.

This suggestion was unanimously passed and such a form of appreciation was engrossed on heavy parchment, bound in book form and, accompanied with a copy of the certificate issued by the Committee in connection with the President's Proclamation, was presented to the

HONORABLE WOODROW WILSON

PRESIDENT OF THE UNITED STATES OF AMERICA

In Recognition of his Humanitarian Act in Proclaiming

THE JEWISH RELIEF DAY

JANUARY TWENTY-SEVENTH, 1916

CENTRAL COMMITTEE FOR THE RELIEF OF JEWS SUFFERING THROUGH THE WAR

HARRY FISCHEL. *Treasurer*
LEON KAMAIKY, *Chairman*
ALBERT LUCAS, *Executive Secretary*
RABBI I. ROSENBERG, *Vice Chairman*
MORRIS ENGELMAN, *Financial Secretary*
RABBI MEYER BERLIN, *Vice Chairman*

COMMITTEE

Bernard Bernstein
John L. Bernstein
Stanley Bero
N. H. Borenstein
Louis Borgenicht
Guedalia Bublik
Moses Davis
Rev. Dr. Bernard Drachman
Julius J. Dukas
C. Joshua Epstein
E. W. Lewin-Epstein
William Fischman
Louis Friedman
Aaron Garfunkel
Jacob Ginsburg
Henry Glass
Rabbi Samuel Glick
Rabbi Herbert S. Goldstein
Mendel Gottesman
Rabbi Benj. B. Guth
Isidore Herschfield
Albert Herskovitz
Joseph Horwitz
Nathan Hutkoff
Rev. Dr. Moses Hyamson
Samuel I. Hyman
Rev. Phillip Jaches
Louis I. Kapit
David Kass
Edwin Kaufman

Wolf Klebansky
Rabbi Philip Klein
Rabbi Joseph Konvitz
Nathan Lamport
Rabbi B. L. Leventhal
Rabbi M. S. Margolies
Rev. Harris Masliansky
Samuel Mason
Rev. Dr. H. Pereira Mendes
Rev. H. S. Morais
Samuel W. Moskowitz
Moritz Neuman
Rabbi M. Peikus
Moses H. Phillips
Hon. N. Taylor Phillips
Nathan Roggen
J. Rokeach
Abraham Rosen
Nathan Rosensweig
G. S. Roth
Ignatz Roth
Jacob Rubin
Hon. Leon Sanders
Ezekiel Sarasohn
Rabbi J. Seigel
Hon. Isaac Siegel
Rabbi Aaron Teitelbaum
Leon Tuchmann
Jonas Weil
Peter Wiernik

WOMEN'S PROCLAMATION DAY COMMITTEE

Mrs. Samuel Elkeles, *Chairman*
Mrs. Henry Kraft, *Treasurer*
Mrs. David Kass
Mrs. Emanuel Elzas
Mrs. L. W. Zwissohn
Miss Sara X. Schottenfels

Honorary Secretaries

Mrs. Joseph Mayor Asher
Mrs. Albert Canfield Bage
Mrs. Julius Baran
Mrs. Simon Baruch
Mrs. Julius Beer
Mrs. Meyer Berlin
Mrs. R. L. Bernstein
Mrs. Elmer Black
Mrs. J. Blau
Mrs. L. Block
Mrs. Alfred Blumenthal
Mrs. Henry Bodenheimer
Mrs. Isaac Boehm
Mrs. Solomon Boehm
Mrs. Sidney C. Borg
Mrs. William Grant Brown
Mrs. Clarence Burns
Mrs. A. N. Cohen
Mrs. Virginia Danziger
Miss Katherine B. Davis
Mrs. M. Deiches
Mrs. Haryot Holt Day
Mrs. Bernard Drachman
Mrs. E. W. Dreyfus
Mrs. Julius Dukas
Mrs. William Einstein
Mrs. Morris Engelman
Mrs. Edward Epstein
Mrs. E. W. Lewin-Epstein
Mrs. Harry Fischel
Mrs. Samuel Floersheimer

Mrs. Samuel Frankelstein
Mrs. B. L. Friedman
Mrs. Henry Glass
Mrs. J. Goldey
Mrs. Samuel Goldberg
Mrs. David Goldfarb
Mrs. Edward Goodman
Mrs. Herbert S. Goldstein
Mrs. Eugene J. Grant
Mrs. Benedict J. Greenhut
Mrs. Rudolph Grossman
Mrs. Daniel Guggenheim
Mrs. Daniel P. Hays
Mrs. Moses Hyamson
Mrs. M. Isaacs
Mrs. Leon Kamaiky
Mrs. Abraham Kassel
Mrs. Edwin Kaufman
Mrs. Julius Keller
Mrs. Philip Klein
Mrs. Samuel Koenig
Mrs. Lazarus Kohns
Mrs. Alexander Kohut
Mrs. Irving Lehman
Mrs. M. L. Levenson
Mrs. Philip Lewinsohn
Mrs. Harry Lilly
Mrs. Edward Lissman
Mrs. Benjamin Leerburger
Mrs. Albert Lucas
Mrs. M. S. Margolies

Mrs. Marcus M. Marks
Mrs. Samuel Marks
Mrs. Samuel Mason
Mrs. F. DeSola Mendes
Mrs. H. Pereira Mendes
Mrs. Mortimer M. Menken
Mrs. Percival Menken
Mrs. Frederick Nathan
Mrs. Moritz Neuman
Mrs. Charles J. Oppenheim
Mrs. Laurent Oppenheim
Mrs. A. M. Palmer

Mrs. Max Phillips
Mrs. Leopold Plaut
Mrs. N. Taylor Phillips
Mrs. William Scheuer
Mrs. Samuel Schulman
Mrs. William Solomon
Mrs. Harold Spielberg
Miss Carrie Tekulski
Mrs. Israel Unterberg
Mrs. Henry Villard
Mrs. Thomas J. Vivian
Mrs. Fred Wachtel

Miss Mary Wood

A delegation from the Central Relief Committee was then appointed to go to Washington and formally present this token of its gratitude and esteem to the President. This delegation consisted of the following: Leon Kamaiky, president; Harry Fischel, treasurer; Albert Lucas and Morris Engelman, secretaries, and Rabbis M. S. Margolies, B. L. Leventhal, Meyer Berlin, Israel Rosenberg and Aaron Teitelbaum.

In addition to this delegation, one from the Women's Proclamation Day Committee, the women's auxiliary of the Central Relief Committee that had worked with the parent body in bringing about the success of the Jewish War Relief Day, also was named and included Mrs. Harry Fischel, Mrs. Albert Lucas, Mrs. Samuel Elkeles, Mrs. Leon Kamaiky and Mrs. David Kass.

The two delegations called jointly on President Wilson at the White House on February 17, 1927, and were presented to the President by Rabbi Silverstone and Rabbi Benjamin Gross, both of Washington. The members were received with the greatest courtesy by the President who stated in his acceptance of the Committee's gift that he deemed it a great privilege to have been afforded the opportunity of lending his assistance in such a worthy humanitarian cause. A photograph of the two delegations was taken on the White House steps before their departure.

While it was generally recognized that the Central Relief Committee, with Mr. Fischel's aid, had been responsible for bringing about the President's proclamation and his naming of a day for a national Jewish War Relief collection, no ill-feeling was created among the other relief committees.

On the contrary, on February 21, 1916, Mr. Fischel received the following letter from Jacob Billikopf, at that time Executive Secretary of the American Jewish Relief Committee in Kansas City.

Mr. Harry Fischel,
Treasurer of the Central Relief Committee,
63 Park Row.
Dear Mr. Fischel:

I suppose that you have received a great many congratulations upon your suggestion to Senator Martine of New Jersey which resulted in the President's setting aside January 27th as the day on which to collect money for the suffering Jews. I want to add my sincere congratulations and to express the conviction that it is in consequence of your initative that at least a million dollars more has been raised throughout the Country for the suffering Jews than would otherwise have been collected.

I regret exceedingly that you found it impossible to stop over in Kansas City on your way to the coast. It would have given several of your admirers great pleasure to have entertained you. I trust that we may have the privilege of entertaining you in the near future, and with kind regards, I am,

Sincerely,

JACOB BILLIKOPF

Mr. Fischel at this time received many other letters and telegrams of the same tenor from prominent Jews all over the United States.

As treasurer of the Central Relief Committee Mr. Fischel had occasion at various times to sign checks for sums as high as two hundred and fifty and five hundred thousand dollars each and one check for a million dollars, a photograph of which is herewith reproduced.

CERTIFICATE ISSUED BY THE CENTRAL RELIEF COMMITTEE

In connection with the Jewish Relief Day Proclamation by President Woodrow Wilson.

CHAPTER XXVII

THE JEWISH ASSEMBLY OF 1917

By the year 1917, as the result of three years of effort by the various commtitees making collections for the work of Jewish War Relief, which had been accompanied by almost continuous appeals to the public, there was a noticeable slackening in the response on the part of the people despite the fact that the need was, if anything, more urgent than at any time since the beginning of the war.

The public was, in short, tired of giving and had grown callous to the reiterated pleas made in behalf of the sufferers in the war zones whose plight had become worse than ever and who, it was no figure of speech to state, faced annihilation through privation and want.

It was apparent that some drastic step must be taken to re-awaken the public interest and to induce contributions in larger numbers and amounts than had even thus far been secured. Accordingly the leaders of the three committees determined to call an Assembly of the representatives of the various committees throughout the United States to be held at the Spanish and Portugese Synagogue in New York, the date for which was fixed as October 28, 1917.

More than 1500 delegates from every section of the country responded to the summons and took part in the Assembly, following which the entire number were the guests of Mr. Felix M. Warburg, chairman of the Joint Distribution Committee, at one of the largest dinners ever held in the Hotel Astor.

On October 25, three days before the dinner, Mr. Fischel received the following letter from Mr. Warburg:

Dear Mr. Fischel:

I take pleasure in appointing you as chairman of the dinner and one of the speakers at the dinner and conference which will be held on Sunday evening at the Hotel Astor. The subject you are to talk about is "The Orthodox Jew and Relief Work." I hope you will accept the appointment to make this address which I am sure will be very interesting to the delegates.

Very sincerely yours,

FELIX M. WARBURG
Chairman Joint Distribution Committee.

Mr. Fischel regarded this assignment as of such great importance that he decided not to rely upon extemporaneous remarks but to prepare his address in advance, making the following speech on this occasion:

THE ORTHODOX JEW AND RELIEF WORK

The subject assigned to me is "The Orthodox Jew and Relief Work." In order to make myself clear on this subject, I thought it advisable to change my usual custom of speaking extemporaneously and instead to read my remarks to you.

The Orthodox Jew, by reason of his faith, has been taught never to close his ear to the cry of the unfortunate and those in need. The greatest of our sages were wont to give a small coin to the poor before each prayer, thus fulfilling the injunction, "As for me, I will behold thy face with charity."

The records of the Central Relief Committee, of which I have the honor to be the Treasurer, show what the Orthodox Jew in this country has done in aid of his unfortunate brethren in the war zones. We have collected nearly $2,500,000 and the money, in the main, came week in and week out, not from the rich, but from the poorest of the poor. The shoemaker, the tailor, the baker, the newsdealer, the pushcart owner, the small storekeeper; in short, the very class that feels most what it means to struggle for a living. The Orthodox Jew, as a rule, when he gives, gives not from his surplus but from his small principal.

The Orthodox Jew is enjoined to give quickly when there is a demand. A story is told in the Talmud of a man named Nachan Ish Gamzoo, who, laden with wealth, was making a journey one day. He was met by a poor man, who asked him for help. The wealthy man said to him, "I am busy with my wares, wait until I have time." In the meantime the poor man died. When the wealthy man heard what had happened he was stricken by the shock, and never recovered. We may be ever so busy with our daily tasks, but we cannot, and must not say to the ever increasing destitute men, women and children: "Postpone your starving until the end of the year when I take stock." No, we must give and keep on giving, now.

An interesting case of raising money for war relief occurred in a small town. A campaign was held there, about $400 was collected. The question arose as to who was to bring the money to the Central Relief Committee in New York. This was recognized to be an honor worth bidding for. Three of the committee bid for this honor. One bid $25, another $30, and still another $25. When the bidding was over, the Rabbi, according to the law laid down by our sages, decided that bids made for charity must not be withdrawn. The instruction, therefore, was that each one must pay his offering, and since each one had to pay the amount of his bid, all of the three came to New York with the money. In this way not only was $90 added to the Fund but the spirit in which the Orthodox Jew gives his charity was proven.

It is not so long ago that the Orthodox Jew was charged with not doing his share towards relieving the conditions of the poor. Nothing can better disprove this false accusation than the record of the Central Relief Committee. The Orthodox Jews have not alone given in proportion to their means, but they have given far beyond their means. In many instances large sums were realized by virtue of the fact that our immigrant settlers have headed the lists of subscribers.

You know the ancient teachings of our Sages who said:

"He who saves one life is as if he were saving a world, for each man is a little world in himself."

The Jewish people in the war zones are now in a most critical position. Like the patient who is seriously ill, and concerning whom the physician says to his friend, "If we can tide him over for another week he will become well," so it is with our people, starving both physically and spiritually. They need temporary aid. If you give it, they will come out well, if not, Jewry of Russia, Roumania and Palestine will be depleted.

Let me say a word here of appreciation and thanks to the Rabbis present, also to the Presidents of Congregations, Chairmen of Committees, and all other workers for war relief. It was their task to keep the enthusiasm alive by their constant agitation, to awaken that Jewish Consciousness, which, once aroused, remains a dominant power for good. It was with their assistance, that the Central Relief Committee was able to raise and help in raising large sums, although insufficient to put away the sight of starvation, which is continually staring our unfortunate brethren in the face. That is why this conference has been called. What was done is history. What is yet to be done depends upon you.

In addition to war relief which it has been your work to perform, it is most essential that you devote your best energy also to constructive relief work which must necessarily embrace the work of building up the Jewish Centers, and thus, preserve the Jewish spirit. We are satisfied that you will continue to work harder and harder, so that in the end, the results becoming greater and greater, will enable our Orthodox brethren to boast of a record which the Central Relief Committee is anxious to preserve for its constituents. In that way, Orthodox Jewry in America will be enabled to enjoy the pride and satisfaction of knowing that it has done its full duty.

Our Committee feels it their duty also to thank our beloved Government and its leaders for the human interest it has taken in the affairs of Jewry abroad. Our Government has listened to every plea of ours and has carried out every demand possible and in time.

I believe the generosity of our beloved President Wilson, who proclaimed January 27th, 1915, the day for Jewish Relief, which made it possible to raise a large sum of money for relief, is still fresh in your minds. While all the Committees reaped the benefit of this day, however, this proclamation was declared by our President through the efforts of the Central Relief Committee.

We also wish to render thanks in our name, and in the name of our branches, to the Government, for its work in forwarding money to relatives and designated institutions in Palestine. Thanks are due to Ambassadors Morgenthau and Elkus, also the American Consul at Jerusalem, Dr. Otto Glazebrook, for their efforts in our behalf, in this special direction.

We must never forget our allegiance and wholehearted devotion to our country. The Orthodox Jew, who is commanded by the observance of his faith to remain true to his God, must necessarily be loyal to his country. In looking up the definition of religion, I found that it is defined as obedience to a higher order of things. Citizenship is defined as respect for law and order. Religion and citizenship overlap each other, to be a religious Jew is synonymous with being a loyal citizen.

I am certain that the Orthodox Jew, liberal as he is, in trying to save his co-religionists in the different parts of the world, is likewise discharging his full duty to the Stars and Stripes. This day, being set aside as a day of prayer, by the Proclamation of President Wilson, let us all meditate and fervently pray that the year 1918 will bring victory for America, and thereby assure Democracy to the World, as well as justice to the Jew.

On October 29, the day following the dinner, Mr. Fischel received the following letter from Mr. Felix M. Warburg:

My dear Mr. Fischel:

That the Assembly and dinner last evening was such an unqualified success was due in a large measure to your efforts and I desire to express to you my heartfelt appreciation therefore.

Cordially yours,

FELIX M. WARBURG

In addition to other steps taken as a result of the Assembly, (possibly the most notable gathering of Jews of every shade of opinion in the history of the country,) was the appointment of a Committee of Five to consult with the different collecting agencies throughout the United States, with a view to formulating a plan for further unifying the work of the existing relief committees and of systematizing and increasing the collections. Mr. Fischel was named by the chairman, Dr. Cyrus Adler, of Philadelphia, as one of the members of this special committee.

Through his connection with the war relief work and his many other activities Mr. Fischel's name was, by now, widely known not only in America but throughout Europe and Palestine, having in fact reached to the smallest communities. The reputation which he had earned by so many years of effort in widely diversified philanthropic and commercial activities, was to largely increase his opportunities for future service.

THE CENTRAL COMMITTEE

FOR THE RELIEF OF JEWS SUFFERING THROUGH THE WAR

154 NASSAU STREET

No. 10124

New York, December 18, 19 19

Pay to
the order of JOINT DISTRIBUTION COMMITTEE

$1,000,000.00

ONE MILLION - - - - - - - - - - - - - - - - - - 00/100 Dollars

THE CENTRAL COMMITTEE FOR THE RELIEF OF JEWS
SUFFERING THROUGH THE WAR

Harry Fischel
TREASURER

Guaranty Trust Company of New York
New York
1-107

To

DO NOT DETACH

THIS CHECK IS IN FULL PAYMENT OF THE FOLLOWING
ACCOUNT AND THE PAYEE ACCEPTS IT AS SUCH.

DATE	PARTICULARS	AMOUNT
FOR GENERAL RELIEF		
	TOTAL	
	DEDUCTIONS	
	NET	

THE MILLION DOLLAR CHECK

*For Jewish War Sufferers signed by Mr. Fischel as Treasurer
of the Central Relief Committee.*

CHAPTER XXVIII

BEGINNINGS OF YESHIVA COLLEGE

EARLY in the year 1915 Mr. Fischel was afforded the privilege of lending fresh impetus to a cause that had always lain closest to his heart, that of higher Jewish religious training.

From the efforts put forth at this time the foundation for the great Yeshiva College, that in later years was to be one of the most important achievements of Orthodox Jewry in America, was actually laid.

The Yeshiva Rabbi Isaac Elchanan Theological Seminary, of which Mr. Fischel was Vice President and to which he had always found it possible to give a considerable part of his time and energy, was housed at this time in a building at 156 Henry Street.

The war had indirectly placed additional responsibilities on this institution as in the early days of the conflict many of the students in European Yeshivas managed to leave their native lands and had come to America where they sought to continue their studies. As a result the building occupied by the Theological Seminary, an old and unsuitable structure, had become greatly overcrowded and many applicants had to be denied admission to the institution.

Mr. Fischel was requested to look for a site on which to erect a new building. He was at this time also associated with the Yeshiva Etz Chaim, at 85 Henry Street, having in 1895 served as the Chairman of its Building Committee, when it was provided with the home it occupied at this time. This Yeshiva also was badly overcrowded and in need of a new building, and, as a number of its directors, like Mr. Fischel, were also directors of the Yeshiva Rabbi Isaac Elchanan, it was possible for the two institutions to be brought together in a satisfactory merger.

Mr. Fischel was selected as Chairman of the Building Committee to seek a site and prepare plans for a new building which should house both institutions. In the early part of 1915 he was successful in purchasing two houses at 9-11 Montgomery Street. He immediately started to convert this property into a modern and fireproof educational building, having every facility needed to carry on the work.

The cornerstone of the New Yeshiva building was laid by Mr. Fischel on July 1, 1915. The event was celebrated by the Orthodox Jews of New York as a holiday as it was the first time in the history of the city that a building had been constructed solely for the purpose of imparting Talmudic knowledge. Many of the leaders in Jewish education, as well as prominent Rabbis, made addresses appropriate to such a significant occasion.

Much stress was laid both in the English and Jewish press on the incentive to Talmudic knowledge contributed by the new Yeshiva building. The account of the occasion appearing in the Hebrew Standard is herewith reproduced:

CORNERSTONE FOR YESHIVA LAID

JULY 1ST, 1915

The cornerstone for the new Rabbinical College of the Rabbi Isaac Elchanan Theological Seminary and the Yeshibath Etz Chaim was laid last Thursday afternoon in the presence of a notable gathering of rabbis and prominent Orthodox laymen. The exercises consisted of a prayer by Rabbi M. S. Margolies, a greeting by the president, Mr. Jacob Hecht, and addresses by Borough President Marcus M. Marks, Rev. Dr. Bernard Drachman, Commissioner of Education, I. M. Levy, Rabbi S. E. Jaffe, Rabbi Herbert S. Goldstein and Mr. Harry Fischel.

After the singing of Hatikva, the cornerstone was laid by Mr. Fischel, the honor being conferred upon him in recognition of his preliminary work in assuring the success of the institution.

Mr. Fischel said: "We have assembled this day for the purpose of celebrating the laying of the cornerstone of a new institution, an institution which was established to fill a want that has long been felt, not only by the Jewish community of New York City, but by Jews all over the United States.

"The new Rabbinical College, whose birth it is now our privilege to witness, holds forth as its object 'Orthodox Judaism and Americanism,' that is, its aim shall be to educate and produce Orthodox rabbis who will be able to deliver sermons in English, so that they may appeal to the hearts of the younger generation, and, at the same time, who will be thoroughly qualified to occupy positions with congregations demanding conformity with the strict requirements of Orthodox Judaism.

"At this point I wish to emphasize strongly that the Rabbinical College does not intend to set itself up in opposition to, or in competition with, the Jewish Theological Seminary of America, of which Professor Schechter is president. On the contrary, it is our earnest desire to cooperate with that institution as far as is possible for us to do so. It is true that the Jewish Theological Seminary is accomplishing splendid results in sending forth rabbis who are able to deliver good English sermons, but these rabbis, with very few exceptions, do not meet the requirements of Orthodox congregations. It is the purpose of this new Rabbinical College, not only to produce rabbis who are thoroughly versed in rabbinical culture and who can deliver sermons in English, but they must also have the authority to decide ritual questions, technically called Torath Haw rawooy.

"The new Rabbinical college is unique in its creation. Although new in its plans and purpose, yet it begins its career upon a solid foundation. This is due to the fact that it is a combination of two long established institutions which have been in existence for over twenty-five years, namely the Yeshibath Etz Chaim and the Rabbi Isaac Elchanan Theological Seminary. These two institutions not only have the confidence of the Jews of the City of New York, but they have the support and backing of the country at large and therefore the success of this new undertaking is assured.

"My friends, as we are sitting here in comfort, enjoying the rights and privileges of peace and liberty under the protection of the Stars and Stripes, our brothers in the war zones are dying by the thousands. Not alone should we mourn the fate of all those who are losing their lives in the death struggle of nations, but especially should we mourn the loss of the scores of Jewish young men who are being killed on the battle fields, from whom this country has been nourished with Talmudical knowledge and who have supplied the material for such rabbis as this institution seeks to develop and produce.   Since the supply of students which we could expect from the foreign countries has been reduced, it is therefore our duty to interest young American boys in the study of rabbinical culture, and these young boys should not alone fill the loss which we have sustained through the war, but they should make better material for this institution because they possess the American flow of language which should enable them to better appeal to the younger element.

"It is our aim to produce educated rabbis, yet we are mindful of the fact that in order to produce ten rabbis it is necessary to educate at least one hundred young boys, so as to have material from which to select those who are eligible to take up the study of rabbinical culture.   The rest will possess enough knowledge to fill many other high positions in Jewish educational institutions.   It is our intention to bring up the students of this Rabbinical College in the utmost religious environment and to enable them to devote their undivided time to their studies, without being compelled to earn their livlihood.   We have therefore provided in this building an up-to-date kitchen and dining room, where the students will be supplied with food and, in addition thereto, they will be furnished with the necessities of life, so that they may concentrate all their energies on their religious work and acquire the title of Rabbi in as short a time as possible. I wish to say further that this building will contain well lighted and ventilated class rooms and all the latest sanitary improvements.   We have spared no effort to equip this institution in as efficient a manner as possible."

Other addresses were made by Rabbis H. Masliansky, B. M. Leventhal; A. L. Alperstern; M. J. Pelius; J. Rosenberg; J. Kanovitz; Meyer Berlin and I. Siegel.   The proceedings were concluded with a prayer by Rabbi Wolf Margolies.

Among the subscribers to the institution are Mr. and Mrs. Harry Fischel $2,000; Mr. Nathan Roggen, $1,250; Jacob H. Schiff $1,000; Estate of Joseph Oshinsky, $1,000; S. Heller, $1,000; M. Friedman, $500; Jacob Hecht, $500; Nathan Lamport $500; Mr. Kommel $500; and I. Rokeach $500.

The new institution will be under the supervision of Dr. Bernard Revel, an eminent pedagogue, who was born in Kovno, Russia, in 1887.   He is the son of the famous scholar Nahum Shraga, who was rabbi in Pren and Linkovo and son-in-law of the great Gaon Rabbi Moses Isaac, of Peneves. He received his Jewish education and was ordained Rabbi in 1901. He also received a collegiate education in Russia and came to America in 1907. He studied law at Temple University, Philadelphia, Pa. and received the degree of M.A. from the New York University, and Ph.D. from Dropsie College. He is the author of "Bachya Ibn Pakudah, Karaite Halakah" and a contributor of articles to the Jewish Quarterly Review and other English and Hebrew publications. He was associate editor of the Hebrew Encyclopedia "Ozar Israel." Dr. Revel is a member of the Union of Orthodox Rabbis and was its secretary 1908-9. He is a member of the American Orthodox Oriental Society and other institutions.

No time was lost in the construction of the building under Mr. Fischel's direction so that a dedication commensurate with the importance of the event took place on December 15th of the same year and attracted nation-wide attention. The dedication was attended by the Acting Mayor of the City, the Hon. George McAneny and many other officials, noted Rabbis, educators and prominent laymen.

The celebration in connection with the dedication, lasted for an entire week. It was generally looked upon as one of the most important in the history of the Jewish people in the United States, for the completion of the building marked the taking of a notable step for the advancement of Talmudic knowledge.

As Chairman of the Building Committee it devolved upon Mr. Fischel to present the key of the new building to Mr. Jacob Hecht, president of the institution, with an appropriate address. The newspapers again devoted much space to the institution and the vast importance it spelled to the future of Orthodox Judaism in America. The following article appeared in the Hebrew Standard:

NEW RABBINICAL COLLEGE OPENED

The dedication of the building of the Rabbinical College No. 9-11 Montgomery Street took place last Sunday afternoon. The opening marks an important step in Jewish history in the United States for it is the first Orthodox institution which seeks to train English-speaking rabbis.

Mr. Harry Fischel presided and the exercises were opened with Jewish melodies by the band of the Hebrew Orphan Asylum. Rabbi M. S. Margolies delivered a prayer and then explained the importance of the occasion. Mr. Fischel, as chairman of the building committee, presented the key to Mr. Jacob Hecht, president of the institution, and delivered an address which included the report of the committee. Mr. Fischel said among other things:

"My friends, this building which we are dedicating today is simple in design, yet beautiful in its construction. Our Building Committee took special pains in providing this building with the most modern improvements, so that it is strictly fireproof, has plenty of air and light, and contains all the latest sanitary devices, including shower baths of the newest design.

"It is true that this building is extremely small in proportion to the demand made upon us by the Orthodox congregations all over the United States, but we are told by our sages that the reason we begin the lighting of one candle on the first night of Chanukah and increase the number of candles every night thereafter is because, in everything that is Holy, we should always increase and never decrease, which was the theory of the School of Hillel. So with our Yeshivah, while we are beginning with a comparatively small building, yet we hope that it will grow in strength and usefulness from year to year until we achieve the great result for which we are aiming, and it is our hope that, like a seed which is carefully planted in fertile soil, this institution will grow into a flourishing plant, whose fruit will refresh and revive Judaism in the whole of the United States.

"Now, Mr. President, I am prepared to deliver the key of this building to you on behalf of the Board of Directors. Before doing so, however, I believe it is my duty to give a brief statement of the cost of the construction of the building.

"I want to emphasize the fact that although the amount expended in altering this building is only the nominal sum of a little over $16,000 yet I am proud to state that, with the exception of the two side walls, this building is entirely new and is equal in every respect to a new building which would have cost more than twice the sum. This was due to the great efforts of the Building Committee."

Mr. Hecht in accepting the key thanked the Chairman of the Building Committee for his efforts in completing the building at such low cost.

Hon. George McAneny, acting Mayor of the City of New York, delivered an eloquent address, in which he thanked the institution for relieving the city of work and responsibilty in undertaking its splendid educational project. Isidore Montefiore Levy, Commissioner of Education, emphasized the fact that the Board of Education welcomes institutions of this kind. The Rev. Herbert S. Goldstein called upon the younger generation to make some sacrifices for Judaism, and to take up the work of the Rabbinical College. He also made an urgent entreaty to the public for funds. The Chanukah lights were lit by Cantor Rothman, and the prayer was chanted by the assembly. An address by the Rev. Harris Masliansky followed, and Dr. H. Pereira Mendes closed the exercises for the afternoon session by delivering the benediction.

The exercises continued in the evening and eloquent addresses were delivered by the Rev. Dr. Philip Klein, Rev. Dr. Bernard Drachman, Rev. Meyer Berlin, Rev. Jos. Konowitz and Mr. M. Finesilber.

CHAPTER XXIX

SEEING AMERICA WITH A PURPOSE

FOLLOWING the laying of the Yeshivah cornerstone in the summer of 1915, Mr. Fischel, who, for a long period had been continually engaged with many exacting duties, determined it would be advisable to take a vacation but one that should at the same time give him the opportunity to keep in touch with the war relief work throughout the nation and be of help in stimulating collections in the communities he planned to visit.

He decided, in other words, to tour the country. He had several times visited Europe but, like many other Americans, had neglected to see America first, not having gone further west than St. Louis in the year of the World's fair in that city. With his wife and two unmarried daughters, Bertha Marion and Rose, he decided, therefore, on a trip across the continent to San Francisco planning while en route to visit the leading cities of the country, including in his itinerary Yellowstone Park and the Jewish Home for Consumptives at Denver, Colorado.

The Fischels left New York on a Thursday. In order not to desecrate the Sabbath by traveling it was arranged to remain in Chicago over Saturday. On his arrival in Chicago early Friday afternoon, Mr. Fischel was met at the station by a local committee representing the Hebrew Sheltering and Immigrant Aid Society, which informed him of plans to hold a dinner in his honor. Mr. Fischel advised the Committee that he could not at that time accept such an invitation but promised the members that on his return from the Pacific Coast he would remain in Chicago for a longer time and would then take up the matter of such a function with them.

The party left Chicago on Sunday morning and were due to arrive in San Francisco on the Wednesday evening following.

When they reached Denver, however, Mr. Fischel decided that this was an opportune time to visit the Jewish Home for Consumptives, in which he had long taken a very keen interest.

Following an inspection of the institution Mr. Fischel found that his party would be compelled to remain for the night as the Superintendent had arranged an entertainment in their honor.

At this entertainment Mr. Fischel was called upon to make an address and expressed his sympathy for the patients. Many sufferers from the same disease, he pointed out, were without any such aids to their recovery as were here afforded.

The party proceeded the next morning on their journey to San Francisco where they were scheduled to arrive at noon on Friday. On Thursday at about six o'clock in the evening, when the train had reached the Great Desert, the conductor informed Mr. Fischel they were twelve hours late and could not possibly reach San Francisco before Friday at midnight.

Mr. Fischel was beside himself at this news. For the first time in his life and while on a pleasure trip, he would be compelled to desecrate the Sabbath, a temptation he had avoided in all his life even when facing the utmost poverty and want.

The thought occurred to him that it might be possible to leave the train and stop at some small place over the Sabbath but when he asked as to this he was told that as they were on the desert there was no place at which the train would stop until it arrived at Sacramento, which was only four hours from San Francisco and where they were not due until eight o'clock on Friday evening, still too late to prevent the desecration of the Sabbath.

As a way out of his dilemma, Mr. Fischel was reminded of the expression, "money will move mountains" and thought to himself that if this was true, certainly money ought to be able to make a train move faster. He was ready, indeed, to pay any amount to the trainmen if he could accomplish his purpose of arriving in San Francisco before sunset the next day, but he realized that it would be difficult for him to impress upon the conductor the urgency of his demand if he attempted to explain to him the religious motive by which he was actuated.

Accordingly, he summoned the conductor and told him he had a very important appointment in San Francisco at six o'clock on Friday evening and that it would be worth any amount of money to him to reach there by that hour.

The prospect of earning such a reward naturally appealed to the conductor but he told Mr. Fischel that unfortunately he could not take advantage of it for the reason that he was quitting the train at midnight and his place would be taken by another. He agreed, however, that when this man relieved him he would try to arrange some way by which Mr. Fischel's wish could be realized and the two employes would divide the money, a considerable sum, between them.

Mr. Fischel, needless to say, remained up to meet the second conductor as arranged and it was agreed by him to do everything possible to accelerate the speed of the train which rushed along at the rate of probably sixty miles an hour until, at two o'clock Friday afternoon, it was approaching Sacramento. It required but four hours from there to complete the journey to San Francisco. At this time, however, the train's speed began to slacken and Mr. Fischel and his family were prepared, if need be, to remain in Sacramento over Saturday.

When that city was reached the temperature was 120 degrees in the shade, something the Fischels had never experienced in their lives. Mr. Fischel scarcely knew what to do. Fearing that to remain in Sacramento in such heat might endanger the health of his wife and daughters he again consulted the conductor and upon being informed that the train would arrive in San Francisco not later than seven o'clock he decided that his only course was to continue on the journey. As a matter of fact the train arrived in San Francisco at six-thirty.

On arrival the party was met at the station by a delegation from the San Francisco Branch of the Hebrew Sheltering and Immigrant Aid Society. They found that this committee had prepared an apartment for their stay in that city where they might faithfully observe the dietary laws.

Although Mr. Fischel's purpose in making this trip was primarily for rest and recreation he learned that a war relief meeting had been arranged in advance of his coming by Rabbi Bernard Drachman, a director of the Central Jewish Relief Committee and Morris Engelman, its secretary, which meeting he was, of course, expected to attend.

This meeting, participated in by many of the Jewish leaders of San Francisco, occurred on August 2 and following an appeal made by Mr. Fischel and the other speakers, resulted in the collection of a large sum of money and the securing of many pledges. The meeting formally launched the relief work in San Francisco on a systematic basis.

The Fischels remained in San Francisco about three weeks deciding to return by the way of Yellowstone Park to view the beauties of that wonderland of nature. Their first stop was at Portland, Oregon, where they were met by a representative of the Jewish Tribune, at that time the leading English-Jewish publication of the West, who informed Mr. Fischel that he had been assigned by the editor to accompany him on his trip and to report his activities while in the west.

From Portland the party went to Seattle, Washington, thence to Spokane, to Yellowstone Park, to St. Paul and back to Chicago. In every city they were met by welcoming committees.

In many of these cities Mr. Fischel was asked to give his advice on some particularly intricate and puzzling local question, as, for instance, in one city it was how a loan might be raised to build water works, in another, how the school conditions might be improved and in a third, what could be done toward making the city more beautiful.

One such experience he had in Seattle, Washington, is of especial interest. On arriving in that city, Mr. Fischel was met by a committee representing the Seattle Branch of the Hebrew Sheltering and Immigrant Aid Society. This Committee was headed by a Mr. Kessler, the president of an Orthodox Congregation, which had just completed the construction of a beautiful new synagogue.

Mr. Kessler related that the Congregation had always been scrupulous in its observance and that the new synagogue had accordingly been so constructed that its seating arrangements provided for the separation of the sexes, with a gallery for the women and the lower floor to be occupied by the men.

With the completion of the structure, however, a quarrel had arisen over these provisions, their being some of the trustees who were not so strictly Orthodox in their views as others. Mr. Kessler informed Mr. Fischel that as President of the Congregation and as the one who had devoted his entire time to the undertaking for the past two years he could not consent to having the sexes mingle at worship.

He declared that he felt sure from what he knew of Mr. Fischel's views on religion he would support him in his position against this desecration of the building. Mr. Fischel replied that inasmuch as he did not know a single member of the congregation it would be rather an embarrassing and delicate matter for him to exert pressure to decide such an issue but that, as a question of religious principle was involved, he would do all in his power to help solve the difficulty.

Mr. Kessler then called a meeting of the directors of the local branch of the Hebrew Sheltering and Immigrant Aid Society, most of whom it happened were also trustees of the Congregation, to meet in the Synagogue and to be addressed by Mr. Fischel.

Mr. Fischel first reviewed the general immigration problems and told of the work done in the main office in New York, after which he took advantage of the opportunity to try to persuade the directors of the Congregation who were present to adhere to the original plan for separation of the sexes in the structure. In the course of his argument Mr. Fischel said:

"Many congregations today, Orthodox in other respects, are

seeking to amend the ancient Jewish tradition which provides for the separation of the sexes during religious services.

"This tradition is as essential to the preservation of our faith as any other. It is not intended to place women in a position inferior to man, but is aimed primarily at the man, rather than the woman, its purpose being to enable the man to worship in true purity of thought and undisturbed by the distractions of feminine proximity during services."

The manner in which Mr. Fischel put the matter succeeded in its purpose and on his return to New York he received a letter of thanks, with a resolution signed by the trustees expressing their gratitude for his efforts in causing the Congregation to come to an agreement in accordance with the traditions of the faith.

On the Fischel's arrival in St. Paul they were met by a committee of war relief workers who also had arranged a meeting in that city. At this meeting Mr. Fischel made an appeal resulting in the collection of a large sum of money which was at once forwarded to New York.

Returning to Chicago, Mr. Fischel was compelled to fulfill his promise to the members of the Hebrew Sheltering and Immigrant Aid Society in that city to attend a dinner given in his honor. The Fischels finally came back to New York during the month of September.

CHAPTER XXX

REVOLUTIONIZES REAL ESTATE FINANCING
WITH PLAN FOR MORTGAGE AMORTIZATION

It was on his return from his tour to the Coast that Mr. Fischel put forth a new business idea which was to largely revolutionize the system of real estate financing as then in force and was to exert a large influence in the prevention of future periods of real estate depression.

This plan, as it came into general use, also protected the small investor from loss and had the effect of stabilizing the realty market in a degree that no previous expedient had accomplished.

The plan, which, in a word, was the introduction of the system of mortgage amortization, was worked out by Mr. Fischel during the hours he spent in the long train journeys from city to city while on his vacation, and again showed that, large as was his contribution to communal, philanthropic, educational and religious undertakings, his business acumen and judgment were productive of equally important results.

Mr. Fischel had given a great deal of thought to the causes leading to the recurring financial panics of different years, particularly as these panics affected the stability of real estate securities. In reviewing these periods of depression, through which he had been so fortunate as to pass practically unscathed, he was especially impressed with the fact that the panic of 1893 was virtually forgotten in less than a year and normal conditions restored in a year and a half. Following the panic of 1907, however, eight years had elapsed with little or no improvement, insofar as real estate conditions were concerned.

Every business other than real estate had gone back to normal, but realty, instead of recovering, was, if anything, in a worse situation than in the panic's darkest days. What could be the basic cause of such a wide discrepancy in the effects of the two periods of financial stress, Mr. Fischel pondered.

He finally concluded that the answer was to be found in the wholesale calling of mortgages as soon as they were due.

Mortgages were called in, either in their entirety or there came the demand for large payments toward their reduction or for their renewal, demands which the owners of real estate were given no time to satisfy or else were not in a position to meet.

When these demands were not met the mortgages were immediately foreclosed, with the result that the property was bought in by the mortgagee, the owner of record frequently losing his entire equity.

The solution for this situation, Mr. Fischel decided, was the adoption of a plan for amortizing mortgages over a long period, rather than the summary call for payment for the entire amount or for an unreasonable reduction on short notice.

Such a plan Mr. Fischel worked out in detail, giving it to the public through the Associated Press on November 7, 1915. This plan in full was as follows:

THE REAL ESTATE PROBLEM IN NEW YORK CITY

A SUGGESTED SOLUTION

Nov. 7th, 1915

(Addressed particularly to Mortgagees

By MR. HARRY FISCHEL)

It is a well-known fact that real estate in the City of New York has suffered more than any other business or investment. The New York real estate market passed through several dangerous periods in the last few decades, namely in 1873, 1893 and 1907, but at no time were the conditions as critical as they are today. The panic of 1893 was not limited to real estate alone. Naturally, real estate suffered in common with all other business. But the panic lasted only one year. Confidence was soon restored. Activity in the real estate field increased and investments were made more freely than before. The panic proved to be merely an acute sickness and the man of finance administered the cure rapidly and effectively by placing plenty of money in the market on liberal terms. The best proof of recovery was that there were abundant purchasers for real estate both at public auction and private sales where property could be bought at reasonable prices.

It is quite remarkable how different was the panic of 1907, which still continues its depressing influence. Almost nine years have elapsed and not only is no sign of relief in sight, but conditions are getting worse each year.

The sickness has become chronic!

Men with money will invest in speculative transactions even at low rates of interest, but refrain from investing in real estate, which would yield a good income and be a much safer investment.

There are two questions which arise from this state of facts.

1. Why do such conditions exist?

2. What is to be done to remedy this chronic evil?

While realty owners are suffering considerably from the many persecutions of the various city and state departments, which compel them to make considerable expenditures, nevertheless, this would not have deterred real estate investors, because the income from real estate is too tempting. There must be some other reason why hundreds of millions of dollars are lying idle in vaults, or at very low rates of interest in trust companies. The owners of this money would gladly invest it in real estate but they are afraid to do so.

THE REASON IS THAT THEY ARE NEVER SAFE WITH THEIR INVESTMENT, ON ACCOUNT OF THE MORTGAGEES, WHO HAVE MADE IT A PRACTICE TO DEMAND PART OF THE MONEY AS SOON AS THE MORTGAGE IS MATURED—no matter if the mortgage debt amounts to a very small percentage of the value of the property.

There was a time when investors were safe in buying property by investing from 25% to 40% of the value of the purchase, but today, conditions are such that even 50% or 60% of the value is not safe, because you do not know how soon the mortgagee will demand part payment. If the real estate owner has not the ready cash to meet this demand, and if there are no ready purchasers to buy the property at any price, the natural result is that his entire investment is lost, and the property goes to the mortgagee. There is no doubt that the mortgagee as a rule does not want the property, but is compelled to take it against his own wishes. It is the old story of the dog in the manger. Such is the state of affairs existing today.

I have spoken to many of the largest money lenders in the City of New York, and not a single one could give any reason for demanding that the mortgages be reduced. It was simply a case of doing what the other fellow does. It can be readily understood that this fact not alone has withheld hundreds of millions of dollars from being invested in real estate, but it has brought matters to such a pass that all the financial institutions are stocked up with a lot of real estate, which is frequently managed by incompetent men, whereas, had the owner of the property been let alone, he could have managed it in a much better way, to the advantage of all concerned. This cannot be denied by anyone who is at all cognizant of the real estate situation.

Now as to the cure. There is only one way to remedy this existing evil, and that is, by a united effort of all the largest money-lenders in New York to have their mortgages amortized. To explain—every mortgagee should demand regularly, the payment of 2% of the amount of the mortgage each year, so that every real estate owner should be compelled (and would gladly do so) to add the amount of the amortization to the annual running expenses of the property. In this way, he would be prepared to meet the demands of the mortgagees without feeling any hardship. By paying regularly the amount of 2% each year, the owner would have less interest to pay each year, and the mortgagee would be paid off, without any difficulty on the part of the owner. In addition thereto, instead of the mortgagees being compelled to take the property, there would always be a big sum of money flowing into their hands, which could be placed on new buildings or expended in the construction of new improvements, so that this system would stimulate activity in the erection of new buildings and in real estate in general.

I can readily understand that this plan may be opposed by many of the attorneys for the mortgagees whose income would be reduced in this branch of their profession. By having the mortgages remain, they lose their fees in replacing the amount of the mortgage elsewhere, searching titles, etc. But they should stop to consider that a large sum of money would come annually into the hands of their clients from the amount of the amortization, which money could be replaced and, in addition thereto, real estate investors, knowing that they would not be called upon to pay off the mortgage, this would stimulate real estate transactions, increasing the income of the attorneys.

Therefore, for the reasons stated herein, I hope that the time will soon come when the money lenders will realize that it is to their advantage to accept the suggestion herein contained.

Mr. Fischel's proposals for a solution of this difficult problem were favorably received and secured the endorsement of many of the most prominent bankers, heads of real estate companies and others who were experts in this field of finance. The plan, furthermore, evoked many columns of newspaper discussion and comment.

The headings of some of the principal New York newspapers, many of which carried Mr. Fischel's proposal in full, are given herewith.

NEW YORK HERALD

"Mr. Harry Fischel an old-time real estate man calls on money lenders to relax their grip on the realty market. He advocates long term amortizing loans. He says that indiscriminate, unwarranted reduction and calling of mortgages is direct cause of realty's distress. Millions of dollars withheld because of fear that element of safety is missing."

NEW YORK TIMES

"Amortized mortgages plan grows in favor. Plan proposed by Harry Fischel, real estate man and builder."

NEW YORK TRIBUNE

"Harry Fischel finds solution for relieving big problem in financing. His plan will release more money for city's development."

So much discussion was, in fact, aroused over the plan and so many questions were asked regarding it that Mr. Fischel prepared a supplementary article answering some of these questions. This article follows:

The Effect of the Amortization Plan Upon the Owners
of Small Mortgages

(A Supplementary Article)

After presenting my suggestion to the public through the courtesy of the press, the following question was put to me:

"How can the trustees and other owners of small mortgages dispose of the annual payment which is to be made on account of the principal if they loan their money on a mortgage having the amortization plan in it?

My answer is that there would be two methods of reinvesting this money.

First, title companies today are loaning out money and issuing certificates in which these small investors could invest the amount of money which they receive annually on the amortization plan. It is true that these certificates are not liquidable, but should this amortization plan come into effect, the title companies would undoubtedly arrange some method whereby these certificates might become liquidable upon, say, sixty or ninety days' notice. It should be remembered that a large sum of money would always come from the annual payments of the principal according to the amortization plan, which would be more than sufficient to meet any demands of these holders of certificates who might desire to liquidate them.

Secondly, should this amortization plan be generally accepted, there could be, and I am certain there would be, strong financial companies organized, for the special purpose of obtaining money from small investors, on the basis of some such plan as suggested for the title companies.

Experience has shown that the demand regulates the supply.

I wish to say that while it is practically impossible to amortize ALL mortgages in the city of New York today, however, this should not affect the large majority of mortgages, which are held by the big financial institutions, such as the life insurance companies, trust companies, savings banks, etc., of which there are many in the City of New York, and which have many millions of dollars invested in mortgages. Thes mortgagees would always receive enough during a short period, to make another loan. Hence, they would be enabled to loan at least fifty per cent more annually than they can do under the present conditions, without impairing any interest of their own, and certainly without impairing any interest of the owners of the property. In this way, new buildings would be encouraged in neighborhoods which are being entirely neglected today, on account of the impossibility of obtaining loans. Therefore, although there may be a small number of mortgages to which the amortization plan would not apply, nevertheless, this fact should not affect the acceptance of the plan by the large mortgagees.

In conclusion, I desire to point out that under the present practice of demanding part payment to be made upon the maturity of a mortgage, the owners of the small mortgages and trustees of estates are in no better position today, with the small amount which they receive when the mortgage matures. On the contrary, their position is worse, for they are not certain whether they will receive this payment and may be compelled to take in the property.

As the immediate result of Mr. Fischel's suggestion, he received scores of letters, many of them from officials of the title companies, and executors of estates, in addition to owners of property.

More important yet, however, his suggestions were at once acted upon by many of the larger institutions as well as by individual lenders of money on bond and mortgage so that the amortization principle came into general use and is being practiced to the present day.

The easing of the mortgage money market, largely accomplished as a result of this suggestion, brought about an immediate improvement in real estate conditions generally, so that prosperity in this field has continued to increase and the security of real estate has never been greater than today both as an investment for the owner and for the mortgagee.

A cause for even larger gratification was the fact that a way was found by this plan to help many poor people to retain the savings of many years which they had invested in real estate and which, under the old system, were in constant jeopardy.

ONE OF THE EARLIEST OF GREAT APARTMENT
HOUSES ON FASHIONABLE PARK AVENUE
Erected by Mr. Fischel in 1915.

CHAPTER XXXI

EARLY APARTMENTS ON PARK AND FIFTH AVENUES

ANOTHER important milestone in Mr. Fischel's career, on its business side, occurred in this year, that of 1915, when he engaged in his first building operations on Park and Fifth Avenues.

Here again, he was among the pioneers in the construction of the earliest of those great apartment structures which now line these thoroughfares and which were to completely change their character, providing homes for hundreds of the wealthiest and most socially prominent families in New York.

In returning to business activity on an extensive scale at this time, Mr. Fischel was chiefly moved by the fact that his war relief work had made exceptionally heavy demands upon him and he was anxious to be placed in a position where he could continue unabated his philanthropic endeavors.

As had been true throughout his life the opportunity was again presented to him. It had been his experience in the past that the more he contributed to charitable causes, the greater was his prosperity in material affairs and, as his influence continued to grow in the field of philanthropy, so he also loomed larger as a leader in the financial and business world. One result of this was that promising business propositions were continually being brought to his attention.

America, had not at this time yet been drawn into the war, nor was there then the belief that she would be. On the other hand, many persons were being made rich as the result of business enterprises due to the war and with the sudden acquisition of wealth sought to live in a manner befiting their new circumstances.

Mr. Fischel learned that Park Avenue was the street most likely to be favored for the future homes of the rich and that large apartment houses on that avenue would be in demand. In order that he might have a part in this new housing development he decided to seek a site on this Avenue on which to carry out his plans.

The opportunity came to him to secure from the New York Central Railroad a long lease of the entire block fronting on Park Avenue, from Fiftieth to Fifty-first streets, and, by an odd coincidence, the lease for this property was signed on the same day on which Mr. Fischel laid the cornerstone of the new Yeshivah Building. Having acquired this plot, Mr. Fischel proceeded to make an intensive study of the city's leading apartment structures with the result that he was able to erect on this site a building containing many improvements over the finest apartment houses that had been built up to this time.

Before leaving on his trip to see America, Mr. Fischel commissioned the well known architects, Warren and Wetmore, architects for the New York Central Railroad Terminal, to prepare plans for this great new apartment building and these were subsequently drawn in accordance with a sketch Mr. Fischel left with them.

The plans were completed on Mr. Fischel's return but did not meet with his entire approval. Despite the great knowledge and reputation the firm of Warren and Wetmore enjoyed, they welcomed every suggestion Mr. Fischel made to them and on one occasion, in the presence of Mr. William Newman, vice president of the New York Central Railroad, Mr. Wetmore took occasion to say, "I have learned more from Mr. Harry Fischel than from some of my work in college."

During Mr. Fischel's absence from the city the foundations for the building were completed by his associate Mr. Joseph Ravitch, and, on his return, following his approval of the amended plans, the work of construction rapidly proceeded. While this was Mr. Fischel's first experience with high class apartment buildings, he gave close attention to the requirement of tenants of the type ready to pay the high rentals that were asked and

introduced a number of improvements which other buildings of
the same class lacked. As a result, when the building was finished the news rapidly spread among the brokers having charge
of the rental of apartments of this character, that it was the
best constructed building of its kind on Park Avenue. In consequence, before the building was completed in September, 1916,
and in spite of the fact that America's entrance into the World
War was by that time assured, nearly all of the apartments were
leased to some of the wealthiest families in the city.

On June 23, 1916, Mr. Fischel entered upon a new real estate
proposition, transferring his activities from Park to Fifth Avenue, where he purchased the famous mansion of Mr. Alfred
Duane Pell at the corner of Seventy-fourth Street. On this
site, in association with Mr. Joseph Ravitch, he erected another
fine apartment house but before the structure was fully completed in 1917 the United States entered the war and it looked
as though the undertaking would prove a failure.

Fortune was again with Mr. Fischel, however, and despite the
predictions of many, the building, as soon as finished, was completely leased and has always remained a highly profitable
investment.

CHAPTER XXXII

CORNERSTONE LAID FOR NEW HOME OF THE DAUGHTERS OF JACOB—HONORS TO A VENERABLE JEW
COMPLETION OF CENTRAL JEWISH INSTITUTE

LARGELY as Mr. Fischel's time was occupied with war relief work and business undertakings in these years, this did not preclude a continuance of his interest in local communal affairs and participation in events connected with them.

On October 26, 1916, he was one of the committee which laid the cornerstone of the new building of the Home of the Daughters of Jacob, occupying the block on 167th Street from Findlay to Teller Avenues, the Bronx. When Mr. Fischel laid the cornerstone for the first building of this institution on October 6, 1907, at the corner of East Broadway and Scammel Street, he expressed the hope in his address as chairman of the Building Committee, that the time would come when the institution would grow to such size that it would occupy an entire block. That this prediction should have so soon come true filled him with unusual happiness.

It was in Mr. Fischel's residence, it will be remembered, that this institution for the care of dependent aged men and women saw its beginning in 1896, when Mrs. Fischel with six other women organized the Home and became its charter members. It was quite natural, therefore, that Mr. Fischel should always have taken an especial interest in its work and should have given a great deal of time, energy and money for its advancement, as he always considered it one of the worthiest among all the charitable institutions of the city.

During the same year the Central Jewish Institute was erected.

A PORTRAIT OF MRS. FISCHEL,

Who, among her countless other philanthropic activities, was one of the founders of the Home of the Daughters of Jacob.

After the building had been constructed as far as the roof it was found necessary to suspend work because of the lack of funds. Mr. Fischel then came forward with a proposition to the president, the late Samuel I. Hyman, that if Mr. Hyman would get nine additional men to loan the institution $3,000 each, Mr. Fischel would be the tenth, which would provide sufficient funds with which to insure the building's completion. Mr. Hyman accepted the proposition with the result that he procured nine men among the Board of Directors, each of whom loaned $3,000. This, together with Mr. Fischel's loan, amounted to $30,000, with which the structure was finished. The institute was dedicated with appropriate ceremonies on April 7, 1916.

In November of this same year, the Hebrew Sheltering and Immigrant Aid Society decided to pay appropriate honors to the venerable American, Mr. Simon Wolf, on the occasion of his eightieth birthday. Mr. Fischel was appointed chairman of the committee to arrange a dinner to Mr. Wolf, who had for many years been the representative of the Society in Washington and had had charge of all immigration cases requiring special official action by the government.

During his long period of service to the Society, Mr. Wolf had won the respect and confidence of many Presidents of the United States and Mr. Fischel felt highly honored at being designated to take charge of the arrangements for the testimonial.

The dinner took place at the Hotel Savoy, New York, on November 28, 1916. To Mr. Fischel was entrusted the task of presenting the guest of honor with a Bible, commemorative of the occasion. In making the presentation Mr. Fischel made the following remarks:

The other day the great statesman, Senator Chauncey M. Depew, made a statement that King David had created a feeling among all men that when a man has reached the age of 70 he is no longer useful to the world, and, therefore, those who believe in

King David's philosophy, when they reach the age of 70 lose interest in everything.

I am justified this evening in disagreeing with Senator Depew, because our guest of honor, Mr. Simon Wolf, is a striking illustration of the fact that some men over 70 are not alone active, but their acts are marked by that mature deliberation which age brings with it.

My opinion of the meaning of King David is, that after a man has reached the age of 70, and his years have been used only for his personal benefit and to satisfy his animal instincts, he is naturally bound to lose interest in the world, but when a man has reached the age of 70 but has spent very little of his time for personal benefit, and most of his life for the good of humanity, he is not old even at the age of 80 and there is no better witness to this fact than our beloved friend, Mr. Simon Wolf.

Now, Mr. Wolf, in behalf of our Committee of Arrangements of which I have the honor to be Chairman, I herewith present to you this Bible. It is our sincere wish, that just as the Bible, although thousands of years old, is still recognized by the entire world as the fount of wisdom, so too shall your name be perpetuated, not alone by the present generation but by many generations to come.

I therefore present to you, the man of men, the Book of Books and it is my earnest wish that you shall use this Bible for at least 20 years to come.

The Bible was accepted by Mr. Wolf with many expressions of his joy and appreciation.

MR. FISCHEL AT THE AGE OF FIFTY.

CHAPTER XXXIII

PALESTINE AND THE BALFOUR DECLARATION

SINCE visiting Palestine with his daughter in 1910, Mr. Fischel had been more than ever interested in the hope of the Jews the world over to re-establish in that country a homeland which would be a haven for the oppressed of their faith of every nation and to which they might migrate in large numbers with the purpose of securing the right to self expression and self government.

Until the introduction in the British Parliament, on November 11, 1917, of the Balfour Declaration, the way toward this end had been beset with many difficulties and Mr. Fischel, up to this time, had felt that Palestine as a recreated Jewish homeland could not succeed. His reasons were that the majority of Jews who had migrated there had done so chiefly with the idea of dying on Holy ground and that charity alone was the foundation upon which the colonization plan was built.

So long as Palestine was under Turkish domination and rule the undertaking, Mr. Fischel believed, lacked the elements of business security, as investments were necessarily unsafe. With the Balfour Declaration, however, all this was changed. The opportunity for profitable enterprises, which Mr. Fischel had noted on his visit in 1910 and had commented upon in interviews on his return to America at that time, now needed, he was convinced, only capital for development.

Mr. Fischel believed that this was the time for the millions of Jewish people throughout the world to show their appreciation of the Balfour Declaration and its significance by investing a part of their savings in the project of the upbuilding of Palestine, which could be done with the assurance of the protection of the British government for such investments.

Accustomed to dealing in a big way with big projects, Mr. Fischel devoted considerable thought to the Palestine problem with the result that within less than a month after the Balfour Declaration had been made public, he evolved a plan for the financing of the development of Palestine, which, had it been carried into effect, would undoubtedly have met the entire needs of the situation for many years to come.

This plan was none other than the floating of a Jewish Liberty Loan of $100,000,000 to be subscribed to by the Jews of America and Europe.

It so happened that at this time the Zionist Organization was holding its annual convention in Baltimore, presided over by United States Supreme Court Justice Louis D. Brandeis, with whom Mr. Fischel had become well acquainted through their association in the work of organizing the American Jewish Relief Committee.

Mr. Fischel accordingly decided to take this opportunity to communicate his plan to Justice Brandeis, sending him the following letter, in which he submitted the full details of his proposal:

Hon. Louis D. Brandeis,
Washington, D. C.   December 13, 1917.

My dear Judge:

I herewith enclose a copy of my plan for the proposal to float a Jewish Liberty Loan of $100,000,000 for the development of Palestine. I have been informed that the Zionist Organization will meet in Baltimore and will no doubt take up some sort of financial proposition to help build Palestine. I therefore feel that this is the proper time to consider this plan. While the amount is large, there are, however, at least five million Jews the world over who can subscribe on the average of $20 each for this purpose, and in order to make a beginning I pledge myself to subscribe the sum of $10,000 in accordance with the suggestion made in my plan. I may increase this sum as the necessity arises.

Yours very truly,
HARRY FISCHEL.

The plan, as proposed by Mr. Fischel was as follows.

PLAN FOR $100,000,000 LIBERTY LOAN ISSUE FOR THE PURPOSE OF UPBUILDING PALESTINE

The news covering the success of the English army in capturing Jerusalem and practically all of Judea, and the declaration that a Jewish State in Palestine is much favored, has naturally filled me with pride and satisfaction.

This is not an ordinary incident, and it carries with it the Finger of God. The event having taken place on the first day of Chanucah makes it particularly significant, because on that day, nearly two thousand years ago, the Maccabees entered the Temple.

Every Jew, proud of his tradition, must raise the question, what should be the next step? How should this historical event be celebrated? Shall it be by simply rejoicing in the same way as we have till now mourned the loss of Palestine. No progress was ever made merely with tears, therefore no progress will be obtained by simply rejoicing. It is our duty to do something practical and in a concrete form, to assure the proper development of this wonderful country of our forefathers, which was known to be abundant with milk and honey. Something will have to be done quickly in order to change the entire status of that country, as thousands upon thousands of people will be glad and eager to go there. Till now, most of our people went there to die, few went there to live; today the reverse must be the case, they must go there to live, and do their best for the development of that country.

I had the privilege of visiting a good portion of Palestine a few years ago. I came back enthused with the possibilities that our Holy Land affords development of industrial and commercial enterprises, to say nothing about the agricultural promise that it held out at that time, and which has naturally increased. The country has a vast amount of natural resources and therefore permits not alone of the exploitation of these resources but also the establishment of factories, using as a basis, copper, brass, coal, petroleum, asphalt and quite a number of chemicals that may be used for medicinal and other purposes. The Orient, apart from being attractive to tourists, also has a number of places that permit of being turned into curative resorts. In short, everything that was done in the new colonies under the British domain, like Canada, Brazil, Australia, and later on in Egypt, it is possible to expect of Palestine. The stimulation of business, the construction of buildings, the reconstruction of towns requires a stupendous, yet easily obtainable fund.

Now that everybody is hopeful that a Jewish state in Palestine is no longer a dream, it is well "to make hay while the sun shines." Nothing can be done unless financial backing is secured, and everyone should be willing to give his share.

I am of the opinion that the time is at hand when a $100,000,-000 Liberty Loan can be floated and easily subscribed to by the Jews of America, and that such a loan should be underwritten by our leading Jewish bankers. In order to induce subscribers to make their subscriptions as large as possible, I would suggest that these subscriptions be made payable in five years, in installments of 20 per cent each year, because it would take fully that time before all the money subscribed would actually be required.

I fell that it is a great privilege to start this subscription with my pledge of a large sum on the plan above mentioned. I have every reason to believe that while the enthusiasm is great among all the Jews throughout the United States, it is worth while "To strike while the iron is hot" and let each one show his enthusiasm by the amount of bonds for which he is willing to subscribe. In this way many sympathizers will follow my suggestion, and I have no doubt that this loan of $100,000,000 if properly handled, will be over-subscribed in a very short time.

The following from the New York Times is typical of the newspaper articles which followed this suggestion:

$100,000,000 Loan by Jews Urged to Develop Palestine

Harry Fischel Wants Issue of Hebrew Liberty Bonds—Pledges
First $10,000—Writes Plan to Justice Brandeis—
Subscriptions to be Paid in Five Years

Harry Fischel, well known philanthropist and real estate man, has writen to Justice Louis D. Brandeis, of the Supreme Court of the United States, suggesting that the Jews of America raise a Jewish Liberty Loan of $100,000,000 for the rehabilitation of Palestine. Mr. Fischel is willing to subscribe $10,000. Meetings at which the project will be discussed will be held in Baltimore today and tomorrow. (Here follows Mr. Fischel's plan in full.)

Immediately following publication of Mr. Fischel's suggestion he was in receipt of a large number of telegrams and letters from all parts of the United States inquiring where and how the Jewish Liberty Loan bonds might be purchased.

One telegram in particular, gave him much satisfaction. It was from Nathan Straus and read:

"I note with pleasure your plan of raising $100,000,000 Liberty Loan for the upbuilding of Palestine. Your proposal to start the loan with $10,000 and increase it later is very admirable. It shows that your heart is toward Palestine. May your example be followed by many of our Jewish people in subscribing to this worthy cause. Appreciating your generosity.

NATHAN STRAUS.

Had the Zionist Organization taken advantage of the large degree of enthusiasm among the Jewish people created by the Balfour Declaration and had it acted at this psychological time when Mr. Fischel proposed the $100,000,000 Loan, there can be little doubt but that a very large sum of money would have been subscribed by Jews in the United States and all over the world.

The imagination of the people was at this time fired by the capture of Jerusalem and the pledge of Great Britain for the establishment of a true Jewish homeland, for which the Jews had yearned for more than 2,000 years. It would have required relatively little effort to transform this enthusiasm into terms of money for Palestine's upbuilding, but the Zionist Organization, for reasons of its own, failed to act on Mr. Fischel's plan and the great opportunity was lost. It was inevitable that, as time went on, the enthusiasm should diminish and what might have been accomplished immediately after the Balfour Declaration could never again be duplicated, although many individuals have continued to make large personal sacrifices in order that the dream of the Jewish homeland should be realized.

While Mr. Fischel's hope for floating a great loan for this purpose was doomed to disappointment he continued to give a great deal of thought to the question of how he might raise money to support the industries of Palestine and thus give employment to the Jewish people there, so that they might be self-supporting and become producers.

It was his firm opinion, as a result of what he had personally observed while there, that with a stable government, money could be invested in Palestine with profit, and, at the same time could be made to accomplish results that would be of the largest benefit in helping to realize the greater object of upbuilding the country.

Mr. Fischel, with this idea in mind, on January 21, 1919, called a conference at his home, then at 118 East 93rd Street, at which he proposed the formation of a Palestine Development Corporation, the purpose of which was to initiate and to afford assistance to various Palestinian industries. The conference was attended by business men engaged in varied lines of activity, and a number of Rabbis.

At this meeting, Mr. Fischel advised the conferees they had
been called together for the purpose of helping to upbuild Palestine. He had, he told them, informally discussed the problem
with a number of men deeply interested in the future of the
Holy Land, as a result of which conversations he was convinced
the time was opportune for the formation of a large corporation
which should engage in establishing the several industries
essential to the welfare of the people.

This should be undertaken, he declared, not as a charity but
strictly as a business proposition, and in such a manner that
those who invested their moneys in the corporation should receive a profit.

Incidentally, the people already residing in Palestine, with
those who should in the future migrate there, would, of course,
be greatly aided through such a plan, Mr. Fischel stated, as it
would mean that employment would be found for them. It
would be especially beneficial to the Jews compelled, because of
intolerable conditions, to leave Russia, Poland, Galicia, Roumania and other parts of Central and Eastern Europe.

The occasion was ripe for such a corporation, Mr. Fischel
continued, inasmuch as American Jews were taking a larger interest in Palestine than formerly and were economically better
situated than the Jews of any other country to invest in such an
enterprise, despite the fact that there had already been formed a
Palestine Development Corporation abroad, with many investors,
notably in Russia. Surely, he contended, the Jews of this country would not wish to do less for Palestine than the Jews of
Russia.

The fact that there was considerable doubt as to what the
attitude of America would be toward immigration for a number
of years after the war, Mr. Fischel pointed out, would place
heavy demands upon Palestine as a land of Jewish refuge and
made it extremely desirable to prepare for all future eventuali-
ties. In order to do this it was essential that the work in Palestine be thoroughly organized and systematized with the view,

first, of caring for the people already on the ground, and second, of preparing the land for those who might in the future be compelled or wish to settle there.

As a result of Mr. Fischel's representations the Palestine Development Corporation was formally organized with a capital of $10,000,000 made up of 100,000 shares of stock of the par value of $100 a share. At a subsequent meeting of the incorporators, held on February 5, 1919 at the Central Jewish Institute the following statement of the objects of the corporation was formulated and adopted:

"The object of the Corporation shall be the upbuilding of the Holy Land by the development of industries. This would include the raising, canning and exporting of fresh, dried and canned foods; the growing and manufacturing of cotton and wool; the growing of sugar cane; manufacturing and exporting of sugar; the raising of cattle; the sale of hides and leather; the manufacture of leather and leather goods; the sale of asphalts and other dead sea products; the refining of oils; the manufacture of perfumery and soaps; the development of olive wood and mother of pearl industries; the opening of the petroleum fields.

"The building of houses and factories, assisting capable and enterprising men who have knowledge of industry, but have not sufficient funds to enter into business on their own account, by supplying them with all necessary machinery and raw materials, upon such terms as they may live up to, and to take from them in payment thereof, their manufactured products for export purposes.

"Palestine being the junction of Europe, Asia and Africa, can and should be made the center of purchase, sale and exchange of products of the three continents, for example, its central position should make it the ideal market for furs that are exported from Persia, Smarkland and Turkastan, and likewise for the oriental rug industry."

While the formation of the Palestine Development Corporation was in progress, Mr. Fischel secured the opinions of many men regarded as experts in Far Eastern matters and who, without exception, expressed the view that there was ample scope for such an undertaking, which should be exceedingly profitable.

Among such expressions was a letter received by Mr. Fischel from Dr. Otis A. Glazebrook, American Consul-General in Jerusalem. Dr. Glazebrook while in this country and just before his departure to Palestine to resume his diplomatic post, wrote Mr. Fischel as follows:

Mr. Harry Fischel,
51 Chambers Street,
New York, N. Y.   319 West 59th Street, New York, N. Y.
                                           February 14, 1919.

My dear Mr. Fischel:

I have read with great interest the prospectus of the Palestine Development Corporation. The proposition appeals to me in every particular as feasible. My acquaintance with Palestinian conditions and possibilities justifies the opinion that this enterprise philanthropically will be of great benefit to the unemployed and, I should think, if properly managed, it might prove a good investment.

As an American consular officer I hail with gratification the introduction of American industrial appliances in Palestine. It will be my duty and pleasure to foster in every way such undertakings.

Very faithfully yours,

(signed) OTIS A. GLAZEBROOK.

Mr. Fischel at this time retained as counsel to the corporation former Ambassador to Turkey, Abram I. Elkus, to whom was entrusted the task of conducting necessary negotiations with the British and American governments for obtaining the consent of both countries to the corporation's proposed activities. While the organization proceeded quietly, without publicity or propaganda of any kind, nearly a quarter of a million dollars was privately subscribed by those who had become interested in the enterprise.

With the situation affecting the corporation in this satisfactory condition, Mr. Fischel called upon Mr. Henry Morgenthau, former Ambassador to Turkey, who had just returned from Palestine and to whom he outlined his plans. Mr. Morgenthau, on the occasion of this meeting, discouraged the project but the following day called Mr. Fischel personally on the telephone and asked that he have tea with him at five o'clock that afternoon.

When Mr. Fischel arrived at Mr. Morgenthau's residence, he found the latter had changed his attitude toward the new corporation and was ready to give his assistance in every way possible. It was after this conference that Mr. Fischel authorized Mr. Elkus to complete the legal details involved, but, for some undivulged reason, Mr. Elkus did not proceed as fast as Mr. Fischel wished.

At this time, Mr. Fischel called on Federal Judge Julian W. Mack, then president of the Zionist Organization of America. While Judge Mack lent a great deal of encouragement to the plans, he nevertheless requested Mr. Fischel to delay further steps until after the conclusion of the drive of the Palestine Foundation Fund, just then in progress.

On the next Saturday night, while attending a dinner given by the Central Jewish Relief Committee in honor of the late Albert Lucas, secretary of the Joint Distribution Committee, Mr. Fischel met at the function Mr. Jacob H. Schiff, always an early attendant at affairs of this kind, and related to him the plans of the Palestine Development Corporation in detail. Mr. Schiff gave his entire approval to the project but suggested that Mr. Fischel meet him for another conference at his office before proceeding to obtain a charter for the corporation.

At this subsequent meeting, after Mr. Schiff and Mr. Fischel had discussed the matter from every angle, the former requested that the launching of the enterprise be postponed to a future time when, he said, conditions would be more favorable.

Following his talks with Mr. Schiff and other Jewish leaders who endorsed his idea but felt the time was not opportune for it, Mr. Fischel decided to be guided by their advice and judgment and to delay further action until he might himself again visit Palestine and decide what might be done to provide a home there for the thousands of Jewish people denied the privilege, under the existing immigration laws of the United States, of making their abode in this land of freedom and opportunity.

CHAPTER XXXIV

PURCHASES THE HOLLAND HOUSE

THE scarcity of labor during the war had greatly curtailed activity in the building industry, not alone seriously affecting housing conditions but creating a dearth of business accommodations as well.

With the signing of the Armistice there was great need for a resumption of activity in this field. Mr. Fischel, although he continued to devote a major part of his time to his communal and philanthropic interests, considered that it was not proper for one who had the ability to be a producer to remain idle at such a time and accordingly looked around for some enterprise which would utilize his experience and resources.

One of the old and famous landmarks of the city was the famous hotel known as the Holland House, at the corner of Fifth Avenue and Thirtieth Street, where for nearly a generation many noted people had made their residence. This hotel, a ten story building erected in 1892, was one of the first strictly fireproof hostelries to be built in New York, and was of the highest class and most expensive type of construction. It was justly celebrated for its staircase of Carara marble, especially imported, and was also known for years as a favorite stopping place for couples on their honeymoons.

With the passage of the Eighteenth Amendment and the Volstead Act, however, the Holland House, in common with many other hotels, came upon lean days, for a large part of its revenue had depended upon its bar, and now that liquor could no longer be legally dispensed it had been forced to go out of business as a hotel. The property was on the market for a long time but no one could be found who would chance operating it again for its original purpose and the building was too expen-

THE FAMOUS OLD HOLLAND HOUSE.

*Fifth Avenue and 30th Street; for a generation, one
of New York's leading hotels, converted
by Mr. Fischel into an office building in 1919.*

sive and modern to be torn down with the object of erecting a
new structure on the site.

Mr. Fischel, sensing an opportunity, decided the hotel could
be profitable transformed into an office building.

Accordingly he purchased the Holland House in November 1919
at a very reasonable cost and by extensive alterations, which he
himself planned and supervised, succeeded within a period of
four months, in converting the hotel into a high class office
building, practically all the space in which was rented before the
alterations were completed.

The building having a very central and convenient location,
Mr. Fischel arranged a suite of rooms for his own offices which
he still maintains there. The transaction proved one of the most
successful building operations of his entire career.

The four upper floors of the building were leased as the
headquarters of the American Baptist Foreign Missionary
Society. Shortly after this organization had been installed in
the building, its general manager, Mr. Hutchinson, called on Mr.
Fischel and put to him this question.

"How is it that the Jewish people do not engage in any missionary work in foreign fields."

Mr. Hutchinson was apparently under the impression that the
Jews could obtain converts from among the heathen more readily
and economically than the Christians.

Mr. Fischel replied to him in this wise:

"Entirely apart from the financial aspect of the successful
conduct of missionary work, in which it may be true that Jews
might excel; from the religious standpoint, our Jewish law pro-
hibits our attempting to convert anyone to Judaism. Indeed, we
are instructed by law that should one of a different religion come
to us voluntarily with the purpose of becoming a Jew, we should
do everything in our power to dissuade him.

"We are instructed to exert every effort and expend all the
money at our disposal for the purpose of giving religious instruc-

tion to our own people to acquaint them fully with our religion in order to have them remain as Jews.

"As to my own experience, I have always found that if a Jew becomes converted to the Christian religion, he must necessarily have been a bad Jew, else he would have remained true to his faith. Therefore, I do not feel that Christian missionaries who seek to convert Jews to their own beliefs are ever very successful in their undertaking and I believe that the money which is spent in this way cannot bring good results, even from the Christian point of view."

THE ASTOR LIBRARY.

A New York landmark at Lafayette Street near Astor Place, acquired by Mr. Fischel in 1919 as the Home of the Hebrew Sheltering and Immigrant Aid Society of America, and reconstructed by him, as Chairman of the Building Committee.

CHAPTER XXXV

ASTOR LIBRARY ACQUIRED AS HOME FOR THE HIAS

FROM the time of the signing of the Armistice to the end of 1919, the Hebrew Sheltering and Immigrant Aid Society directors realized that with the actual end of the world conflict there would be a large influx of immigrants for which the Society in its existing quarters at 229 East Broadway, would be unable to care.

From the beginning of the war in 1914, when immigration at once ceased, the Society largely devoted its efforts to enabling the stricken refugees in the war zones to communicate with their families in America and its building was almost entirely occupied by executive offices, with accommodations for only a few casual wayfarers. Practically no provision was made for the large number of immigrants, now to be expected.

Considerable thought had been given by the directors to plans for increasing the capacity of the Society's building either by purchasing the adjoining property and erecting a new building or moving to another part of the city. The consensus of opinion was that it was desirable to move to a neighborhood affording better transit facilities and Mr. Fischel was appointed chairman of a Committee to secure a desirable site.

With thousands of immigrants ready at once to migrate to America, there was no time to await the construction of a new building if the immigrants were to have accommodations on their arrival. It was therefore decided to look for a completed building that could readily be converted to the needs of the moment.

By what appears as the intervention of the Almighty, Mr. Fischel was approached on November 18, 1919 by the real estate firm of Brown, Wheelock and Company, through their representative Mr. Simon Neuman who proposed to Mr. Fischel the purchase by him for investment of the famous Astor Library building on

Lafayette Street and which had been discontinued as a library
on the opening of the new public library at Fifth Avenue and
Forty Second Street.

With his mind centered on the necessity of a home for immigrants the idea at once occurred to Mr. Fischel that this building would be ideal for the purpose, inasmuch as it could be quickly converted at a reasonable expense. The price asked for the
property, however, was $350,000. While Mr. Fischel regarded
this as a low figure, he felt it involved too large a sum to be expended by the Society at that time and decided to buy the building himself, solely as a business proposition. Accordingly, he
made an offer of $325,000, having still in his mind the idea that
should the offer be accepted he would turn the building over to
the Society, if the directors later decided they cared to purchase it.

Subsequently, Mr. Fischel called together the members of the
Building Committee, to whom, in conjunction with the Board of
Directors, he submitted the proposition. They regarded it, however, as too large a project financially, for the Society to undertake, although several of the directors individually were in favor
of it.

The day following this meeting Mr. Fischel was advised by
Mr. Neuman that at a meeting of the executors of the estate his
offer for the property, had been accepted, despite the fact much
larger offers had been made in the interim. Inasmuch as the contract had been drawn and the executors had agreed to the price,
the property, he was told, was regarded as his. Mr. Neuman
then offered Mr. Fischel a large profit if he would sell the contract. To this, Mr. Fischel replied:

"I cannot accept any offer for the reason that I have bought the
building for the purpose of a home for immigrants and I am
certain that I will, in the end, be able to convince the directors
that while the amount is a large one, its purchase will be better
for the Society than buying ground and erecting a new building,
besides which it has the advantage of placing the Society in the

position of at once being able to accommodate the influx of immigrants."

The next day Mr. Fischel received offers of a still larger profit, to all of which he turned a deaf ear, instructing Mr. Neuman to have the contract drawn in the name of the institution, rather than in his name personally, as he felt sure that the directors would realize their mistake and ratify the agreement.

It so happened that Mr. Albert Rosenblatt, an influential member of the Board of Directors, was informed at this time that a friend of his had made a much larger offer for the property than that at which it had been offered to the Society through Mr. Fischel. This friend had been told the property had been sold, although the name of the purchaser had not been disclosed by the estate.

Mr. Rosenblatt went to Mr. John L. Bernstein, president of the Society, and related what he had learned, with the result that Mr. Bernstein immediately called on Mr. Fischel and asked him to bring about another joint meeting of the Building Committee and Board of Directors in order that the matter might be reconsidered.

At this meeting those who had originally opposed the purchase were insistent that the building be acquired even though it became necessary to pay a large profit to the new owner. In short they asked Mr. Fischel to buy it at almost any price at which it might be obtained.

Mr. Fischel asked that the decision of the Board be expressed by an unanimous vote. Mr. Leon Kamaiky, who had most strenuously opposed the proposition at the earlier meeting, then made the motion that Mr. Fischel be empowered to buy the property. The resolution was passed without dissent.

Mr. Fischel then arose and took from his pocket the signed contract made out in the name of the institution and presented it to the president. The scene which followed was dramatic in the extreme. The directors could scarcely believe their own eyes, so carefully had Mr. Fischel guarded his secret. Nor did they become convinced until they had examined the contract in detail and finally approved it in its entirety. The profit sacrificed by Mr. Fischel through having the contract made in the name of the institution, although the directors had originally rejected the proposition, was a very large one, but he had no regrets in view of the knowledge that he had been enabled to meet the situation with which the Society was confronted.

The action of the Board of Directors did not, however, finally decide the question because it was regarded as desirable to consult Mr. Jacob H. Schiff, always a great friend of the Society, concerning the wisdom of the step. Mr. Bernstein called on Mr. Schiff and informed him of the purchase, as well as the fact that a large sum of money would be required to convert the building to its new uses.

As a banker and accustomed to carefully weighing the ability of institutions to assume new financial burdens, Mr. Schiff at once stated that he felt the obligation was entirely too great for the Society to assume. This opinion, coming from Mr. Schiff, caused a number of the directors to share his view and they were ready to cancel the contract and return the property to Mr. Fischel.

Although he could have profited largely through its resale Mr. Fischel declared that he had confidence in the Jewish people of America and was sure they would respond to an appeal issued by the Society in behalf of the immigrants and that enough money would be raised in this manner to successfully carry out the plans. He then suggested that he would like to be one of a committee to call upon Mr. Schiff again.

Mr. Bernstein, the president, Judge Leon Sanders, a former president, and Mr. Fischel then visited Mr. Schiff and Mr. Fischel, approaching the proposition from an entirely new angle, asked the famous financier and philanthropist this question:

"How are we going to care for the large number of immigrants who are arriving daily? Can we afford to let them take the chance of going astray without our protection? Furthermore, our present building is very old and is a veritable fire-trap."

The best, quickest and cheapest way to meet the problem was, Mr. Fischel informed Mr. Schiff, to alter the Astor Library building. For this purpose, he declared, all that was needed was $100,000 with which to take title and $75,000 for alterations making the building ready for immediate occupancy, as the estate had agreed to take back a mortgage for $225,000 covering a long period of years.

Mr. Fischel sought to convince Mr. Schiff that inasmuch as the Hebrew Sheltering and Immigrant Aid Society was a national organization, with well organized branches throughout the United States, there would be little difficulty in raising the $175,000 needed for this worthy purpose.

Mr. Schiff then put the question: "Have we a right to burden the institution with a mortgage of $225,000?" To this Mr. Fischel promptly replied:

"We represent the Jews of every state of the Union. If the government has the right in an emergency to mortgage the nation to the extent of more than twenty billions of dollars, as was done during the war, then we have a right to mortgage the Jews of the United States for the small sum of $225,000 to meet this need."

When he had heard this argument, Mr. Schiff was convinced it was correct and not only gave his immediate consent to the purchase of the property but, with the interest he always showed in the immigrant situation, promised to make a large contribution with which to start the appeal.

This change of attitude on the part of Mr. Schiff was all that was needed to command the support of every director and Mr. Fischel was immediately authorized to prepare plans for the alteration of the building.

The next annual meeting of the Society, always an event of large general interest and attended by prominent officials both of the state and of the United States, took place on January 11,

1920. On this occasion, after reading his annual report as treasurer, Mr. Fischel was requested as chairman of the Building Committee as well, to make a report on the purchase of the Astor Library.

This report was as follows:

At the previous annual meetings of our Society, time and again mention has been made of the necessity for a new building in which the work of our organization might be carried on in keeping with its growth. Its present building, at 229 East Broadway, has not only become inadequate, but, due to its age and lack of facilities, it has become unfit either to shelter the immigrants or to provide for the ever-increasing administrative work. The old building, though improved from time to time, could not be made satisfactory, and every dollar spent upon its improvement was practically wasted. Moreover, it was felt that the Society should have a building in keeping with its unique standing in American Jewry and its international character. For, as you well know, the purpose of the Society is to transform the immigrant to America, by proper guidance and education, into an American citizen of the highest type.

The old structure has always been a source of great worry to us, it being virtually a fire-trap. Moreover, it must not be forgotten that, while ten years ago it was located in the center of the Jewish population, conditions have so changed that we are warranted in moving to a new location in order to be nearer to the mass of our people in Greater New York.

We felt that the headquarters of the Hebrew Sheltering and Immigrant Aid Society should be, as it were, a monument to its effort in behalf of the foreign born Jew in this country.

We are most fortunate to be able at this hour—our annual meeting—to announce that the Society has acquired the old Astor Library, located on Lafayette Street and facing the colonial homes that at one time sheltered the greatest literary men of America and Europe, as well as several presidents of the United States. The neighborhood is replete with historic recollections, and it is only fitting and proper that a building which long radiated knowledge shall henceforth be devoted to the noble task to which the Hebrew Sheltering and Immigrant Aid Society is dedicated.

The Astor Library is centrally located. It is near the subways, the Second and Third Avenue "L's", and crosstown street cars, and can, therefore, be easily reached from every part of Greater New York. The people who come to us from every part of the city for inquiries will henceforth find it much easier to do so than in the past.

The building housed the first public library in America. In style of architecture, it has been regarded as one of the civic monuments of New York. In appreciation of what America has meant to the immigrant we are therefore glad indeed to be able to acquire this building for our future needs and to preserve it, though remodelled in the interior, as one of the city's most valued relics.

The size of the lot is 249 feet long by 130 feet deep. The building is 200 feet wide and 110 feet deep, with 25 feet on each side for open space and ventilation. It is a three-story fireproof structure and the rooms, without exception, have high ceilings and are laid out with good taste. The beautiful architecture commands the respect and attention of the passerby, and its interior, too, is calculated to fill those whom it may attract with a spirit of welcome and appreciation of true brotherhood.

As Chairman of the Building Committee it gives me pleasure to report to you that we have acquired this unique and historical property practically at one-half of its value.

The land on which this building is erected is worth at least $400,000 and the building could not be erected today for less than $300,000, a total value of at least $700,000. We have been fortunate enough to purchase the land and buildings for the sum of $325,000.

We expect to remodel its interior to enable us to carry on the vast and manifold labors to which our Society is devoting itself and to the additional work that may become ours as time goes on. This reconstruction work will involve an additional sum of $75,-000. The present owners of the property—the New York Public Library Association—have consented to carry a mortgage of $225,000 and its Directors have, by their sympathy for our work, accorded us every courtesy and consideration.

One of our eminent philanthropists, in a conversation with me, suggested that it was presumptuous on our part to mortgage the

Jews of the City of New York for the sum of $225,000. My
answer was that we are not a local but a national institution. We
represent the Jews of every state in the Union; therefore, if our
Government had the right to mortgage the Nation to the amount
of over twenty billions of dollars during the war, we, the Directors of the Society, feel that we also have the right to mortgage
American Jewry for the paltry sum of $225,000 and we have
full confidence in our members that this mortgage will be paid
in a very short time and that we will be assisted to a great extent by those whose families we are going to reunite.

The Society has no endowment funds or any resources upon
which to draw. The annual income has always been just sufficient to meet the needs of the moment. There was never any
money to spare. The Society now looks to its members, and to
all of American Jewry, as never before. It has commanded the
confidence of American Jewry and the respect of the leading men
of this country, including high officials, presidents of universities
and editors of newspapers and magazines. This confidence has
been manifested again and again in many ways and this gathering
today proves absolutely the hearty recognition of the work of
our Society, on the part of the people at large.

As Chairman of the Building Committee, as well as Treasurer
of this organization, I feel it my duty to inform you that a call
for contributions to the Building Fund will be made shortly, and,
from former experience, I have no doubt that the members will
respond nobly.

In conclusion, I take this means on behalf of the Building
Committee to congratulate the members, as well as Jewry in
general, upon the purchase of this historic building, and it is our
hope that it will be completed and ready for occupancy within
the next six months.

At the first meeting of the Board of Directors following this
annual meeting the decision was reached that inasmuch as the
building when completed would serve the needs of the Society
for many years, no expense should be spared in converting it into
a national home which might be utilized not alone for its primary
object of housing Jewish immigrants but for other communal
purposes as well.

The Directors expressed the view that once an appeal for funds was launched it would meet with a generous response from all parts of the country. This prediction was happily more than realized. Nearly half a million dollars poured into the treasury of the Society from every city, town and village in the country, so enthusiastic did the Jewish public become over the idea that the famous Astor Library was to be a national home for immigrants.

Much of the success of the campaign was, of course, due to the generous treatment it received at the hands of the press of the entire country which filled endless columns of space with news of the undertaking, sketches of the history of the library itself and accounts of the work done in behalf of Jewish immigrants from the very inception of the Society.

Of these articles the following from the Jewish Tribune of October 8, 1920, is especially interesting.

The Old and the New
Astor Library Building

Harry Fischel, Treasurer of the Hebrew Sheltering and Immigrant Aid Society, Tells the Story of the Purchase of the Historic Landmark to be the Society's new Home.

Whoever is familiar with the history of the first Jewish settlers in New York, when the total population of our present metropolis hardly amounted to one thousand and five hundred, way back in the second half of the seventeenth century, will remember that Peter Stuyvesant, the "Strong-headed," then Governor of New Amsterdam, reluctantly admitted the first twenty-three Jewish refugees from Brazil who came here to seek refuge from the "Holy" Inquisition. They were finally permitted to land on the condition that none of them be allowed to become a burden to the community, and the Jews of New York have kept their vow ever since.

When about thirty-five years ago, the situation of the Jews in Russia and Roumania became unbearable and they began to come to this country in larger numbers than ever before, Amer-

ican Jewry felt that an organized effort was necessary to meet
the new immigrant, to extend a brotherly hand to him, to guide
him during the first few weeks and months of his stay here, to
help him find his bearings, to make a good prospective American
citizen of him. The result of this sentiment led to the formation
of two organizations, The Hebrew Sheltering Society and the
Immigrant Aid Society, which about eleven years ago merged
into the present Hebrew Sheltering and Immigrant Aid Society
of America.

The readers of the Jewish Tribune have already more than
once been made familiar with the work of the Society, with its
ever increasing activities, with the truly motherly care it gives
to the strangers at our gate, with its recent successful effort to
reunite upwards of 30,000 heads of families with their kin in
Eastern Europe. Our readers also know that the present home
of the Society at 229 East Broadway, has proven inadequate, and
that the Society has therefore purchased the Astor Library building at 425-437 Lafayette Street, to be the new home of the
Society.

Harry Fischel, who has been treasurer of the Society since
its very inception and who has always given of the best of his
ability, energy, heart and soul to the welfare of the Society, has
given the Jewish Tribune the following account of the plans for
the property:

"In planning alterations in the building, there were several
problems to be solved. The first was that we had to deal with a
large immigration and to provide for it sufficient temporary
accommodation, a large dining room and two kitchens, since
our institution has always strictly upheld the dietary laws. We
also had to take care of separating the immigrants from wayfarers, as we have always done even in our old building, because
the wayfarers would exert an undesirable influence on the immigrants, making them feel rather pessimistic towards the opportunities offered by their adopted fatherland.

"The new building, after it has been remodelled, will be a
perfect specimen of what a home for the temporary accommodation of Jewish immigrants should be and the Astor Library building, with its great traditions of all that is noble in American
citizenship, will become the greatest monument to American
Jewry's achievements when occupied by our Society.

"A special feature of the building will be an auditorium which which will accommodate about 600 people and will be used for lectures on America, naturalization classes and as a synagogue on the Sabbath and Jewish Holydays.

"On the whole, I may safely state that this building, when completed, will not only be one of the finest edifices in New York, but will be a pride and glory for all Jews of America who have helped transform it into a home for immigrants."

Mr. Fischel added that part of the building will be completed by the first of the year and the entire building will be finished during the early part of the Spring before the Passover holidays, provided the Jews of America respond and contribute liberally to the Building Fund.

The writer left Mr. Fischel with the impression that American Jewry will heed the appeal of the Society that has been doing its work so zealously and devotedly for so many years, a work which helps build up a happier, better Jewry, not in this country alone, but the world over.

CHAPTER XXXVI

DEDICATION OF THE NEW HIAS BUILDING

THE work of transforming the Astor Library building into the home for immigrants was commenced by Mr. Fischel in March 1920 and from that time until the middle of 1921 he devoted practically his entire time to this undertaking.

On the completion of the alterations he received the commendation not only of the directors but of all those who inspected the building. Finally the time arrived when the new Immigrant Home was ready to be dedicated and formally opened to the public.

As the only institution dealing with immigrants which was officially recognized by the government, it was decided to invite the President of the United States, the late Warren G. Harding, to attend the dedication ceremonies. A committee was accordingly appointed to visit President Harding at the White House and to extend the formal invitation of the Society.

The directors of the Hebrew Sheltering and Immigrant Aid Society named as members of this committee Judge Leon Sanders, Mr. Leon Kamaiky and Mr. Fischel. The delegation went to Washington on May 18, 1921. The occasion marked the second time that Mr. Fischel had personally called upon a President of the United States in behalf of this organization and the third President he had visited in relation to philanthropic activities.

President Harding received the delegation, which was introduced to him by Congressman Chandler, with his accustomed cordiality. He expressed great admiration for the work the Society had done during the war and for its aid to Jewish immigrants at all times since it was founded. Although Mr. Harding declared he would like to attend the dedication of the new

MR. FISCHEL VISITS THE WHITE HOUSE

Delegation from the H. I. A. S. with the late President Harding, Washington, D. C.,
May 18, 1921.

building, he expressed his regret that he could not leave Washington on the date fixed, June 5, 1921, because of the pressure of his official duties owing to the still complicated international situation.

Mr. Harding said, however, that he would be willing to officially open the building by pressing an electric button installed in his executive offices and would deliver an address over the telephone. He then appointed as his personal representatives to attend the function the Secretary of Labor, the Hon. James J. Davis; the Assistant Secretary, Edward Henning, and the Solictor of the Department of Labor, the Hon. S. Risley.

Before the Delegation took its leave the President acceded to a request that he have a picture taken with the members and the White House photographer took the photograph which is herewith reproduced.

The dedication of the building on June 5 was generally recognized as one of the most important events in the history of American Jewry. It was attended by the national directors of the Society from every part of the United States as well as by leading officials of the government and many other men and women of prominence in public and private life.

When, at three o'clock, President Harding pushed the button at the White House, causing the building to be illuminated from top to bottom, the famous structure was filled with the largest throng ever within its doors. Immediately thereafter the President began his address through the telephone, and this was transmitted by amplifiers so that it was heard by every person in the vast audience.

The programme arranged by the Society then followed. Mr. Fischel made the address of welcome after which, as Chairman of the Building Committee, he turned the key of the new immigrants' home over to the President of the Society, Mr. John L. Bernstein. The celebration attendant upon the opening of the structure lasted for a week, during which time the building was visited by thousands of persons from all parts of the country.

The following article reproduced from the Hebrew Standard of June 10, 1921, gives a complete and accurate account of the occasion.

HEBREW SHELTERING AND IMMIGRANT AID
SOCIETY DEDICATION IMPRESSIVE CEREMONY

President Harding Officially Opens New Home.   Mr. Harry Fischel, Chairman of the Building Committee, and Mr. Albert Rosenblatt, Chairman of the Building Fund Committee, Deliver Notable Addresses.

The dedication of the new home of the Hebrew Sheltering and Immigrant Aid Society of America at 425-437 Lafayette Street, which began on Sunday afternoon and lasted all this week, was marked by impressive ceremonies.

At 2:30 Sunday afternoon a bell tinkled in one of the rooms in the Astor Library building and John L. Bernstein, president of the Hebrew Sheltering and Immigrant Aid Society announced that the bell had been sounded by President Harding in Washington and that the building was thus formally dedicated to the usage of the Society.

The President of the United States then delivered the following message over the telephone:

"I wish to express to you my congratulations and good wishes on the occasion of the opening and dedication of the new home of your society. Your organization has for more than a score of years carried on a most useful, patriotic and humane service, and I join with you in the hope that with the enlarged facilities you are now securing, you will be able to expand and improve it. The charity and liberality of the Hebrew people always have been peculiarly noticeable and an inspiration to others. I want you to know of my earnest wish for the continuance and enlargement of the splendid work you have done.

"I am informed that the purchase of the new home was made possible through gifts from persons who came to America as immigrants. It seems to me there could be no more emphatic testimony to the usefulness and effectiveness of your society's work for Americanization."

The new home is the culmination of over 30 years of work

of the Hebrew Sheltering and Immigrant Aid Society of America and this fact was strikingly brought out on Sunday. Mr. Harry Fischel, treasurer of the Building Committee, was instrumental in securing the purchase of the Old Astor Library and it was due to his untiring efforts that the Society has so magnificent a structure.

Mr. Leon Kamaiky, first vice-president, welcomed the large and distinguished assembly. He said:

"It is with great pleasure and pride that the officers, directors and Jews of America open this magnificent building for the service of the immigrant and the stranger.

"When King Solomon recited his prayer at the Dedication of the Temple, he said:

" 'Also to the stranger who cometh of a far-off country, for he heard of thy name and the outstretched hand, mayest thou listen and do according to all that the stranger will call on thee for.'

"The Directors of this institution have adopted this prayer as their motto, namely to do all for the stranger that he calls for.

"When the World War broke out and the call came from our brethren refugees in Japan, we stretched our hand across the Pacific and helped them with food and shelter and communicated with their relatives in this country who sent them money for passage so that almost everyone who was eligible according to the law was transferred to America. Thousands of families are now happily reunited.

"When peace was declared in Europe, the Hebrew Sheltering and Immigrant Aid Society sent a commission to Europe to unite those families whose bread-winners were in this country.

"The commission, consisting of Mr. Jacob Massell and myself, had a very hard task. When we came to Europe in February, 1920, we found that there were no shops, no railroads and no way to send money. After hard work we found a solution and we may say with pride, that we have united upwards of 30,000 families.

"Although our work will be somewhat hampered by the new immigration law, there remains plenty of work to do for our unfortunate brethren on the other side, and we hope to accomplish more good with your cooperation and help.

"In the meantime when our work increased, we found ourselves cramped for room. The home on East Broadway became inadequate and many times we had to go out at night to find a place where the newly arrived immigrants could be sheltered.

"The Board decided on a new home. After a long search we decided to buy this building and make it suitable for our work. We found this location, an admirable one on account of its being accessible by elevated, subway and street railways. We have rebuilt it and furnished it at a great cost, as you have probably seen by going through it.

"We dedicate this building today and hope to proceed with our enlarged work here to the glory of American Jewry."

In transferring this building and its key to the Society, Mr. Fischel delivered the following address:

"On behalf of the Building Committee, I extend to you our heartiest welcome to this new and splendid home for immigrants. My friends, I have had the good fortune to be connected with this institution from its infancy to the present day, from the time it was organized in the basement of 68 Essex Street. I had the privilege to participate in the purchase of its first house at 210 Madison Street in the year 1890, thirty-one years ago, at which time I was elected treasurer of the institution, and have successively held this office until the present day. I was also privileged to participate in the purchasing of the two houses at 229-231 East Broadway, through the generosity of the late Mr. Jacob H. Schiff, on which occasion I also had the honor of being the chairman of the Building Committee.

"On the occasion of the opening of the new building at 229-231 East Broadway, in 1908, when I delivered the key to the president, the late Mr. Nathan Hutkoff, who had been president of this institution for many years, I well remember expressing the hope that I might live to see the time when that building should become too small for our various activities and that our next building would be three times the size of that one. My friends, my hope has been more than fulfilled. Our institution has grown so big that our old building cannot accommodate even one-quarter of our present activities, and I have lived to see it. Since the Almighty has given me the privilege to bring about the purchase of this historical Astor Library building and also the privilege of reconstructing it into this palatial home for immigrants, I will use this occasion to thank the Almighty for all that He has done for us by delivering a blessing. 'Blessed art Thou O Lord our God, King of the Universe, Who has kept us in life and has preserved us and has enabled us to reach the opening of this building.'

"I believe you all remember the story in the Bible when God ordered Moses to build a tabernacle. Moses being the great leader of the people was occupied with many problems, and could not spare the time for the building of the Tabernacle. He therefore appointed the great master Bezalel as chairman of the Building Committee together with the best men available to help him. The great master, with all his ability and with all the instructions given to him by Moses, did not know how to build the tabernacle until God Himself showed Bezalel a complete model of the structure, with all its details, decorations and even the draperies. Having been shown this model, having the money required at his disposal, having no unions to deal with, he had no difficulty in accomplishing his task. Our committee, however, did not have any model by which to be guided, nor did we find any other institution anywhere of this kind by whose experience we could benefit. Under these circumstances our committee had many problems to solve.

"My friends, in order to acquaint you with some of these many problems, I will give you a brief resume of the different activities for which comfortable space has been provided in this, our new building.

"First came the necessity of separating the immigrants from those who have been in America for many years, but who, through adverse circumstances, are compelled to seek shelter in our home for a short time until they obtain employment.

"While the number of these is not many, this condition however, exists. The reason for the separation is obvious. The Jewish immigrant on leaving his native country pictures America not only as a land of refuge, but a land of true democracy and opportunity. On arriving in our institution, should he meet those unfortunates, either male or female, who are compelled to call at our home for temporary shelter, he will be entirely disillusioned, and immediately become disappointed. Therefore, in order to prevent the meeting of these two classes we have provided separate entrances, separate registration rooms, separate reading rooms, even separate showers and bathrooms.

"The Building Committee has given a good deal of thought and consideration to provide the necessary accommodations and comforts for both male and female, such as separate quarters for men and women, spacious and airy dormitories, separate reading and writing rooms, separate bath rooms and all other sanitary accommodations which were impossible in our old building on account of lack of space.

"Another great problem which our committee solved was to provide separate rooms for entire families, that is special sleeping quarters for husbands, their wives and children. In our old home, we were compelled to separate husbands from their wives and children for the same reason, that of not having enough space. The committee is therefore very happy that all these conditions are thoroughly remedied in our new home.

"A great deal of attention has been given by our committee to providing the necessary room for educational work. The spacious auditorium will be used for lectures, which will be given to the immigrants, illustrating through moving pictures the different parts of the country, with its splendor and resources, the possibilities and opportunities offered to them there, and through such pictures, an effort will be made to induce them to spread out all over the United States.

"This auditorium will also be used as a synagogue on Saturdays and Holy Days, while a smaller room will be used for daily religious services. On the second floor we have a number of classrooms for the purpose of teaching the immigrants English and preparing them for American citizenship. There are thousands of American Jews who come to the headquarters of the Society for information on various matters connected with immigration. In the spacious room west of the waiting room we will be in a better position to take care of our patrons than was possible in our old home. Various activities of the Society, as represented by the Executive and Administrative departments, the Bureau of Work in Foreign Countries, the Bureau of Advice, the Bureau of Oriental Jews, etc., will be housed in offices fitting both the important work performed by our Society and the great number of applicants who come for advice and information.

"The dietary laws prescribed by our Jewish religion have always been most rigidly observed in the home of our Society, and the observances have been approved by the most representative men and women in this country and abroad. In order to more carefully carry out these observances, we have provided in this building separate kitchens, with the best up-to-date modern kitchen equipment under the most sanitary conditions, one for dairy and the other for meat cooking; we have also provided separate pantries as well as separate dish-washing machines and separate refrigerating rooms, so that the necessity of supervision of Kashruth will be reduced to a minimum. There will be no danger of mixing the dishes, since there will be no connection between the two kitchens.

"In conclusion I wish to say that in planning this building not a stone was left unturned to provide sanitary conditions and cheerful surroundings, bearing in mind that the immigrant having emerged from an environment where gloom and unhappiness prevailed, must be made to feel as soon as he enters our home that everything has changed for the better and that he now has a chance to start life anew, under new conditions, in happier surroundings, as symbolized by the Hebrew Sheltering and Immigrant Aid Society of America.

"I take this means of extending my sincere thanks and appreciation to every one of the members of the Building Committee who have always been ready and willing to respond to my call for consultation and advice, and I feel that were it not for their devotion to this work, in spite of the fact that I have given to this building all my time, my energy and my long experience in the construction of buildings, I could never have accomplished the great work which was necessary to transform the old building into this home for immigrants.

"Last, but not least, special thanks are due to Mr. Fain, our general manager, for the great assistance he has been to me in the performance of my work. I feel certain that when you are guided through this building and see all the departments, you will agree with me that this building of ours is not alone a source of honor and pride to those who have contributed to the building fund, but it will redound to the glory of American Jewry.

"I am now ready to deliver to you the key of the building. I regret this building has been completed at the same time the new immigration law has gone into effect, thereby preventing us at once from making full use of our facilities. However, we need not be discouraged, as this building has not been built for one

year, but rather for many years to come. Furthermore, when
our Committee was in Washington to invite the President to the
opening of this building, I had the honor and privilege of meeting
those officials who have been given the power to carry out this
immigration law, namely, the Hon. James J. Davis, Secretary
of Labor; the Hon. Edward Henning, Assistant Secretary, and
the Hon. S. Risley, Solicitor of the Department of Labor, the
last of whom we have with us this afternoon. All these are big
men with hearts as big as themselves. My impression after
meeting them is that they are in full sympathy with the immigrant
and will give them the benefit of every doubt in order to admit
them.

"Mr. President, under ordinary circumstances if I were only
the chairman of the Building Committee I would say to you that
my work has ceased, and your responsibility has increased, but
being also the treasurer of this Society, I feel that my responsibility together with yours has increased. It is therefore, our duty,
together with the Board of Directors to put our shoulders to the
wheel and work much harder in order to raise the funds necessary to maintain this large institution.

"My friends, one word more. I want to point out to you the
interesting fact that this building has been built by immigrants
with money collected from immigrants, to be used as a haven of
refuge for immigrants."

Mr. John L. Bernstein, in accepting the building and the key,
paid a high tribute to Mr. Fischel. He said:

"On behalf of my brother directors and on behalf of the 40,000
members of this Society, I take pride and pleasure in receiving
from you this symbolic key of our new building. You, as a man
who was one of the first organizers of the Sheltering House; you,
who took part in the organization of the other society, the Hebrew
Immigrant Aid Society; you, who were present at the merger of
these two organizations into one; you, who have at all times stood
as a pillar of this institution, it is but fit and proper that you
should be the one to present this key, not to me alone, but to the
Board of Directors, to the 40,000 members whom I have mentioned and to the Jews or America.

"If there was ever a time in the history of Jewry or in the
history of America when a building of this kind was necessary,
when work of the kind that we are doing was necessary for the

welfare, not only of Jews, but of humanity at large, this is the time, and you, working as you have for the past thirty years for all things that were good and kind, for all things that were helpful, it is but fit and proper that now, when you have passed middle age, that you should be standing here before this great assembly and be able to say to them and to me and to the others, that this, the latest work that you have done, perhaps transcends everything else that you have ever accomplished.

"You are an exemplification of the Jewish immigrants of America. You came here poor. You came here from a land where you and your forefathers were persecuted. You came to these United States, the land of liberty, which opened the doors to you and you, as a man, you as a Jewish immigrant, have understood what America has done for you, that it has but lent to you, that it is up to you to repay in good citizenship, in service to humanity, to your fellowmen and to your fellow Americans.

"You have done that this many years, and this latest service (I know it will not be the last) is, but a culmination of the life of usefulness which you have led, the life of kindness, loving kindness, that you have led.

"I am proud that you are a member of our Board. I am proud that you are here today presenting me with this key, and I hope that your efforts on behalf of the less fortunate of your fellow beings will not lessen, that your advancing age will not take away from you the energy which you have always displayed in helping your fellow beings. And I know that this Ark, this holy Ark which you and Mrs. Fischel have contributed, which was one of your contributions to this building, will ever bear testimony to the interest you have taken in the religion of our fathers and in the principles of America."

Addresses were also made by Oscar S. Straus, formerly Secretary of Commerce; Solicitor Risley, Leon Sanders, Mr. Jacob Massel, Congressman Isaac Siegel and the Hon. Judge Hugo Pam of Chicago, Ill., who has just returned from Europe as one of the Society's European commissioners.

Mr. Straus said it was a great tribute to the immigrants who came here that they organized the Society, now with 40,000 members, in order to make the task of those who came after them somewhat easier.

He said there was a kind of compensation in history and declared it was significant that John Jacob Astor, who came to this country in the latter part of the eighteenth century, got his start by becoming the employee of an immigrant Jew named Levy, who taught him the trade of furrier, from which position Astor laid the foundation of his great fortune.

Although, he said, the conditions that resulted in fixing a limit on immigration were extraordinary and the policy probably has good reasons behind it, he declared that "'whatsoever the conditions" the policy was contrary to the historic spirit of the country.

Mr. Risley explained the necessity for the present limitation of immigration and said that Americanization was an educational and political growth which must ultimately supplant preconceived opinions, "and this progress may be seriously retarded by a suspicious or hostile attitude toward the alien." He made a plea for a "square deal" for the immigrant.

Telegrams were read from Governors of twenty-eight States, and other officials.

Rabbi Herbert S. Goldstein delivered the opening prayer and Rabbi M. S. Margolies gave the Benediction.

Cantor Josef Rosenblatt recited the Dedication Psalms.

ARK OF THE SYNAGOGUE

Presented to the New Home of the Hebrew Sheltering and Immigrant
Aid Society by Mr. and Mrs. Fischel
on the occasion of its dedication, June 5, 1921.

CHAPTER XXXVII

NEW BUILDINGS FOR THE RABBI ISAAC ELCHANAN YESHIVA

THE principal institutions with which Mr. Fischel had identified himself in the very earliest days of his communal work were all destined, it seemed, to grow in public estimation and usefulness, so that with the passing of the years they required new and larger accommodations with which to carry on their work.

This had been successively true of the Beth Israel Hospital, the Hebrew Sheltering and Immigrant Aid Society, Uptown Talmud Torah, Hebrew Free Loan Society and Home for the Daughters of Jacob and was now to be true of the Rabbi Isaac Elchanan Jewish Theological Seminary.

In the five years which had elapsed since the dedication in 1915 of this institution's new building at 9-11 Montgomery Street, it had, under the leadership of Dr. Bernard Revel, already outgrown its facilities and was unable to care for but a small part of the number of students who sought admission to its halls.

Mr. Fischel was again appointed chairman of a committee to purchase a site for a new structure or preferably to acquire a building already in existence, if a suitable one could be obtained.

The Home of the Daughters of Jacob had completed its new building at 167th Street, Teller and Findlay Avenues, the Bronx. Mr. Fischel, who was also chairman of the Building Committee of that institution, suggested to the directors of the Home that they sell their former building at 301-303 East Broadway to the Yeshiva, with the result that in November, 1920, this transaction between the two institutions was consummated.

Mr. Fischel then undertook the task of converting these buildings into a suitable structure for the Yeshiva, expending upon the operation six months of his time and energy, so that the new Yeshiva building was ready to be dedicated on April 3, 1921.

In his capacity as Chairman of the Building Committee, Mr. Fischel on that date turned over the keys of the building to the President and in his remarks called attention to the fact that when it was constructed for the Home of the Daughters of Jacob he had prophesied the next building of the Home would occupy an entire block. This prophecy had come true, Mr. Fischel pointed out, and it was his expectation that the next home of the Yeshiva likewise would occupy an entire block.

Once again Mr. Fischel's glimpse into the future proved an accurate one for this Yeshiva now owns nearly three whole blocks on upper Amsterdam Avenue, where, on a part of the property, three buildings are already under construction covering nearly a full block.

A week was given over to the dedication of the East Broadway building, each day being marked by a celebration conducted by a different organization, including those of the Rabbinate, educational institutions and the Yeshiva's alumni.

This event, as was the dedication of the first Yeshiva building, was hailed by the public and by the Jewish and English press as an occasion of the utmost importance to the future of traditional Judaism. One of the many articles which appeared at the time is herewith reproduced from the Jewish Tribune of April 9, 1921.

NEW YESHIVAH BUILDING IS DEDICATED

Sunday afternoon the new home of the Rabbi Isaac Elchanan Theological Seminary, 301-303 East Broadway, New York City, was dedicated. The ceremonies began with a march of the directors, members of the faculty and students from the old building, 9-11 Montgomery Street.

Harry Fischel, chairman of the building committee, presided and delivered a brief address, Rabbi M. S. Margolies delivered the opening prayer. He was followed by Nathan Lamport.

Gustave S. Roth was presented by Mr. Fischel with a gold key, with which he opened the new building.

Cantor Josef Rosenblatt sang several appropriate liturgical selections and recited a prayer in memory of Rabbi Isaac Elchanan Spector—the celebrated Rav of Kovno, after whom the institution is named. Those assembled marched into the building where speeches were made by the Rev. H. Masliansky, Rabbi J. Levenson and others.

Sunday evening a banquet in honor of the dedication was given, Rabbi Herbert S. Goldstein acting as toastmaster. Addresses were made by Rabbi M. S. Margolies, Rabbi Meyer Berlin, Rabbi Bernard Drachman, Rabbi Philip Klein, Sol Rosenbloom of Pittsburgh, and Julius Siegel, senior student of the Yeshivah. The sum of $20,000 was contributed by those present.

The ceremonies continued throughout the week, addresses being delivered on other days by Rabbi B. L. Leventhal of Philadelphia, Rabbi Solomon E. Jaffe, Rabbi E. M. Preil of Elizabeth, N. J., Dr. Meyer Waxman, Rabbi N. H. Ebin of Buffalo, Rabbi Sol Friedman of Pittsburgh, Rabbi Aaron D. Burack of Brooklyn, Rabbi D. B. Zvirin of Philadelphia and others.

Rabbi B. Revel, president of the faculty, owing to severe illness, was unable to take part in the celebration.

CHAPTER XXXVIII

LIVING UP TO A TRUST

WHEN in 1885, Mr. Fischel emigrated to America, his brother, Philip, with the latter's wife and three small children, two girls and a boy, remained in Russia in no better worldly condition than were his father and mother.

In December, 1890, Mr. Fischel decided to help his brother provide for his family and accordingly brought him to America where after several months he was able to earn a living. It was not long, however, before the Almighty saw fit to afflict him with typhoid fever and within a week after contracting this disease he was taken to the better world. His last words to Mr. Fischel were: "I am leaving my family in your hands."

Deeply mindful of the obligation imposed upon him, Mr. Fischel sent for his brother's wife and children, ranging in age from three to eight years, and settled them in Chicago, where Mrs. Philip Fischel had a brother, sister and several other relatives. From that time until his sister-in-law remarried and was able to care for the children herself, Mr. Fischel provided for the family's needs. After a few years the mother died and the three children were left orphans. The two girls then kept house for their brother, continuing to live with him even after his marriage.

Having promised his brother always to look out for his children, Mr. Fischel determined that when either of the girls should marry he would attend the wedding and lead them to the altar in place of their departed father. The younger sister, Mary, was the first to find a suitable helpmate and Mr. Fischel, who attended her marriage, which took place in Chicago, represented his late brother in every way.

Two years later the elder sister, Bessie, informed her uncle that she had become engaged and that her marriage was set for August 20, 1920. On this occasion, Mr. Fischel, with his wife and two unmarried daughters, Bertha and Rose, made the journey to Chicago for the wedding and were met at the station by the bride and groom to be. At the same time a committee of the Chicago branch of the Hebrew Sheltering and Immigrant Aid Society, headed by its president, Mr. Adolph Copeland, met them and extended an invitation to Mr. Fischel to attend a meeting at the Hebrew Sheltering House on Monday evening, August 23, for the purpose of giving the Chicagoans a first hand report concerning the purchase of the Astor Library Building.

Although reluctant to accept this invitation for the reason that he had expected to leave Chicago in time to keep an important business engagement in New York on that evening, Mr. Fischel saw the opportunity to secure a large contribution for the building fund of the H. I. A. S. and accordingly decided it was his duty to remain over. What was his surprise on reaching the hall to find a committee in evening dress waiting to escort him to a spacious dining room where tables were set for a repast for several hundred persons.

Following Mr. Fischel's report and his appeal to the gathering, a large sum of money was contributed by those present toward the building fund.

CHAPTER XXXIX

MARRIAGE OF HIS THIRD DAUGHTER

In view of Mr. Fischel's strenuous activities in communal life, he had formed the habit of spending a few days out of each month in Atlantic City, as a means of conserving his energy.

It was on December 31, 1920, while on one of these brief vacations, accompanied by his devoted wife and his two daughters, that his daughter Bertha met Dr. Henry A. Rafsky. There was a mutual attraction from the moment they met. After an unusually brief courtship they became engaged in February and were married on April 10, 1921. This union Mr. Fischel believes was certainly ordained by the Almighty.

The wedding was solemnized in the Congregation Kehillath Jeshurun, by Rabbis M. S. Margolis, Elias A. Solomon and the bride's brother-in-law, Rabbi Herbert S. Goldstein. Like the previous weddings in the family, it was attended by many outstanding leaders in American Jewry.

The ceremony was followed by a wedding supper in the home of Mr. and Mrs. Fischel. In honor of this happy occasion, Mr. Fischel made a contribution of $5,000 towards the Building Fund which was being raised at that time for the Hebrew Sheltering and Immigrant Aid Society of America.

Once more Mr. Fischel found occasion to express his gratitude to the Almighty for all His blessings, not only for giving him the means and the opportunity to serve his fellow men, but for vouchsafing to him the happy marriage of his children and enabling them to follow in the path laid down by him, both in religious and communal work.

Dr. Rafsky is connected with Lenox Hill and Beth Israel Hospitals. He is president of Medical Board of the Home of the Daughters of Jacob, and is the author of many papers on gastro-

MR. FISCHEL'S THIRD SON-IN-LAW,
Dr. and Mrs. Henry A. Rafsky and their children.

enterology. Besides his professional activities, he has found time to be an active trustee in the Congregation Kehillath Jeshurun. One of the unique accomplishments growing out of his endeavors in behalf of Orthodox Judaism, was his successful reorganization of the Jewish community in Beechhurst, Whitestone, L. I., into a unified Congregational Center which he effected during a short stay while on a summer vacation there.

Mrs. Rafsky is a member of the Religious School Committee of the Council of Jewish Women and a directress of the Home of the Daughters of Jacob, a member of the Executive Board of the Women's Branch of the Union of Orthodox Jewish Congregations of America; a directress of the Hebrew Day Nursery of New York and a member of the Women's Committee of the Yeshivah College Dormitory Fund. She is also affiliated with the Federation of Jewish Charities and the New York Chapter of Hadassah.

The couple have a strong inclination for communal work, with the result that they are giving a great deal of their time and service for the betterment of humanity.

CHAPTER XL

DEPARTURE FOR A SECOND VISIT TO PALESTINE

MR. FISCHEL had never entirely given up his thought of accomplishing something toward the development of Palestine, despite the fact that he had, in accordance with the wishes of Jewish leaders, abandoned for the time being his plan for the organization of the Palestine Development Corporation. With the completion of the building of the new Home for Immigrants, he determined to visit the Holy Land for a second time, with a view to determining from personal observation, what might best be done to advance the cause of the Jewish homeland. Accordingly on June 29, 1921, he engaged passage for Palestine for his wife, his youngest daughter, Rose and himself.

Although Mr. Fischel did his utmost to keep his sailing a secret, in some manner it leaked out and the directors of the Hebrew Sheltering and Immigrant Aid Society took advantage of the opportunity to tender Mr. Fischel a dinner in appreciation of the work he had done as Chairman of the Building Committee as well as to wish him bon voyage on his departure for the Holy Land.

The dinner, which was held in the auditorium of the reconstructed Astor Library Building, which had been dedicated only three weeks before as the new Immigrant Home, was the first social function arranged there and was attended by the directors of the institution, and their wives, the heads of a number of other institutions with which Mr. Fischel was affiliated, as well as by many public officials and others prominent in Jewish affairs in the city. The toastmaster was Judge Leon Sanders and addresses were delivered by Judge Otto A. Rosalsky, Hon. Samuel Koenig, chairman of the Republican County Committee of New York, Congressman Isaac Siegel and Rabbi Herbert S. Goldstein, who spoke on behalf of the Fischel family.

Mr. Albert Rosenblatt, chairman of the committee which succeeded in raising nearly half a million dollars for the new building, presented Mr. Fischel with a loving cup which bore the following inscription:

"Presented to Harry Fischel by the Building Committee of the Hebrew Sheltering and Immigrant Aid Society of America in recognition of his services as Chairman—Monday, June twenty-seventh, nineteen hundred and twenty-one."

At the conclusion of the banquet the President of the Institution, Mr. John L. Bernstein, who was the last speaker, took Mr. Fischel completely by surprise by unveiling a magnificent oil painting of the guest of the evening, which was presented to him in recognition of his work as a member of the Board of Directors. Mr. Bernstein in making the presentation, however, stated that it was the wish of the Board that Mr. Fischel should permit the portrait to be hung in the Board of Directors' Room and to remain the property of the institution.

Mr. Fischel was too overcome to respond to the President's remarks, and Rabbi Goldstein accepted the portrait in his behalf, giving it back to the Board to be used in the manner they had requested.

The following, which was published in the Hebrew Standard in its issue of July 2, 1921, describes the occasion succinctly:

HIAS GIVES FAREWELL TO HARRY FISCHEL,

ITS MOST LOYAL WORKER

The Board of Directors of the Hebrew Sheltering and Immigrant Aid Society of America tendered a dinner to Harry Fischel in recognition of his services as Chairman of the Building Committee of the new home and on the occasion of his departure on a visit to the Holy Land, Monday evening, at the HIAS building, 425-437 Lafayette Street.

Judge Leon Sanders was toastmaster and speeches eulogizing the work of Mr. and Mrs. Fischel were delivered by Judge Otto A. Rosalsky, Congressman Isaac Siegel, Albert Rosenblatt, Chairman of the Building Fund Committee, and John L. Bernstein, the president. The latter presented Mr. Fischel with a magnificent loving cup as a tribute from the members of the Building Committee. Rabbi Herbert S. Goldstein spoke for the family, after which an oil painting of Mr. Fischel was unveiled. The portrait is being placed in the Board room of the Society. Mr. Fischel in his response spoke of his desires and hopes and said his forthcoming visit to Palestine was dictated by a wish to be of some service to his people. Mr. Fischel donated $5,000 to the Building Fund. In the official program, the following tribute was paid to Mr. and Mrs. Fischel:

AU REVOIR

"The members of the Board of Directors, in bidding a temporary farewell to their colleague, have in mind the fact that Mr. Fischel has been the treasurer of the Society for more than 30 years and during that period has given loyal service.

"Mr. Fischel had for years had the vision of a beautiful home for the Society and the HIAS building at 425-437 Lafayette Street is the realization of that vision.

"Mrs. Fischel accompanies Mr. Fischel. She is the first vice-president of the Rose N. Lesser Auxiliary, affiliated with the Society and has thus energetically furthered our cause.

"May their journey be a most pleasant one and may they witness and participate in the rebuilding of Zion."

Mr. Fischel, accompanied by Mrs. Fischel and Miss Rose Fischel, sailed Thursday. They will be gone about three months.

On the day Mr. Fischel sailed for Palestine he received a number of telegrams and letters wishing him Godspeed, among them communications from the President of Beth Israel Hospital, addressed to Judge Sanders, from the Rabbi Isaac Elchanan Theological Seminary and from President Bernstein of the Hebrew Sheltering and Immigrant Aid Society, formally acknowledging Mr. Fischel's additional contribution of $5,000 made to the Building Fund on the eve of his sailing. These communications are given herewith.

Judge Leon Sanders, Chairman,
Dinner to Harry Fischel,   June 27th, 1927.
Hebrew Sheltering & Aid Society

Mrs. Cohen and I regret exceedingly that my illness prevents us from doing our share towards honoring Mr. Harry Fischel on the eve of his departure for the Holy Land. Knowing Mr. Fischel as I do, I am convinced that his trip to Palestine has not been planned solely for his personal pleasure and if the result of his journey will be as fruitful for good for Jews and Judaism in the Diaspora, Universal Israel will be the gainer even though his friends will have to forego the pleasure of his society during his absence. That his trip be blessed by God is the wish of his sincere friend.

JOSEPH H. COHEN, President
Beth Israel Hospital.

RABBI ISAAC ELCHANAN THEOLOGICAL SEMINARY

Mr. Harry Fischel,   June 28, 1921
276 Fifth Avenue
New York City
My dear Mr. Fischel:

Permit me to address to you a few lines on behalf of the Yeshivah and those who are anxious for its welfare and progress.

The faculty and student body, as well as all in the office feel their indebtedness and gratitude for your active work and assistance given the Yeshivah, during the period of constructing our new building, and for all you have done during the long time of your connection with it and wish to express to you their sincerest gratification and indebtedness.

At the time of your leaving this country for an extended trip to our Holy Land, they all wish you their sincerest Bon Voyage. May the Lord Almighty crown your visit to the Holy Land with success for the future of Palestine, and may He send you health on the trip and bring about the realization of your plans.

I am writing this letter upon the request of the Faculty and the student body and I need not tell you that I, personally, share these sentiments with them. I only hope that with your return from the Holy Land you will devote even more time to the

Yeshivah, the institution which is so dear to you and to which you are so devoted.

It is the unfortunate position of the Yeshivah that it could not make an elaborate farewell to you as other institutions did, but you surely have the good wishes and blessings of all of us, the blessings which come from our innermost hearts and which will be accepted by you, I hope, the same way.

Reiterating our thanks and best wishes and ardently hoping that the trip will be a healthy and a successful one for you and yours, I beg to remain,

Most respectfully yours,

SAMUEL L. SAR, Manager.

Mr. Harry Fischel   New York, June 29, 1921.
276 Fifth Avenue
New York City

My dear Mr. Fischel:

I beg to acknowledge the receipt of your favor of this day, enclosing check for $5,000 as your further contribution towards the building fund of the Hebrew Sheltering and Immigrant Aid Society.

You ought to be proud of the fact that yours is the largest contribution to the building fund, with the exception of that of the late lamented Mr. Jacob H. Schiff.

All through my life I have tried very hard not to be envious of other people, but I must admit to you that I would have considered myself very happy if I could emulate your example and match your contribution. I, of course, bear in mind not only the money contributed, but your contribution of the expert knowledge, indomitable energy and months of time which you were able to give to the erection of what, everybody agrees, is the greatest institutional building of its kind in the United States.

I am sure that all the members of the Board do appreciate the services which you have rendered in the cause of alleviating the sufferings of the Wandering Jew for the past thirty years, and especially, during the last few years, when to their knowledge you have given a great deal of your substance and all of yourself to that cause.

It is my sincere wish that the part that you will take in the upbuilding of the Jewish Homeland may be no smaller than that part you have taken in the upbuilding of HIAS.

May I in all solemnity exercise my prerogative as direct descendant of Aaron, the High Priest, and ask you to take with you upon your journey the priestly benediction of old.

With kind regards to Mrs. Fischel, I remain,

Yours sincerely,

JOHN L. BERNSTEIN, President.

The Fischels embarked on July 4 on the S. S. Berengaria, for Palestine. In accordance with Mr. Fischel's insistence on observing the dietary laws when traveling on either land or sea, he arranged with the Cunard Steamship Company, as in the case of his previous voyage to Europe, for facilities to this end.

Through the courtesy of Mr. W. H. Allison, General Caterer of the Cunard Line, a separate kitchen, with new cooking utensils, a Jewish cook and a Jewish waiter were provided. Mr. Allison even came from his home in the country the day prior to the sailing to see that these arrangements had been carried out.

Mr. Fischel received permission from the Captain of the Berengaria to use his private reception room as a temporary synagogue. Religious services were conducted there three times a day throughout the voyage and were attended by many of the Jewish passengers in the first and second class cabins.

The Fischels landed at Cherbourg and the day following arrived in Paris. The steamer on which they were scheduled to leave for Port Said was to depart on Friday, July 15, so that the party was compelled to wait in Paris until Thursday the fourteenth.

Mr. Fischel employed this time to visit the Paris branch of the Hebrew Immigrant and Sheltering Aid Society where he observed with satisfaction and interest, the work being done in behalf of refugees from many countries, compelled to remain in

Paris until their passports were vized by the American Consul. Accompanied by Mr. Shapiro, Manager of the Branch, Mr. Fischel and his wife and daughter, also visited the Rothschild Hospital and many other Jewish institutions in the French capital.

The party reached Marseilles on Friday to board the steamer "Nalderea" for Port Said and Mr. Fischel was just beginning to wonder how he should be able to observe the dietary laws on this part of his journey when, much to his surprise, he learned on boarding the vessel that instructions from Mr. Ballin, Chief Steward of the Cunard Steamship Company, had preceded him and that practically the same arrangements which had prevailed on the "Berengaria" had been provided for himself and the members of his party on the "Nalderea."

They reached Port Said on July 20 and proceeded by train to Cantarra where, crossing the Suez Canal, they took the train for Jerusalem, reaching that city on July 22.

Mr. Fischel was much impressed with the tremendous improvements which he beheld on every side. The city of Jerusalem was, indeed, almost unrecognizable to him as the place he remembered from his previous visit to the Holy Land, eleven years before.

For the first few days following his arrival he occupied his time with visits to the various institutions with which he had become acquainted on his first trip and everywhere was happy to note the great progress which had taken place under the British administration of the country.

CHAPTER XLI

MR. FISCHEL'S RECEPTION BY SIR HERBERT SAMUEL —PROVIDES HOME FOR CHIEF RABBI

THE news of Mr. Fischel's arrival reached the ears of His Excellency, The High Commissioner, Sir Herbert Samuel, as a result of which on Sunday, July 24th, Mr. Fischel was visited at his hotel by a military officer who presented to him an invitation to call upon the High Commissioner, at the Government House, on the following day.

In accordance with the English custom, this officer read the invitation before formally handing it to Mr. Fischel. The invitation said:

"His Excellency, The High Commissioner, requests the pleasure of your presence at the Government House on Monday the 25th at 2:30 P. M. Should this time be inconvenient for you, you are requested to name an hour that will be satisfactory."

Mr. Fischel, of course, accepted the appointment for the hour fixed by Sir Herbert, welcoming the opportunity of consulting the Commissioner as to what steps might best be taken to carry out the principal objective of his visit, that of aiding in the upbuilding of the Jewish Homeland.

On arriving at the Government House the following day Mr. Fischel was ushered into the private office of the High Commissioner, whom he found a modest English gentleman attired in ordinary civilian clothing.

Mr. Fischel had been warned by the High Commissioner's Secretary that owing to the great number of visitors, Sir Herbert was compelled to insist on a time limit of twenty-minutes for each audience. In order, therefore, to accomplish the utmost in the time allotted to him, Mr. Fischel counted every moment.

When the twenty minutes were up the Secretary entered the

apartment and informed the Commissioner that a certain official
was waiting for him. His answer was that this official should be
referred to Mrs. Samuel who would entertain him until he was
disengaged. Mr. Fischel's interview lasted an hour and three-
quarters, during which time, despite the Secretary's interruptions
at the expiration of almost every twenty-minute period, Sir Herbert disposed of all his callers either by sending them to Lady
Samuel or to someone else.

Mr. Fischel was greatly pleased with the results of his visit
to the High Commissioner, who suggested that he make a tour
through the Holy Land, visiting the principal towns and cities
and meeting the people and upon his return to Jerusalem that
he should again call upon him.

Mr. Fischel found that not only was Sir Herbert a man with a
true Jewish heart, ready and anxious to help the Jewish people
to establish their homeland, but that he was especially interested
in Chief Rabbi Abraham I. Kook, of whom he spoke in the
highest terms.

Sir Herbert pointed out to Mr. Fischel that whereas the Chief
representative of other religions in the city of Jerusalem each
occupied a suitable residence, Rabbi Kook was compelled to live
on the second floor of an old and dilapidated building where the
proper reception to visitors was impossible. He stated that this
residence ill-befitted the dignity of the high office of the Chief
Rabbi of Palestine. He therefore advised Mr. Fischel that he
would be glad if on the latter's return he would try to interest
a few wealthy Americans for the purpose of building a more
suitable home for the Chief Rabbi.

Upon reaching his hotel, Mr. Fischel placed the problem before
his wife and daughter, with the result that, after short deliberation, they reached the decision to build a home for the Rabbi
entirely at their own expense.

Mr. Fischel then called on Rabbi Kook and informed him of
his conversation with the High Commissioner and the determination he had reached. Rabbi Kook at first declined Mr. Fischel's

offer but after a great deal of persuasion finally agreed to accept the gift, not as a personal tribute but as one made in recognition of his office.

Mr. Fischel then questioned the Chief Rabbi at length as to his requirements. In a very modest way Rabbi Kook replied that his personal needs were small but that inasmuch as it was Mr. Fischel's wish to provide a residence for the Chief Rabbi of Palestine, rather than for an individual, such a building should comprise the following: a salon to receive special guests, a meeting room for the reception of the general public, a succah or tabernacle, a synagogue with a separate room for women, a dining room, kitchen, three bedrooms and bathrooms and rooms for male and female servants.

Mr. Fischel, following his interview with the Chief Rabbi went at once to an architect and instructed him to prepare plans in accordance with the latter's suggestions.

On terminating his interview with the High Commissioner Mr. Fischel had requested the privilege of presenting to His Excellency a number of Americans who had accompanied him to Palestine and who also were desirous of aiding in the upbuilding of the Jewish Homeland.

Sir Herbert at once granted this request and on July 27, Mr. Fischel had the honor of presenting to the High Commissioner, in addition to Mrs. Fischel and his daughter, Rabbi Aaron Teitelbaum, Mr. and Mrs. Max Abrams, Mr. and Mrs. Joseph Horowitz, Mr. Jacob Levy and son, Mr. and Mrs. Charles Werbelowsky, Mr. and Mrs. Max Hirschenoff, Mr. and Mrs. Hyman Goldman and son of Rochester, New York, and Mr. and Mrs. Abram Mazer.

Sir Herbert, in person, escorted the entire party through the Government House and expressed to them his hope for the formation of an American business corporation, having as its purpose the development of the country in behalf of the Jewish people.

A few days after this interview Mr. Fischel and his party left Jerusalem in several automobiles for a trip through the Holy

Land.   Upon reaching Nazareth the party found the chief official
of that place awaiting a visit from the High Commissioner, with
soldiers drawn up in military array for review.   Cavalry had
been stationed along both sides of the highway, forming a long
line, and when the Fischel party in its cars reached the beginning
of this line, it was mistaken for the High Commissioner's en-
tourage so that it was accorded military honors and was saluted
for the entire distance until the hotel in Nazareth was reached,
where, for the first time, they learned the occasion for this unexpected reception.

About half and hour later the High Commissioner with his
escort arrived at the same hotel and Mr. Fischel enjoyed the
great pleasure of seeing a Jewish Prince, the First Prince of
Israel since the destruction of the Temple 1900 years before,
received with the high honors befitting a ruler of the people.

After a tour through all of Palestine, the party returned to
Jerusalem where Mr. Fischel again called upon the High Commissioner and informed him of the plans he had arrived at, as a
result of his inspection of the country.   Mr. Fischel told the High
Commissioner that on his return to America he would undertake
the formation of such a commercial company as Sir Herbert had
declared was necessary for the development of the country and
also for the first time advised him of his intention to build a
residence for the Chief Rabbi, the cornerstone of which would be
laid before Mr. Fischel left for America.   This news was received
by Sir Herbert with expressions of great satisfaction and pleasure.

As soon as Mr. Fischel returned to Jerusalem he called a conference of the most representative Jews, to discuss with them
various questions concerning the proposed home for the Chief
Rabbi.   It was the consensus of opinion that the Chief Rabbi's
residence should be centrally located so that it might be easily
accessible to all the people of the city.

Represented at the conference were the directors of the organization known as the Central Committee Knesseth Israel, which
owned a number of buildings and much land in Jerusalem.

Among the holdings of the Knesseth Israel was a one story building occupying a large plot in the center of the city, facing the Rothschild Hospital.

The President of the organization suggested that the Chief Rabbi's residence be erected on the foundation of this building, which suggestion Mr. Fischel accepted because it seemed to him to insure the quickest and most practical way of carrying out the entire plan.

The cornerstone of the Chief Rabbi's residence was accordingly laid on Monday, August 15th. The ceremony was attended by the High Commissioner and his aides and many other officials, all in full military uniform, as well as by practically every Rabbi and the representatives of all the Jewish institutions in the Holy Land.

The exercises lasted throughout the entire day. On the following day, August 16, having seen this work begun, Mr. Fischel and his party left Palestine.

The return trip was planned so that Mr. Fischel was able to be present at the Zionist Congress at Carlsbad beginning September 4th to which he had been appointed a delegate by the Mizrachi, the religious branch of the Zionist Organization.

Before the Congress convened, Mr. Fischel attended many sessions of the delegates for the purpose of working out the program for the Congress and was named as a member of the Budget Committee, the work of which gave him an intimate knowledge of the scope and aims of the Zionist Organization.

Mr. Fischel, up to this time had not taken any active part in the executive work of the Zionist Organization and this was the first Zionist Congress he had attended. He was greatly impressed by the fact that such a large number of delegates had traveled thousands of miles with the sole purpose of extending their assistance in the upbuilding of Palestine, and he became more than ever anxious to carry out his earlier intention of using all his strength and influence to accomplish this end.

He was determined to assist in every way in helping to provide a refuge in Palestine for the thousands of Jews of nearly every land who were forced by circumstances to leave their homes and who looked to the Holy Land as their one haven, now that the doors of America were practically closed to them through the immigration restrictions which were imposed following the end of the war.

The final session of the Zionist Congress took place on Wednesday, September 7. The Fischels had already booked their return passage on the "Berengaria," on which vessel they had made the trip to Europe and which was scheduled to leave Southampton on Friday afternoon, September 10.

In order to arrive on time the Fischels left Carlsbad on September 6, reaching Paris on Wednesday the seventh. They were but a few hours ride from Cherbourg, from which port the "Berengaria" was to leave on Saturday afternoon. As embarking on the steamer on Saturday would have necessitated the desecration of the Sabbath, they decided instead of taking a train from Paris to Cherbourg, to go to London, and from there to Southampton, where they were able to board the steamer on Friday afternoon.

They found on reaching the "Berengaria" that the same arrangements which had been made by the Cunard Steamship Company for the observance of the dietary laws on their outward voyage had again been made for their return home.

They arrived at Sandy Hook on Friday morning, September 16th. Mr. Fischel was met at quarantine by a large number of reporters who were anxious to get his impressions of Palestine and particularly to secure his views of the British High Commissioner, Sir Herbert Samuel.

The purport of this interview was published in the Jewish Tribune of September 23rd, when the following article appeared:

SIR HERBERT AND AMERICA
HARRY FISCHEL MAKES INTERESTING DISCLOSURES
ON PALESTINE'S HIGH COMMISSIONER

Harry Fischel, prominent Jewish philanthropist, just returned with his wife and daughter from a summer spent in Palestine, is "enthusiastic over the future because of the idealistic spirit of the courageous settlers there and ready to use all my energy and a goodly part of my fortune for the development of the Jewish Homeland. Furthermore, I advise my friends to do the same."

Received shortly after his arrival by the High Commissioner, Mr. Fischel had several long conferences with Sir Herbert Samuel, in which the affairs of Palestine and development plans were discussed thoroughly and frankly. Few men have had such candid discussions with the High Commissioner as Mr. Fischel and with few men has the High Commissioner ever discussed affairs of the country so intimately and frankly. Here are Sir Herbert's views on the future of Palestine, particularly America's part in its making, as he gave them to Mr. Fischel and as Mr. Fischel reported his statement:

"Americans are always coming here and saying what they are going to do, but they never do it.

"With reference to the pogroms in Jaffa and Jerusalem: The Zionist Commission was so enthusiastic about the Balfour Declaration that it forgot a tenant was still occupying the premises. In order to move in, it was necessary either to buy out the tenant or fight. I am against fighting. When the Arabs heard of the Balfour Declaration they were frightened. It was explained how it would benefit them and bring money into the country; how the land would be improved; how work would be made for everyone. Instead, little money came from America, and the labor, which came in from Europe, was unskilled and competed with the Arabs taking their work away from them.

"The only way to prevent a recurrence of the trouble is to take the Arab in as a partner in everything you do in Palestine and show him a genuine friendly spirit. This can only be done, of course, if America supplies the money to start developing the country. Palestine needs money for business, not for charity. Charity will never build Palestine."

Mr. Fischel informed us that he will soon call a conference of his friends, at which time he will tender a complete report of his findings in Palestine and of his interviews with the High Commissioner, also a complete plan for the formation of a company to help develop Palestine.

CHAPTER XLII

$5,000,000 BUILDING AND LOAN COMPANY FOR

PALESTINE FORMED

THROUGHOUT his homeward voyage Mr. Fischel concentrated his thoughts upon the manner in which the formation of the commercial development company suggested by Sir Herbert Samuel might be accomplished, so that on his arrival, just before the Holy Days, he had already formulated complete plans for this ambitious undertaking.

He lost little time in putting these plans into action and immediately after the holidays issued an invitation to a number of representative men in the real estate field and other branches of industry to meet with him at his residence, 118 East 93rd Street, to discuss the steps to be taken.

This meeting, which was held on October 31, 1921, was largely attended and after Mr. Fischel had related the impressions he had gained from his observations in the Holy Land and had told of his interviews with the High Commissioner and his talks with people in every walk of life, he broached his plan for the organization of a $5,000,000 Palestinian Building and Loan Company.

The plan was immediately approved and there was not one among those present who did not agree to subscribe to the stock of the proposed corporation.

The plan, in detail, as Mr. Fischel then gave it and as it was later given to the press on November 25, 1921, was as follows:

When the Balfour Declaration was made public, I felt it my duty to help develop Palestine. I called together a number of prominent men in every line of industry and explained to them the advisability of organizing a Palestine Development Corporation.

245

It took little time to convince them that besides helping to build Palestine, this corporation would pay from a business standpoint. That same evening we decided to organize the Palestine Development Corporation with a capital of $10,000,000. Several hundred thousand dollars were subscribed by those present.

A committee was appointed to prepare a prospectus. We decided to go slowly until we should get the approval of some of the most influential men in America. We laid the proposition before Judge Julian W. Mack, the late Jacob H. Schiff, Nathan Straus, Henry Morgenthau, Judge Abram I. Elkus, and the American Consul to Jerusalem, Otto A. Glazebrook, who was then in New York. Those gentlemen were all enthusiastic about the proposition and promised their cooperation.

One day Mr. Schiff and Judge Mack, then President of the American Zionist Organization, requested me not to proceed with the organization, because the sale of the stock would interfere with the Palestine Restoration Fund, for which a campaign was then being waged. Knowing the interest Mr. Schiff and Judge Mack had in all matters of this kind, our committee decided to comply with their request and wait for a more opportune time.

No Housing Facilities

When Dr. Chaim Weizmann arrived in America, one of the points which he emphasized most strongly was that Palestine had no housing facilities. It could hardly accommodate the present population. Therefore, before any substantial immigration could be started, houses would have to be built on a large scale. The situation touched the inner strings of my heart, I felt that this being in my line, it was up to me to do all in my power to help build Palestine. I immediately decided that as soon as the "Hias" building would be completed, I would make the journey to Palestine and see what I could do.

Realizing that one man alone, with the best of intentions, could not accomplish much, I made every effort to persuade some of our successful builders to join me in that work. Those whom I approached on the subject, were willing to help both morally and financially, but not many were ready to make the trip with me. Finally I succeeded in interesting Jacob Levy of Levy Bros., well-known builders of Brooklyn, Joseph Horowitz, Charles Werbelowsky of Brooklyn, Max Abrahams of New York, as well as Rabbi Aaron Teitelbaum, representing a proposed Palestine Building Corporation.   While on the steamer we met Max Hirschenoff, Abraham Mazer of Brooklyn and Hyman Goldman and his son of Rochester, N. Y., who were also going to Palestine, and they joined our party. After several conferences with these gentlemen on the steamer, we unanimously agreed to unite to help build Palestine.

FEW WANT CHARITY

At Cantarrah, Egypt, we had an opportunity to interview many of the Chalutzim from all over Europe, who were also on their way to Palestine; young men and women from the richest families of Europe with the highest education. By their enthusiasm they reminded me of our Forefathers, who on receiving the Torah at Mt. Sinai said—Nah-ase Ve Nishma—"We will first take upon ourselves to do all that is required of us, and we will then hear what we are to do." This same spirit existed among these young men and women. They were ready and willing to make every possible sacrifice to help build up a Jewish Homeland in Palestine.

From the time we arrived until the hour of our leaving Palestine, I had occasion to see and converse with people of every kind, from the poorest unfortunates to the principal business men. All sorts of propositions were brought to me for consideration. What impressed me most was that only a small number wanted charity money, everybody wanted the opportunity to be a producer instead of a consumer.

We arrived in Jerusalem on Friday. On Sunday morning a messenger from the High Commissioner, Sir Herbert Samuel, came with an invitation, asking me to call on him at his residence in the Government House on Monday. Upon my arrival at the Government House I was immediately introduced to the High Commissioner, who made such a great impression upon me that at the moment, I felt it necessary to extend to him the message and blessing of the Jewish people of America, which I did, and for which he was very grateful.

The Government House is the finest building in Palestine, erected by the German Kaiser as his residence, at a cost of at least $5,000,000. The story goes that in building this residence, the Kaiser decreed that no Jew should perform any work on it. Is it not remarkable that this residence, in which no Jew was allowed to labor, is now occupied by the Jewish High Commissioner of Palestine? It certainly points the finger of God. It simply shows that the Messiah period is coming near to realization, and that the world at large is recognizing that the time has come for the Jewish people to come back to the land which was originally promised to them, and which they once occupied.

The High Commissioner informed me that Dr. Chaim Weizmann had communicated with him by letter and cable to make every effort to give me all assistance possible, in order to help me realize my desire to improve the housing situation in Palestine. We discussed at length every problem which confronts Palestine.

The next morning our party started out on an automobile tour of the entire country, to acquaint ourselves with all its resources. We visited every city in Palestine, large and small, as well as many of the colonies. We studied Palestine from every angle, the political, industrial and the housing situation.

AMERICAN BUILDING NOT PRACTICABLE

We started our investigation first in Jerusalem, where some building is being done by Jews. In Jaffa, building is projected on a much larger scale, because it is a port city, and also because the building material resources are better than in Jerusalem. In Haifa and Mount Carmel, some building is going on, and there are some factories for the manufacture of building material.

After a thorough and careful investigation everywhere, we came to the conclusion that the building of houses by American builders is not advisable, nor is it practicable. Instead of our building houses, we decided to help others to build, by loaning them from 50 to 60 per cent of the cost of the houses for a long term of years, payable in small installments, but at a fair rate of interest of from 6 per cent to 8 per cent, according to the location. At present, loans on real estate are difficult to obtain, and the interest is from 12 per cent to 18 per cent.

The reasons for our conclusions are as follows:

1.—We found several men in each city interested in the building trade and thoroughly capable of carrying on the building of houses on a large scale. It would, therefore, be useless for American builders to go into competition with them, except that I found that the laying out of the plans could be improved upon economically. This I did personally with the approval of the architects.

Arabs Profited

2.—We found several groups of men in the different cities, business men, recent immigrants and government officials, who had purchased large plots of ground. These groups are anxious to start building homes for themselves, but the largest majority of them have only half of the amount required for building deposited in the banks. All they need is a loan of the second half, which they will be able to pay off in small installments. Most of these families are now occupying rooms in houses owned by the Arabs, who are taking advantage of the shortage of houses. This shortage has been caused by the influx of about 10,000 Jewish people during the last two years, without any proportionate increase in housing facilities. These Arabs are charging as much as $20 a month for a two-room apartment with no water, nor even a bathroom. A number of Arabs are adding an additional story to their occupied houses by taking two or three years' rent in advance, and with that money they almost pay for the cost of an additional story.

More Building Possible

3.—The most important reason is that for the same amount of money which would be required to build one house, we would be helping to build nearly three houses, then, too, the investment would be so much safer, and we would be making room for a much larger number of families.

Therefore we decided that if American Jews expect to take advantage of the Balfour Declaration and are willing to help build a Jewish Homeland in Palestine, immediate steps should be taken to organize or to reorganize the several Palestine development companies which have lately been organized, into one large Building Loan Company, with a capital of at least $5,000,000, for the sole purpose of loaning from 50 to 60 per cent on houses to be built in and around the cities of Jerusalem, Jaffa, Haifa, Tiberias and Safed. These loans to be made for a long term of years and payable in small installments, at a rate of interest of from 6 to 8 per cent in accordance with the location.

Palestinian Jews Help

We have already arranged with several influential men, three in Jerusalem, three in Jaffa and three in Haifa, who have agreed to subscribe personally to the stock of this corporation, and serve on the board of directors. Each group in these cities has volunteered to do all the work required in connection with the making of the loans in their cities gratuitously in order to minimize the expense.

After going over the entire political and economic situation with Sir Herbert Samuel, he explained to me the benefits of the Balfour Declaration to the Jews of the world, also his expectation of the whole-hearted support of the Jewish people. He went on to say that he could not expect financial assistance from the Jews of Europe, on account of the low valuation of their money, but they were doing their share toward the upbuilding of Palestine by sending over strong and healthy men and women, the sinew of the country, full of energy and vigor, and ready to make any sacrifice.

Sir Herbert Disappointed

Sir Herbert expressed his disappointment in the American Jewish people. He stated that many Americans are coming to Palestine, laying before him all sorts of plans, but as soon as they leave they forget all about them, whereas the European Jews make no promises, but put their shoulders to the wheel and are making all sorts of sacrifices to help build the country.

I explained to him that the European Jew, upon leaving his country, severs all connections with it. Naturally, upon his arrival in Palestine, he has to make the best of it, as he has no other country to which he can go back. Whereas, the American Jew, upon his return to America, finds every hand outstretched to him, glad to receive him back under the protection of our beloved Stars and Stripes, and before he will extend his assistance to Palestine by investing his capital there, he wants to be assured that his investment will be protected.

APPROVES BUILDING COMPANY

I then laid before him our plan for the Building Loan Company, which met with his entire approval. He emphasized the fact that one of the reasons he was compelled to stop immigration into Palestine, is because there are no houses for the people to live in. To use his own words: "I do not desire to make Palestine a sanatorium, with people living in tents. Houses must be built before I will allow extensive immigration." He also remarked that the Building Loan Company would induce many people to build homes on a large scale, and it would supply occupation for a large number of immigrants in the building trade, skilled labor and unskilled labor. He further assured me that in order to safeguard our investment, he would see to it that the corporation laws of Palestine were modified, so that they might conform with the by-laws of the Building Loan Company.

After many conferences in Palestine with men in every walk of life, and later with several of the leaders at the Zionist Congress in Carlsbad (to which I was a delegate), and above all, after a long conversation with Dr. Weismann on the question of building in Palestine, I came to the following conclusion, which was agreed to by the High Commissioner.

THE ONLY WAY

If we wait for Palestine to be built by Palestinian Jews alone, Palestine will never be built. If we should wait until Palestine be built by European Jews, it will take a very long time. Even if we should wait to build Palestine with money collected in America from a charitable point of view only, Palestine will never be built.

The only way Palestine can be built, and should be built, is by American Jews, with American money invested on a solid business basis. And steps must be taken immediately in this direction, or we may lose this opportunity for which the Jewish people have been waiting for so many years.

One thousand dollars loaned will help build a home for a deserving family. One million dollars will help build homes for 1,000 families, and at the same time will furnish employment for several thousand people. Besides, the money collected from installments on the mortgages will again be invested in new mortgages, making it possible to help build more homes.

So favorable was the reaction to these plans by all those who attended the conference at Mr. Fischel's home, that he proceeded at once to the work of organizing the Corporation and called together at his office a Committee of those who had attended the first meeting. This Committee consisted of Jacob Levy, Joseph Polestein, Henry D. Weil, Joseph Ravitch, and S. A. Israel.

Steps were then taken to secure a charter and Judge Abram I. Elkus, former Ambassador to Turkey, was retained for this purpose.

At about this time the Annual Convention of the American Zionist Organization took place at which a number of prominent members severed their connection with that Organization. Among these was U. S. Supreme Court Justice Louis D. Brandeis, Federal Judge Julian W. Mack, Nathan Straus, the late Sol Rosenbloom, Robert Szold, Jacob DeHaas, Samuel J. Rosensohn, Julius Simon and Mrs. Joseph Fels.

This group then formed a corporation under the name of the Palestine Cooperative Company for the purpose of helping to establish different industries in Palestine. The main feature of this Company's program, however, was to form a Building, Loan and Mortgage Company on practically the same lines as had been decided upon by Mr. Fischel and his Committee.

In November, Jacob DeHaas, who was the Secretary of the new Brandeis faction among the Zionists, called upon Mr. Fischel with the suggestion that his Committee should join with this group with the aim of forming one strong corporation, rather than to have two separate organizations engaged in virtually the same work.

This plan appealed strongly to Mr. Fischel for the reason that he believed much quicker results could be obtained by taking advantage of a corporation already in existence, particularly where such men as Justice Brandeis, Judge Mack and Nathan Straus were interested. He therefore called his Committee together and laid the suggestion before them.

The members of Mr. Fischel's Committee were all real estate

men and favored a corporation they themselves should manage personally but since Mr. Fischel was convinced that the interests of the people of Palestine would be much better served through a merger of the two organizations, he arranged a meeting with Justice Brandeis, Judge Mack and Mr. DeHaas. At this meeting it was agreed that the Palestine Cooperative Company should form a subsidiary Company under the name of the Palestine Building Loan and Savings Association with a capital stock of $250,000 of which sum the Brandeis group should subscribe for shares to the extent of $125,000 and the remaining $125,000 of stock should be subscribed by Mr. Fischel and those working with him.

The Company was accordingly organized and Mr. Fischel was elected as Chairman of the Palestine Building, Loan and Savings Association. He started immediately to secure subscriptions to the stock with the result that the allotment of $125,000 which he and his Associates were to take was soon made up through Mr. Fischel's personal subscription of $25,000 and $100,000 subscribed by a number of his friends.

The late Mr. Sol Rosenbloom of Pittsburgh, one of the organizers of the Palestine Building Loan and Savings Association, at this time volunteered to go to Palestine in order to inaugurate the work of the corporation there. Before his departure he was tendered a dinner by the officers and directors of the Corporation which was held at the Hotel Astor on January 8, 1922.

At this dinner Judge Mack told of the great interest Mr. Fischel had taken in the formation of the Palestine Building, Loan and Savings Association and declared that he had been largely instrumental in the success of the project. Judge Mack expressed the hope that Mr. Fischel, with his wide knowledge of conditions in Palestine, would be able to go there personally to complete the organization of the Association in accordance with American methods and system.

The press gave considerable space to the dinner to Mr. Rosenbloom, the New York Times on January 9, 1922, containing the following account of the function:

SOL ROSENBLOOM ENTERTAINED

Palestine Development Council Entertains Pittsburgh Banker—
Receives $75,000 Cash and Large Pledges

The departure this week of Sol Rosenbloom, Pittsburgh banker, for Palestine, where he will undertake the establishment of the Credit Union Bank, was signalized last night by a dinner in his honor at the Hotel Astor. It was given by the Palestine Development Council, of which Mr. Rosenbloom is Treasurer. A large gathering of noted New York Zionists attended the dinner.

Supreme Court Justice Julian W. Mack, Chairman of the Council, who presided, declared that "if Palestine is to be built up as a Jewish homeland it must be built up in an orderly and businesslike way. Unless business can be conducted there, there can be no future to the land. It is necessary that agriculture, industry and commerce be conducted in Palestine as it is in other lands and Palestine can in that way maintain a self-sustaining and self-respecting people."

Rabbi Stephen S. Wise said that he had finally recuperated from the meetings at Cleveland last June, when the present officers of the Palestine Development Council ceased to remain heads of the Zionist Organization of America.

"This is a peace meeting," he said. "There can be peace only when men or groups have been at war. We have not quarreled. We have dared to insist upon the maintenance of certain moral standards in and for Palestine and we have dared to be insistent in our demands because Palestine is deserving of our best. We believe that the only way to serve and to build up Palestine is to insist upon the highest in the standards and in the conduct of those who are entrusted with leadership."

Subscriptions to the council were announced. Some were contributions and others were the purchase of stock in the organization. Harry Fischel of New York pledged $100,000 and gave $25,000 cash. Sol Rosenbloom gave $50,000 and pledged $200,-

000 more in the course of ten years. A pledge of $60,000 from Mrs. Mary Fels was announced. Other pledges of almost fifty thousand dollars were also reported.

Nathan Straus was scheduled to speak but he asked to be excused because he was not feeling well. Other speakers were Miss Ruth Franklin, Julius Simon, Harry Fischel, Louis S. Posner, Captain Alexander Aaronsohn and Mr. Rosenbloom.

CHAPTER XLIII

ADVANCES PLAN FOR HOUSING AMERICAN WORKERS —BUILDS AGAIN ON BROADWAY

AT the time that Mr. Fischel was giving a large part of his attention to Palestine and its problems he also was giving considerable thought to the housing situation in New York which had become increasingly difficult for a large part of the population owing to the scarcity of certain types of living accommodations and the high rentals that were being exacted.

This condition affected particularly the working people and others in moderate circumstances. While there was an over-production of the middle class and more expensive apartments, the poor man, able to pay not more than $8 or $9 a room, could scarcely find a place in which to live at this price. This condition had existed during and since the war and not only was it impossible to find homes in the city proper at these rentals but even in the suburbs they were not to be had.

Applying himself to this problem as he had previously applied himself to the matter of relieving the financial situation affecting real estate through the amortization of mortgages, Mr. Fischel suggested a solution of the new difficulty. Many proposals for relieving the acute housing situation in New York were made at this time, one of them by Mr. Samuel Untermyer, and Mr. Fischel's plan, differing largely from that of Mr. Untermyer, naturally attracted wide attention.

His thought was, that if those engaged in the building trades were to build for themselves with their own labor, they would be able to save a large part of the cost of construction, thereby not only adding to the housing facilities and bringing a substantial reduction in rentals, but making it possible for the workers, in

THE FISCHEL BUILDING

*A modern mercantile structure on upper Broadway,
at the southeast corner of Broadway
and 37th Street. Erected by Mr. Fischel in 1922.*

time, to become the owners of their homes through such cooperative building.

This proposal was heralded generally as being a practical one
that would be productive of most beneficial results. The New
York Times, among other papers, in its issue of December 23,
1921, announced the plan, extensively as follows:

HOUSING PLAN FOR BUILDING TRADES
BUILDER WOULD HAVE LABOR ERECT AND OCCUPY OWN HOUSES.
COST REDUCED BY 25%

Workers, Constructing Own Apartment to Cost $60,000, Would
Supply $20,000 in Day Labor

Workers from the various building trades unions, acting on a
co-operative basis, could, with the help of a financial institution,
successfully erect their own tenements at a cost reduction of 20
to 25 per cent, according to a plan outlined yesterday by Harry
Fischel, the well-known builder.

The reduced cost, Mr. Fischel said, would represent the contribution of the artisans, who would, of course, be working without pay.

Mr. Fischel said he drew up his suggested plan after finding
what he said were some fundamental objections to Samuel Untermyer's $100,000,000 tenement-building project.

An outline of the plan has been sent to Mr. Untermyer and to
the President of the Building Trades Council. Discussing the
plan, yesterday, Mr. Fischel said:

"I have been watching very carefully the progress made by
Mr. Untermyer for increasing the housing facilities in the City
of New York. Mr. Untermyer has certaintly accomplished a
whole lot in getting the Metropolitan Life Insurance Company
to agree to loan a large sum of money for the purpose of building
cheap houses near New York for a class of people who cannot
afford to pay more than $8 or $9 a room.

"I believe it is a good, humanitarian act on the part of the
officers of the Metropolitan Life Insurance Company to go out
of their way to comply with his request. It is also praiseworthy

on the part of the Thompson-Starrett Company to offer to construct a large number of buildings without any profit, and it is certainly praiseworthy of the building trades unions, the members of which are willing to work six hours a week without pay.

OBSTACLE TO UNTERMYER PLAN

"I would like to call to Mr. Untermyer's attention the fact that no institution will make a loan on a house before said house is nearly finished, even if the institution shall agree to make such loan in the form of a building loan; it will, likewise, not advance any money until the building is at least one or two stories high.

"Under the circumstances, did Mr. Untermyer stop to think that it is necessary to have some one who is going to buy the land and furnish the necessary capital to bring those houses to such a position that an institution will be able to make a payment on the loan.

"Furthermore, no insurance company, nor any other institution, would loan more than 60 to 65 per cent of the cost of the building. While it is true that the offer of the Thompson-Starrett Company and the offer of six hours a week of labor free would reduce the cost of the building 10 to 15 per cent, which may make it possible for an institution to loan 75 per cent of the cost, and while it may make it somewhat easier, there must be some one who would be willing to take the big initial responsibility in carrying such a project into effect.

"Under the circumstances it is clear that unless such individual or corporation is available, this proposition with all its merits and the generosity of the Metropolitan Life Insurance Company and the Union men could not be accomplished.

"I am personally very much interested in the housing situation. In fact, I am responsible for the amortization of mortgages, which has been adopted by a good many institutions, and which gives people a chance to pay off their mortgages gradually, instead of calling for the entire amount when it is due.

"I have therefore given a great deal of consideration to this housing situation, and would suggest the following proposition, which I believe could be carried out in a very short time.

"Make arrangements with the building trade unions to organize groups of different trades for the purpose of owning and building a house for each group on a cooperative plan.

A 24 PER CENT. REDUCTION

"A house which is to accommodate twenty families should be built by fifteen men from the different building trades. All these men are to furnish the labor for all the houses free of charge. In this way almost the entire labor on the building could be supplied without the necessity of investing any money for same, which will amount approximately to about 20 to 25 per cent of the cost of the building. This would give a chance to each one of those men to own an apartment without putting in any money; furthermore, they would be able to buy the material for such houses at a much lower rate than the prevailing market price.

"When each house will be completed fifteen families will be able to have their own apartment. Having taxes free for the next ten years, all they would have to pay would be the interest on the mortgage, water, taxes and insurance. The five apartments left could be rented and would bring enough to cover the interest charge on the house with all other expenses.

"To take a concrete example, a five-story house, 50 by 100 feet, with four families on a floor, each having four or five rooms and bathroom, would cost approximately $60,000. Under ordinary circumstances an institution could loan two-thirds, namely $40,-000. The labor on such a house and the deduction of any builders' profit would equal the other $20,000 necessary for the operation.

"The interest on $40,000 at 6 per cent would mean $2400 and together with the insurance, water charges and incidentals would bring the running expenses on the house up to $3000 a year.

"The five apartments which would be left for renting would pay not alone the necessary expenses of running the house, but would even be sufficient to amortize the mortgage somewhat.

"While to carry out this plan would also require a substantial amount of money, it would not be anywhere near the amount required under the first plan. All that would be necessary is a small sum to pay on the land and some money for incidentals to carry up the foundation.

"For this purpose, I suggest that a call shall be issued to a group of public-spirited men, who shall subscribe to the stock of a corporation which shall be organized for that purpose, with sufficient capital to begin buying land and start building several houses.

"I would also suggest that each one of the apartment owners shall pay from $20 to $25 per month for the purpose of paying off the money, advanced by the corporation.

"When that is all paid up, the payment of this nominal rent can be continued until the entire mortgage will be paid up, which would take less than ten years. Under this proposed plan, each workingman in the building trade, by simply sacrificing a few weeks of his time, can own an apartment without paying any money, and have the benefit of free rent forever.

"I am fully convinced that a capital of $500,000 would be sufficient to buy land and start a number of houses, as demanded by the trades unions, and the number of houses can be increased."

In order to extend the scope of his charities and to meet the many additional calls which came to him with each succeeding year, Mr. Fischel decided at this time to endeavor to increase his wordly possessions so that he might better keep pace with the ever growing demands upon him.

He therefore determined to renew his building operations with another large construction enterprise. On January 15, 1922 he succeeded in obtaining possession of a large parcel of land on the South East corner of Broadway and 37th Street, immediately opposite the site of the building he had erected in 1913, nine years previously, and which he had sold to Mr. Ruben Sadowsky.

When Mr. Fischel erected the Sadowsky Building it was the first mercantile building in this section of Broadway. Since that time the locality had rapidly developed into one of the best neighborhoods for business in the city and he decided to erect on the new site a sixteen story building for use of the best type of merchants.

The acquisition of this property, one of the most expensive locations in New York, with Mr. Fischel's plans for the building he proposed to erect, created a great deal of interest in the real estate world and, as was to have been expected, evoked a considerable amount of comment.

The New York Times on January 18, 1922, contained this announcement of the project:

"BROADWAY CORNER IMPROVEMENT WILL INVOLVE $7,500,000

Harry Fischel to Pay $6,000,000 to Hoe Estate For Use of 37th St. Site: To Spend $1,500,000 on Building

The group of old buildings at the southeast corner of Broadway and Thirty-seventh Street is finally to give way to a big business building, a structure that will cost $1,500,000 to build. This was decided yesterday after months of negotiations between Harry Fischel, builder, and the Hoe Estate, which has owned the property for the last thirty-five years.

It was reported several weeks ago that Mr. Fischel had secured the corner, but this was denied by Frederick Fox, treasurer of the Robert Hoe Estate Company, the holding concern of the Hoe family. He said that negotiations were pending. These negotiations were concluded yesterday by Frederick Fox & Co., when Mr. Fischel and the Hoe Estate representatives settled the difficulties that had held the deal open. Mr. Fischel takes the property for twenty-one years, with two renewals of twenty-one years, each, at a rental that is estimated will total $6,000,000.

A sixteen-story building will be erected on the property, which has an area of 14,000 square feet. It will extend along Broadway to the Van Ingren property, on the north side of Thirty-sixth Street from Broadway to Sixth Avenue, which the Greenwich Savings Bank secured last spring as a site for a fine building. The Fischel structure design will be influenced by the bank improvement, for it is the aim of the builder and the bank directors to make the block one of the most attractive on Broadway. The south side of the building, which will tower many stories above the bank quarters, will be finished in the same material and with as much care as the street facades of the structure. When the structure has been completed the bank will take a mortgage on it. The building will not cover the Sixth Avenue and Thirty-seventh Street corner, for the Hoe family has other plans for that property. Joseph Ravitch, who has been associated with Mr. Fischel in other building projects, will erect the building. Sommerfeld & Steckler will design the structure. It will be planned especially for the millinery trades."

It was at the insistence of Mr. Joseph Ravitch, who continued to be associated with Mr. Fischel, that this new building, one of the largest in the section, was named the Fischel Building.

In less than a year from the time the undertaking was started the building was completed and occupied by some of the most prominent merchants in New York.

CHAPTER XLIV

AN INTERVAL OF RENEWED WAR RELIEF EFFORT

CONTRARY to the hope of all who for four long years had been engaged in the work of raising funds for the relief of the Jewish sufferers through the war, the signing of the Armistice and the cessation of hostilities failed to lessen the need for assistance.

The post-war period, indeed, increased the calls on America for aid for thousands of Jewish refugees and others who continued to face indescribable hardship and suffering, so that even down to the present day it has been impossible at any time to discontinue the efforts in behalf of these unfortunates.

The ending of actual war-fare, on the other hand, had the effect of turning the public mind in America away from the necessities of the situation and made it increasingly difficult to procure funds, with the result that all of the war relief agencies had slackened their efforts.

The Central Committee for the Relief of Jews Suffering through the War, in common with other Committees, had largely lessened its activities but was confronted with urgent pleas from the Jews in the various devastated areas for further assistance. It was finally decided that a new drive should be undertaken to help particularly the Jewish institutions which were without funds and whose survival was absolutely necessary for the continuance of Jewish life. In accordance with this decision campaigns were again conducted throughout the United States in every city and town, large and small.

Mr. Fischel, who had continued as Treasurer of the Central Relief Committee, in January 1922 received an urgent plea from the Chairman of the Central Committee's drive in New Haven, Conn., to attend the most important conference that had yet been held in that State in relation to aid for European Jewry. This plea, which he felt he could not refuse, was as follows:

SHAPIRO & SHAPIRO
Attorneys and Counselors at Law
SUITE 312 MEIGS BUILDING
BRIDGEPORT, CONN.

Mr. Harry Fischel,   January 23, 1922.
118 East 93rd Street,
New York, N. Y.

Dear Mr. Fischel:

Connecticut is planning the largest and most important conference ever held in our State to precede our new campaign for the war sufferers in Europe, under the auspices of the American Jewish Relief Committee, co-operating with the Central and People's Relief Committee.

Leading co-religionists from twenty-five cities and towns in our State, which has accepted a quota of $150,000, will be present at this conference, which is to take place at the Hotel Taft, in New Haven, next Sunday, January 29th, at two o'clock in the afternoon.

We would consider it a privilege if you could deliver an address on this occasion, which, if my recollection serves me right, will be your first visit to this State in this cause, and I hope that you may find your engagements such that you will be able to accept our invitation.

Colonel Isaac M. Ullman and Judge Jacob Caplan, who are respectively State Treasurer and Secretary, join in this request as we feel that Connecticut, emerging from the industrial depression, wishes to do its utmost towards the success of this campaign and know that your being with us will prove most opportune and of the greatest assistance.

With kindest personal regards, I am

Very sincerely yours,

CHARLES H. SHAPIRO,
Chairman for Connecticut.

Although Mr. Fischel had not made it a practice to speak at public functions he went to New Haven on the date fixed, at which time he made the following address, which in reality formed a complete history of the work of the Central Jewish Relief Committee throughout its several years of existence:

My friends:

The Central Relief Committee, of which I have the honor to be treasurer, was the first Committee to be organized in aid of our brethren abroad, coming into being on October 8th, 1914, by virtue of the efforts of the Union of Orthodox Jewish Congregations of America. We have collected over $9,000,000 in sums large and small, much of which money could never have been raised, but for the fact that in the early days, every Orthodox Jew throughout the country, as many still do, considered it a holy obligation to constitute himself an active worker of the Central Relief Committee. Our people responded to our call, because they knew that our Committee, in particular, represents Orthodox Jewry abroad and that our pressure would surely be used to the end, that Judaism as such, should not be wiped out because of social and economic changes that might take place, but would be strengthened by the manner in which we would see to it, the funds should be distributed. We have always cooperated in Joint Distribution Committee drives as we are now doing.

You can well understand the amount of work entailed in the handling of small amounts, and what a tremendous task it was for us to be able to get in touch with every city, large or small, throughout the United States and Canada, including a few of the South American countries, to say nothing of places where the number of Jews was represented by only one or two families.

The Central Relief Committee is interested in this Drive, because it realizes that the care of the 300,000 or more orphans, has placed upon us a sacred obligation, not alone of caring for them physically but also of making sure that they are so brought up that they will be an asset to real Judaism.

The medical and sanitary aid rendered to communities abroad and calculated to check disease and lessen the death rate, is a work that requires no apology, but its duration is limited because after we shall have equipped the various hospitals with instruments, modern surgical appliances, etc., and have obtained the cooperation of the local physicians, as members of the local sanitary boards, they will be able to continue that work of their own accord without further aid from us.

The Credit Associations,—which are being subsidized out of the funds to be raised largely through this campaign—with the change for the better of industrial conditions everywhere, which we all hope for, will naturally afford to our people abroad the opportunity to regain the position of self dependence which they formerly occupied.

There is one work in particular, however, that concerns the Central Relief Committee most. This task is included in our cultural program, which concerns itself with the preservation of Judaism. We feel that the children as they grow up, must continue to respect our holy traditions and practice those religious rites, without which they must prove, in the years to come, a hindrance and not an asset to Judaism. If we care for Judaism in its broader aspect, we must continue to inspire the feeling of pride in the child; we must instill in the little ones that religious spirit which not alone makes them better Jews, but better men and women, and incidentally, assures their respect for either parent and for the memory of their departed. The Central Relief Committee has recognized that the doing away with the Talmud Torahs, Chadorim and Yeshivas in many instances cannot be permitted to continue. Just as soon as we had an opportunity to learn the exact status of affairs in that respect, we took it upon ourselves to subsidize all the schools in the various countries, and have afforded them the assistance, without which, thousands upon thousands of children would today be compelled to forego schooling to which they are entitled.

In Poland alone, our aid has been extended to 328 cities and small towns and 502 Jewish educational institutions are receiving our grants, 103,000 children thus being looked after. These figures are based upon a report received by us some time ago, and by now, I dare say that, with the additional amounts forwarded to our Committee abroad they have been able to further extend their important work. It is claimed that over 400,000 children in Poland alone require support and if only slightly over 100,000 children are able to be reached the reflection is not one aimed at us, but proves that the Orthodox Jews all over the country have failed sufficiently to recognize this particular work, as their holy obligation.

Two-hundred and ninety-five Talmud Torahs, 15 Talmud Torah Yeshivas, 15 Yeshivas and various other types of schools, including kindergartens, high schools and teachers' institutes were enumerated in the report that I quote from.

The following countries have received direct assistance for cultural work from the Central Relief Committee, and the amounts represent a period of fourteen months only.

Austria	$811.10
Czecho-Slovakia	15150.00
Russo-Carpathia	1850.00
Constantinople	2000.00
Germany	3386.00
Hungary	5400.00
Latvia	11400.00
Lithuania	52320.30
Poland	72869.30
Palestine	118613.30
Roumania	1250.00
Russia & Ukrania	7091.81
Vilna & Vicinity	33250.00
Rabbis	3600.00
	———— $361,391.81

If I had the figures showing how many children have been thus enabled to receive the care and education, which but for us and I might say but for you, would have been impossible, you would indeed feel proud of what you have done and prouder still of the work that you must pledge yourself to do from now on.

We trust that in consequence of the work of reconstruction, which will be done with the money collected through this drive, many of the parents now unable to pay for their children's education, will be able to do so when they are again on their feet. But until then, and it is going to take some time, you must not forget that Judaism is on trial and must fight for its very existence; for it must fight not alone its outer but its inner enemies. You must not forget that whatever governmental support may have been obtained for the maintenance of Jewish schools, has been withdrawn completely. You must also remember that in the so-called Public Schools, where formerly admissions were limited as to the number of Jews, conditions were seldom as bad as now. Even

the small percentage which was formerly admitted was done
away with almost everywhere, except in Hungary where they
have been recently reinstated for the first time.

The condition of the refugees is most deplorable. Many of
the cities from which they came have been destroyed. Many of
the countries from which they came, have nothing to offer to
them upon their return. Many of the countries to which they
might have gone, no longer extend to them the welcome of former
years. In every large city of Europe, in the Jewish quarters,
refugees abound from Ukrania. The stories they have to tell are
too horrible to listen to, and that is why I will not narrate any of
the experiences told to me while abroad last year, because they
would provoke your tears, and I am here not to draw upon them
for they are useless, excepting insofar as they evince sympathy.
What we want you to do is not alone to give of your sympathy
but of yourself by rendering service that will tax all of your
energy, all of your spare time and of your means to an extent that
will truly express sacrifice of the highest type.

When I was in Carlsbad last year, as a delegate to the Zionist
Congress, I met the man who truly represented our people in
various parts of devastated Europe. They all complained that
hard hit as they are, because of conditions, they expected that
with the return of those of our people who left in the early stages
of the war, conditions would become more trying. They emphasized the over-crowding of the schools, the lack of proper buildings, lack of proper apparel, which hinders the child from attending school during the winter, and a thousand and one instances,
reflecting upon the needs of various type and kind.

In the figures enumerated in relation to countries, you will,
perhaps, have noticed that we have devoted more money for
education in Palestine than in any other country. The reason for
that is due to the fact that Palestine has always had the support
of the world at large, and now receives aid mainly, or almost exclusively, from America.

When I was in Palestine last year, I had the extreme pleasure
of visiting the various schools supported by us, and it would have
done your heart good, had you been with me, to see the wonderful progress the children are making. Upon these children we
must concentrate, as never before, because they are our only
hope for the future of that country.

While I came here to talk to you as the Treasurer of the Central Relief Committee, however, I want to impress upon you that in this drive, we have united all our efforts, and have instructed all our representatives throughout the United States, to put their shoulders to the wheel, and work for this united drive. I therefore feel the right to plead with you, not as a representative of the Central Relief Committee only, but as one who is devoted heart and soul, both morally and financially, to this great and probably the last drive for the rehabilitation of these poor war sufferers, and especially for these poor orphans, whose parents have left them in our charge, and we ought to consider it a great privilege to be in a position to help those who cannot help themselves.

It has fallen to the privilege of American Jewry to lift our people out of their struggle and true to our habit as of old, we have done our best. Doing our best is not enough, we must do better. Yours is the opportunity and yours will be the blessing when you have accomplished this task.

As a result of this and other addresses, the meeting was very successful and resulted in the raising of a large sum of money for the new campaign.

CHAPTER XLV

PALESTINE HOME BUILDING PLANS GO FORWARD— THE RUTENBERG HYDRO-ELECTRIC POWER PLANT FOR JERUSALEM

THE bringing to fruition of the elaborate plans for the financing of the contemplated improvements in Palestine required no end of arduous and exacting detail but Mr. Fischel permitted none of his other activities to interfere with the progress of this work, which he regarded as of primary necessity and importance to the future of the Jewish people.

One of the first steps toward the actual functioning of the Palestine Building Loan and Savings Association, organized as a subsidiary of the Palestine Cooperative Company and both of which were constituents of the Palestine Development Council, was a meeting of the representatives of the three corporations. This joint meeting took place at the office of Nathan Straus on February 22, 1922.

The minutes of this meeting which are of historical interest, herewith follow:

A meeting was held at the office of Nathan Straus on the 22nd day of February, 1922, at which the following were present:

On behalf of the Palestine Development Council: Justice Louis D. Brandeis, Judge Julian W. Mack, Dr. Stephen S. Wise, Mrs. Joseph Fels.

On behalf of the Palestine Cooperative Company: Judge Julian W. Mack, Harry Fischel, Bernard Flexner, Robert Szold, Samuel J. Rosensohn and Emil Weinheim, and Jacob de Haas on behalf of the Central Committee.

The following resolutions were unanimously adopted:

1—That the proper officers of the Palestine Cooperative Company be authorized to set aside from its funds the sum of $250,-

000 for the purpose of instituting a Building Loan and Savings Association in and about Jerusalem.

2—That the Board of Directors notify the High Commissioner of Palestine that the Palestine Cooperative Company has the capital necessary for the organization and operation of a Building Loan and Savings Association in and about Jerusalem, and is prepared to begin business.

3—That the Board of Directors transmit to the High Commissioner a proposed ordinance permitting the organization of a Building Loan and Savings Association in Palestine, and providing the machinery for its supervision.

4—That the Building Loan Committee of the Palestine Cooperative Company proceed with the preparation of the plans and details for the operation of the Building Loan and Savings Association.

5—That the Committee consist of the following members:

> Mr. HARRY FISCHEL, *Chairman*
> SAMUEL J. ROSENSOHN
> ROBERT SZOLD
> BERNARD FLEXNER

6—That the committee proceed to give the fullest publicity to the entire plan for the organization and operation of a Building Loan and Savings Association in and about Jerusalem.

It was further resolved that since Mr. Bernard Flexner is shortly to go to Palestine that he and Mr. Rosenbloom are authorized to carry out the plans adopted by the Building Loan Committee, establish suitable offices in Jerusalem, engage the proper manager and begin business as soon as the ordinance is approved by the High Commissioner.

The Board congratulated Mr. Harry Fischel upon his personal achievement not only in completing his immediate task of raising $100,000 in stock subscriptions, but in his efforts to bring the whole plan to a successful conclusion. Mr. Fischel promised to continue his efforts to develop and enlarge the building loan feature of the Company.

> Signed, SAMUEL J. ROSENSOHN,
> Secretary.

Following this meeting formal notification was given to Sir Herbert Samuel, that the Company was now ready to function.

The notification was in the form of a letter addressed to the High Commissioner of Palestine by Judge Julian W. Mack and was as follows:

March 9, 1922.

My dear Sir Herbert:

I am sure that you will be interested to know that the Palestine Cooperative Company now has the necessary capital for launching a Savings and Loan Association, formed primarily for the benefit of wage-earners and other persons of limited means, to enable them to accumulate their savings and thus eventually acquire homes.

Such a company will further the association of persons (in the beginning in and about Jerusalem) to whom the obligation of a small monthly contribution would be a stimulus to continue saving. The amount contributed, increased by legitimate interest, will constitute a fund from which mortgage loans will be made to members to aid them in procuring modest homes. It will thus encourage industry, frugality, saving and homebuilding among its members.

To do this effectively, an ordinance will be necessary to permit the incorporation of Savings and Loan Associations in Palestine. We purpose incorporating a company under such ordinance, if enacted, and are prepared to start operations in Jerusalem. Mr. Sol. S. Rosenbloom, treasurer of the Palestine Cooperative Company, is by this time in Palestine, and Mr. Bernard Flexner expects to be there on April 21, 1922. Each is a director of and together represent the Palestine Cooperative Company. They are ready to organize the Company so that it may begin operations.

As a guide for the necessary legislation, which may, perhaps, be of service to your legal secretary, we attach hereto a suggested ordinance, modeled on the New York Statute, in our judgment the best in the United States.

All legislation of this kind in the United States contemplates the possible payment of some amount in excess of legal interest, called a premium, not for the purpose of securing larger profit to the Association, but as a possible means of determining which of the members should have the loan, and provides that the payment of such premiums should not be deemed a violation of any statute against usury. While it is not contemplated that any premiums will be charged for loans by this company and our proposed by-laws will not provide therefore, the business may so develop that that may be the sole means of determining which of the members should have the loan. For this reason it seems advisable to permit it to be done.

The primary essential to the success of Savings and Loan Associations is proper and effective governmental supervision. In New York, this is secured through examiners under supervision of the Banking Department. We trust that the laws of Palestine will likewise provide for such supervision.

The Palestine Cooperative Company proposes owning stock in the Building and Loan Association to be formed to operate in Jerusalem. Sufficient capital has been secured and set aside specifically for the purpose. A committee of the Palestine Cooperative Company has prepared a general plan of operation and is preparing a detailed set of by-laws. This committee is headed by Mr. Harry Fischel, a very successful real estate operator in New York, who is fully familiar with the operation of Building Loan Associations and with the necessity for buildings in Palestine. Mr. Fischel has been of the greatest assistance in making possible the immediate launching of this venture. I understand from Mr. Fischel that he has conferred with you with reference to such a corporation.

Yours very sincerely,

Sir Herbert Samuel,   JULIAN W. MACK
   High Commissioner,
      Jerusalem, Palestine.

The significance attached to the enterprise on the part of the press and public is reflected in the following article which appeared in the Hebrew Standard of March 3, 1922, together with an article in the Jewish Tribune on March 17th and an editorial on the same date:

Article from the Hebrew Standard, March 3, 1922.

TO INFORM HIGH COMMISSIONER BUILDING LOAN PLAN READY

A plan whereby interest and loan will be repaid within a period of about ten years without unduly straining the resources of the borrower, is the most striking feature of the plan worked out for the establishment of a Building Loan and Savings Association in Jerusalem which is to be established shortly by the Palestine Co-operative Company. At a meeting of the directors of the Company, held last Wednesday, at which were present Judge Julian W. Mack and Messrs. Harry Fischel, Bernard Flexner, Robert Szold, S. J. Rosensohn, Emil Weinheim and Jacob de Haas, and at which the officers of the Palestine Development Council were also present, including Justice Brandeis, Judge Mack, Dr. Wise and Mrs. Fels, the treasurer of the Palestine Cooperative Company was authorized to set aside from its funds the sum of $250,000 for the purpose of instituting the Building Loan and Savings Association in and about Jerusalem.

A special committee, consisting of Harry Fischel, chairman; S. J. Rosensohn, Robert Szold and Bernard Flexner was appointed to proceed with the preparation of the plans and details for the operation of this association, and the Board of Directors were authorized to notify Sir Herbert Samuel, the High Commissioner, that the Palestine Cooperative Company has the necessary capital for the organization and operation of a Building Loan and Savings Association, and is preparing to begin business in and about Jerusalem. In order to facilitate the organization of the association on lines that seem advisable to the New York committee, the directors will transmit to the High Commissioner the form of ordinance that they believe to be desirable for the organization and supervision of this association. The actual carrying out of the details of organization in Palestine, devolves upon Mr. Sol. Rosenbloom, the treasurer, who is now in Palestine ,and Mr. Bernard Flexner, one of the committee who will shortly proceed to Palestine. They will establish suitable offices in Jerusalem, engage the manager and begin business as soon as the necessary legal formalities have been carried out with the cooperation of the High Commissioner.

At the directors' meeting at which these plans were adopted, Mr. Fischel was complimented on his share in raising the necessary capital and his continued effort in the practical work.

Article from the Jewish Tribune March 17, 1922.

LAUNCH BUILDING AND LOAN

Sir Herbert Samuel Advised of Organization of $250,000 Association to Operate in Jerusalem

What has been hailed as the first definite, practical step in the constructive work that must be carried out for the realization of the Jewish National Homeland in Palestine, is the organization of a Building Loan and Savings Association in Jerusalem, with a capital of $250,000, recently announced by the Palestine Co-operative Company.

With the capital already set aside, with Sol. J. Rosenbloom already in Palestine and Bernard Flexner expected there in a month, the directors of the Company who will carry out the details of organization of the Association, which was originated and planned by Harry Fischel as a result of his trip to the Holy Land last summer, will shortly be accepting savings and loaning money to Palestinian settlers so that they can realize their hopes to own their own homes in Palestine.

Announcement of the completion of the Association was forwarded to Sir Herbert Samuel, High Commissioner to Palestine this week by Judge Julian W. Mack, in a letter paying high tribute to Mr. Fischel.

Editorial from the Jewish Tribune March 17, 1922.

MARCH FORWARD IN PALESTINE

On another page we publish a letter from Judge Julian W. Mack to Sir Herbert Samuel, advising the High Commissioner to Palestine of the formation of a Building Loan and Savings Association with a paid-up capital of $250,000, to operate in and around Jerusalem. Everywhere this achievement of the Palestine Cooperative Company has been hailed with satisfaction, for here is a practical, constructive measure for the upbuilding of the Jewish National Homeland, which satisfies the very fundamentals for progress in Palestine—home building.

In addition to its valuable savings and loan features, there is something of even greater significance to it. This association and those that will follow it in the other cities of Palestine, will grant these same opportunities to the Arabs and all other members of the population. Here is a real forward step looking toward that comity of racial units in Palestine which is so necessary to effective progress in the country.

This association was originated by Harry Fischel, who saw the needs for building loan and savings associations in Palestine after his visit there last summer. Judge Mack pays high tribute to Mr. Fischel in his letter to the High Commissioner and THE JEWISH TRIBUNE is happy to add its appreciation of the splendid constructive piece of work that is being carried out largely through the tireless energy and initiative of this ardent Jewish worker.

One of the larger projects of the Palestine Development Council was that for the creation, through the Rutenberg plant, of Hydro Electric power in Palestine.

In order to obtain subscriptions for this vast undertaking a conference was called by Judge Julian W. Mack on June 27, 1922, a report of which is contained in the following article which appeared in the Jewish Tribune of June 30, 1922.

LAUNCH RUTENBERG APPEAL

Palestine Development Council Receives Subscriptions of Almost $900,000

The Palestine Development Council's campaign for the sale of trust certificates for the Rutenberg plan for the creation of hydro-electric power in Palestine, was formally launched last week at a conference at which Judge Julian W. Mack, Chairman of the Council, presided. Addresses were delivered by Dr. L. C. Loewenstein, Pincas Rutenberg, Justice Louis D. Brandeis, Rabbi A. H. Silver and Harry Fischel.

The principal subscriptions announced were:

Palestine Cooperative Company, $125,000; Sol Rosenbloom, $50,000; Justice Louis D. Brandeis and Louis Horowitz, $25,-000; Julius Simon, $10,000; Harry Fischel, Solomon Ulmer, Cleveland; Mrs. J. Guggenheimer, Lynchburg, Va.; Dr. Harry Friedenwald, Baltimore and Sigmund Eisner, Red Bank, N. J., $5000; Mr. and Mrs. Norvin R. Lindheim, $4000; George I. Fox and Dr. Julius Friedenwald, Baltimore, $2000; Dr. Edgar Friedenwald, Baltimore, $1300; Samuel J. Rosensohn, Dr. Julius

Jarcho, Louis H. Miller, Buffalo; Jacob Rosing, Buffalo; Jacob Ginsburg, Philadelphia, Adolph Ginsburg, Baltimore; Benno Kohn, Baltimore; Michael Schloss, Baltimore; Louis S. Posner and Samuel B. Waxman, Baltimore, $1000.

The following state and city pledges, totaling $570,000 were announced:

Brooklyn, Cleveland and Philadelphia, $100,000; Minnesota, $80,000; Baltimore, $75,000; Buffalo and Boston, $50,000; Central New York, $15,000.

In earlier chapters of this biography the marriage of three of Mr. Fischel's daughters was chronicled. Mr. Fischel naturally looked eagerly forward to the marriage of his youngest daughter, Rose, and derived intense pleasure and satisfaction when she informed him of her engagement to Mr. Albert Wald. This betrothal was received with equal satisfaction by Mrs. Fischel and the others of the family.

The formal announcement of the engagement was made on October 20, 1922, the New York Times containing the following item:

"'Miss Rose Fischel, daughter of Mr. and Mrs. Harry Fischel, of 118 West 93rd Street, and Mr. Albert Wald, are betrothed. Miss Fischel is a graduate of Barnard College. During the war she rendered service in a canteen of the Jewish Welfare Board. At present she is assisting in the Americanization work of the Council of Jewish Women by teaching English to bonded immigrants.

"Mr. Wald is a lawyer. During the war he had charge of the welfare work connected with the Housing and Transportation Departments of the United States Shipping Board. Mr. Wald belongs to the New York County Lawyers' Association and the American Institute of Electrical Engineers."

A formal engagement party was held at the Fischel residence on November 12th and was attended by several hundred of the friends of the Fischel and Wald families as well as representatives of many of the institutions with which Mr. Fischel was so actively identified.

CHAPTER XLVI

GROWTH OF BETH ISRAEL HOSPITAL

THE war, with its diversion of funds from local needs, together with the scarcity of labor and high cost of building material, had caused many of the city's philanthropic institutions to forego the construction of new edifices, although imperatively needed.

One of the institutions which, for many years, had required additional facilities for the care of its wards was the Beth Israel Hospital, one of the first institutions with which Mr. Fischel had become identified after entering upon communal work. He had been chairman of the building committee which had purchased ground for the erection of the first hospital at Jefferson and Cherry Streets and for which he had lain the cornerstone on May 1, 1900.

With the passing of the years, this institution had come to be regarded as a model of its kind and had been of ever increasing usefulness to the community. The fact that the hospital had proved of such tremendous service was a source of much gratification to Mr. Fischel, and, as early as December 22, 1913, a meeting had been held at his home, 118 E. 93rd Street, when the question of securing a new site and erecting a larger building had been considered. At this meeting Mr. Fischel had subscribed $10,000 toward a new building fund and a substantial sum had later been raised for this purpose.

At subsequent meetings the project had been held in abeyance for a more advantageous time. Finally the Directors succeeded in purchasing the entire block on Livingston Place, from Sixteenth to Seventeenth Streets, a most desirable and central location, as a site for a new building.

The ground for this building was broken on October 9, 1921, and the cornerstone was laid on November 5, 1922. This great new hospital is now practically completed at a cost of $5,000,000 and will, when opened, be one of the most modern and best equipped in New York.

On November 3, 1922, the American Hebrew published the following article concerning Beth Israel and its work:

THE MAINTENANCE OF A GREAT INSTITUTION

"Detailed plans for financing the new $5,000,000 Beth Israel Hospital, to be constructed at Livingston Place and Seventeenth Street, New York City, were announced recently by Harry Fischel, chairman of the Finance Committee of the Hospital.

"One million dollars has been raised through the Federated Building Drive of the Jewish Federation. The plan for raising the balance is to endow each one of the free rooms of the hospital for $5000. The hospital will have more than 500 individual rooms. Four hundred of these rooms will be assigned to free patients. Many have already been endowed, according to Mr. Fischel, each director being responsible for the endowment of a certain number of rooms. The directors, according to Mr. Fischel, have already underwritten the amount needed for the completion of the building. The endowment of $5000 for each room will be paid in four annual payments at the option of the endower.

" 'Beth Israel Hospital is fortunate in having on its Board of Directors some of the most influential men in every industry,' said Mr. Fischel. 'The directors have contributed large sums of money individually and they will raise the balance through their business friends. The hospital never stops at expense when the welfare of a patient is at stake. The Board of Directors has just made up a deficit of $100,000 for the last two years. This was done through individual contributions made by the directors themselves.

" 'We consider each patient, not as a case but as an individual. We give each patient special care, the poor the same as the rich. Once a patient comes into our hospital he is no longer poor. He receives the same treatment as one who pays $100 a week for a room.'

"Mr. Fischel has been a director of Beth Israel ever since the organization of the Board of Directors of the hospital in 1888. He was chairman of the building committee of the present hospital on Jefferson Street and he is a member of the present building committee. He donated the present laboratory to the hospital and he will supply funds to enable the institution to maintain its present high scientific standard. Mr. Fischel, according to an announcement made by Louis J. Frank, superintendent of the hospital, will dedicate the new laboratory, which will cost $100,-000.

" 'Before 1910 all laboratory work was sent to the Board of Health or to an outside doctor,' said Mr. Fischel in telling of his interest in the laboratory. 'The directors thought there was no use in equipping a laboratory since even at that time they had begun to discuss plans for building a new hospital. Mr. Frank, the superintendent, convinced me of the need and it was at his instance that I installed a laboratory, which has been enlarged continually. We now have one of the ablest men in the country at its head, Dr. Max Kahn. Under him are several assistants. A complete test is taken of every patient. These tests have been the means of saving many lives.'

"The following is inscribed on a tablet which is placed on the wall of the laboratory:

This Physiological-Chemical Laboratory was Erected and Equipped by Mr. Harry Fischel for the Benefit of Suffering Mankind for all Generations.   1912.

"Mr. Fischel has always emphasized the religious side of Beth Israel Hospital. The observance of Jewish dietary laws helps greatly in the return to health of the patients, according to Mr. Fischel. In Beth Israel the Orthodox Jew is given food prepared in the way to which he is accustomed.

"In speaking of the location of the new hospital Mr. Fischel said: 'We are filling a long felt want on the central East Side. There is no other Jewish hospital from One Hundredth Street south to the river. Many come to visit the sick on Saturday, the Jewish Sabbath. Under the Jewish law it is a desecration of the Sabbath to ride on a street car or subway. The new location in the heart of the densely populated East Side will permit friends and relatives of patients to walk to and from the hospital.' "

CHAPTER XLVII

PROGRESS OF WORK IN PALESTINE

MENTION was made in an earlier chapter of the fact that Mr. Sol Rosenbloom went to Palestine in the early part of 1922 to organize and to start the work of the Palestine Building Loan and Savings Association.

After nearly a year of effort, during which he had continuously communicated the results of his labors to the Board of Directors of the Association, he returned to New York for the purpose of making a report on the work which had been accomplished in this period.

His return was marked by a dinner tendered him at the Hotel Astor on January 14, 1923, on which occasion Mr. Fischel delivered the following address:

At the dinner tendered to Mr. Rosenbloom a year ago, before he departed for Palestine, the theme assigned to me was "A Land to Build." Tonight I will take for my theme, "A Land We Are Building."

I believe that most of you assembled this evening, are stockholders in the Palestine Co-operative Company, and are responsible for the Palestine Building Loan and Savings Association, of which I have the honor to be the Chairman.

Those of you who were present at the dinner a year ago, may recollect that at that time, I outlined my plan to help the people of Jerusalem build houses, by loaning them 60% of the cost of their proposed homes on easy payments. I will take this occasion to explain to you why we selected Jerusalem to give the first aid through building loans.

If we had organized our Company for the purpose of making a profit, we would certainly have selected Jaffe or Haifa, as both these cities have a port and business is more prosperous there. Jerusalem, being a city without a port, naturally has less business and a smaller income from real estate. It is therefore much harder to get money on mortgages. Under the circumstances, the people in Jerusalem are more entitled to aid, especially as Jerusalem is a universal city, and is considered the most holy spot in all of Palestine. When our resources will permit, we will extend our loans to other cities as well.

It gives me great pleasure to report to you that at this time, over 100 houses are being built in the City of Jerusalem with our loans, which means your money, since you are the stockholders of the company.

I will take this occasion to explain to you how we have accomplished this. As soon as Mr. Rosenbloom left for Palestine, our building loan committee worked out a complete plan and By-Laws for the Building Loan and Savings Association on the same basis as the Building Loan and Savings Associations in New York State only making such changes as would apply to the Palestinian conditions.

This plan was sent by our President, Judge Mack, to the High Commissioner of Palestine, Sir Herbert Samuel, who gave it his entire approval and had the plan made a part of the laws of Palestine in order to protect our American investments, as he promised me he would do, when I saw him in August, 1921.

As soon as Mr. Rosenbloom reached Palestine, he engaged a manager, opened an office and started to take applications for loans. He organized a local Advisory Committee in accordance with our By-Laws.

Mr. Rosenbloom could not carry out the entire plan of the Building Loan and Savings Association, which included a much broader plan than simply the making of loans. Part of the plan was to give an opportunity to every borrower to become a depositor, by buying a share in the Building Loan Company for $5.00. For every additional $5.00 he could buy another share, and as soon as he should have enough to make up the amount of 40% of the cost of his proposed building, The Building Loan Company would loan him the additional 60%.

Our idea was, that in this way, we would give the people a chance to save money and increase the loaning capacity of the Association. Mr. Rosenbloom with the best of intentions, however, could not carry out this savings proposition at that time, for the reason that he arrived when the mandate was declared and there was a great deal of unrest in the country. In order to show the people that the Americans are ready to invest money in

Palestine, he decided to make loans immediately, without waiting for the Savings Association to be established.

Our Committee never expected that there would be so many people who would have the necessary 40%, entitling them to the loan of the balance of 60% toward their homes. However, to our surprise, applications came in, in great numbers, and our manager had all he could do to select the ones who were most deserving.

While we only set aside the sum of $250,000 to start the Building Loan and Savings Association, deserving applications reached the sum of $350,000 which is $100,000 more than we are able at this time to meet. Under the circumstances, it is necessary for us to put our shoulders to the wheel and sell additional stock for the sum of $100,000 within the next three or four months.

Last spring our Committee completed plans to raise a large sum of money by selling stock in this Company, enough to supply all the demands, not alone in Jerusalem, but in Jaffe, Haifa, and Tiberias. However, we were advised by our leader, Judge Mack, to delay our campaign to a later date, and use all our efforts to obtain subscriptions for the Rutenberg Hydro-Electric project.

Our Committee feels that this electric proposition is of such importance, that it is advisable for us to be contented with what we have already done, until the stock for the Hydro-Electric Corporation is entirely subscribed for.

While I am personally interested in the Building Loan and Savings Association, however, I strongly advise all my friends to invest as much money as they can spare in this electric proposition, for the reason that electricity is what makes a new country. We need electricity in the houses. With electricity we can build the houses much cheaper, through the manufacturing of the material. We need electricity for a quarry to cut stones, and above all, we need electricity for the manufacture of all products.

All those who have come from Palestine lately, have reported that our Building Loan proposition is the only practical work which has so far accomplished anything in Palestine with American money. It has brought remarkable results, by supplying employment for several hundreds of people. The money remains in Palestine, and through its circulation, it has produced a great volume of business. It has supplied living quarters for hundreds of families, and above all, it has done a great deal in cementing the breach between the Arabs and the Jews, for the reason that many Arabs are employed in the building of houses. They do such work as cannot be done by our Jewish people.

In addition, we have made several loans to Arabs on their incompleted houses, which have been standing unfinished since before the war. I have the greatest confidence in this Building Loan and Savings Association for the reason that the money invested in these mortgages is just as safe as money invested in first mortgages in the City of New York, and probably safer. As a real estate man, I know that sometimes in the City of New York, there can be an overproduction in a certain class of houses, reducing the value of the property, which automatically reduces the value of the mortgages, whereas, in the City of Jerusalem, no such thing can happen. There will be no over production for many years to come, and as the City grows, the property will always increase in value, thereby making our mortgages always safer. Furthermore, these mortgages will be amortized, so that within a few years, they will be only 30% of the value, instead of 60% which we are loaning at present.

In order to see with my own eyes how these houses are progressing, to help improve and enlarge this Building Loan and Savings Association, I have engaged passage for Palestine on April 24 for Mrs. Fischel and myself.

I hope with the Will of the Almighty and with your assistance that we shall be able to increase our Building Loan Corporation to such an extent that we will be able to establish branches in every city in Palestine.

CHAPTER XLVIII

WEDDING OF MR. FISCHEL'S YOUNGEST DAUGHTER

MR. FISCHEL'S youngest daughter Rose was married to Mr. Albert Wald on February 18, 1923. The marriage of the youngest child is always a happy and significant event in the lives of their parents. In this case it was particularly so, for Mr. Fischel felt confident that through the union of his daughter and Mr. Wald the family's spiritual heritage would be handed down to the next generation intact.

The ceremony, which took place at the Synagogue of the Congregation Kehillath Jeshurun was performed by Rabbis M. S. Margolies, Henry S. Morais, Herbert S. Goldstein, and the late Dr. Philip Klein. A dinner for the family and friends followed at the home of Mr. and Mrs. Fischel, 118 East 93rd Street. As on all previous happy occasions in the life of Mr. Fischel, he made liberal donations to charities.

Already there has been discerned in the lives of the young couple a strong communal effort along religious lines. The children of Mr. and Mrs. Fischel were reared in an atmosphere permeated by the twofold desire to serve humanity and to carry on the faith. Mr. Fischel is very happy in the thought that his youngest daughter and son-in-law are trying to emulate his example.

Rose Fischel Wald is on the Committee of Religion and Religious Schools of the Council of Jewish Women, on the Women's Committee of the Yeshivah Dormitory Fund, a directress of the Women's Auxiliary of the Central Jewish Institute and is Vice President of the West End Group of the Hadassah.

When visiting in Palestine with her parents just prior to her marriage, she was strongly impressed by the work of the Hadassah Medical Organization and has been actively interested in the organization since that time.

Mr. Wald is President of the Permanent Organization of his Law School Class. Besides his professional and political activities, he is also deeply interested in things Jewish. He is a junior trustee of the Congregation Kehillath Jeshurun. As Counsel for the Yeshivah Rabbi Isaac Elchanan, of which he is a life member, he was eminently successful in procuring from the N. Y. State Education Department, the Yeshivah's right to confer the Degree of Doctor of Hebrew Literature (L.H.D.) He is a member of the Executive Committee of the Union of Orthodox Jewish Congregations of America and participated in the campaign of the Union to prosecute violators of the New York Kosher Law, having acted as the Union's Counsel in the first conviction secured under this law.

MR. FISCHEL'S YOUNGEST SON-IN-LAW,
Mr. and Mrs. Albert Wald and their children.

CHAPTER XLIX

A THIRD VISIT TO PALESTINE

On his third visit to the Holy Land, now to take place, Mr. Fischel had a dual object, acceleration of the work of the Palestine Building Loan and Savings Association and the dedication of the home of Chief Rabbi Kook, for which Mr. Fischel had provided the funds and laid the cornerstone on his previous visit, two years earlier, and which was now practically completed.

Before leaving Palestine on that occasion, Mr. Fischel had deposited the entire amount of money that it was estimated would be required with the Anglo Palestine Bank and had signed a contract for the prosecution of the work, at the same time naming a Committee with power to draw on the money as needed to pay the contractors.

On his arrival home, several weeks later, he received word that the entire sum deposited had been expended but that the work had been only half completed. Although he had not expected any such eventuality, Mr. Fischel at once cabled additional money and ordered the Committee to proceed with the work as speedily as possible.

Building construction, however, is not accomplished in Palestine with the alacrity with which it is done in America and the work proceeded particularly slowly. Thus it was not until the early part of January, 1923, that Mr. Fischel was finally notified that the Chief Rabbi's residence had been finished. At the same time he was informed that the work upon the synagogue, which was a part of the undertaking, had not even been started and that an additional sum of money was still needed for this purpose.

Determined that the work should not halt, despite the much greater expenditure than he had anticipated, Mr. Fischel immediately notified the Committee to proceed on the synagogue, so that it might be dedicated not later than May and before the hot weather should set in, and made his own arrangements to sail for Palestine on April 24.

Accompanying him on this trip, in addition to Mrs. Fischel, were his daughter and son-in-law, Rabbi and Mrs. Herbert S. Goldstein. Rabbi Goldstein, as President of the Union of Orthodox Jewish Congregations of America, had long wished for the opportunity to visit the Holy Land, as does every Orthodox Jew, and Mr. Fischel felt it was most appropriate that to him should be accorded the privilege of formally presenting, in his behalf, the home of the Chief Rabbi to the people of Palestine.

It was Mr. Fischel's good fortune, through his acquaintance with United States Supreme Court Justice Brandeis and through the latter's kind offices, to secure a letter from the then Secretary of State, Charles E. Hughes, introducing him to the American Ambassadors and diplomatic officers in the countries he proposed to visit.

This letter was as follows:

DEPARTMENT OF STATE
Washington

March 26, 1923.

To the Diplomatic and Consular Officers of the United States of America.

Gentlemen:

At the instance of the Honorable William M. Calder, formerly Senator of the United States from the State of New York, I take pleasure in introducing to you Mr. Harry Fischel of New York City, who, accompanied by his wife (Jane Fischel), is about to proceed abroad.

I cordially bespeak for Mr. Fischel and his wife such courtesies and assistance as you may be able to render consistently with your official duties.

I am, Gentlemen,

Your obedient servant,

CHARLES E. HUGHES

The Fischels once more embarked on the S. S. Berengaria on April 24th and, as on their former voyages, the Cunard Steamship Company carried out every request made of them, so that the members of the party might strictly observe the Jewish dietary laws.

Mr. Ballin, the Chief Steward of the Cunard line, had also again arranged for the use of the Captain's private reception room as a synagogue and where, during the entire voyage, services were held three times daily.

On Mr. Fischel's departure, the following article explaining the purpose of his trip appeared in the New York Times:

NEW YORKER GIVES CHIEF RABBI HOME

Harry Fischel Will Sail to Dedicate Palatial Building in Jerusalem

When the "Berengaria" sails from New York tomorrow she will have on board Harry Fischel, donor of a palatial home for the Chief Rabbi of Palestine. He is a multi-millionaire, of 276 Fifth Avenue, Manhattan, conspicuous in numerous philanthropies, and is going abroad especially for the dedication of the building to which he has given so generously of his time and care and money. Mr. Fischel will be accompanied on his journey by his wife, daughter and son-in-law, Rabbi Herbert S. Goldstein, of the Institutional Synagogue, Manhattan, who is President of the Union of Orthodox Jewish Congregations of America.

The Chief Rabbi of Palestine is a picturesque figure to the millions of his faith, and the present holder of this distinction, Rabbi Abraham Kook, endeared himself to Mr. Fischel when the latter visited Jerusalem a few years ago. Mr. Fischel then took up the matter of erecting a permanent chief rabbi's home for the district, with Sir Herbert Samuel, High Commissioner of Palestine.

The result is a monument to Jerusalem, located on the principal square at the intersection of three streets. It is a one-story edifice of Moorish design, built of stone, fronting 150 feet on one street, extending 100 feet on another, measuring 90 feet in width in the rear. It is probably the only house in the city having every modern convenience, and besides living rooms, it also contains a large meeting room and a synagogue. It was started August 29, 1921, and has just been completed. Mr. Fischel's party will arrive in Palestine May 10 and the date of dedication will be fixed immediately afterwards.

Besides his interest in the dedication Mr. Fischel intends to increase the home building activities of his people in Palestine, and which were inaugurated on his previous visit through the Palestine Cooperative Company, a building and loan concern fashioned after American ideas, which has already erected 165 new homes for Jews in Jerusalem.

This also is in the nature of a philanthropy, being conducted by the Palestine Development Council in which the following are associated with Mr. Fischel: Supreme Court Justice Louis D. Brandeis, Federal Judge Julian W. Mack, Nathan Straus, Sol. S. Rosenbloom, Robert Szold, Leo Wolman, C. Lipman and others. Mr. Fischel is chairman of the loan committee.

The party arrived in Paris on May 2nd and on May 4th reached Marseilles, where they boarded the Mediteranean steamer Morea. Again Mr. Fischel had the pleasant experience of being informed by the Chief Steward of that vessel that through the instrumentality of the Cunard Company, facilities had been provided for the party whereby the dietary laws might be observed by them on this part of their voyage.

The party reached Port Said on May 9th and on May 10th arrived at Lud, the station before Jerusalem, where they were met by a delegation of Rabbis sent forward by Chief Rabbi Kook to welcome them and bearing the request that on their arrival in Jerusalem their first stop should be at the new home of the Chief Rabbi, which he was already occupying.

On his arrival at the Chief Rabbi's residence Mr. Fischel was greeted in a manner that left no doubt in his mind as to the appreciation and gratitude his deed had evoked. The Chief Rabbi came forward and, although he did not express his feelings in many words, showed his affection for his benefactor by the warmth with which he embraced and finally kissed him.

The party was then escorted by Rabbi Kook through the entire residence, which had been constructed exactly as Mr. Fischel had planned and of which every part was completed except the synagogue. This still required about two week's work to finish, including the setting up of its furniture, equipment and its holy appurtenances. It was therefore arranged that the dedication of the building should take place on May 27th.

In the intervening period the Fischel party took the opportunity to travel throughout Palestine, Mr. Fischel himself remaining in Jerusalem, however, to give all his time to help completing the synagogue. Mr. Fischel also embraced the opportunity again to visit the various institutions in Jerusalem, including several that had not been in existence on the occasion of his previous stay in the Holy Land.

Among these was the New Diskind Orphan Asylum, and the new Bikur Holim Hospital, in each of which institutions Mr. Fischel dedicated a room.

The electric power plant built by the Rutenberg Hydro-Electric Power Company, which was to supply electricity to Jerusalem, was also completed at this time and Mr. Rutenberg, having been informed of Mr. Fischel's arrival, extended to him an invitation to participate in the ceremony attending the first turning of the large shaft which marked the actual beginning of the operation of the plant.

At this function Mr. Fischel had the honor of helping to turn the gigantic wheel which, once it was set in motion, immediately illuminated all the streets of the city.

This unusual and epoch-making experience, that of helping to flood this ancient city with modern illumination, forms one of the outstanding recollections in Mr. Fischel's life.

During the period when the synagogue was being completed Mr. Fischel spent such time as he could spare in the offices of the Palestine Building Loan and Savings Association and with Mr. Emanuel N. Mohl, the manager, traveled to various outlying districts where the Company, through its loans, had helped to build entire communities.

Mr. Fischel found gratification in the fact that through the Company's assistance several hundred houses had been constructed in the suburbs of Jerusalem. In one such suburb, about three miles outside the city, namely Bone Bayit, which was built entirely with loans made by the Association, an elaborate celebration was held in honor of Mr. Fischel on May 25.

While Mr. Fischel was thus occupying himself, the synagogue was completed and invitations issued for the dedication on May 27.

A copy of this invitation, together with the program arranged for the dedication are herewith reproduced.

We have the honor to invite you to be present

at the ceremony

OF THE CONSECRATION OF THE SYNAGOGUE

AND THE HOUSE WARMING OF THE "BETH HARAV"

which were built with funds contributed by

Mr. and Mrs. Harry Fischel of New York

Ceremony to take place at the Colony Beth David,

on Sunday 27th, May 1923, at 3:30 P. M. sharp.

His Excellency, the High Commissioner has kindly consented

to honour the Ceremony by his presence.

Respectfully yours,

CENTRAL COMMITTEE KNESSETH ISRAEL

Jerusalem

CONSECRATION OF THE SYNAGOGUE
AND WARMING OF RABBI'S HOUSE

by the Central Committee Knesseth Israel, Jerusalem

Order of Program

1. Blind orchestra (directed by Mr. Mizrahy) receives the guests.
2. The Chairman Mr. M. L. Slutzkin opens the meeting on arrival of His Excellency, the High Commissioner.
3. Song of "Beruchim Habaim" sung by the children of the Etz Haim Talmud Torah schools.
4. Sefardic Chief Rabbi Jacob Meir blesses the meeting.
5. Rabbi Abramovitz, representing Central Committee Knesseth Israel, hands over silver key of Rabbi's House to Mr. Harry Fischel.
6. Mr. Fischel hands same over to His Excellency the High Commissioner.
7. Acceptance of key by the High Commissioner.
8. Mismor Shir Chanukath, by Chazan Rivlin's chorus.
9. Address by Rabbi Herbert S. Goldstein.
10. Address by the American Consul.
11. Address by His Excellency the Acting Governor.
12. Address by Dr. Joseph Klausner.
13. Address by Mr. Davis Yelin.
14. Address by Rabbi Glazner, Chief Rabbi of Klausenburg.
15. Address by Rabbi J. M. Charlap.
16. Sermon by Chief Rabbi A. I. Kook.
17. Key of Synagogue is handed over to Mr. Harry Fischel by Central Committee Knesseth Israel.
18. Opening of the Synagogue by Mr. Harry Fischel.
19. "Seu Shearim Rosheichem," sung by the chorus.
20. Minha Service by Chazan Bardaky.
21. Ten minutes interval. Refreshments partaken of.
22. Address by Rabbi Rubin Braz.
23. Address by Rabbi E. M. Tikazinsky.
24. Address by Rabbi M. N. Auerbach.
25. Address by Rabbi J. G. Hurvitz.
26. Address by Rabbi Z. Epstein.
27. Address by Rabbi S. A. Polansky.
28. Address by Rabbi Ch. L. Auerbach.
29. Address by Rabbi Isaac Levy on behalf of "Merkaz Harav."
30. Speech by a pupil of Etz Haim Talmud Torah.
31. "Yigdal" sung by the Chorus.
32. Evening Service.
33. "Hillula Derabannan."

CHAPTER L

CEREMONIES ATTENDING THE DEDICATION OF THE
HOME OF THE CHIEF RABBI OF PALESTINE

THE Ceremony attending the dedication of the Chief Rabbi's home, was one to which not only every Jewish resident of Jerusalem had long looked forward but was of paramount interest to all of Palestine and to Orthodox Jews in every land. It served to emphasize the great importance of the position of the Chief Rabbi and to focus world wide attention upon the religious as well as the material significance attached to the Jewish Homeland.

Preparations for the event, which was regarded as a national holiday, engaged the attention of the populace for many days preceding the celebration. The whole city of Jerusalem was decorated for the occasion. In practically every window appeared the Zionist flag, that was merged in the decorations with the American colors.

The Chief Rabbi's residence, together with the synagogue, occupies practically an entire block, in the center of which is a large courtyard where upwards of a thousand people may be comfortably seated.

This entire courtyard was decorated with banners explaining the full purport of the occasion. On the surrounding walls had been erected large canvasses on which were inscribed suitable prayers and a great platform was placed in the center.

When the great day came this platform was occupied by the highest officials of Palestine, together with the guests of honor and the most prominent rabbis. Among these were Chief Rabbi Kook, for whom the residence had been built, together with the Sefardic Chief Rabbi, the High Commissioner, Sir Herbert

Samuel, the Consular officials representing the different governments, the Governor of Jerusalem, the Mayor of Jerusalem and the Rabbis who were scheduled to be the speakers.

The hour set for the exercises was 3:30 in the afternoon, but long before the appointed time, every seat was filled and thousands of persons who could not possibly be accommodated within, remained on the streets outside the enclosure. In order to keep this tremendous throng in order, military officers were stationed on all sides.

At precisely 4 o'clock, the High Commissioner, Sir Herbert Samuel with Lady Samuel, together with the members of their party and military aides, arrived on the scene. The British and American National Anthems were sung by the immense throng, followed by an impressive rendition of the Zionist Anthem, the Hatikvah.

Since this biography is largely intended as a record to be preserved for the benefit of those interested in the outstanding Jewish events occurring during Mr. Fischel's life, there is herewith given the account of the entire proceedings as prepared by an official government reporter.

Consecration Ceremony of the Beth Harav and Synagogue, Sunday, May 27th, 1923

On SUNDAY, SIVAN 12, 5683 (May 27th, 1923), an impressive consecration ceremony took place at Jerusalem when the Beth Harav and Synagogue especially constructed by Mr. and Mrs. Harry Fischel at their own expense for Chief Rabbi Kook, was consecrated.

The ceremony was a most brilliant event and will remain a red letter day in the annals of Jerusalem.

There were present the elite of the Jewish and non-Jewish communities and also a number of American visitors who then happened to be in Jerusalem. The gathering was graced by the attendance of His Excellency, The High Commissioner and Lady Samuel. That day will long be remembered as it afforded joy and honor to Mr. and Mrs. Fischel and rendered spiritual pleasure to the whole of Orthodox Judaism in Jerusalem.

THE DECORATIONS

The spacious courtyard of the Central Committee Knesseth Israel (Vadd Hakloli) was gaily decorated. At the entrance gate there hung a bluish-white banner bearing the inscription "Beruchim Haboim" (Welcome to the Visitors). On the outside balcony, one observed a signboard in gilt letters "Beth Harav and Synagogue built by Mr. (Israel Aron) Harry and Mrs. Fischel." The interior walls of the courtyard were covered by blue and white colored bunting and banners having inscribed thereon such Biblical verses as "This day hath the Eternal appointed, let us be glad and rejoice thereon." "Bless the Lord O House of Israel; bless the Lord O House of Aron." On the wall facing the gathering there hung two pictures, one of King George V, and the other of the High Commissioner. Immediately beneath these pictures were thirteen tablets in the form of Mogen Dovids (Shields of David) with the lettering of the donor's name—ISRAEL ARON FISCHEL.

About 3:30 P. M. the courtyard was filled to overflowing. The gathering was representative of every class and phase of Jerusalem Jewry—Ashkenazim, Sefardim, Rabbis, Talmud scholars, business men, journalists, teachers—who had all been invited by the Central Committee Knesseth Israel to participate in the consecration ceremony. The stairs and balconies were packed with the women of Jerusalem who had also come to participate in the day's festivity.

THE DISTINGUISHED VISITORS

On a specially arranged platform, there sat on plush armchairs the two Chief Rabbis, Rabbis Kook and Jacob Meir. The first row of chairs was occupied by the American Consul, Mr. Cobb; the Italian Consul, who is a neighbor of the Beth Harav; the American visitors now in Jerusalem, Messrs. Solomon Lamport, Margareten, Horowitz, Levin, Silversweig, and others. Of rabbis there sat on the platform Rabbi Schapiro of Dohbrowitz; the veteran Rabbi Moses Samuel Glasner of Klausenburg; Rabbi Reuben Braz, brother-in-law of Mr. Fischel, Rabbi Joseph Gerson Horowitz, Rabbi Harlap; Rabbi Zorah Epstein; Rabbi M. Tibotzinsky; Rabbi Meir Auerbach; the Wardens of the Central Committee Knesseth Israel; the Mizrachi Rabbis M. Ostrowski and Asof, and others. Among other notables present were Mr.

Sultzkin of Melbourne, Australia, who was chairman of the proceedings; Dr. Judah L. Magnes of New York; Colonel Kisch of the Zionist Executive; David Yellin; Dr. Mazie; Professor Pick; Dr. Wallach; Dr. Salkind; Mr. Joseph Meyuhas and Mr. Kesselman. The organization of the meeting was under the supervision of Mr. J. Amdursky.

At 4 P. M. punctually, Mr. and Mrs. Harry Fischel arrived accompanied by their son-in-law and daughter, Rabbi Herbert S. Goldstein and Mrs. Goldstein. They were followed by the Acting Governor of Jerusalem, Commander Luke and Mr. Edwin Samuel. The guests were received with musical honors.

Soon after, His Excellency, the High Commissioner and Lady Samuel entered the courtyard accompanied by aide-de-camp Mr. Cust and Miss Franklin. The band of the Blind Institution struck up the National Anthem and the whole gathering rose as a mark of respect. The Choir under the direction of Cantor Zalmon Rivlin then sang Beruchim Haboim. The High Commissioner took his seat between the Chief Rabbis and near Mr. Harry Fischel. The proceedings then began.

THE SPEECHES

Mr. Slutzkin, who presided, opened the consecration ceremony by delivering a warm-hearted address. He congratulated Rabbi Kook and Mr. and Mrs. Harry Fischel on this auspicious occasion. He expressed the hope that the Beth Harav would unite all the forces of the Torah and create an impetus for further study and spiritual loftiness.

Chief Rabbi Jacob Meir then rose and in a learned and interesting address, dwelt on the Biblical verses "Honor the Lord out of your wealth" and "Read not thy sons but thy builders." "Hitherto," said Rabbi Meir, "Rabbi Kook had to move from place to place and house to house, involving many difficulties and inconveniences. By Mr. and Mrs. Harry Fischel's munificence, however, Rabbi Kook and his family would now be able to live at ease and comfort in the Beth Harav, which had been erected for them. In connection with the Beth Harav, a House of Learning had also been built for study and worship which would bring honor to the Ashkenazic community." Rabbi Meir warmly shook hands with Rabbi Kook and wished him prosperity. He also congratulated Mr. and Mrs. Fischel, terminating his speech, with

the wish that "we should all be privileged to witness the reconstruction of our National Home, which could be attained only by
the combination of all forces through union and organization."

Rabbi Duber Abramowitz of St. Louis, spoke on behalf of the
Administration of the Vaud Hakloli (Central Committee). He
invited Mr. and Mrs. Fischel to become inhabitants and citizens
of Jerusalem. "Mr. Harry Fischel," he said, "is a great communal
worker in New York and he is also treasurer of the Central Relief Committee which subvents all the Yeshiboth, Talmud Torahs
and Talmudic scholars in Palestine. The reconstruction of Palestine is part and parcel of his life and the erection of the Beth
Harav merits much praise. Other institutions looked forward
to Mr. Fischel's help, one of these was the new building of the
Bicur Holim Hospital which was still roofless and required completion." Rabbi Abramowitz then handed the gold key of the Beth
Harav and Synagogue to Mr. Fischel.

Mr. Fischel, on rising to speak was received with cheers. He
seemed profoundly touched and speaking from notes in Hebrew,
he said:

הוד מעלתו, הרב קוק, הרב מאיר, אורחים נכבדים, גבירות ואדונים
נכבדים.

אין די מילים בפי ברגע זה להביע את הודתי לאלקי ישראל על
שזכני לבנות את בית הרב ואת בית המדרש. יכול אני להביע את
רגשותי על צד היותר טוב רק בברכי את „ברכת שהחתו" הידועה לנו:
ברוך אתה ה' אלהינו מלך העולם שהחינו וקימנו
והגיענו לזמן הזה.

„לבי במזרח ואנכי בסוף מערב". ביתי באמריקה. והיה עלי לעבר
ערך ששת אלפים מיל כדי להשתתף בחגיגה קדושה זו. הבאתי עמי את
אשתי הטובה, את בתי, את חתני את הרב גאלדשטיין ואת אחי אשתי
הרב ראובן בראז, שיקחו חלק עמי יחד בשמחת היום הזה.

ועד הבנין כבדני במפתח בית זה והעיד בזה שהבנין נגמר עתה
מהמסד ועד הטפחות. ואחר שהבית ובית המדרש מיועד לשמש לטובת
תושבי ארץ-ישראל ושהוד מעלתו הוא ראש הממשלה בארץ הזאת, אני
חושב לנכון ולטוב לכבד את הוד מעלתו במפתח וליעד אותו בתור מפקח
על הבנין הכפול הזה. רשאי אני לבקש את הוד מעלתו שיקבל את
מפתח לזהב הזה וישמרהו בתור זכר ומזכרת למאורע השוב זה.

רוצה אני להשתמש בהזדמנות גם כדי להודות להוד מעלתו בקהל-
עם על הכבוד שהנחיל לנו בכבדו את חנוכת הבית הזה בנוכחותיו. יהי
נועם ה' על הוד מעלתו על שלטונו ועל תושבי ארץ-ישראל ויברך אותו
ואותם בשלות השקט בבטחון גמור ובשלום בל ימוט. אמן.

Mr. Fischel then translated his speech into English for the benefit of those who could not understand the Hebrew. It was as follows:

"Your Excellency, Rabbi Kook, Rabbi Meir, distinguished Guests, Ladies and Gentlemen:

"Words fail me at this moment to express my gratitude to the Almighty for granting me the privilege of building this Beth Harav and Synagogue. I can best express my feelings on this occasion by pronouncing the well-known Schecheyanoo prayer 'Blessed art thou O Lord, only King of the Universe, who hast kept us in life and hast preserved us and enabled us to reach this time.'

"While my heart always beats for Palestine, yet my home is in America. I have, therefore, had to travel nearly 6,000 miles to participate in this holy celebration. I brought with me my good wife, daughter and son-in-law Rabbi and Mrs. Herbert Goldstein, and my wife's brother, Rabbi Rubin Braz, to share with me the joy of this day.

"The Building Committee has just presented me with the key of this house certifying thereby that this building is now completed. In view of the fact that this residence and synagogue are to be used for the benefit of the people of Palestine, and that Your Excellency, is the Chief Executive of the land, I therefore deem it fitting and proper to present you with the key, and designate you as custodian of this combined edifice. May I ask you, please, to accept this golden key and keep it as a souvenir and memento of this occasion? I want to take this means also of publicly thanking you for the honor you have bestowed upon us. May God grant you, your administration and the people of Palestine continued security and peace."

The High Commissioner followed and delivered an address, which was regarded by the assembly as of great political importance. He said in effect:

"I congratulate the Chief Rabbinate, Mr. and Mrs. Fischel and the Jewish Community at large on this auspicious day. Among the many problems with which the Civil Administration had to deal on its establishment was the adoption of measures to place the Jewish Community both on its secular and on its ecclesiastical side, upon a permanent and regular basis. The question of the organization of the secular side was not yet fully settled. But the government had been able to establish, on an electorial basis, the Chief Rabbinate, and for the first time after an interval of many centuries, a Jewish Ecclesiastical Authority had been founded upon a permanent footing, based upon the desires of the community itself. It was fortunate that the choice of the community had fallen upon Chief Rabbi Kook and Chief Rabbi Meir, who upheld the dignity of the other religious communities in Palestine. His Excellency expressed the gratitude that was universally felt to Mr. and Mrs. Fischel for the most generous gift of the spacious buildings that they were dedicating on that day.

They were all aware what was the purpose of the policy of the British Government in Palestine in relation to the Jews. That policy had been, was now and would remain, the promotion of the establishment of a Jewish National Home in Palestine. To that end political action must largely contribute. Not less important was the work and sacrifices of the Jews themselves. The erection of buildings such as these was but an instance of that work. More necessary even than bricks and mortar were the numbers of the Jewish population and even more important than numbers was their character. Upon the character of those who already lived in Palestine and those who came from other countries to live there, upon the loftiness of their ideals and the soundness of their principles, depended more than on any other factor the success of the Jewish National Home. That was the key to Palestine.

The High Commissioner's declaration was greeted with applause. The Choir with Cantor Rivlin then sang the Psalm of the Dedication, accompanied by the band.

Rabbi Herbert S. Goldstein, then inspiringly expressed his sentiments in English and his address was translated into Hebrew by Mr. Isaac Abadi. Rabbi Goldstein in the course of his remarks said that it was customary in America for members of the family and relatives participating in such celebrations to speak as briefly as possible. He touched on the past of the Jewish people and pointed out that its future existence depended on the Torah and its loftiness. He mentioned the fact that his father-in-law, Mr. Fischel, had crossed the ocean three times in his endeavors to help in the re-building of the country both materially and spiritually. He concluded his speech with a blessing for Chief Rabbi Kook.

Commander Luke, Acting Governor of Jerusalem, whose remarks were translated into Hebrew by Mr. Abadi, said:

"Permit me to thank the organizers of this celebration for inviting me and to congratulate Rabbi Kook. I hope he will be privileged to enjoy health in this new and beautiful house. I have also the honor of thanking the donors for their wisdom in choosing such a gift. I cannot imagine a finer and more appropriate form of philanthropy for Mr. and Mrs. Fischel, in this city, where the demand for decent residences is so great. It is undignified for persons occupying prominent positions and playing an active role in the people's life, to be troubled year in and year out with the housing problem. I hope that Mr. and Mrs. Fischel's example will be copied by others. I have no doubt that there will arise a Sefardic philanthropist who will also build a house for his Chief Rabbi. It is also possible to hope that the government will also follow suit and provide fine dwellings for its officials."

Mr. Cobb, the American Consul, was then called upon to address the gathering. He said, "It is for me a great and special pleasure that one of our citizens has done something great for Jerusalem. Two years ago Mr. Fischel told me that he contemplated doing great things for the benefit of this country, and his smallest deed is the erection of this house and making it an endowment for the Jewish Community in Jerusalem.

"Since I have been in Jerusalem, and in the course of my work, I have had the honor of coming in touch with Rabbis Kook and Meir. I know the value of the great work they are doing and I also know that many American citizens have been benefited therefrom. I trust that they will be spared for many years to carry on this good work."

At this stage the guests were served with tea and refreshments, and the band played selections.

Dr. Joseph Klausner then congratulated Mr. Fischel. He spoke on the importance of the Beth Harav and other such buildings which tend to strengthen our position in Eretz Israel. Dr. Klausner pointed out the necessity of acquiring more land, as the importance of the National Home the Jews have obtained centered around the forty years' labor to this end and the land already acquired.

Mr. David Yellin congratulated Mr. and Mrs. Fischel and Rabbi Kook on the occasion of the opening of the Beth Harav.

He said that such spacious buildings should also be erected for the Council of the Jerusalem Jews and the Jewish National Council.

The eminent Rabbi of Klausenburg, Rabbi Moses Samuel Glasner, spoke in a quivering and affected voice. He tearfully thanked the Almighty for having privileged him to come to Jerusalem to spend the remaining days of his life. The Beth Harav, which Mr. Fischel erected, would be a pride and an honor to the Jewish Community. He praisingly spoke of Rabbi Kook whom he had known in the Diaspora. He warmly shook hands with Rabbi Kook and also blessed the donors. Rabbi Harlap followed and delivered a learned address spiced with Rabbinical lore.

Rabbi Kook, who was received with great enthusiasm, opened with the Biblical text "What doth the Lord demand of thee but to do good, etc." With his usual profoundness he explained how Jerusalem was the source of joy. "The Key," he said, "that was handed to the High Commissioner, will also be a key to the inner soul of His Excellency wherewith to open up the gates of our Jewish National Home."

THE OFFICIAL OPENING

After the speeches, the High Commissioner and Lady Samuel, Chief Rabbis Kook and Jacob Meir, Mr. and Mrs. Fischel and their family and other prominent guests mounted the stairs leading to the Synagogue of the Beth Harav. The High Commissioner personally handed the golden key to Mr. Fischel who opened the doors of the Beth Hamedrash, throwing it open to the visitors. The Choir sang "Lift up your heads ye gates, and be ye lifted up, ye everlasting doors." That moment was indeed an auspicious and impressive one. The distinguished guests then inspected the beautiful house of the Beth Harav of Chief Rabbi Kook. Around servietted tables the visitors regaled themselves with excellent refreshments and the High Commissioner drank to the health of the Chief Rabbi, to Mr. Fischel and the other rabbis. He then took a friendly leave of the whole company.

In the meantime Mincha was prayed in the Beth Harav by Rabbi Goldstein, after which the festivities were renewed in accordance with the programme. Rabbi Rubin Braz delivered a fine address in Hebrew. He touched on the suffering of our brethren in Poland and the Ukraine, and said that their only hope

DEDICATION OF THE HOME OF THE CHIEF RABBI OF PALESTINE.

Mr. Fischel's gift to the Jewish Homeland, May 27, 1923.
Mr. Fischel presenting the key of the building
to Sir Herbert Samuel, British High Commissioner for Palestine.

was Palestine. His speech was very inspiring and created a deep impression on the gathering. He was followed by Rabbi J. M. Tikotchinsky; Rabbi Menaham Auerbach; Rabbi Joseph Gerson Horowitz; Rabbi Polanski; and a young Talmudic student, Isaac Levi, who spoke on behalf of the students in the Beth Harav Centre. All praised the good efforts of Mr. and Mrs. Harry Fischel. The speeches were concluded by two boys of the Etz Haim Yeshivah who pointed out that they were the most interested parties at the celebration, since they were the future carriers of the Torah.

The evening service was then read, after which the company gave themselves up to festivity. It was late in the night that the beautiful ceremony of the consecration of the Beth Harav was concluded and it made a deep impression on all who had the pleasure of being present. This day was indeed an auspicious one in the life of Jerusalem.

CHAPTER LI

LUNCHEON WITH SIR HERBERT SAMUEL

PRIOR to the departure of the High Commissioner and Lady Samuel, from the dedication ceremonies, an invitation was extended by Sir Herbert to Mr. and Mrs. Fischel, and Rabbi and Mrs. Goldstein to attend a formal luncheon at the Government House at a date to be fixed later. Sir Herbert also extended an invitation to Mr. Fischel to meet him at the Government House for a conference the following day at 2 o'clock.

This conference occupied nearly an hour and a half, during which the two discussed the entire work that had been undertaken by the Palestine Building, Loan and Savings Association. Sir Herbert explained to Mr. Fischel the difficult position in which he was placed as the chief official of the British government and as a Jew, in explaining to the population that his duty necessitated consideration for the needs of all the people, Arabs and Christians, as well as those of his own faith.

The next day the invitation to luncheon with Sir Herbert was delivered to Mr. Fischel by a representative of the High Commissioner. The invitation follows:

"His Excellency, the High Commissioner Sir Herbert Samuel and Lady Samuel extend an invitation to Mr. and Mrs. Fischel and Rabbi and Mrs. Herbert S. Goldstein, for a Luncheon which will be given in their honor at the Government House on Friday, June 1 at 12.45 precisely."

On the day set a Government automobile arrived at the hotel and conveyed the party to the Government House. Upon entering the salon where the High Commissioner received his official guests, the members were introduced to Sir Clayton, Sir and Lady Richmond and a Miss Franklin, a relative of Lady Samuel. The next half hour was taken up in very pleasant conversation.

At 1:30 the High Commissioner, acting as the escort of Mrs. Fischel, Sir Clayton escorting Mrs. Goldstein, Lady Samuel escorting Mr. Fischel and Miss Franklin acting as Rabbi Goldstein's escort, entered the dining room, whereupon Lady Samuel made the following statement before the party was seated: "I wish to inform you that while the Government House is conducted at all times in accordance with the Jewish dietary laws, on this occasion, with Rabbi Goldstein present as the head of the Union of Orthodox Jewish Congregations of America, we have made special preparations and the repast has been prepared under the supervision of a personal representative of Chief Rabbi Kook."

The party while at the table engaged in a general discussion of the great improvements which had taken place for the benefit of the Jewish people in Palestine since the Balfour Declaration and particularly under the administration of Sir Herbert. The High Commissioner took special pains to praise the work done by the Palestine Building, Loan and Savings Association, and took occasion to refer to information he had received from United States Supreme Court Justice Brandeis and Judge Mack as to the part Mr. Fischel had taken in initiating this enterprise.

Following the repast, the members of the party proceeded to the gardens of the Government House, and then were escorted through each apartment, with either Sir Herbert or Lady Samuel giving some incident or anecdote related about each room that proved extremely interesting. It was not until 3 o'clock that the assemblage broke up, after there had been a free discussion of practically every problem connected with Palestine and American participation in the work of upbuilding the country for the benefit of the Jewish people.

Throughout this visit to the Holy Land, Mr. Fischel took every opportunity to travel about the country and to visit the various towns and cities, and on every hand he was greatly impressed with the strides which had been made in the two years since he had previously been there. He was particularly impressed with the

zeal which marked the individual attitude of every Jew helping
to constitute Palestine as the newly created Jewish Home Land.

The magnetic influence exerted upon every visitor to the Holy
Land, and the strong desire of all who have once made the journey
to make it again, emphasizes Palestine's peculiar attraction to
every Jew. The Fischels left Jerusalem on June 7, hoping that the
Almighty might soon again grant them the opportunity to return.

Mr. and Mrs. Fischel had not planned to return until August
25, and so, with ten weeks to spare, they decided once again to
visit the places of their birth—Mrs. Fischel to visit Eishishok,
where she first saw the light of day, and Mr. Fischel to return to
his native town of Meretz.

Although these two towns were only twenty miles apart, a distance that could be easily covered in two hours, Eishishok was at
this time a Polish possession and Meretz was a part of Lithuania.

In order to reach this locality it was necessary for the Fischels
first to journey to Warsaw. The party, including Rabbi and Mrs.
Goldstein, arrived in Alexandria on June 8, where they embarked
on the steamer Diana for Italy. They reached Brindisi on June
10, and from there proceeded at once to Rome.

On arriving in Rome they visited the Vatican, where due to the
office held by Rabbi Goldstein as president of the Union of
Orthodox Jewish Congregations of America, an audience had been
arranged for him with the Pope. The Pope, however, was unable
to grant the audience because of the absence of his Secretary of
State, Cardinal Gasparri, unless Rabbi Goldstein should remain
in Rome for a week longer, when the Cardinal was expected to
return. As the itinerary had already been previously arranged,
this was impossible.

The party left Rome on June 12, proceeded to Venice and then
to Vienna. After a tour of that city they continued to Warsaw,
where they arrived on June 18.

As Treasurer of the Hebrew Sheltering and Immigrant Aid
Society, Mr. Fischel was here afforded the opportunity of observing the work the Society was doing in that city, then the busiest

spot in all Europe as regards emigration activities.   On June
20 the party was invited to the home of Mr. Farbstein, President
of the Mizrachi Organization of Poland as well as a deputy in the
Polish "Sejm".

By a fortunate coincidence, a conference of all the rabbis of
Poland was fixed for the following day, June 21, for the purpose
of preparing plans for participation in the next Zionist Congress
to be held at Carlsbad.   Mr. Farbstein, as President of the
Mizrachi, invited Mr. Fischel to attend this conference of the
Rabbis, a meeting he will never forget, attended as it was by more
than seventy-five rabbis, the leaders of Orthodox Jewry from
every part of Poland.

In the evening a banquet was arranged by the Mizrachi, with
Mr. Fischel as the guest of honor.   In his dual capacity as Treasurer, not only of the H.I.A.S. but of the Central Committee for
the Relief of Jews Suffering Through the War, Mr. Fischel was requested to give a report covering the work of war relief and of
the H.I.A.S. as well as his impressions of his visit to Palestine,
and his recommendations as a result thereof.

With three such vitally important subjects to discuss, Mr.
Fischel's report occupied nearly two hours.   The rabbis expressed
their appreciation of and gratitude for the opportunity to receive
at first hand information on these three subjects, each of great
import to the Jewish population of Poland.

It was Mr. Fischel's privilege at this time to personally meet
the most famous of all rabbis, the venerable Israel Meyer Cagan,
a sage of international renown, who bears the title of "Chofetz
Chaim." Although Mr. Fischel had been in frequent communication with this celebrated figure for many years, it was his first
opportunity to meet him in person.

On June 23, the party separated, Rabbi and Mrs. Goldstein
going to Germany and England from which latter country they
embarked for America, while Mr. and Mrs. Fischel left for Vilna,
preparatory to going to their respective birth places.

CHAPTER LII

MR. FISCHEL RETURNS TO HIS BIRTHPLACE

AFTER an absence of thirty-eight years, Mr. Fischel was now to return to the little town of Meretz where he had first seen the light of day and from which he had departed as a youth for a strange land, almost penniless, unfamiliar with the language of the country toward which his face was set and with only his boundless ambition and the teachings of his parents to sustain him.

He was now returning in middle life blessed with an abundance of this world's goods, his name virtually a household word to the Jewish people of every land. His thoughts comprised a mingling of gratitude for what he had been privileged to achieve in the passing of the years and of sadness because his beloved parents would not be a part of the familiar scene to greet him.

Arriving in Vilna on June 26, it was the plan of Mr. Fischel to proceed at once to Meretz, and Mrs. Fischel to go to her birth place, Eishishok. As they had, however, but one passport between them, it was necessary to secure individual passports in order to reach their respective birth places, which were now under the control of two different governments. Mr. Fischel soon learned that in Poland, where a new government had only recently been set up, the obtaining of a duplicate or individual passport would ordinarily require at least a month's time before it received the approval of the various departments that had to pass upon it.

He accordingly determined to seek out some friend who could help him out of the difficulty, and it occurred to him that while in Carlsbad in 1921 attending the Zionist Congress, he had made the acquaintance of Rabbi Rubenstein, who was now a Senator in the Polish Parliament. Mr. Fischel therefore called upon Rabbi Rubenstein and much to his surprise was greeted with a kiss.

He explained his difficulties, and Rabbi Rubenstein at once exerted all his influence to assist him, with the result that on the same day he received the necessary passport.

Before proceeding on his journey, Mr. Fischel went with Mrs. Fischel to a monument maker in Vilna to obtain a suitable tombstone for the grave of Mrs. Fischel's mother, who was buried in the town of Eishishok. This stone was later put in place in their presence. On the day following, Mr. and Mrs. Fischel separated, the former leaving for Meretz, now a part of Lithuania, and the latter for Eishishok, that was under Polish rule.

Arriving at the frontier at about noon, Mr. Fischel was required to show the sum of money he had taken out of Poland, it then being a rule of the Government that no one should depart from its borders with more than 500,000 marks, amounting to only about $5 in American currency. This law was due to the impoverished condition of the country. As Mr. Fischel had 850,000 marks in his possession, the officials retained the excess of 350,000 marks until he returned at a later date.

Mr. Fischel arrived in Riga at about 10 o'clock in the evening, leaving for Kovno, the capital of Lithuania, the same night and arriving there the following morning.

On reaching Kovno Mr. Fischel went at once to the office of the Hebrew Sheltering and Immigrant Aid Society, where he deposited his belongings. He spent the entire day in reviewing the work of this local branch that was enabled to extend its aid to thousands of emigrants and in the evening was called upon by a committee headed by Mr. Rosenbloom, Minister of Jewish Affairs in the Lithuanian Cabinet, and who only that day had been appointed to this high office.

The purpose of the committee's call was to secure from Mr. Fischel a report on conditions in Palestine and on the work of the Hebrew Sheltering and Immigrant Aid Society in America and it was one o'clock in the morning when they departed.

The next day, June 29, at 9:00 A.M., Mr. Fischel left by automobile for the town of Meretz, upon which he had not laid eyes since his memorable departure thirty-eight years before. As he passed through the various nearby towns, Rumshishok, Yesna, Pren and finally Alita, all of which reminded him of his boyhood days and when his thoughts naturally turned to the memory of his parents, he counted the moments when he should again at last gaze upon the scenes of his youth.

Finally, the chauffeur told him that he was only twenty-five miles from Meretz. It was but a short time later when his conveyance reached the first house on the outskirts of the town, one of a row of entirely new homes that had been built by the Joint Distribution Committee upon the ruins of those devastated during the war. A moment more and he was at Mark Place, a landmark of the ancient town, which seemed strangely unfamiliar to him, as it appeared much smaller than the picture he had retained in his memory.

At this point he was greeted by a committee made up of the most representative men of the place who were accompanied by a large number of the townspeople. He was escorted to the home of Chaim Izchok Lukenizky, the wealthiest man in Meretz. Mr. Fischel was met at the threshold by Mr. Lukenizky, whom he recognized immediately, as well as by the latter's wife and son, who extended a most cordial welcome. A large crowd had followed Mr. Fischel to the door of the residence, and Mr. Lukenizky pleaded in vain with this throng to remain at a distance until Mr. Fischel should have been entertained at lunch.

His host was finally compelled to close the doors in order that privacy might be obtained. Following luncheon, the doors were opened, and one by one the townsmen extended the "Shalom Aleichem" greetings. This reception lasted for several hours. A committee was then organized to act as Mr. Fischel's bodyguard during his stay in Meretz. Mr. Fischel advised his former neighbors of the purpose of his visit, which was to unveil a tombstone which he had previously ordered erected over the graves of his father and mother.

Some time later, Mr. Fischel was escorted to the cemetery,

about half a mile distant, and the road to which lay upon a steep hill. This walk, together with the excitement attending his mission, all but exhausted Mr. Fischel, but when he arrived at the graves of his parents he forgot his physical weariness, which was supplanted by a great peace and contentment.

In his imagination, it seemed his parents were still living and that he was able once again to talk with them. He finally realized, however, that he was, after all, only standing beside their graves. Uttering a prayer that their souls might rest in peace, Mr. Fischel returned to the town, announcing that the unveiling of the tombstone would take place the following Sunday morning.

As Mr. Fischel returned to Meretz and passed the different homes and other landmarks, the memories of his youth came back with full force and he even recalled the names of nearly all the families that had occupied these houses at the time he had left for far off America.

Although most of these friends of his boyhood had since died and a new generation had grown up, the houses nevertheless remained much the same, except for those which had been destroyed during the war, and Meretz, as a whole, was little different than it had been for hundreds of years.

Escorted by the Committee, Mr. Fischel walked through every street and was greeted by the residents who called to him from the windows or welcomed him from their small stoops. Finally he reached the house that had been occupied by his parents at the time he had left Meretz for America. He was greatly touched when an aged woman shouted to him at the top of her voice "Archick, (his pet name as a boy), is it you? Do you remember me?"

While the woman had greatly changed in appearance and her hair was now almost white, Mr. Fischel immediately recognized her, and replied, "Yes, Dobke" (the pet name by which he had known her in his youth). As a girl, this now elderly woman had been a close neighbor of the Fischels, and Mr. Fischel had been strongly attracted to her. It was not improbable had he remained in Meretz that they would have been married.

On leaving his old home, the party was met by the Shamas, who cried out, "In Shool Erein," which meant that it was an hour before sunset and time to light the candles and repair to the synagogue. The men were thus informed that they had half an hour to close their places of business and get ready for the Sabbath. Before the thirty minutes had elapsed, however, every Jewish man in the town and every boy from the age of six years up was on his way to synagogue. Mr. Fischel forthwith fell into line.

When he had reached the synagogue, he was escorted to the seat which had been occupied by his father from the time the synagogue was erected until the latter's death. Following the services, the congregation filed past Mr. Fischel's seat, one by one extending to him the customary greeting of "Good Shabbos."

After the Shabbos supper at the home of Mr. Lukenizky a number of townsfolk whom he had not previously seen, some of whom had been absent on his arrival, called upon him and extended their welcome. Mr. Fischel then conferred at length with Mr. Lukenizky as to the needs of the town, it being his desire to make some substantial contribution in memory of his father and mother. Mr. Lukenizky informed Mr. Fischel that what the town most needed was a Talmud Torah building. There were, he stated, more than two hundred children in Meretz who were compelled to receive religious instruction in scattered and out of the way buildings and in rooms unsuited to the purpose.

On Saturday morning Mr. Fischel went again to the synagogue where he once more occupied the seat his father had had before him and, after chanting "Maftir," announced his decision to build a Talmud Torah on the site of what had been the largest synagogue in Meretz, and which had been destroyed during the war.

Tremendous enthusiasm greeted this announcement and Mr. Fischel received expressions of gratitude from all present. Following the services, the line again formed towards his seat, with more expressions of "Good Shabbos," and additional thanks for the building he had pledged.

Following dinner, the Committee from the Talmud Torah called upon Mr. Fischel and invited him to review the work of the children in the various religious schools. Mr. Fischel was greatly impressed with the scholarship shown by the children as in each class he was greeted by one boy who addressed to him a poem, delivered in Hebrew, after which copies of the several poems were presented to him.

Mr. Fischel enjoyed every moment of this day, and indeed, all the time he spent in Meretz. On Saturday afternoon he abandoned his usual custom of taking a nap and took advantage of the opportunity to walk through the town by himself. On his return to the residence of his host, he intended to take a short rest, but found a committee awaiting him from the Keren Hayesod, which requested him to come with them to the Synagogue to give them a report on Palestine.

On reaching the synagogue he found the building crowded to the doors. He spoke for about an hour. Following this address, "Mincha" services were held, after which the congregation went to Sholesh Sudas. Before this repast was finished, a committee from the Folk Shule called upon Mr. Fischel for assistance.

After a conference, during which the committee explained the sort of education that was given to the children, Mr. Fischel pointed out his dissatisfaction with their course of instruction and suggested that the Shule should combine with the Talmud Torah, to which program the committee gave virtual assent. Mr. Fischel then named a committee of six persons, four from the Talmud Torah and two from the Folk Shule, with the Rabbi as Chairman, which was to enter upon the task of working out a suitable program for combining the two activities.

The following day, Sunday, Mr. Fischel arose at 5:30 and went to the first services in the synagogue which began at 6 A. M. As he left his room he had a most unusual experience. He noticed a small woman nearly ninety years of age, feeble and wizened, standing near his door. As she saw him emerge the woman struck her thin hands together, in kind and motherly fashion, crying out "Is this you Artchick, my child?"

At first thought Mr. Fischel conceived the idea in his already excited mind that it was his mother. Again he recalled, his mother was dead.

Turning to the woman he asked, "Who are you?"

She answered, "I nursed you for a time when your mother was unable to do so."

Seeing before him the woman who had given to him of her life blood, Mr. Fischel was overcome. He could hardly express his feelings in words.

Standing before him was, in a sense, his foster mother and all he could think of was "Does she need my aid?"

When he asked if she required anything she at first replied "No." Then on his insistence that he be told if he might do something for her she answered that the only thing she needed was "ausrichting," meaning in translation, a shroud for her burial. Mr. Fischel at once gave her the sum required for this purpose whereupon she thanked and repeatedly blessed him. He left her sitting near his room, declaring that he would find her upon his return, but he never saw her again.

It so happened that this Sunday, the 17th of Tamuz, was Mr. Fischel's 58th birthday.

Following the Synagogue services and accompanied by a large gathering, Mr. Fischel proceeded to the cemetery to unveil the monument dedicated in memory of his father and mother.

These services, in which virtually the entire town took part, were most impressive and formed a fitting requiem for a man and woman who, throughout all their lives, had been noted for their piety and charitable deeds and for their personal service and sacrifice in behalf of all their neighbors, although they themselves had not been endowed with a large share of this world's goods.

Indeed, for the more than sixty years Mr. Fischel's parents

MR. FISCHEL PRAYING AT THE GRAVES OF HIS PARENTS

Tombstones marking the last resting place of his Father and Mother in their native town, Meretz.

were married, no element of schism or discord ever arose between them and they set an example to all Meretz in the way of love, respect and sacrifice for each other until the day they finally parted.   May their souls indeed rest in peace.

As Mr. Fischel did not expect soon to visit this hallowed spot again he had a photograph taken of the monument so that he might have it always before him.

From the cemetery he went once more to the Rabbi's house to perfect the details for the building of the new Talmud Torah. On the advice of the Rabbi he appointed a Committee with power to arrange the plans for the new building and also to let the contracts and to proceed with the work.

This Committee was given authority to draw on the money that Mr. Fischel deposited for the purpose with the local branch of the Hebrew Sheltering and Immigrant Aid Society in Kovno. Mr. Fischel before leaving Meretz, laid the cornerstone of the new building in the presence of a large audience that assembled without special invitations or other notice.

When Mr. Fischel returned to the United States he was notified by the Committee appointed to carry out the work that the cost would be almost three times the amount which he had pledged.   Although he was naturally surprised at this information, Mr. Fischel, determined that, as the structure was intended as a memorial to his parents, no deficit should interfere with the progress of construction.   Accordingly he at once cabled the additional sum to the Committee, instructing it to proceed with the building.   Not even this sum, however, proved to be sufficient for the needs as they arose and before the project was completed another check was required.

When, however, Mr. Fischel later received in America a photograph of the completed building he felt the money had been well expended and he was thankful for the opportunity that had been afforded him to thus commemorate the holy, sacred and devoted lives of his father and mother, in his native town.

When the time came for his departure from Meretz an automobile awaited him and he left carrying with him the cheers, blessings and Godspeed, of all the inhabitants.

In addition, Mr. Fischel received on his return home, a great many letters of gratitude and was particularly proud of one received from the Meretz Relief Association in New York. This letter was as follows:

MERETZ RELIEF ASSOCIATION

Mr. Harry Fischel,
118 East 93rd Street,
New York City.   New York, May 24, 1924.

Dear Sir and Brother:

It gives us great pleasure to remit this, the united congratulations and thanks of all our members at their last meeting, May 18, 1924, at 79 Delancey Street, New York.

Taking great pride in your inestimable philanthropy in this country, in your inexhaustible energy in work devoted solely for the benefit of the needy and poor, weak and helpless, young and old; your participation actively in educational enterprises for our own Holy Faith and for the furthering and steady advancement of Americanization of our people; for the incessant stream of funds, for the masterly organization of many co-workers and millions of contributors for our starving brothers in Europe, we feel joyful to have you as one of ours, and pronounce and hail you as King of Industry, Prince of Charity and Father to millions of helpless here and abroad.

What prompts us to express, (hardly enough) our long cherished opinion of your noble deeds, is this. We have learned from our home town, Meretz, that on your recent visit you have erected an eternal statue to your credit by organizing and financing the erection of a new fireproof, up-to-date Talmud Torah in Meretz; a building which will accommodate hundreds of students, who will be trained under modern Orthodox instructors to *respect*, *know* and *cherish* our Torah, Bible and all of Hebrew Literature. Not only have you given them the entire sum of money to build,

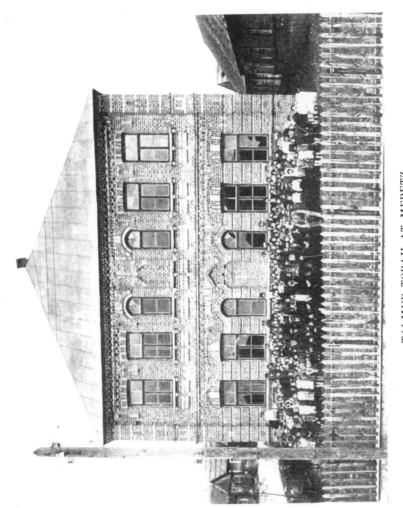

TALMUD TORAH AT MERETZ

Presented by Mr. Fischel to his birthplace in memory of his parents.

complete and furnish the building, but you have even pledged partial support of maintenance.

It is our united wish that in compensation of your untiring efforts for Meretz and the Jewish community in general, that our Great God bless you with everlasting health, happiness to the extent of your own wishes, great joy for you and yours now and ever.

Very truly yours,

MERETZ RELIEF ASSOCIATION

SIMON HORWITZ, Pres.

SEAL   A. S. BLOCK, Secy.

Leaving Meretz, Mr. Fischel arrived in Kovno on July 2, on his return trip. He was received at once at the home of the famous Rabbi Abraham Shapiro, Chief Rabbi of Lithuania, in whose company he had the privilege of visiting practically every Jewish institution in the capital of that country, taking especial pleasure in his visit to the Yeshiva in Slobodka.

Returning from Kovno to Riga, Mr. Fischel had an unusual experience indicative of the obstacles placed in the path of travelers who sought to go from one country to another.

While on the train he was awakened at 3 A. M. by an official of Latvia who told him that his passport was only vized to leave Latvia and not to enter it. According to this interpretation of the law, Mr. Fischel was made to understand that all that could be done was to allow him to leave the train at the next station.

Understanding conditions as he did, however, he parleyed with this official, finally asking how much money would be required to cause him to change his mind. Mr. Fischel was told that a sum equal to $10 in American money would solve the problem. Paying this amount and again retiring he was awakened in another half hour by another official who stated that the $10 he had given to the previous dignitary was only for the purpose of permitting him to remain on the train and that when he reached Riga he would be placed in the custody of the authorities.

Mr. Fischel then asked what sum would finally clear him of his heinous crime and was advised that if he would part with an amount equal to $25 in American money, all would be well. He gladly paid this sum.

When Riga was reached, however, he found two officials awaiting him at the station who escorted him to the Police Commissioner. Fortunately, Mr. Fischel had upon his person the letter from Secretary of State Hughes. Upon perusing this document, the mien of the police officers changed at once and the Commissioner began to apologize. He then wasted no time in vizeing Mr. Fischel's passport without further ado.

From Riga Mr. Fischel returned to Vilna and from that city went via automobile to Eishishok, his wife's birthplace.

Eishishok is located but a few miles from the town of Radin, where the foremost sage, Rabbi Israel Meyer Cagan, (the Chofetz Chaim) lives in the celebrated Talmudical college of that place, known the world over.

Mr. Fischel had been only a few hours in Eishishok when Rabbi Cagan was informed of his presence and at once sent an automobile bus used for the purpose of conveying students from the station at Radin to the Yeshiva, to take him there. Accompanying the bus was a Committee of students.

Mr. Fischel was met at a considerable distance from the Yeshiva by the Rabbi, then 86 years of age, who personally escorted him to his home and then through the Talmudical college. Although Mr. Fischel had met Rabbi Cagan before in Warsaw, a deep impression was created upon him through his visit to his home and to the Yeshiva where the Rabbi had spent virtually his entire life in preparing his many writings which had exercised so great an influence upon Jewish religious culture and thought.

Mr. Fischel was particularly impressed with the fact that so eminent a man and one who had contributed so much to the thought of his time, should live in such a modest environment.

From Eishishok, Mr. and Mrs. Fischel returned to Warsaw

where they remained until July 15th. There was still six weeks or thereabouts remaining before August 25, the date fixed for their sailing for home, and Mr. and Mrs. Fischel decided to go to Carlsbad, where they might be able to attend the Zionist Congress of that year, to which Mr. Fischel had been elected a delegate by the Mizrachi Zionist organization in Warsaw.

While Mr. Fischel had attended the Zionist Congress in 1921, the Congress of 1923, nevertheless, proved a most impressive event to him.

CHAPTER LIII

MEMORIAL TO PRESIDENT HARDING IN CARLSBAD

On August 3rd, the sad news was received in Carlsbad of the death of the President of the United States, Warren G. Harding. This tragic information caused every American great grief and in order that their sentiment might be properly expressed, a memorial meeting was at once arranged at one of the large hotels.

The invitation to this meeting was issued by Morris Engelman, Financial Secretary of the Central Jewish Relief Committee, who happened to be in Carlsbad at the time and a notice was posted in every hotel, so that on August 5th a large assemblage of Americans met in the Hotel Kroh for the purpose of giving voice to the great loss sustained by the nation.

The Committee that arranged the meeting was headed by Morris Engelman and included Charles Garfiel, Adolph Kulptman, Samuel Markowitz, Louis Roggen, Cantor Josef Rosenblatt, Morris Rothenberg, Jacob W. Wertheimer and Mr. Fischel of New York; Henry Spira of Cleveland and Louis Topkis of Wilmington, Delaware.

The minutes of the memorial meeting are given herewith:

Minutes of the Memorial Meeting held by American Citizens, pursuant to the call hereto annexed, at Hotel Kroh, Carlsbad, Czecho-Slovakia, on August fifth, Nineteen Hundred and Twenty-three, at three o'clock in the afternoon.

The meeting was opened by Mr. Morris Engelman, who suggested that Judge Samuel Strassburger of New York, act as chairman of the occasion. Judge Strassburger addressing the assemblage said in part:

"Ladies and Gentlemen; Fellow Americans, residents of Czecho-Slovakia and representatives of the different nations present: It is with deep sorrow that we are gathered here today to express our heartfelt sympathy and sadness caused by the terrible shock of the unexpected death of our dearly beloved President of the United States, Warren G. Harding. It is not for me to make any extended remarks at this time. We l..ve present a number of representative men and women who will address you and I will call upon them to express the sorrow we all feel so keenly."

The following then spoke: Mr. Samuel Markewich of New York, Mr. M. V. Joseph of Birmingham, Ala., Mr. Henry Spiro of Cleveland, O., Mr. Harry Fischel of New York, Dr. Bernard Kaufman of San Francisco, Cal., Mr. S. B. Kamaiko of Chicago, Ill., Dr. Armand Kaminka of Vienna.

The eulogies were eloquent, heartfelt and sincere. The gathering was largely attended and fitting resolutions were adopted and ordered to be cabled to Washington and a copy of same forwarded to the family.

At the suggestion of one of the young American women present, the audience rose and with bowed heads remained silent and in prayer.

The following prayer was then uttered by Chief Rabbi Samuel Reich:

Warren G. Harding, President of the United States of America is dead. We, prostrate in prayer, Almighty God, beseech Thee to receive him in grace in Thy Heavenly regions. Thou art called in the Holy Scriptures, the father of the orphans and the oppressed. We pray to you to look down and see how America has proved itself the kindhearted mother of the unfortunate victims of the late World War. We praise Thee every morning for that. Thou clothest the naked, Thou liberatest the fettered, Thou comfortest the oppressed and broken-hearted and Thou helpest the destitute. All these virtues have America's great and noble people exercised in Europe under the administration of the departed President. America has stars in its National flag. When Europe was enveloped in darkness and despair, the American star of charity spread forth its shining light of hope and relief. Thy homeless and expelled children of the old country have been received with love and kindness in America and now that the soul of the deceased President flies from this world into Thy Heavenly domains, we unite in prayer to Thee to take him up into Thy grace and love and grant him eternal peace and rest. Father in Heaven, give Thy blessings to this great nation, unequalled in human history, which is the hope for the future of the entire world. May the many tears the American people have helped dry in Europe fall as mild dew on the work of President Coolidge and his advisors, so that America may continue with glory to flourish and to prosper. Amen.

At the conclusion of the meeting it was voted unanimously to send a cable to the Secretary of State in Washington, conveying the resolutions that were passed unanimously, and the Committee defrayed the cost of this cable which was as follows:

TO THE SECRETARY OF STATE,
WASHINGTON, D. C.

At a meeting of American citizens, held on August fifth, Nineteen Hundred Twenty Three, at Hotel Kroh, Carlsbad, Czecho-Slovakia, the following was unanimously adopted:

RESOLVED, That we, citizens of the United States, deeply mourn the loss of our beloved President Warren G. Harding and join with our fellow citizens at home in the nation's sorrow.

The sudden death of our beloved President is not only a severe blow to our nation, but, as we believe, an irretrievable loss to all humanity throughout the entire world.

Our heartfelt and deepest sympathy is herewith extended to Mrs. Harding, Dr. Harding, the father, and to all the members of the family of our late lamented President.

A large number of newspapers both in Europe and America commented at length upon this meeting, which was one of the first memorial meetings held in Europe in honor of the late President of the United States.

Among these articles was the following appearing in the London Chronicle of August 10th:

HARDING MEMORIAL MEETING

Carlsbad, August 6th.

A memorial meeting to the late President Harding was held here yesterday. Judge Strassburger presided. The portrait of President Harding, framed in oak leaves, was prominently displayed.

Rabbi Reich referred to the gigantic relief activity which has been organized by the United States, under President Harding's administration, on behalf of stricken Europe. The Rabbi concluded with a prayer to God to be gracious to the soul of President Harding who had sought to bring about world peace.

Mr. Markewich spoke of the liberty and prosperity enjoyed by all American citizens without any distinction of race. The whole world, he said, mourned the loss of the American nation.

Mr. Harry Fischel said that they had lost not only a President but a friend of humanity and of the whole world. President Harding had more than once personally ordered that immigrants who were refused admission to the United States, because the quota figures were exhausted, should be allowed to land. He had taken immense interest in the welfare of the immigrants. On one occasion he had allowed himself to be photographed together with members of the Hebrew Sheltering and Immigrant Aid Society. Mr. Fischel proposed that a telegram of condolence should be addressed by the meeting to Mr. Secretary Hughes, and through him to the whole American nation and to Mr. Harding's family.

Mr. S. B. Kamaiko, of the American-Lithuanian Chamber of Commerce, related that a few weeks ago, just before he had set out on his visit to Lithuania, he had met President Harding who had spoken to him of his hope that the new States of Europe would learn the lesson of liberty from the United States. In the same way, when Professor Masaryk, the President of Czecho-Slovakia, was on his visit to America President Harding had spoken with him of his hope that Czecho-Slovakia would always pursue the paths of humanity and of right, and would accord full protection to her minority nationalities.

Other speakers were Dr. Kaufman, President of the American Medical men in Vienna; Mr. Joseph Birmingham, a non-Jew; Mr. Spiro and Miss Engelman, on behalf of the American women.

In the proposal of Mr. Spiro, a telegram of condolence has been sent to Marion, President Harding's native town.

While Mr. and Mrs. Fischel had only to take a train from Carlsbad to Paris and then go a short distance to Cherbourg to board the steamer on which they were leaving for the United States, they were confronted once again, however, with the problem that faced them on their previous visit to Europe in 1921, namely, that they would be compelled to desecrate the Sabbath were they to board the vessel at that port, as the steamer was to arrive in Cherbourg on Saturday morning and to leave on Saturday afternoon.

They took advantage, accordingly, of their previous experience and journeyed to London so that they might reach Southampton and board the vessel on Friday afternoon.

While on the way from Carlsbad to London they visited Holland. Going from Amsterdam to the Hague, they particularly enjoyed the opportunity of visiting the World Peace Tribunal. To do this they had to secure special permission from the American Legation. Mr. Fischel here again presented his letter from Secretary Hughes which secured for him a great degree of courtesy and attention. They were escorted by the Secretary of the Legation through every part of the building, and formed the conclusion that the structure was one of the most impressive and most beautiful in the world.

From the Hague they went to Rotterdam and from Rotterdam to Antwerp. Leaving Antwerp by boat, they went to Harwich, England, from there to London and then to Southampton, where they reached their steamer on Friday, August 24, again finding that arrangements had been made by the Cunard Line to enable them to observe the dietary laws on their return voyage.

CHAPTER LIV

REPORTS ON JEWISH HOMELAND BUILDING

Arriving back in America once more, Mr. Fischel found the Jewish public eagerly awaiting a report on the progress that had been made in the upbuilding of the Jewish homeland in Palestine. The Fischels reached port on Saturday, September 1, but in order not to desecrate the Sabbath did not land until the evening of that day.

Mr. Fischel was visited on ship-board by many newspaper representatives who requested an interview on his impressions gained while in Europe and Palestine but he refused an extended statement at that time, because of his intention later to prepare a complete and detailed report for submission to the stockholders of the Palestine Cooperative Company and the Palestine Building Loan and Savings Association, as constituents of the Palestine Development Council.

Several months later, on October 21, these organizations arranged a reception for Judge Julian W. Mack, Emanuel N. Mohl, and Mr. Fischel, that was held in the Hotel Pennsylvania and on which occasion Mr. Fischel delivered the following report:

Two Years of Great Progress in Palestine

In order to show the progress in Palestine, I will review briefly the situation as I found it two years ago as compared with its present condition.

My interest in Palestine, as far as the economic side is concerned, dates back to 1910 when I made my first pilgrimage to the Holy Land, and purchased a grove for oranges, esrogim, lemons, almonds, etc. Immediately after the promulgation of the Balfour Declaration, together with some friends, I planned a Palestine Development Corporation, to include in its scope every form of

325

commercial and industrial enterprise. We were advised at that time to defer action.

Disturbed that it was not my privilege to do something concrete for the upbuilding of our Holy Land, I determined two years ago, to make a second trip, to examine the situation and see what could be done. Together with Mrs. Fischel and some friends, I left for Palestine prayerfully hoping that the Holy One, Blessed Be He, would show us the path of duty.

We left on Independence Day, 1921, and arrived in Jerusalem on July 21. A few days later I received an invitation from His Excellency the High Commissioner to visit him. Upon inquiry he advised that we first make a tour through Palestine, and then decide what ought to be taken up immediately. We heeded his advice and spared no pains to thoroughly investigate the possibilities of the country. Needless to say, we visited the large and small cities, the old and new colonies. Being for so many years a real estate operator and builder, I was naturally more interested along these lines.

Upon investigation I found frightful conditions. From the close of the war to the date of our arrival, about 20,000 Jews had migrated to Palestine. No provisions, whatsoever, had been made to house them. The people in the larger cities, especially in Jerusalem, were in danger of contracting disease due to overcrowding. Not a single house had been built from the beginning of the war up to that time, 1921. The old houses, owned largely by the Arabs, contained no sanitary improvements whatsoever. The newcomers had to pay a very high rental, and were forced in many instances to deposit in advance rental for three years, which money was used by the owner for constructing an additional story to his house. All this was due to the lack of room and to the more important fact that little or no money could be obtained on mortgages on real estate, in spite of the fact that the owners were ready to pay from 18 per cent to 25 per cent interest. Naturally under such conditions no houses could be built or even attempted.

Upon my return to New York, I called a conference of many of the most successful real estate men and builders in New York. I laid the proposition before them. We then formed a company for the purpose of making building loans in Palestine. It was to be known as the Palestine Development Corporation.

It so happened, at the same time, that the eminent Jurists, Justices Louis D. Brandeis and Julian W. Mack and Mr. Sol Rosenbloom of Pittsburgh, Mr. Jacob deHaas, the well known Zionist worker and many others had withdrawn from the Zionist Organization of America, in order to do practical work in Palestine. As luck would have it, they were informed of our plans and invited us to join with them and work together in the same direction. Since our motive and sole purpose was to help relieve the terrible congestion in Jerusalem and its outlying districts, we accepted the proposition and amalgamated. Half of our initial capital was furnished by the Palestine Cooperative Company, known as the Brandeis-Mack Company and half by my associates and myself. Then Mr. Sol Rosenbloom went to Palestine and organized the Palestine Building Loan and Savings Association. We were fortunate to obtain the services of Mr. E. N. Mohl, an able and most enthusiastic worker in the building line, to act as our Palestine manager. No time was wasted and applications for loans were received immediately.

While the general opinion always prevailed that all the Jews of Palestine are dependent upon charity, this was entirely disproved by the fact that in a very short time the applications for loans from a very large number of Jewish home seekers amounted to over $400,000. This represented 60 per cent. of the cost of construction for new houses. Almost every one of these borrowers was ready to furnish the additional 40 per cent. of the cost of the building, in accordance with our requirements. Since our capital was limited, only the most deserving applications for loans were accepted, and these amounted to over $300,000 which amount we were then able to supply. In a short time we were deluged with applications from every part of Palestine. Since the amount we appropriated had been exhausted, the only thing for us to do was to sell more stock in our Company in order to grant more loans.

As Chairman of the Building Loan Committee I felt that before we made an effort to sell more of our stock, it would be advisable for me to go to Palestine and see with my own eyes what had been accomplished; what the immediate and future requirements were; how many of the new applicants were able to furnish the 40 per cent. of the building cost; how many were ready to start building; whether enough material was obtainable, whether the

houses which were being erected could be improved upon by
American methods; whether the cost of the buildings could be
reduced; in short, I wanted to make a general survey of the entire housing situation so as to make my first report of our progress and needs.

Accordingly, accompanied by Mrs. Fischel, I left New York
on this April 24, for Palestine, arrived in Jerusalem on May 9,
and started to work immediately. I will not at this time speak
of the general beauty of Palestine nor of its magnetic power to
attract people to come again once they have visited the Holy
Land, nor will I dwell on the benefits from the Balfour Declaration, or the duty of every Jew in America to help build a homeland for the hundreds of thousands of Jewish sufferers from
devastated Europe. I will limit my report to a picture of the
Building Loan and Savings Association, which the Almighty has
given me the privilege of helping to organize, and the Association's accomplishments for Palestine; the effect it has had on the
housing situation; on general business; in furnishing employment; in lowering the prevailing interest rate and in cementing the
ties of friendship between the Arabs and the Jewish people.

MY IMPRESSIONS

The office of our Company, namely the Palestine Building Loan
and Savings Association, occupies two rooms in a so-called office
building in Jerusalem. I spent several days going through all
the books, the form of mortgages, the form of building loans, the
contracts, plans and specifications of buildings in course of construction, as well as the general work of the Company. As one
who has had 37 years experience in the real estate and building
business, I was very pleasantly surprised and satisfied to find
the entire system in such splendid working order. As Mr. Mohl,
who introduced American methods in a country where such things
were unknown, is giving all his time to this work gratis, there is
practically no expense except that of a stenographer and an office
boy.

After examining all this work in the office, Mr. Mohl took me
to the several districts where the houses are being built with our
loans, namely, Boni Baith, Talpiot, Romamo and several houses
scattered throughout the city of Jerusalem, as well as Bath Galim

in Haifa, none of which locations are more than thirty minutes walk from the city of Jerusalem or from the city of Haifa and about ten minutes ride by a bus line which has already been established for the benefit of the settlers.

Words fail me to express my amazement and pleasure at what our building loans have accomplished in such a short time and with the small amount of capital invested by our Company. Mountains of rocks have been transformed into cities, wildernesses into beautiful gardens.

We first reached Romamo, the settlement nearest to the city of Jerusalem. I did not believe my own eyes when I saw this beautiful piece of land, developed where had been nothing but heaps of stones, probably since the destruction of Jerusalem, now made into wide streets, divided into large building plots, upon some of which beautiful residences have been erected by the so-called Bal-ha-Batim or the richer class of Jerusalem. While not all of the homes are being built with our loans, however, this section has been started through the impetus given by our organization. General Allenby, when he entered Jerusalem, had stopped at that part of the city and for that reason a beautiful boulevard was laid out and a splendid monument is being erected at the entrance to the boulevard.

We then proceeded to Talpiot, which is a beautiful piece of land on the road to Hebron. Its position is most glorious, with a view of the entire city of Jerusalem as well as of the Dead Sea. This land was bought by a group of business men several years ago, but they were unable to start building until our Company was ready to make building loans. Almost every house in that section, with the exception of probably four or five, are being built with our loans and a large number of persons are waiting to commence operations as soon as we are ready to grant more loans.

We then proceeded to a district which I consider the most beautiful and picturesque place near Jerusalem, namely Boni Baith. If I had the ability of Rabbi Jehuda Halevi, I would be able to adequately express the pleasurable emotions which I experienced on that spot. A large mountain of rocks in the shape of a horse shoe had been transformed in less than six months into a most beautiful town. Fifty-nine houses were being constructed, many of which are now completed. Every one without exception is being erected with our loans and there are three times that number ready to be built if we could only make more loans. The mountain has been converted into large terraces with houses built in such a way that the houses on the upper terraces overlook the tops of those on the lower. There are fine entrances with beautiful gardens in front of every house and each house has a remarkable view of Jerusalem and the entire Judean mountains.

Although these houses are not of the very expensive kind, the architectural designs displayed are very picturesque and are beyond my limited power of description. No two houses look alike. The owners of these houses, all of whom are of the intellectual class, namely teachers, bank clerks and Government employees, exercised their own love of beauty in preparing the plans. They paid special attention to the laying out of the lawns, gardens and flower beds. They quit their work in the offices at about 3 in the afternoon, for they begin work at 7 in the morning. When they reach home, they spend the rest of the day, to as late as 9 at night, working to help finish their homes, especially the lawns and gardens. It would do your heart good, as it did mine, to see the pleasure they derive in doing this work.

They sing the most melodious Hebrew songs and appear to be very happy. They enjoy their little homes much more than many a multi-millionaire in America enjoys his mansion. I asked several of them how they can stand the strain of so many hours additional work after finishing their regular daily tasks and the answer was unanimous—"I am now realizing the dream of my life which is to have my own home. Besides, I am not only building my own house, I am also helping to build Palestine, the home of the Jewish people."

A feeling of this kind prevails, not only in this settlement of Boni Baith, but in every section where houses are being erected. The joy in the thought that they will soon move from the old dilapidated houses without any sanitary facilities, situated in the narrow streets of the congested city, into their own modern homes with beautiful gardens, open spaces, large grass plots and plenty of sunshine, gives them the courage and strength to carry on until the completion of their new abodes. The beautiful verandas in the new homes are used as dining rooms by those who have already moved in and where, through the enjoyment of the fresh air, they forget the scantiness of their meals for which they spend very little, using every dollar to improve their homes. Anticipating all this, it is no wonder that they overlook the great hardships until the joyous moment arrives when they may actually take possession of these homes.

In forming our Building Loan Company, we decided that we would first confine our activities to the city of Jerusalem and its surroundings, having in mind that this universal city is the most overcrowded, being the first place in which foreigners settle. However, we could not refuse the cry for loans from a group of business men who had bought a large plot of land in Haifa, near beautiful Mount Carmel, which land faces the beach of the Mediterranean Sea. This place is called Bath Galim, meaning the Daughter of the Waves. We made loans on only thirty houses in this settlement, but through our impetus, twice this number of houses are being built and many more are ready to be built if we will extend loans to them.

The same condition prevails in every settlement. There were many people who were ready to start building with their own money, but were unable to proceed individually for the following reason: To start a building proposition in a new district requires the combined effort of a large number of people and an outlay of a large sum of money in order to provide roads, water and transportation facilities for material and labor and many other necessities, the cost of which is prohibitive to the individual. When we formed our Company we foresaw these conditions and accordingly made loans in large numbers for each section. Consequently the cost of providing all the preliminary needs were apportioned among all the borrowers and the expense to each individual was nominal. As soon as all the preparations were made and work started on these buildings, many individuals took advantage of this activity and also started building homes in these sections but without our assistance.

It gives me pleasure to point out that besides the four settlements above mentioned, our company, at the suggestion of the High Commissioner and the Governor of Jerusalem, made many loans to the influential Arabs on their homes in the City of Jerusalem. These houses were started before the war but could not be finished due to the lack of funds.

Justice Brandeis has stated on many occasions that I am the Mother of this child, namely the Building Loan and Savings Association. And as such, I will endeavor briefly to express my joy and pleasure in finding that this young child was able in a very short time and with comparatively small capital to accomplish this great practical and useful assistance in Palestine in the following manner:

1.   Every dollar which we loaned on these buildings remains in Palestine. Thousands of people in every business and industry are benefited by this money. It circulates from the laborer to the merchant and from the merchant back to the colonist who produces the food and sells it to the laborer.

2.   Our Company made employment possible for a large number of men in the building line, both mechanics and unskilled laborers.

3.   Our Company helped build several hundred houses, thereby enabling a large number of the Jewish population to move from the overcrowded and unsanitary houses in the city to beautiful country homes. As a result of relieving some of the congestion, the rents in the city were automatically reduced to less than one half.

4.   Our Company, by bringing $300,000 into Palestine and placing same on long term mortgages, caused the prevailing high rates of interest on real estate loans, ranging from 18 per cent. to 25 per cent. to be reduced to as low as 10 per cent. This was a great achievement. I believe it is in place for me to mention at this time that our present interest charge is 8 per cent., six per cent. to meet our dividend obligations and two per cent. for expenses incurred in Palestine. At the same time I would like to impress on you that the expenses of selling stock and other charges in America are defrayed by individual donations. Therefore, every dollar of stock which you buy in our company is invested in mortgages and will bring six per cent. interest.

5.   Our Company was instrumental in creating a better feeling between the Arabs and the Jewish people in two ways: First, by making a number of loans to the better class Arabs who have a large following and are the owners of the houses in the city. Second, by giving them employment, as the cutting of stones in the quarry and the delivery of building material is done by Arabs.

An interesting incident happened while I was in our Jerusalem office. An influential Arab of a well known family came in to pay the interest due on his mortgage. Mr. Mohl introduced me as one of the organizers of the Palestine Building Loan and Savings Association. The Arab fell to his knees and prayed to Allah for my health and the success of our Company. He expressed his appreciation and that of his friends, for the good our Company has done for them. Our Building loans were their only chance to complete their houses.

The day before I left Palestine, this Arab called at the office with a friend to extend an invitation to my family for a dinner which he had arranged in our honor. In his speech of invitation, he expressed his brotherly love for our Jewish people, as we, together with them, said he, are the children of Abraham, and therefore ought to dwell together in peace. I informed him that it would be impossible for us to accept his invitation because we were to leave Palestine the next day. He was sorely disappointed because he was deprived of the opportunity of showing his appreciation and that of his friends in the form which they had arranged. It took me some time to convince him that it was impossible to change our plans and could not accept his invitation. He was finally contented with my promise and hope to return soon again, and the hope that our Company will soon have sufficient funds to grant all deserving loans for which applications are made.

The amortization enables the borrowers to pay off the whole loan in about 15 years, when they will own their property free and clear, yet we have so arranged this detail as to provide us with a certain amount of new money for loans every six months. I stress this point. Not only does the owner's equity increase annually by his payments, which adds to our security, but the extension of operations conducted conservatively, should improve the value of the equity so we will be helping people to save as well as to build homes by our simple system. I believe that everyone here will agree with me that we should set our faces sternly against all artificial increases in values. We want no land booms in Palestine. Therefore, when I speak of increased values I mean only those which are the natural result of better facilities, the demand for better living conditions and the natural increase of population.

There is no doubt in my mind and I am authorized to express the opinion of the High Commissioner, Sir Herbert Samuel, as well as that of many other influential men in Palestine, that the work of our Building Loan and Savings Association has aided

the development of Palestine in a marked degree. But we will be
of far greater assistance as soon as we shall be able to grant more
loans for which applications have been filed.

In order to raise additional money, required for the many applications, it is our intention to invite those men and women whom
God has blessed with wealth and the Jewish heart which beats
for Palestine, to invest part of their spare cash in stock of our
Company. For that reason I deem it my duty to acquaint our
future stockholders with the methods adopted in making our
building loans, so that they will be able to see for themselves the
safety of their investment.

SAFETY OF INVESTMENT

Our main object is to help establish new settlements near the
city of Jerusalem where a number of people desire to build homes.
We are loaning them 60 per cent. of the cost of their home, not
including the land for which they have already paid. The largest
amount loaned on one house is L600 amounting to about $3,000.
The cost of the building of these houses is no less than $5,000
and in many cases as high as $8,000. They are to pay about
12 per cent, of the loan annually, which amount includes interest
and the installments and amortization of the mortgage. In no
case is the amount of the payment more than the rent which they
are compelled to pay for three rooms in an old house in the congested part of the city without any improvements. Not alone
have they the benefit of the improved conditions, but they are, at
the same time, paying off the mortgage on their home in about
15 years.

While we loan 60 per cent. of the cost of the building, however, our loan becomes a smaller percentage of the collateral every
year as the borrowers pay off a portion of the loan semi-annually.
In addition, thereto, every new house which is erected in that
section makes those houses more valuable, so that our loans
do not average more than 40 per cent. of the actual value of the
house on which the loan is made.

I believe it is known to every one familiar with real estate that
savings banks in the small towns, loan 60 per cent. of the value
on real estate. This amount is considered by them as perfectly
safe. Our Company is loaning in and around Jerusalem on the

average less than 40 per cent of the value and this is being reduced from time to time. Isn't that a perfectly safe investment?

The work of the Palestine Building Loan and Savings Association is felt all through Palestine and is almost the only practical and productive work there. Considering the international
reputation of the men who represent our Company, it should have
accomplished much more even in the short period of its existence.
These men should have no difficulty in raising the money necessary to meet all the loans applied for. This condition has been
called to my attention by some of the leaders of the world's Jewry,
including the High Commissioner. My answer was that our
Company was organized to do practical work on a business basis.
Before we could recommend to the public that it invest its money,
we wanted to make reasonably sure that the investment was safe.
It is for this reason also, that I went to Palestine to see whether
these building loans made by our company are safe and whether
the company will be in a position to pay the 6 per cent. dividend
to its stockholders.

Although, I had every confidence in this enterprise from its
inception, I am convinced now more than ever of the soundness
of our proposition. Every dollar invested in the Building Loan
is just as safe as any loan made on real estate in the City of New
York. It is, therefore, the duty of the influential men connected
with our Company as well as everyone who can help, to put his
shoulder to the wheel and buy stock of our Company for himself
and also sell stock to his friends thereby enabling us to raise
sufficient funds to carry the work so nobly commenced to complete success. There are a great number of Jewish people in
America who have money lying idle or even deposited in Savings
Banks upon which they receive $3\frac{1}{2}$ per cent. or 4 per cent. Can
they find a safer and better paying investment than by buying
stock in our company, either for cash or in four installments of
25 per cent. each?

In conclusion, let me say that returning to Palestine after an
interval of two years, I was happy to see the great changes which
have taken place in every branch of industry as well as in agriculture. Many fields in the colonies and around the city, which
had been uncultivated and covered with stones, are now cultivated and covered with vegetation. Many new homes are also

being built in the colonies, thus making more room for immigrants and more facilities for employment.

The opportunities for success in every industry are great no matter what business one will start, provided that he knows his business and is familiar with local conditions. There were several men who started industries and did not succeed. This was not the fault of Palestine, as the High Commissioner expressed it, but it was the fault of themselves, because they came to Palestine unqualified to manage the industries started by them. Besides they began on a scale, much larger than the capital they possessed warranted.

All that is necessary is, that our American brethren should have a little more confidence in Palestine. They should invest part of their capital on a business basis. Not alone will they receive a good income on their capital, but they will also help to prepare a haven of refuge for the thousands of Jewish people of Europe who cannot come to our beloved United States of America, but who ought to be relieved of the oppression and pressure they meet with in some of the European countries.

I appeal to the conscience of every Jew and Jewess in America to help us further the good work of providing homes for worthy Jewish families in Palestine. The sooner the money is invested, the sooner will we be able to direct our Jerusalem manager to extend further loans and thus we hope that the foundation will have been permanently laid for the home of our Brethren in the Holy Land.

While in Palestine and Europe, largely as a result of the strain under which he had labored for many years, together with the excitement incident to the journey to his former home, Mr. Fischel's health, already far from robust, suffered further inroads.

He went to Carlsbad hoping to obtain a complete rest and upon arriving there was examined by a physician who informed him that he was a victim of diabetes, a disease then regarded as almost incurable. While he took the treatment prescribed in Carlsbad, he received only temporary relief so that on his return to America he determined to make every effort to care for his health. He was ordered by his physician to take things easy and not to unduly exert himself and was advised that it was essential that

he move to a corner apartment where he would receive the benefit
of as much sunlight as possible and at the same time avoid the
necessity of climbing stairs.   Although Mr. and Mrs. Fischel
were both greatly attached to their home at 118 East 93rd Street
which they had occupied for twenty-two years, after a family
conference they reluctantly agreed to part with it and secure another residence.

On June 10, 1924, Mr. Fischel purchased a plot of land on the
southwest corner of Park Avenue and 80th Street, one of the
finest corners on that exclusive Avenue, where he planned to
erect a fourteen story apartment in keeping with the standards of
the locality and having its main entrance on Park Avenue.

It was in this structure he arranged to have his own home,
occupying the second story, with a separate entrance on Eightieth
Street, giving him virtually a private house with all the sunlight
and ventilation possible, and at the same time affording him the
convenience of an apartment.

In the meantime, Mr. Fischel was in the care of the late Dr.
Max Kahn, specialist in diabetes and was ordered to the Battle
Creek, Michigan, Sanitarium for complete rest and treatment.
He was, however, so far from well upon his departure that his
son-in-law Dr. Henry A. Rafsky, would not permit him to make
the trip alone.

Upon Mr. Fischel's and Dr. Rafsky's arrival at the institution
they were met by Dr. John W. Harvey Kellogg, head of the
Sanitarium and a personal friend of Dr. Max Einhorn, with whom
Dr. Rafsky is associated.

Mr. Fischel's stay in Battle Creek, lasted five weeks, the vege-
tarian diet upon which he was placed causing his condition to
greatly improve.   This was also largely due to the personal care
of Dr. Kellogg.

During the five weeks spent in Battle Creek, Mr. Fischel's
health was largely restored, so that he was enabled, on taking up
his residence in a temporary home at 68 East 86th Street, to
enter upon the great task of building the new Yeshiva College of
which an account will be given in another chapter.

CHAPTER LV

CHIEF RABBI KOOK OF PALESTINE VISITS AMERICA

An outstanding event in the annals of American Jewry was the visit to the United States, early in 1925, of Chief Rabbi Abraham I. Kook of Palestine. This visit was brought about through the efforts of the Central Committee for the Relief of Jews Suffering Through the War, of which Mr. Fischel was the treasurer and had as its primary purpose the stimulating of collections in behalf of the hundreds of thousands of the Jews of Europe whom the war had left destitute and whose institutions were without funds to function properly.

Following the armistice, the task of securing contributions for this cause had grown increasingly difficult, so that it finally became necessary, in order to stimulate giving anew, to bring here some commanding personality who should be able to re-vitalize the enthusiasm of Orthodox Jewry toward the continuance of the obligation resting upon it.

In order to accomplish this purpose it was decided to endeavor to induce Rabbi Kook to come to America.

This effort, in view of the urgency of the situation, was successful and Rabbi Kook arrived here on March 19, 1925.

Mr. Fischel enjoyed the great honor of meeting the Chief Rabbi of Palestine at the steamer and headed a welcoming throng of at least 10,000 persons who came both on foot and in automobile to escort the Chief Rabbi from the steamer to the City Hall, where he was officially received by the then Mayor, John F. Hylan.

Rabbi Kook remained in America from March 19 to November 12th of that year, during which time he visited the principal cities of the country and through his appeals to Orthodox Jewry at large, the additional sum of nearly $400,000 was raised for the specific purpose of helping to maintain the Yeshivas and Talmud Torahs of Europe.

Mr. Fischel gave a farewell dinner at his residence for Rabbi Kook, prior to the latter's departure for Palestine.

This dinner was held on October 28, 1925, and was attended by the most prominent Orthodox Rabbis of America and the leaders of the Jewish institutions in New York.

On November 12th, Mr. Fischel, accompanied by a large number of prominent Jews, escorted Rabbi Kook to his steamer, where the assemblage wished the latter Bon Voyage and Godspeed.

CHAPTER LVI

GREAT YESHIVA COLLEGE HAS ITS BEGINNING

OF all the many and diversified interests, communal and business, which had engaged Mr. Fischel's attention throughout the years, that of Jewish religious education had, perhaps, remained uppermost in his thoughts.

There still remained in this field of endeavor the largest and most ambitious undertaking of his career, the effort to establish the great Yeshiva College, that was to insure the preservation of Orthodox Judaism in America for all time and to which task he now gave himself with all his strength.

For twenty-seven years Mr. Fischel had been active in the work connected with the Yeshiva Rabbi Issac Elchanan Theological Seminary and the Yeshiva Etz Chaim, his interest dating back to 1900, almost to the birth of these institutions.

In this period, the institutions had merged and had moved at various times from 1 Canal Street to 85 Henry Street, thence to 9-11 Montgomery Street and finally to 301-302-303 East Broadway.

In each instance Mr. Fischel had served as the chairman of the Building Committee which had secured for the Yeshiva its several homes and he had also taken a very great interest and part in framing the educational program.

The institution was the only one in America with a complete High School course, conducted in conjunction with its facilities for a Talmudic education and which had received the approval of the State Board of Education, so that it had come to be classified by the authorities as a Parochial Institution.

The school was recognized not only for its high standards of religious instruction but as one of the finest High Schools in secular learning in the State.

As a result of these facilities, the school was enabled to graduate its students at a much lower age than any other High School, as the students found that in acquiring Talmudic knowledge they also obtained a much more ready insight into their secular studies.

The school finally became so favored that it was impossible to accommodate anywhere near the number of students who applied for entrance. With a capacity of only 400 students an effort was made to provide room for 550. The consequent congestion had grown from bad to worse and it finally became imperative that some way be found to increase the accommodations.

The problem was accentuated by the fact that following the armistice many of the European Yeshivas, which had been fountains of Talmudic knowledge and had produced large numbers of scholars of merit, had been compelled to close and their students had immigrated to America with their parents.

These young men naturally sought to complete their studies here and as their previous training gave them the capacity quickly to acquire the English language they at once came to this institution to obtain the opportunity to graduate as Rabbis or religious teachers or even to pursue other professions.

With this situation in mind the Directors of the Yeshiva Rabbi Isaac Elchanan Theological Seminary determined that the High School course of the institution was not sufficiently broad, especially for those desiring later to enter the Rabbinate and that it would be necessary to provide additional courses.

The problem was one which troubled the Directors acutely for some time, until finally the President of the Faculty, Dr. Bernard Revel, suggested at a meeting of the Board that there was only one way out of the dilemma and that was either to allow the future generation of Jewish youth to be brought up in ignorance of Talmudic law or to establish a college where they might receive both a Talmudic and secular education under one roof, and under the same environment.

It seemed exceedingly difficult to accomplish this objective as the resources of the institution were limited. It was, however,

impossible to conceive of permitting the future generations of
Jewish young men to remain in ignorance of their faith and it
was determined that a parochial college must be established, even
though the institution at the start should be a small one in accordance with the means available.

At this meeting of the Board of Directors, a campaign was
launched to raise enough money to purchase four lots in a central
location for the purpose of erecting a college thereon and a Committee to secure such a site was appointed.   The late Samuel
Greenstein, who had been a worker in the institution for many
years, was appointed chairman of this Committee, the first meeting of which was held on October 21, 1923.

At this meeting the question of a suitable campaign for funds
was discussed.   Some of the conservative members of the committee were of the opinion that a million dollars was the full
sum that should be asked of the public.   Others, who saw further
into the future, claimed that if the undertaking were to be entered upon at all $2,000,000 should be asked.

While this debate was in progress, Mr. Fischel reminded himself of an incident which occurred earlier in his career when the
Hebrew Sheltering and Immigrant Aid Society purchased the site
of the old Astor Library on Lafayette Street, with the object of
transforming it into an Immigrant Home.

It will be remembered that at that time, the Committee, of
which Mr. Fischel was one of the members, called upon Jacob H.
Schiff, for his advice and cooperation and that Mr. Schiff suggested that the investment, involving half a million dollars, was
too large to enter upon.

On that occasion, Mr. Fischel said to Mr. Schiff: "If the Congress may burden the people of the United States with a debt of
twenty billion dollars for war purposes, our Board of Directors
has the right to mortgage our people for the sum required to
accomplish our purpose."

Mr. Fischel felt that the Yeshiva, like the Immigrant Home,
was not purely a local object, but one affecting the entire Jewish

people of the United States and that the Directors had the right
to appeal to the Jews of America for a fund sufficient to build a
Yeshiva College that should, when completed, be an honor and
credit to all the Jews of America.

He, therefore, then and there, suggested that the sum of $5,-
000,000 rather than one or two millions, should be the goal. Some
of the directors took the view that he had gone out of his mind
in suggesting such a sum. Mr. Fischel, however, insisted that
five million dollars was none too large an amount to accomplish
the purpose in view and in order to start the ball rolling he subscribed at once $10,000 with the pledge of an additional subscrip-
tion of $5,000 for each million dollars collected, making his total
pledge $30,000 if the full amount were secured.

This offer created a large degree of enthusiasm among those
present with the result that Mr. Greenstein immediately followed
with a pledge of the same sum and several other members fell
in with subscriptions of $10,000, so that a total of $155,000 was
subscribed among the few men present at this initial meeting.

Having such excellent success at the first meeting the Committee decided to acquire for the proposed college a plot comprising
ten city lots and some of the members even went so far as to
propose that twenty city lots be secured.

A long time was expended in searching for a site in a suitable
location and in the meantime, on Sunday, December 4, the annual
graduation exercises of the Yeshiva Rabbi Elchanan Theological
Seminary took place in the Congregation Kehilath Jeshurun, 117
E. 85th Street.

At these exercises Rabbi Herbert S. Goldstein made the announcement that it was the Committee's intention to build a
college in connection with the Yeshiva and that the sum of
$5,000,000 would be sought from the public.

This announcement, coupled with the news that subscriptions
of $155,000 had already been secured, was seized upon by the
press as of large public interest and the New York Times, the
the next day, published the following article:

PLAN JEWISH COLLEGE HERE
TO BE INCLUDED IN SEMINARY FOR WHICH $5,000,000
CAMPAIGN IS NOW IN PROGRESS

With a total of $155,000 already subscribed in the $5,000,000 campaign for the Rabbi Isaac Elchanan Theological Seminary, Rabbi Herbert S. Goldstein, president of the Union of Orthodox Jewish Congregations of America announced the seminary will include a Jewish college, the first institution of its kind in this country.

The list of subscribers is headed by two $30,000 contributions from Harry Fischel and Samuel Greenstein. Other contributors are Morris Glaser, Mendel Gottesman, S. A. Israel, Nathan Lamport, Joseph Polstein, and Gustave S. Roth $10,000 each; Nathan Roggen, Leon Kamaiky, Samuel Bayer and Roggen Brothers, $5,000 each; Mark Hurewitz, M. W. Levine, Abraham Levy, Abraham Cohen, J. Siegel and Arthur Lamport, $2,500 each.

START IMMEDIATELY

"The campaign will be launched at once," Dr. Goldstein declared, "so that the seminary with its modern high school and college buildings, dormitories and gymnasium, as well as with its completely equipped buildings for Jewish learning, can open in the fall of 1928 and take care of the large waiting list.

"This list includes a considerable number of European students, whose lot is precarious in those benighted countries, where persecution is now rampant and whose facilities for study have in many cases been wiped out by the war and post-war conditions.

"Orthodox Jewry in America has always depended upon Europe for its spiritual leaders. Whatever of Jewish learning we have in America is of European origin. American Jewry has not produced a single great rabbi or great Jewish scholar in the true sense of greatness.

Need American Rabbis

"We can no longer depend upon Europe for our rabbis for it is no longer possible to secure them from abroad, as it will be years before our higher institutions of learning there will again function properly.

"Furthermore, the present generation of American born Jews requires leaders who have lived and been educated in this country, who understand the life and methods of America.

"The Rabbi Isaac Elchanan Theological Seminary the oldest and largest Orthodox Jewish institution of its kind, in America, plans to fill this want by making Jewish learning self-sustaining in America."

The realization this would be the first Jewish college in America that should prepare young Jewish men for spiritual leadership served to create tremendous enthusiasm, so that the committee determined to seek a site that should occupy an entire city block of twenty lots.

For nearly a year the committee continued its efforts to find a suitable location, during which time the chairman, Mr. Samuel Greenstein, who had for many years devoted his life to the cause of the Yeshiva, unfortunately passed away. Upon his death, Mr. Fischel was elected in his place as chairman of the Committee on Site.

With his ability to envision the needs of the future as well as of the present, Mr. Fischel decided that the plans for this great enterprise should be of a most comprehensive character. The Committee accordingly went vigorously to work in preparation for a much larger undertaking than the originators of the project had conceived. After several months of additional search, during which time the Committee visited what appeared to them every desirable location throughout the confines of Greater New York, it finally succeeded in purchasing two square blocks on the east side of Amsterdam Avenue, reaching from 186th to 188th Streets, and comprising not twenty but approximately sixty ordinary city building lots.

From every viewpoint this location seemed highly desirable for the erection of a great educational institution. Many strategic advantages were attached to the situation finally decided upon, among which was the fact that it was in the center of a group of large educational institutions including Columbia University, The College of the City of New York and New York University. Furthermore, the site chosen was situated upon an elevation 300 feet above the Harlem River and affording a magnificent view of this body of water and at the same time surrounded by city parks on two sides. The site of no educational institution in New York surpassed it, and leading educators as well as the press were quick to praise the selection as the finest that could possibly have been made.

CHAPTER LVII

NATHAN LAMPORT FAMILY AND MR. FISCHEL
SUBSCRIBE $100,000 EACH

FOLLOWING the signing of the contract for the purchase of the property for the new Yeshiva College on December 15, 1924, a Building Committee, comprised of many of the most prominent Jewish builders of New York, was organized, of which Mr. Fischel had the honor of being chosen the chairman. The appointment of this committee, with its noted membership, was generally hailed as insuring the success of this great project, possibly the greatest single educational undertaking that had ever been attempted by American Jewry. Among the many newspaper articles which appeared at the time is the following from the New York Tribune of December 16, 1924:

MANY BUILDERS WILL ASSIST IN ERECTION OF JEWISH SEMINARY

Religious Education Center on Washington Heights Will Put Up a Great Combination Building

Construction of the $5,000,000 Jewish seminary and college—the Yeshiva of America—which will be built on Amsterdam Avenue between 186th and 188th Streets, will be in charge of a committee of leading real estate operators and builders, Samuel Levy, chairman of the executive committee of the building fund announces.

Harry Fischel has been chosen chairman of the building committee; Jacob Levy, Louis Gold and Leon Fleischmann, vice chairmen; Joseph Polstein, secretary and Abraham Levy, honorary secretary. The other members include Congressman Sol Bloom, Henry Friedman, Benjamin Winter, Joseph Golding, Philip Meyrowitz, Joseph Ravitch, Harry Schiff, Samuel Minskoff, Jacob Leitner, A. Bricken, Conrad Glazer, Max N. Nathanson, Jacob Goell, Samuel Levy, G. S. Roth, Meyer Vessell, Leon Sobel, Nathan Lamport, Nathan Wilson, Pincus Glickman, Ben Benenson and Isaac Polstein.

The officers of the committee, together with Messrs. Sobel, Benenson, Wilson, Glickman and Isaac Polstein, will make a survey of educational facilities for the institution of higher Jewish learning, whose construction will start in the spring.

To provide the initial funds so that the building operations can be started this spring, a dinner will be held at the Hotel Astor, at which a campaign to raise $1,000,000 among the Jews of New York, will be launched. The $5,000,000 is to be raised over a five-year period. The dinner, which is to be given by the site committee, will celebrate the taking of title to the three city blocks.

The five buildings of the institution, to be known as the Yeshiva of America, will be built in the style of architecture in vogue during the reign of King Solomon 3,000 years ago in the Holy Land. The principal building, the Seminary and Teachers' College, is designed in part after King Solomon's Temple. When completed, the institution will provide for over 2000 students. The present institution, known as the Rabbi Isaac Elchanan Theological Seminary and located at 301 East Broadway, is taxed to capacity with an enrollment of 500 students and it is to provide for its large waiting list that the new institution is being built. When completed, it will be one of the greatest Jewish institutions of higher learning in the world.

On December 18, almost immediately after the purchase, title was taken to the property, and in order to fittingly commemorate this great event, generally recognized as by far the most significant undertaking in the history of Orthodox Jewry, the Committee on Site, under Mr. Fischel's chairmanship, completed plans for a campaign dinner. This function, which was held at the Hotel Astor on Sunday, December 21, the first day of Chanukah, commemorating the lighting of the Menorah, a ceremony which signalized the re-dedication of the Temple in Jerusalem by the Macabbeans, was attended by more than 300 persons.

This was in every respect the most notable day in Mr. Fischel's entire life, for the reason that he saw about to be realized his dream of a great Jewish college, the equal of any institution of learning in America. He was able to visualize the scene that was later to be witnessed, when thousands of Jewish young men would enter this institution and would leave it prepared to bear aloft the banner of Orthodox Judaism, carrying its message to every part of America.

Mr. Fischel, however, realized that it was one thing to have an ambition, and another to see it carried out and, as he was seated at the guest table and surveyed the audience, he began to wonder how the great sum that would be needed would be obtained. He decided that it would be necessary to undertake much intensive personal effort in order to secure the funds with which a real beginning might be made. Accordingly, he took it upon himself to talk to Mr. Samuel C. Lamport, a son of Nathan Lamport, the President of the Yeshiva Rabbi Isaac Elchanan Theological Seminary, a most enthusiastic and active communal worker, in order to enlist his interest and support. This he did together with Judge Otto A. Rosalsky.

Mr. Fischel frankly told Mr. Lamport that the result of the campaign for the Yeshiva College would largely depend upon the elder Lamport and himself, and that the entire Jewish community looked to them to make contributions of sufficient size to be an inspiration to others.

The fact that Mr. Lamport, Senior, was president of the institution and Mr. Fischel was Vice-President and chairman of the Building Committee, was an additional reason why their example would be looked up to and followed by others. He further told Mr. Lamport that, as it was generally known that both his father and Mr. Fischel were blessed by the Almighty with the means to give, that upon their action depended the entire future of the campaign. They could either make or break it by the example they set.

Although Mr. Fischel already had subscribed the sum of $30,-
000 he declared himself ready to match any sum that the entire
Lamport family, all of whom were wealthy, might be ready to
give. Mr. Fischel further told Mr. Lamport the latter's family
need have no fear as to the amount it might decide to contribute,
as the total sum would not be required at once.

Under these circumstances, he explained, it was only necessary
to draw a check upon the Bank of Heaven and to have confidence
in the Almighty that He would see to it that they would be enabled to make good their pledge; in other words, that the Almighty would bless them with health and strength and the ability
to pay the obligation contracted in His name, and to fulfill His
purpose.

Mr. Lamport was tremendously impressed with this strong
argument and asked only that he be given five minutes to consider the question. He then conferred with his father while still
at the dinner, and in a few moments returned to Mr. Fischel
saying, "Harry, I am going to surprise you. We are ready to
subscribe a much larger sum than you have in your mind." Mr.
Fischel replied, "No amount will be too large for me. I will
match anything you do." Mr. Lamport then revealed that the
Lamport family had decided to subscribe the sum of $100,000.

Without any further consideration and even without consulting
the members of his family who were also present, Mr. Fischel
at once accepted this challenge and declared that he, too, would
contribute $100,000, assured in his own mind that his wife and
all of his children not only would agree to this act but that it
would be more than a source of gratification to them.

Mr. Lamport and Mr. Fischel then immediately conveyed
their intentions to Judge Rosalsky, the principal speaker who
was to make the appeal of the evening.

No sooner was the announcement made than the entire room
was in an uproar. So great was the enthusiasm evoked that in
a few moments the sum of nearly $800,000 was subscribed by

those present, by far the largest sum any Orthodox movement in America had ever been successful in raising at one time.

An intermission was then called, when Mr. Lamport, surrounded by his family, assembled at a table and the Lamport pledge of $100,000 was signed. This act was at once followed by a similar ceremony attaching to the subscription of Mr. Fischel and his family.

After Mr. Fischel had signed his name to the document, which marked his largest single gift to a religious and philanthropic cause, he offered a silent prayer to the Almighty, expressing his gratitude that he was in a position to give so large a sum, and asked that he be blessed with the health and strength to continue his labors in behalf of so noble and inspiring a cause. He also prayed that, as chairman of the Building Committee, he might be granted the privilege of seeing the building of this greatest of Jewish religious institutions finished. He was convinced the institution would produce the necessary incentive for hundreds of young men to continue to bear aloft the insignia of Orthodox Judaism, so that it would for all time wield a commanding influence upon the thoughts and lives of the Jewish people of America, and so, do lasting honor and credit to those who had conceived the noble and holy work.

Few events in the history of Jewry in America have commanded more public attention than this auspicious launching of the campaign for the Yeshiva College. Hundreds of columns of newspaper space were occupied by the announcements of the project and an account of the unusual collection which was taken up at the dinner.

An article in the American Hebrew of December 26, an editorial in the New York Times on the same day and an account appearing in the Jewish Monitor of Fort Worth, Texas, on January 16, 1925 are herewith given:

From the American Hebrew

NATHAN LAMPORT AND HARRY FISCHEL CONTRIBUTE $100,000 EACH TO YESHIVA COLLEGE CAMPAIGN

The dinner given by the Site Committee of the Yeshiva College Building Fund, Sunday, at the Hotel Astor, to celebrate the taking of title to the two city blocks upon which the Yeshiva Seminary and College will be built, turned out to be the greatest surprise in the history of Orthodox Judaism in America.

The dinner was given as a joint celebration of the acquisition of the site for the proposed Yeshiva Seminary and College and also to launch a campaign to raise one million dollars by February 1 so that building operations could be started in the spring.

The committee expected that several hundred thousand dollars of this amount would be realized from the two hundred loyal workers of the Yeshiva present. But when Nathan Lamport, venerable president of the Yeshiva and one of its most ardent workers, in accepting the deed for the site from Harry Fischel, chairman of the Site Committee, announced that he would make a contribution of $100,000 toward the Building Fund, the audience was electrified.

"The Yeshiva is my life," Mr. Lamport declared, "and if necessary I will mortgage my life in order to make this $100,000 contribution toward the great institution of learning which is our hope and our dream."

Then Mr. Fischel, another of the Yeshiva's indefatigable workers, jumped to his feet and fired the group to an even higher pitch of enthusiasm by announcing that his contribution would likewise be $100,000.

The two hundred workers present, fired by the examples of Mr. Lamport and Mr. Fischel, began doubling and trebling their original contributions until the first million dollars was practically assured. Almost $800,000, it was announced, was raised at this initial meeting, the largest sum ever raised at a single meeting for a Jewish educational project and the greatest single contribution Orthodox Jewry itself had ever made.

Samuel Levy, chairman of the Campaign Executive Committee with his father-in-law, Meyer Vesell, made a contribution of $50,000. Other of the large contributions follow:

$25,000—Joseph Polstein, Louis Gold, Jacob and Nathan Levy, S. A. Israel, Philip Meyrowitz, Samuel Greenstein estate; $12,000—Mendel Gottesman & Sons; $10,000, A. Bricken, Elias A. Cohen, Morris Glazer, Samuel Kaufman, Bernard Reich, Nathan Roggen & Sons, G. S. Roth, Joseph Ravitch, Leon Sobel, Pincus Glickman, Morris Greenstein, H. B. Rubin, and one anonymous from a friend; $5,000—Samuel Bayer, Henry Friedman, Morris Friedman, Paul Herring, Albert Herskowitz, Leon Kamaiky, Harris Mandelbaum, Isaac Polstein, Harry Schiff, Ben Shapiro, Israel Sapiro, Albert and Harris Sokolski, Philip Weinstein, M. W. Levine, Joseph Horowitz, Jacob Richman and Abraham Levy; $3,000—Julius and Bernard Bernstein, Samuel Kamlet.

The speakers of the dinner included Samuel Levy, who presided; Judge Otto A. Rosalsky, Samuel C. Lamport, Rabbi Herbert S. Goldstein, Rabbi M. S. Margolies, Dr. Bernard Revel, president of the Yeshiva Faculty and Harris L. Selig, director of the campaign.

Editorial from the New York Times

For Jewish Education

American Jewry seems to have been skeptical of the ability of Orthodox Jewry to raise the millions necessary to build the proposed Yeshiva and College on three city blocks in New York. Orthodox Jews had never before raised such an amount for so stupendous an undertaking and no such ambitious project had ever before been attempted on behalf of any educational institution.

We did not think it possible to squeeze another thrill out of a drive for funds, but at the dinner held last Sunday to launch a campaign for one million dollars by February first, things happened.

When Nathan Lamport, venerable president of the Yeshiva, announced that he would contribute $100,000 toward the Building Fund, the audience of 200 workers was electrified.

"The Yeshiva is my life," declared Mr. Lamport, "and if necessary I will mortgage my life in order to make this $100,000 contribution toward the great institution of learning which is our hope and dream."

Harry Fischel, another of the Yeshiva's indefatigable workers, matched the first gift of $100,000 and before the banquet was over almost $800,000 was announced.

This is the largest sum ever raised at any single meeting for a Jewish educational project and the greatest single contribution Orthodox Jewry itself has ever made. The committee rightly feels that it has effectively answered the doubts of American Jewry.

From the Jewish Monitor, Forth Worth, Texas

$100,000 YESHIVA CONTRIBUTIONS OF HARRY FISCHEL AND NATHAN LAMPORT MARK REALIZATION OF DREAM BORN 40 YEARS AGO IN POGROM-SWEPT RUSSIA

When Nathan Lamport and Harry Fischel, leaders in New York communal life and prominent real estate operators, each contributed $100,000 at the opening of the building fund campaign of the Yeshiva of America, a hope which was born in the Ghettos of Russia during its bloody days over forty years ago was turned into reality.

Messrs. Lamport and Fischel were then students in two famous Yeshivoths in widely separated Ghettos in Russia, Lamport at Navaradok, and Fischel at Meretz. Then came the anti--Jewish reign of terror which swept over Russia and Lamport and Fischel, with thousands of other hopeless victims of the Russian excesses, were uprooted from their homes and escaped to America. Here, after the usual years of vicissitudes, they prospered in business, but their first love, the sacred Torah, was never neglected.

Those Yeshivoth days were vivid in the lives of young Fischel and Lamport and when they were established in New York, they dedicated themselves to the one purpose of founding in this country a model Yeshiva, where the Jewish youth who wished to become learned in the law, might study under ideal conditions, so different from the dismal and fearsome days in the pale of blackest Russia.

When the Rabbi Isaac Elchanan Theological Seminary was established forty years ago on the Lower East Side, Fischel and Lamport, then just recent arrivals in America, aided it as best they could. The Seminary was founded along the lines of the

Ancient Yeshiva, which for three thousand years has been the center of Orthodox Jewish life throughout the world. As the Seminary's fame grew and more and more students were attracted to it, it became greatly overcrowded and its waiting list began to grow from year to year.

Still fired by the dream of their boyhood, Lamport and Fischel continued as ardent workers for the Yeshiva, and have been among its chief financial supporters for many years. They were the pioneers in launching this year the movement to establish a great Orthodox Jewish Center of higher learning in America as an outgrowth of the Isaac Elchanan Theological Seminary at a cost of $5,000,000 to be raised over a five year period. When the campaign was launched they practically assured its success by their contributions of $100,000 each, an unprecedented sum in the history of Orthodox Judaism in this country. So inspired were the supporters of the Seminary by their gifts, that at the opening banquet, given to only the workers in the campaign, a sum of $800,000 was realized, being the largest sum of money ever raised at one time for any Jewish educational project in America or elsewhere.

The $5,000,000 Yeshiva of America will be built on two city blocks on Amsterdam Avenue between 186th to 188th Streets, New York. Its five buildings are modelled after the style of architecture which prevailed in the Holy Land three thousand years ago during the reign of King Solomon, and the main building is designed in part after Solomon's Temple. The plans for the institution include a college, giving degrees and courses similar to other American institutions and which will be the first Jewish college established in America. When completed the Seminary and College will be one of the world's foremost institutions of higher Jewish learning.

It is doubtful if any event in Mr. Fischel's life created a greater impression upon him than this dinner in behalf of the Yeshiva College. Upon looking over the faces of the people assembled, he was thoroughly convinced that the Jews of New York, comprising the largest Jewish population in America and who invariably reflect the sentiment of the Jews of the entire country, would not fail to support this ambitious but greatly needed enterprise. He was particularly proud that his recommendation for a $5,000,000 drive had been accepted without question, and that those present had done more than give their passive assent to the program, having proven by their immediate response to the appeal for contributions that they were not only willing but eager to aid the program to a much larger extent than had ever before been vouched for a Jewish educational purpose.

From this moment on Mr. Fischel determined to dedicate his effort, his time and energy, also a large portion of his wealth, to the carrying out of this vast undertaking. From that day, December 21, 1924, to the present day, Mr. Fischel practically divorced himself from every other activity, both his business and communal interests, to this end, except of course, he continued to attend the meetings of directors of other institutions with which he was affiliated, and he continued also to act as treasurer for the Hias and the Central Committee for the Relief of Jews Suffering Through the War.

CHAPTER LVIII

ADDITIONAL LAND PURCHASED FOR YESHIVA COLLEGE

Considering the magnitude of the enterprise, rapid progress was made on the plans for the Yeshiva College from the time the first land was acquired for the site and, as these plans matured, it was soon determined that the two city blocks that had been purchased would be insufficient to the needs of the great institution that was contemplated.

The first step of the Building Committee was to engage architects. This was a considerable problem, inasmuch as it was determined that the structure should not only be erected in accordance with the most practical plans that might be devised for the purpose for which it was intended, but that the exterior of the building should be unique in character and should reflect the purpose of the institution. The architects to be chosen, it was determined, should be men who not only possessed the greatest possible knowledge of educational requirements, but who should be successful in carrying out the ideas of the committee as to architectural dignity, beauty and impressiveness.

The first meeting of the Building Committee was held on March 5, 1925 at Mr. Fischel's office, 276 Fifth Avenue. At this meeting the committee selected Charles B. Meyers as the architect, with Henry Beaumont Hertz, a specialist in Jewish architecture, as his consultant. In selecting these two men the committee was convinced the combination of their talents would result in buildings that would not only be a credit to the Jewish people who were to give of their means for their construction, but that they would obtain the utmost possible in both utility and beauty.

The architects, upon accepting the commission, informed the

committee that before proceeding they wished to consult with a committee of experts thoroughly familiar with the needs of such an institution who would be able to give them advice and information as to the exact layout required and the space to be occupied by the various departments.

After due deliberation, such a committee was named and comprised Dr. Bernard Revel, President of the faculty of the Yeshiva Rabbi Isaac Elchanan Theological Seminary, Dr. S. Safir, also a member of the faculty, Albert Wald, who was familiar with the requirements of the State Department of Education, Jacob Levy and Leon Fleischman, members of the Building Committee and Rabbi Herbert S. Goldstein, as president of the Union of Orthodox Jewish Congregations of America, with Mr. Fischel as an ex-officio member.

This special committee met at Mr. Fischel's temporary home, 68 East 86th Street, on March 18th, when the needs of the institution were discussed from every angle, and a consensus of the committee's views was then transmitted to the architects. As a result of extensive conferences, it was the unanimous opinion of the committee that the institution would require even more ground than had already been acquired for it, and Mr. Fischel was entrusted with the task of continuing to act in the dual capacity of chairman of the Building Committee and chairman of the Committee on Site, which latter committee was instructed to secure additional space.

The Site Committee, after considering the needs from all viewpoints, determined to purchase additional land on the west side of Amsterdam Avenue, opposite the site previously chosen, and where three additional plots were secured in due course. The first additional property acquired was the southwest corner of 187th Street and Amsterdam Avenue, a plot, 100 x 107 ft., after which a plot, 175 x 100 ft. on 187th Street, adjoining the corner, was purchased, and finally the northwest corner of 186th Street and Amsterdam Avenue, a plot 100 x 107 ft. These three parcels gave to the institution seventeen city lots in addition to the original purchase, and the fact that this step was considered necessary increased the confidence of the public in the entire project.

The acquisition of this additional land further resulted in a great deal of public notice.

The New York World of April 26, 1925, contained the following article relative to this decision:

YESHIVA PLANS READY FOR START

Leading Builders to Rush $5,000,000 Jewish Intellectual Centre on Heights

Harry Fischel, as Chairman of the Building Committee, announced final plans yesterday for the $5,000,000. Yeshiva of America, Jewish College and Seminary to cover three blocks on Amsterdam Avenue from 186th to 188th Streets.

Construction of five buildings will start at once after groundbreaking exercises on May 24. Charles B. Meyers has been appointed architect, with Henry B. Hertz consulting. A high school will provide for 2,500 students. A dormitory with 175 double rooms, twenty-five single, will house 375. The Yeshiva, or seminary building will take care of 600 students. The college building, with laboratories, class and lecture rooms, is planned for 1,000. The Library is expected to house one of the most extensive collections of Jewish books in the world. Part of the campus overlooking Harlem River, will be utilized for a stadium, playgrounds and athletic field.

"The high school, which is to be completed first because of the overcrowded condition of the Rabbi Isaac Elchanan Theological Seminary on East Broadway, will have four stories," said the Chairman. "It will contain an auditorium seating 2500 to be used as a synagogue on high holidays, thus helping to relieve congestion in other synagogues during these important Jewish events. Designed in most modern style, it will include classrooms limited to thirty-five students each, laboratories, gymnasium, study hall and library for 200.

"The dormitory, built by the Jewish women of America, who

are raising $250,000, will rise five stories, with a study room on each floor, so that students need not study in their bedrooms; two dining rooms, one with cafeteria for 500 students who are non-residents, the other with regular service for its own students. A small synagogue is planned also for the dormitory as well as an infirmary, club room, laundry, etc.

"In the Seminary Building will be a large study, the Talmud Room, for 400 students, twelve classrooms, seating 50 each, reference library and special administrative offices.

"Yeshiva, college and library buildings will stand on the east side of Amsterdam Avenue, the high school and dormitory on the west side. Nearly all of the leading Jewish metropolitan builders are to take part in the construction."

CHAPTER LIX

AMERICAN COMMITTEE FORMED TO AID
JERUSALEM YESHIVA

WHILE Orthodox Jewry was largely concentrating its attention
on the plans for the great Jewish college to be established in
New York, steps were simultaneously taken, nevertheless, for
American aid to be extended to a similar institution of learning
that had been started in Jerusalem by Chief Rabbi Abraham I.
Kook of Palestine. Mr. Fischel was in the forefront of this movement as well.

Rabbi Kook, during his visit to America for the purpose of
stimulating the post-war campaign of the Central Relief Committee, had informed Mr. Fischel that he had established in
Palestine a Jewish Theological Seminary.

Before Rabbi Kook's departure from the United States, Mr.
Fischel had promised him that so soon as the project of the
Yeshiva College here had been properly launched he would make
an effort to organize an American Committee to raise funds for
the Yeshiva in Palestine.

On Sunday, April 5, 1925, a meeting for this purpose was held
at the Congregation Kehilath Jeshurun and at which were present Rabbi M. S. Margolies, Rabbi B. L. Leventhal of Philadelphia, Rabbi Aaron Teitelbaum, Harris Mandelbaum, Meyer
Vesell, Joseph Polstein and Mr. Fischel and a Committee was
organized with Rabbi Leventhal as chairman and Mr. Vesell as
the treasurer.

On this occasion Mr. Fischel had the privilege of contributing
the sum of $10,000 toward the building fund for the Yeshiva to be
erected in Jerusalem.

The Jewish Daily Bulletin of the following day, April 6, 1925, published the following account of the action taken at the meeting.

AMERICAN COMMITTEE FOR TALMUDICAL ACADEMY IN JERUSALEM FORMED

Founders Intend to Revive Traditions of Sura and Pumbedita

An American committee for a Central Jewish Theological Seminary in Jerusalem, the site for which was recently purchased there, has been formed, according to an announcement made yesterday by the headquarters of the Orthodox Central Relief Committee.

The idea of establishing in Jerusalem a Central Jewish Theological Academy was first broached by Rabbi A. I. Kook, Chief Rabbi of Palestine, at the farewell reception tendered in his honor by the Kehilath Jeshurun Synagogue, of which Rabbi M. S. Margolies is the spiritual leader, shortly before his return to Palestine from his American tour. It was decided that the contribution of the membership of the Kehilath Jeshurun to the Central Theological Academy should be $50,000, which was pledged by those present as the initial contribution toward the establishment of the seminary. Chief among the donors were Harry Fischel $10,000; H. Mandelbaum $5,000; Meyer Vesell $5,000; Joseph Polstein $3,000.

Rabbi B. L. Leventhal of Philadelphia was chosen temporary chairman and Meyer Vesell temporary treasurer.

It is the intention of those who are interested in the new seminary in Jerusalem that its curriculum shall be above that of the existing talmudical academies and shall revive the glories of the academies of Sura and Pumbedita.

CHAPTER LX

THE ONE THOUSAND DOLLAR A PLATE DINNER

Every effort was put forth by the campaign committee for the Yeshiva College in New York to have sufficient funds in hand to start the actual work of construction as soon as the architects should have completed their plans for the first of the structures to be erected.

It will be recalled that at the dinner at which this great undertaking was publicly launched, a few men subscribed about $800,-000. While this was a splendid beginning, the campaign committee, of which Mr. Harris Selig was the General Manager, determined that it was necessary at once to enlist the financial support of as many others as might be possible.

It had been the custom in fund raising, especially since the war, to secure subscriptions for philanthropic projects by bringing together a large number of persons at a dinner or other public function, explaining to them the purpose in view and thus enlisting their support and securing their contributions.

Mr. Selig suggested that such a dinner should be held in aid of the Yeshiva. He proposed that not fewer than a thousand persons should be invited, each of whom would be asked to pay $1,000 a plate, or a total of $1,000,000 for the privilege of attending.

When this plan was first suggested it appeared impossible of accomplishment. A dinner of such magnitude, for which the public should be taxed so large a sum, had never before been attempted for any public cause.

Mr. Selig explained the plan was not so hopeless as appeared upon the surface, for the reason that the Yeshiva College had already enlisted the enthusiastic support of Orthodox Jewry throughout the United States and had generally received the commendation of the press, leading educators and that part of the general public which should rightfully be interested.

The Committee was finally induced to accept Mr. Selig's recommendation, fantastic as it at first seemed, and started an intensive effort to sell 1,000 tickets at $1,000 each, for the proposed dinner.

The very audacity of the undertaking and its novelty attracted widespread attention and secured a tremendous amount of publicity. Coupled with these aids, was the fact that business was exceedingly prosperous at that time and most people were ready and willing to give a portion of their wealth in support of a worthy object.

The date fixed for the function was May 24, and the dinner resulted, as had been hoped, in contributions totalling nearly a million dollars. This, in addition to the $800,000 subscribed at the first dinner, brought to the Yeshiva College treasury a total of approximately $1,800,000, a sum sufficient to warrant approval of the plans and an early start on the work of construction.

At a meeting of the Building Committee held on September 15, the architects, who had meanwhile been working constantly, submitted their final plans for the first three buildings, to be known as the Group A buildings. These received the Committee's approval with instructions to prepare for the giving out of contracts.

So deeply engrossed was Mr. Fischel in this work and so great a part of his energy and time did it consume that in that year he was unable to take his usual summer vacation and only interrupted his personal attention to the project for a sojourn of three weeks at Saratoga. During his brief absence, Mr. Jacob Levy, First Vice Chairman of the Building Committee, acted in his stead.

CHAPTER LXI

MR. FISCHEL CONTRIBUTES TO A RELIGIOUS SYMPOSIUM CONDUCTED BY THE AMERICAN HEBREW

"The American Hebrew" for several months during 1926 conducted a symposium in its columns on the question "Are Jews Losing Their Religion?" Some of the foremost Jews in the country contributed their views to this series of articles and among them Mr. Fischel was asked to express his opinions on this vital topic.

He particularly welcomed this opportunity for the reason that the majority of the readers of the American Hebrew were known to be un-orthodox in their sentiments and he wished to place before them his conception of what constitutes Orthodox Judaism and its bearing upon the life of the Jew in America ,today. The article he prepared and which appeared in the American Hebrew of December 17, 1926, is herewith reproduced in full.

"I must first point out that my statement on this subject is concerned with Orthodox historic, traditional, loyal Judaism. This Judaism has withstood the test of inquisition, philosophy, and science. Today, Orthodox or Thora-treu-Judaism is gaining adherents rather than losing them.

"To make clear and convince your readers that I am not arguing from theory but from practical knowledge, I will cite a few examples which I have noticed in my experience in communal work.

"In the ten years between 1880 and 1890, when the religious persecution started in Russia, many families came to this country, who knew no other religion than the Orthodox. Many of them brought with them grown-up sons and daughters, who had been reared to strictly observe the Orthodox religion. Upon arriving here, they found themselves in an entirely different environment. In starting their career and in looking for positions or professions, they found great hardship, as observance of the Sabbath and religious questions interfered.

"The parents, who were unable to support their children, naturally had very little influence over them and instead of trying to find a way to maintain the good will of their children and wait for more opportune times to come, they refused any compromise. They agreed to disagree with them. They allowed their children to drift away from them entirely with the result that the parents went one road and the children another. As time rolled on, they married women of the same views as themselves, with the result that they were lost entirely to Judaism.

"Fortunately this condition did not exist with all those who arrived in America. There were many families who did not separate. The children clung to the religion of their parents and after a great deal of difficulty, they found positions where they were able to keep the Sabbath and the Jewish holidays. And they practiced the Orthodox Jewish religion in every form. These young men and young women have married and live quite a different life. They have combined Americanism with Judaism. Their children eventually came to the age where they had to decide for themselves as to their religious beliefs. Naturally, having been brought up under a religious environment, the parents and the children agreed, with the result that a new generation of observant Jews had arisen.

"These have not desecrated the Sabbath, nor violated any of the dietary laws, but, on the contrary, have beautified religion and have made it a thing to be admired. It appeals to them and they are carrying the religious gospel into the institutions of learning. They are not ashamed to join religious clubs in the colleges, and above all they are patronizing the kosher restaurants, which were established in several colleges under the auspices of the Union of Orthodox Jewish Congregations of America.

"We have at this time three generations of Orthodox Jews.

"The first generation represents the Jews who came with their children and who have not changed. They went through their critical periods of suffering, even to near starvation and did not waiver in any shape or form, neither in observing the laws nor any of the customs of their faith. They are the Jews who are now the standard bearers of hundreds of synagogues in this country.

"The second generation represents the sons and daughters of those who came with their parents and have suffered many hardships together with them, but have remained loyal to our traditions. They acquired American methods. They worked during the day and went to school at night. Later they interested themselves in charitable and communal work, building new synagogues, Talmud Torahs and Yeshivas.

"In the same period between 1880 and 1890, there also arrived another type of young men and women, in which class my wife and myself are included. They came to America alone, without parents to guide them. However, they were imbued with sufficient religious spirit to remain loyal to our faith, in spite of the many hardships they had to endure. Many of these young men married women of the same religious belief, with the result that their offspring are added to the ranks of the observant Jews.

"The third generation represents the children who were born of the first and second generations. They had the full benefit of American education, which their parents missed, and in most cases they enjoyed the benefit of the hard work performed by their parents. They had easy traveling on the wide road laid out for them by their parents, economically and educationally. Having been brought up in a religious environment, which was beautified and moulded in accordance with American life; having found strictly Orthodox synagogues; the beautiful restaurants conducted in strict accordance with the dietary laws; the most important banquets in the large hotels made strictly kosher; Jewish collegiate societies, and other Jewish influences in the colleges, these children did not find it a hardship to remain good Orthodox Jews. Religion was not a burden to them. In fact, it was a source of joy.

"One point which proves quite forcefully that the Jews in America are not losing their religion is the fact that so many Orthodox young men and young women can be found in the synagogues on Sabbath and the holidays. I will admit that there are several synagogues in the Lower East Side, Harlem, Bronx and Brooklyn which are attended only by the older men and women and the young children below the adolescent age. These synagogues do not attract the young people, simply because they are of the old type, lacking cleanliness, decorum and an English speaking Rabbi.

"The synagogues of the modern type, such as the Institutional Synagogue on 116th Street and all the Young Israel Synagogues, are composed almost entirely of the young men and young women who take a vital interest not only in the service but in every activity which is in any way connected with the synagogue. Many of the young men in these institutions even attend daily services before going to business in the morning. This does not sound as if Judaism is on the decline.

"To prove that Orthodox Jews are not losing their religion, one should observe the number of Talmud Torah and Yeshiva buildings which have been erected during the last ten or fifteen years in the City of New York. These institutions have been built by the second generation. They realize that the methods and conditions under which they received their religious education in Europe cannot be tolerated by their children. Cheders of old will not appeal to their children born in America, who are attending public schools with plenty of fresh air and sunshine. They therefore put their shoulders to the wheel and used all their energy to provide for their children new school buildings with all the latest improvements, light and sanitary classrooms; a new system of education.

"The Hebrew School has been put on a par with the Public School, with the result that these schools have appealed to the children and through the children their influence has spread into the homes of the parents. The effect of the religion has penetrated even the homes of those parents who for economic reasons kept their business houses open on the Sabbath and did not observe the Jewish dietary laws.

"I am personally familiar with many cases where the children have refused to eat at home until all the dishes were thrown out, new ones substituted and Kashruth established. I know of many cases where the parents were compelled to close their business on Saturday, through the influence of the religious training received by the children in the Hebrew Schools. I also know of many cases, where, through the influence of the children, the fathers were compelled to begin to lay the tephilin. The Hebrew Schools have been a great factor in increasing religion not only

MR. FISCHEL'S PRESENT RESIDENCE

*In the apartment building erected by him at the southwest corner
of Park Avenue and 80th Street, showing the private
Succah (Tabernacle) constructed for his own use.
The first such edifice on Park Avenue.*

among the Orthodox Jews, but have also exerted a great influence on the so-called Conservative Jews. What has been accomplished in the City of New York has been followed in all the large cities throughout the United States of America.

"The fact is that there are now more Talmud Torahs and Yeshiva buildings in America, with a Jewish population of about three millions, than there were in all of Europe before the war, with a population of about fourteen millions.

"In conclusion and to prove conclusively that the Orthodox Jews in America are not losing their religion, but have every reason to be optimistic about their religious future in this country, I will mention the fact that we are now erecting on Amsterdam Avenue, from 186th to 188th Streets, the Yeshiva College of America at a cost of over five million dollars. This is being done in order to provide an institution which will give a thorough Jewish education, not only to those who wish to become Rabbis or teachers, but also to enable young men who are entering trades or professions to receive a splendid secular as well as religious training.

"In answer to your question 'Are the Jews in America losing their religion?' I emphatically say 'No'."

CHAPTER LXII

THE FIRST SUCCAH ON PARK AVENUE

It remained for Mr. Fischel, who ever since he had been able to enjoy a home of his own had maintained a tabernacle or succah in his residence, to construct the first such private place of worship to be built on the now fashionable Park Avenue.

In planning his present home in the apartment building at Park Avenue and 80th Street, Mr. Fischel decided that the succah to be installed there, should be the most beautiful that he had yet attempted.

In accordance with the Jewish law, it is required that such a place of worship be built so that a clear view of the sky shall be in no way obstructed; in short that nothing be built over it. The new apartment, was a 14 story building, his residence occupying the second floor. In order, therefore, that the succah should comply with the Jewish law and the roof be exposed to the sky, Mr. Fischel omitted one room on each of the twelve floors of the structure above his own apartment on the second floor, entailing a loss in rentals of about $12,000 a year. Throughout his life, Mr. Fischel had found, however, that he had never had cause for regret in living up to every tenet of his faith, no matter what financial sacrifice was, at the time, involved.

Mr. Fischel moved into his home on September 8, 1925, immediately prior to the Feast of the Tabernacles, the first evening of which holiday was celebrated by him in his own succah surrounded by all of his children and his grandchildren.

During his long connection with philanthropic and other communal affairs, it was the custom of the various institutions with which Mr. Fischel was affiliated, to hold meetings and entertainments in his home for the raising of funds and in his new Park

AN INTERIOR VIEW OF THE SUCCAH IN MR. FISCHEL'S HOME.

Avenue residence, Mr. Fischel constructed a special meeting
room for this purpose.

This place of assemblage was finished in the beginning of January, 1926, and in order that it might be properly dedicated he
called a meeting of the Building Committee of the Yeshiva College to take place there on January 19, 1926. At this meeting
the architects brought with them the completed plans for the
Group A. Buildings, as well as a general perspective for all of
the buildings eventually to be erected on the campus.

Mr. Fischel also arranged for a religious dedication of his
completed home that took place on May 2, 1926. A source
of especial gratification to him, was the presence of Chief Rabbi
Ezekiel Lifshitz of Poland, who was then on a visit to America
and who gave his formal blessing to the household.

On such occasions of family rejoicing it had always been Mr.
Fischel's custom to make some special contribution to charity and
in this instance he subscribed the sum of $15,000 to the fund
being collected by the United Jewish Campaign for the Relief
of Jews suffering Through the War, the largest sum he had ever
contributed to this particular cause.

Mr. Fischel's strenuous work in behalf of the Yeshiva College,
coupled with the fact that he had taken practically no rest for
more than a year, brought about a recurrence of the diabetes
from which he had suffered in 1924 and on June 8, 1926, he left
for a second period of treatment at the Battle Creek Sanitarium
of Dr. Harvey W. Kellogg. He remained only three weeks but
in this short period his health was restored.

During his previous stay in the sanitarium, Mr. Fischel had
arranged to hold religious services for the Jewish patients in his
room each Saturday. These services were greatly appreciated
and also commanded the respect of Dr. Kellogg and others who
were not of the Jewish faith. On his second visit, Mr. Fischel
engaged two rooms, one of which was set aside exclusively for
synagogue purposes. Here daily services were attended by all

the Jewish patients, regardless of whether they were Orthodox, Conservative or Reform.

While the patients hailed from different parts of the United States, these services brought them very close together. In this relationship and bound by the afflictions they held in common, they did not hesitate to reveal the history of their lives and the early struggles which had attended their individual efforts to grasp the opportunities afforded in these great and beloved United States.

On June 29, while still in the sanitarium, Mr. Fischel celebrated his 61st birthday, when he was the recipient of telegrams of congratulation from the directors of many of the institutions which he had helped during his long career in communal labor.

This sudden flood of messages, all arriving on the same day, aroused the curiosity of many of the patients who asked Mr. Fischel the occasion for them. When they were informed that it was his birthday, a Committee was organized among those who had attended the religious services Mr. Fischel had made possible, and he was presented with a bouquet of flowers containing 61 roses, one for each year of his life. The committee also requested that Mr. Fischel consent to be photographed with them in a group picture so that each might have the opportunity of taking this memento of the occasion home with him.

The group arranged themselves on several benches for this purpose and while the photographer was focusing his camera, Mr. Harris Salit of Brooklyn, N. Y., one of the patients, handed Mr. Fischel an envelope which he suggested should be shown in the photograph. Mr. Fischel could not quite understand the meaning of this act but after the picture had been taken and he opened the envelope he found enclosed in it a resolution signed by Dr. John Harvey Kellogg, the institution's head, as well as by many of the attending physicians and twenty of the men who had been in constant attendance at the religious services.

Mr. Fischel highly appreciated the sentiment prompting the resolution, a copy of which is herewith appended:

THE BATTLE CREEK SANITARIUM

Battle Creek, Michigan

Tuesday, June 29th, 1926

A Little Expression of Affection

To our dear friend Mr. Harry Fischel of New York:

We, your undersigned friends at the Battle Creek Sanitarium, Mich., wish you many happy returns of this day. Affectionate thoughts and every good wish go to you on this your birthday. May each succeeding year bring to you the satisfaction which we trust life holds in store for you.

Your friends,

Joseph Aaron, Brooklyn, N. Y.   John Harvey Kellogg, MD. LLD
Sam Adler, Youngstown, O.   Samuel J. Littenberg, N. Y.
Jos. Alruninsky, N. Y.   M. Plant, Vancouver, B. C.
R. V. Ashley, M.D.   Oscar Rosenzweig, Akron, O.
Max Bild   Albert Rosenzeig, Akron, O.
H. Cohen, New York City   Harris Salit, Brooklyn, N. Y.
Morris Effron, Topeka, Kansas. Harry Sandler, New York City
Joseph Frey, Ph.G., St. Louis   H. Siegel, Chicago
Rabbi Isidore Goodman   M. Siegel, Chicago, Ill.
Abe Hubby   I. Sokol, Akron, O.
C. O. Hubby, M.D.   Wm. Telscu, Chicago, Ill.
Harry Katz, Passaic, N. J.   M. A. Turner
M. L. Vitch, Brooklyn, N. Y.

CHAPTER LXIII

SYSTEM EMPLOYED IN AWARDING YESHIVA
CONTRACTS

On his return to New York, Mr. Fischel again devoted himself largely to pushing the work of the Yeshiva College.

The Building Committee for the Yeshiva at this time consisted of about forty members. When the committee had approved the plans of the architects, the services of so large a number seemed no longer to be required and it was arranged that the contracts should be awarded and the details of construction passed upon by a subcommittee, as it was felt that a small body could accomplish quicker and more effective results than a large group. Mr. Fischel suggested that four vice-chairmen be appointed to assist him in executing the practical part of the undertaking and recommended for the posts Mr. Jacob Levy, Mr. Louis Gold, Mr. Joseph Ravitch and Mr. Henry Friedman, all of whom were engaged in the building business.

The committee accepted this recommendation and from that time until the present day, Mr. Fischel, together, with these vice chairmen, have met regularly, never farther apart than once a month, sometimes every two weeks and, when necessary to take immediate action upon some point, as often as every week. Only when a large and important matter or policy was to be considered, was the larger committee called together.

In proceeding with the work of construction of the Yeshiva College, Mr. Fischel and the committee of vice-chairmen charged with the responsibility of awarding the contracts, proceeded along entirely new lines which resulted in substantial savings.

It is usually the custom in such undertakings to give out either a general contract to a single contractor, covering the project in its entirety, or else to engage a building firm to let the contracts for various parts of the work to subcontractors. Either procedure involves a considerable overhead expense. In the case of a general contract, a profit of from five to ten per cent is usually charged on the work alloted to each sub-contractor and when a building firm is engaged to give out the contracts an overhead of from six to ten percent on the total sum expended is usually involved. In the case of so costly an enterprise as the Yeshiva College, this profit to a general contractor or overhead to a building firm would have amounted to several hundred thousands of dollars.

Although it necessitated a much larger amount of work on the part of the Building sub-committee this cost was saved by the committee itself awarding the several contracts, just as an individual would do if engaged upon a building operation for himself.

More than this, however, the personal interest taken by the members of the sub-committee, effected not only a money saving, but greater efficiency and a higher quality of workmanship.

The first contract, that for the foundation, was awarded on May 6, 1926. From that time up to the present date, $1,400,000 worth of contracts have been signed by Mr. Fischel as Chairman of the Building Committee.

In a publication known as the Cornerstone, the following appreciation of the work accomplished by the building committee, appeared on March 4, 1927.

How Building Committee Is Accomplishing Its Great
Task of Construction

*Men of Vision Who Direct Construction of the Yeshiva College
of America—An Edifice in the Solomonic Style of
Unique Architectural Beauty*

One of the major functions of the Yeshiva College Building
Fund during the period of the construction of the Yeshiva College naturally fell to the Building Committee. This committee,
composed of men whose high calibre has been proven by long
experience in the constructive processes of life, had to deal with
the plan, the scope and the character of the edifice which is to
house the great institution for higher Jewish learning. It required vision and an actual knowledge of material possibilities to
arrive at the plans for the great structure. The raising of a
building fund is either a difficult or simple task. All that is
necessary is to present the appeal to the man of means, to convince him of the worthiness of the purpose, of the effectiveness
of the contribution and, when everything goes well, so many dollars have been placed at the disposition of the Building Committee.

How these funds are to be expended in order to insure the
visioned purpose, how best to express the intention of all the
contributors, how to pay regard to the actual needs of the Yeshiva
College, how to provide for its further expansion, how to devise
a plan which would express the soul of the idea and raise the
structure in an appropriate style consonant with the character of
the Yeshiva and, at the same time, provide for the needs of an
institution of learning—these were the tasks with which the
building committee of the Yeshiva Building Fund were charged.

It was not enough to purchase the land, to buy the steel, to
provide the bricks, to hire the labor, to consult the engineer, to
invoke the counsel of the architect. In the case of other buildings the constructors are responsible to themselves and to a limited number of people who have an interest in the building.

The construction of a Yeshiva College for the Jews of America
involves a responsibility not only to the contributors, not only to
the students and the faculty, but also a great moral debt to the
community as a whole. Nay, not only to the Jewish community,

LAYING OF THE CORNERSTONE FOR THE GREAT YESHIVA COLLEGE of the Rabbi Isaac Elchanan Theological Seminary, Amsterdam Avenue, 186th to 187th Streets, New York City, May 1, 1927.

but also to the country at large. A country is judged by its public edifices and to raise the Yeshiva College to such a high architectural level of beauty and power of expression, is an undertaking that might well tax the foresight and knowledge of leaders of men.

Harry Fischel, who himself contributed $100,000 toward the Building Fund, headed the building committee which has considered, weighed and decided upon the plan and its execution. He was aided by Jacob Levy, Louis Gold, Joseph Ravitch and Henry Friedman, vice-chairmen of the Building Committee; Joseph Polstein, secretary; Albert Wald, counsel; Harris L. Selig, director; and Samuel Bayer, A. Bricken, Henry Friedman, Conrad Galzer, Pincus Glickman, Joseph Golding, Mendel Gottesman, Paul Herring, S. A. Israel, Nathan Lamport, Abraham Levy, Rabbi M. S. Margolies, Julius Miller, Samuel Minskoff, Isaac Polstein, Judge Otto A. Rosalsky, Samuel R. Rosoff, G. S. Roth, Harry Schiff, Leon Sobel, Meyer Vesell, Nathan Wilson, Max Wilson and Benjamin Winter; representing the faculty and student body, Dr. Bernard Revel, Rabbi Herbert S. Goldstein, Rabbi N. H. Ebin, Dr. S. Safir, Rabbi J. S. Schwartz; representing the dormitory, Mrs. N. H. Ebin Mrs. Harry Fischel, Mrs. Herbert S. Goldstein, Mrs. A. Levitan, Mrs. Abraham Levy, Mrs. Jacob Levy, Mrs. Elias Surut.

As the first group of buildings of the Yeshiva College of America is emerging, the character of the work accomplished under Mr. Fischel's chairmanship and with the aid of the architects, Charles B. Meyers and Henry B. Hertz, is becoming more and more evident. The public will be able to view and appreciate the beauty of the structure which will be a distinct contribution to American architecture and a notable departure in the construction of Jewish public buildings on this continent.

The buildings were designed in a style resembling that of the Solomonic period. The committee, including experienced realtors, immediately agreed that no endeavor was to be made to erect high buildings of a skyscraper type. For an institution like the Yeshiva College of America something more than a useful type of building is to be sought. Something more than convenient accommodations must be looked for—it must be a building with a soul, a house worthy of the name Yeshiva College of America.

Group A. which is now in the process of construction, consists of three buildings, a high school, an auditorium and a dormitory.

These three buildings will, until that time when the other five buildings are completed, house the Yeshivah in all its departments. It is the hope of the Building Committee that it will be in a position to present the complete Yeshiva College of America to the student body and the faculty in the very near future.

MEMBERS OF THE BUILDING COMMITTEE

Of the Yeshiva College, of which Mr. Fischel is chairman.

CHAPTER LXIV

CORNERSTONE IS LAID FOR YESHIVA COLLEGE
BEFORE AUDIENCE OF 30,000

INTEREST in the Yeshiva College grew apace among all sections of Jewry as the time approached for the ceremony of the cornerstone laying for the Group A. buildings. It was generally recognized that this function would mark the most notable step yet taken in America for the advancement of Jewish religious education and for the preservation of Orthodox Judaism.

In view of the fact that the chief burdens of the undertaking had fallen upon the Building Committee, this committee, quite naturally, was entrusted with the honor of arranging the details of the observance, the date for which was finally fixed for Sunday afternoon, May 1, 1927.

It was determined by the Committee that the cornerstone laying should be a ceremony fully befitting the dignity and significance of the occasion and many meetings were held to plan the details and to secure the cooperation and attendance of the most notable figures in the fields of Jewish education and in public life generally.

An invitation was finally prepared and sent to 25,000 prominent Orthodox Jews, not only in New York but throughout the country, as it was held by the committee, the Yeshiva College constituted a national, rather than a local institution, and the occasion was one that should properly be brought to the attention of American Jewry as a whole.

This invitation was as follows:

The Building Committee of the Yeshiva College cordially invites you to attend the laying of the cornerstone of the Group A. buildings which will take place on Sunday afternoon, May 1,

1927, at two o'clock on Amsterdam Avenue and 186th-187th Streets, New York City.

As a leader in your community and a friend of the Yeshiva, we hope you will attend.

Harry Fischel
Chairman of the Building Committee.

Building Committee

Officers:

Chairman, Harry Fischel
Vice Chairmen: Jacob Levy, Louis Gold, Joseph Ravitch, and Henry Friedman
Secretary, Joseph Polstein
Designing and Supervising Architect, Charles B. Meyers
Consulting Architect, Henry B. Hertz
Counsel, Albert Wald
Director, Harris L. Selig

Samuel Bayer	Philip Meyrowitz
A. Bricken	Hon. Julius Miller
Rabbi N. H. Ebin	Samuel Minskoff
Conrad Glaser	Isaac Polstein
Pincus Glickman	Dr. Bernard Revel
Joseph Golding	Samuel R. Rosoff
Rabbi Herbert S. Goldstein	Judge Otto A. Rosalsky
Mendel Gottesman	G. S. Roth
Paul Herring	Dr. S. Safir
S. A. Israel	Samuel L. Sar
Nathan Lamport	Harry Schiff
Judge Max S. Levine	Leon Sobel
Abraham Levy	Meyer Vesell
David Levy	Nathan Wilson
Samuel Levy	Max Wilson
Rabbi M. S. Margolies	Benj. Winter

Representing the Dormitory

Mrs. N. H. Ebin	Mrs. Abraham Levy
Mrs. Harry Fischel	Mrs. Jacob Levy
Mrs. Herbert S. Goldstein	Mrs. Elias Surut
Mrs. A. Levitan	

Acceptances were received from practically every large city in the United States, giving promise of a very large attendance, so that arrangements were made accordingly.

The grandstand for the occasion, with a seating capacity of more than six thousand persons, was erected by the Municipal government through the courtesy of the Hon. Albert Goldman, Commissioner of Plant and Structures, of the City of New York.

Even this provision, thought to be ample, proved inadequate, however, as when the great day came and although the ceremonies were not scheduled to begin until two o'clock in the afternoon, the grandstand was nearly filled as early as eleven o'clock in the morning. As the hour for the exercises drew near every seat was occupied and many thousands of persons who could not be accommodated, remained standing in the vicinity throughout the entire proceedings.

More than 1200 gaily decorated automobiles, containing the officers of different institutions, formed in line at the Jewish Center on West Eighty-sixth Street, several hours before the time set for the cornerstone laying, leading a great parade which wended its way to the scene of the festivities.

This procession was headed by Mr. Nathan Lamport as President of the institution and Mr. Fischel, as Chairman of the Building Committee, and was escorted along the entire route to 186th Street and Amsterdam Avenue, by motorcycle police. On entering the grounds of the Yeshiva, the procession was greeted by cheer upon cheer from the throats of the thirty thousand spectators who by that time had assembled.

The ceremony of the laying of the cornerstone made an indellible impression upon the thousands of persons who were present. It was the general opinion of all those who attended, that such an event and such a celebration had never previously been held either in the City of New York or elsewhere in the United States, which, indeed, is a fact, for no similar institution of the size and importance of the Yeshiva College has heretofore been established anywhere in America. The cornerstone laying marked the beginning of what must be regarded as a new epoch in Jewish religious education in America. It proved that American Jewry appreciates the need and desirability of the establishment of a Jewish Parochial College where the Jewish youth shall, under one roof, obtain both the Talmudic and secular knowledge essential to the upbuilding of Jewish character and to the preservation of Jewish traditions in America.

Not only was this viewpoint expressed by the Jewish leaders and educators of the community, but such noted non-Jewish educators as Dr. John H. Finley, former Commissioner of Education of the State of New York, Dr. Frederick Robinson, President of the College of the City of New York, Dr. James C. Egbert, representing President Nicholas Murray Butler of Columbia University, and many others. A letter from the President of the United States stressed the great importance to the American people at large, of giving the Jewish youth this opportunity of embracing Talmudic and secular knowledge under proper religious environment and under the auspices of a single institution. This letter was written after Congressman Sol. Bloom and Rabbi Herbert S. Goldstein had caused the undertaking to be brought to the President's attention.

In addition to the remarks of the educators, the leading officials of the State and City, including United States Senator Royal S. Copeland, the Acting Mayor, Joseph V. McKee, President of the Board of Aldermen and Julius Miller, President of the Borough of Manhattan, together with other high officials, expressed their appreciation in behalf of the State and City for the facilities which generous and public-minded Jews were to provide through this great institution.

In order to have a complete record of the ceremony the report of the occasion appearing in the Jewish Daily Bulletin of May 3, 1927, is given herewith.

Yeshiva College Cornerstone Laying Is Witnessed by 30,000

President Coolidge lauds Institution blending Jewish and secular
learning; Prominent Leaders and educators participate
in Solemn Exercises.   Additional $200,000
raised at National Committee Dinner

The cornerstone laying exercises for the first group of buildings of the Yeshiva College of America, an institution sponsored by Orthodox leaders for the purpose of combining Jewish and secular education for the training of rabbis, teachers and lay professionals, were held Sunday afternoon at the Yeshiva site in the presence of an audience exceeding 30,000.   An automobile parade from the West Side Synagogue on Eighty-sixth Street to the Yeshiva grounds at Amsterdam Avenue and 186th Street, preceded the exercises.

The ceremonies were begun with an address by Harry Fischel, chairman of the building Committee and donor of $100,000 to the Yeshiva College Building Fund.   He said:

"Ladies and Gentlemen:

"On behalf of the Building Committee I herewith extend to you a hearty welcome.   We have assembled here this afternoon to celebrate the greatest event in Jewish history, the laying of the cornerstone of The Yeshiva Isaac Elchanan and the first Jewish college ever built in America.   I will therefore say with the Psalmists 'This is the day which the Lord has made, let us be happy and rejoice thereon.'

"We consider this the happiest day in our lives, for we have lived to see our dream realized.

"My friends.   In looking back 33 years, I remind myself of the time when we bought an old private house at 85 Henry Street.   We were then contented.   It was fifteen years later that we first found the need of a new building.   We then bought two old houses at 9-11 Montgomery Street which we transformed into a school building.   We were again contented.   However, our institution grew, and with it our pride in it.   Only five years elapsed before we bought the building at 301-302-303 East Broadway, and converted it into a first class school building which was equal to the needs of that time and which buildings we still occupy.

"It is now three years since a handful of men saw the vision of a modern Yeshiva College building. At that time we had in mind a building occupying about ten city lots. However, our enthusiasm grew daily until we bought the present site. We went far beyond our expectations. The site on which we are erecting the present buildings, occupies a space of 15 city lots. In addition thereto, we own these two beautiful square blocks facing us, consisting of nearly 70 city lots. On these two blocks, we expect to erect in the near future; the Yeshiva Building, a College Building, a Library, a Teachers' Institute, a Gymnasium, a Dormitory for college boys, also all other necessary buildings required for a complete university.

"The buildings we are now erecting are as follows: A High School to accommodate over 1500 boys; an auditorium with a seating capacity for nearly 2500; a dormitory building to accommodate about 200 out of town attendants of high school grades.

"These buildings when completed will house all our activities until the time comes and, I hope in the very near future, when we shall be able to complete our entire plan.

"I take this occasion to extend my thanks to the Almighty for giving me the privilege of acting as Chairman of the Building Committee for every building which the Yeshiva Rabbi Isaac Elchanan Theological Seminary has ever built or altered. I am especially grateful to the Almighty for having the privilege once again to hold the same position in connection with present buildings.

"Before I conclude, I will say that I would be derelict in my duty, were I not to publicly express my appreciation for the splendid cooperation I have received from my four Vice Chairmen, namely: Mr. Jacob Levy, Mr. Joseph Ravitch, Mr. Louis Gold, Mr. Henry Friedman.

"I also extend my thanks to the entire building committee who have helped to prepare the plans for the present structure.

"I am likewise grateful to the Campaign Fund Committee, with Mr. Samuel Levy, as Chairman, for their devotion and energetic labor in providing the funds to pay for the buildings.

"I am very thankful to Mr. Abraham Levy, the Chairman of

FIRST GROUP OF THE YESHIVA COLLEGE BUILDINGS.

Of which Mr. Fischel was Chairman of the Building Committee.

the Arrangements Committee, who has performed his duty in a manner that is a credit not only to the Building Committee, but to the entire Jewish Community.

"Last but not least, I am grateful to the Architects, Mr. Charles B. Meyers and Mr. Henry B. Hertz for the great skill they have displayed in planning these buildings.

"My friends, in accordance with the Orthodox Jewish custom on festive days, I will conclude with the traditional Schehecheyanu prayer.

" 'Blessed art Thou O Lord our God who has kept us in life and hast preserved us and enabled us to reach this occasion of the laying of the cornerstone.'

"I further pray to the Almighty that I, as well as everyone who is assembled here this afternoon, will be privileged to share in and be present at the completion of all the buildings, not only on this side but on the other side of the street as well."

A Megillah in Hebrew and English was deposited under the cornerstone, relating the history of the first Yeshiva in America and of the developments leading up to the rise of the present structure. The exterior of the first group of buildings is already completed.

The ceremonies were attended by many Orthodox Jewish leaders, rabbis and contributors to the Fund, as well as by representatives of the National, City and State governments. Samuel Levy, as chairman of the Executive Committee of the Yeshiva College, was master of Ceremonies.

Joseph V. McKee, Acting Mayor and president of the Board of Aldermen, bringing the greeting of the municipality, said that the Yeshiva will do for its future pupils what modern universities are failing to do when they neglect the "immortal souls" of their student bodies.

"Our universities are teaching physical facts and forgetting to discipline the wills of their students," he declared. "Thus they are bereft of the fruits of a full education. You Jews here are making better men for yourselves and for your country by not ignoring the needs of the soul. After establishing yourselves as leaders of commerce, politics, and finance you are making yourselves leaders in education as well."

Senator Royal S. Copeland said the planning and building of the Yeshiva project should be a cause for great satisfaction to

American Jewry, calling attention to the literal meaning of Yeshiva, a "Meeting" or "Session." Senator Copeland said the new college was in line with an American tradition which began in the New England meeting house of the Seventeenth century.

Professor James C. Egbert, director of the University Extension at Columbia University, brought the greetings of Columbia and of President Nicholas Murray Butler. Dr. John H. Finley, former Commissioner of Education, welcomed the new college because, he said, it would preserve the gifts of Jewish religion and culture for future generations in America.

Dr. Bernard Revel, the Rosh Yeshiva, president of the institution's faculty, delivered the principal address.

The cornerstone was laid by a committee of six which included Nathan Lamport, Harry Fischel, Adolph Lewisohn, Frederick Brown, Meyer Vesell and Samuel Levy. They were assisted by Morris Asinoff, Samuel Bayer, Joseph H. Cohen, Jacob Fabian, Henry Friedman, Pincus Glickman, Louis Gold, Mendel Gottesman, Maurice Greenstein, Samuel Kamlet, M. W. Levine, Abraham Levy, David Levy, Jacob Levy, Nathan Levy, Isaac Liberman, Samuel Minskoff, Isaac Polstein, Joseph Polstein, Joseph Ravitch, Harry Roggen, Judge Otto A. Rosalsky, Gustavus S. Roth, Max Silberman, Louis Topkis and Benjamin Winter.

A letter from President Coolidge addressed to Dr. Revel was read. In his letter the President said:

"I regret that it is impossible for me to be present at the laying of the cornerstone of the new buildings of the Yeshiva Rabbi Isaac Elchanan, marking as they do a new era in the development of your institution of higher education, which stands for culture, learning and scholarship and for religious training so vitally essential to the welfare of our country. The exercises on Sunday have a peculiar significance to all true Americans. Long eminent in philanthropic, social and communal work, the Jews of America, through the increased advantages at the disposal of the Yeshiva, will be able to broaden their field for the training of scholars and religious leaders for their people. This is of importance, not only to them but to our national life as a whole.

"I send my congratulations, greetings and best wishes."

CHIEF RABBI ABRAHAM I. KOOK, OF PALESTINE

With Mr. Fischel at the entrance to the Chief Rabbi's home in Jerusalem, during Mr. Fischel's fourth pilgrimage to the Holy Land, June, 1927.

A cablegram of congratulations was received from Rabbi Abraham I. Kook, Chief Rabbi of Palestine.

The Hebrew text of the Megillah was read by Harris L. Selig and the English by Gustavus A. Rogers.

Music was furnished by the Hebrew Orphan Asylum Band and singing by the Jewish Cantors Association of America, led by Louis Lipitz, president, and Cantor Pinchas Jasinowski. An additional fund of $200,000 was raised at the dinner given in the Grand ballroom of the Hotel Astor Sunday evening in honor of the National Yeshiva Committee.

CHAPTER LXV

A FOURTH VISIT TO PALESTINE

THE cornerstone of the Yeshiva College having been laid and the most important contracts for the construction of the Group A. buildings having been let, Mr. Fischel once more turned his eyes toward Palestine. He was anxious again to visit the Holy Land both for the spiritual inspiration he invariably received from this source and for the reason that he had in mind a definite program that he believed would be beneficial both to the Yeshiva College here and to the Yeshiva Chief Rabbi Kook had established in Jerusalem, known as the Universal Yeshiva.

This plan was to arrange an exchange of professors between the two institutions and also to afford the graduates of the Yeshiva College in America the opportunity to go to Palestine and take a post graduate course in higher Talmudic learning in Rabbi Kook's institution. This latter institution was being conducted in the synagogue Mr. Fischel had erected in connection with his gift of a residence for the Chief Rabbi several years earlier.

Mr. Fischel entrusted to the Vice Chairmen of the Building Committee of the Yeshiva College the work of proceeding with the construction of that institution and, with Mrs. Fischel, took passage for Palestine on May 17, 1927.

It was their privilege on this occasion to be accompanied by Rabbi M. S. Margolies, Dean of the Orthodox Rabbinate of America, who was paying his first visit to the Holy Land, an experience that gave this venerable Rabbi, the greatest joy.

Arriving in Palestine, the party, before reaching Jerusalem, was met by a committee representing the several institutions, which was sent by Chief Rabbi Kook to welcome them. This committee escorted them to the Chief Rabbi's home. A little distance from their destination they heard the melodious sound of the students' voices in the Yeshiva as they studied the Talmud.

At the residence of the Chief Rabbi, they found assembled a large number of Rabbis, heads of institutions and business leaders who had arranged a formal reception for them. The Chief Rabbi was especially cordial in his greetings to Rabbi Margolies, whom he presented to the gatherings as the leader of Orthodox Rabbis in America, at the same time taking advantage of the opportunity to relate the manner in which Mr. Fischel had provided the Chief Rabbi's home and Synagogue and the efforts he had put forth in behalf of the Universal Yeshiva, with his contribution of $10,000 to the latter cause.

The party reached Jerusalem three days before Shevuoth, (the Feast of Weeks) and, in accordance with his practice on his previous journeys, Mr. Fischel paid his first visit to the oldest synagogue in the city known as the Churva Rabbi Jehuda Ha-Chasid, which is 700 years old. He at once noted that the interior of the edifice had been entirely redecorated and presented a beautiful appearance. Looking toward the center, however, he was surprised to find, in view of the spic and span appearance of the rest of the building, that the Bimah, or centre-platform, was broken and dilapidated. Curious to know why this should be he inquired of the President of the Congregation, the reason for the discrepancy.

He was informed that during the decoration of the ceiling, which is about 75 feet high, the scaffolding broke. Two painters fell and were not even hurt but in the descent of the scaffold the pulpit was struck and shattered to pieces. Asking why it had not been repaired, Mr. Fischel was told the Congregation believed this was inadvisable as the ancient pulpit did not conform to the rest of the remodeled structure. What had long been desired was an entirely new pulpit. The cost, however, would be $1,000 and the Congregation did not have this sum to spare for the purpose.

Mr. Fischel at once offered to contribute this amount, announcement of which, when made to the Congregation by the President, was received with expressions of joy and gratitude.

On this visit, the Fischel party remained in Palestine four weeks, going from one end of the country to the other, visiting the people and the institutions. Mr. Fischel found that since his previous visit four years earlier, notable progress had been made on every side and many important improvements had been completed, which, more than ever, caused him to have confidence in the future of the Jewish Homeland. Many of the institutions, however, faced economic difficulties which Mr. Fischel sought to remedy by his financial assistance.

While in Jerusalem he organized a Free Loan Society among the students of the Universal Yeshiva, starting the fund with a substantial amount so that it might immediately function and afford loans to students when in need.

On the evening of June 29, the day before their departure, Chief Rabbi Abraham I. Kook, together with the teachers and students of the Yeshiva, arranged a farewell reception in honor of Mr. and Mrs. Fischel. This function was held in the Yeshiva Building and was attended by the representatives of many of the institutions of Jerusalem. Mr. Fischel was greatly touched by this expression of affection and respect and publicly gave his thanks to the Almighty, for having been privileged to lend his assistance in both the religious and material upbuilding of the Jewish Homeland, which he fervently prayed he might visit many times again and might continue to aid.

CHAPTER LXVI

AN INTIMATE VIEW OF HARRY FISCHEL, THE MAN

No biographical work is complete or satisfactory that does not attempt to visualize to the reader something more of the personality of the individual than is contained in the mere chronicle of his public activities. For this reason, it is sought to give, in the final chapter of this book, a glimpse of Mr. Fischel in his every day life, in his home and office, with his family, friends and business associates, in order that the reader may come to know the man himself, not merely the astute and sagacious business leader or even the philanthropist and ardent communal worker.

It is Mr. Fischel as husband, father and friend that this chapter will seek to make known to those who have followed the history of his achievements as set forth here.

What sort of man is it, then, who has emerged in middle life from the crucible of a boyhood spent in hardship and privation in a primitive Russian hamlet; who, as a youthful immigrant in a strange land, struggled to preserve his ideals and to win a livelihood against overwhelming obstacles and who, in later life, triumphing over poverty and discouragements, attained material prosperity and a record of service to his fellow man undreamed of in his most extravagant early imaginings.

To begin with, the dominant traits of Mr. Fischel's character, his unassuming manner, supreme gentleness, sympathy with and understanding of the needs of others, and his reliance upon his faith, have remained unaltered with the passing of the years and during the transition from poverty to affluence. Today he is as easily approachable, as ready to do a service, as democratic and kindly in his attitude toward all he meets as he was when an obscure and friendless youth. Nor have the fires of his enthusiasm, his belief in human nature or his zeal for his religion been in any way abated.

The worldly power which wealth of necessity brings, the association with outstanding leaders in every walk of life, the opportunities for opulent living, have left him unaffected. His tastes are as simple, his wants are as easily satisfied as when frugality was imposed by circumstance. Service to his fellow man, the advancement of Judaism remain the things closest to his heart.

Mr. Fischel has permitted publicity to be given to his work in behalf of the great Jewish institutions with which he is affiliated, his strivings in the interests of religious education for the Jewish youth, his efforts to upbuild the Jewish homeland in Palestine, in order to stimulate others. On the other hand, Mr. Fischel's private gifts, and these have been innumerable, have remained a secret between himself and those whom he has aided.

A pen picture of Mr. Fischel's physical characteristics and mode of living may not be inappropriate here. Although slight of build and of medium height, he enjoys that durable type of constitution which is sometimes defined as "wiry." He is, as his career indicates, possessed of a great reserve of nervous energy so that, despite the exactions of a life continually at the service of others, he is enabled to meet extraordinary demands upon his vitality and perform a vast amount of labor. His capacity for work is heightened by his ability to concentrate his entire attention upon the matter immediately before him until it has been disposed of, leaving his mind free to devote to the next problem. Mr. Fischel's sandy hair, closely trimmed beard and soft blue eyes indicate the determination of the man, no less than his kindliness.

His method of living is methodical and he is abstemious almost to the point of asceticism. He does not use liquor or tobacco in any form, except as wine is partaken of and only occasionally as part of the ritual of his faith. His regular habits, close observance of the dietary laws and generally simple living have enabled him to preserve his health and strength and to throw off illness when it has assailed him.

Arising daily at six-thirty o'clock it is Mr. Fischel's invariable practice to repair at once for morning worship to the Synagogue of the Congregation Kehillath Jeshurun. Following the services, Mr. Fischel, together with a few other devout souls, spends half an hour in religious group study of the Mishna, led by Rabbi M. S. Margolies, after which he goes home to breakfast. This procedure is never broken, no matter at what hour Mr. Fischel returns to his home the night before from meetings or other functions and even though he is unable at times to retire until the early hours of the morning.

Following breakfast, Mr. Fischel devotes his mornings until lunch time exclusively to his charitable and public undertakings, visiting institutions, calling upon those in distress, studying reports, planning new undertakings, in short, laboring as assiduously to relieve the necessities of others as many men slave over their desks to advance their own fortunes.

After luncheon Mr. Fischel goes to his office, usually arriving there about two o'clock and remaining until five or six. It is between these hours that Mr. Fischel sees most of those who daily come to him for assistance or advice in one form or another. These callers are legion and come from every walk in life. His office is never closed to any person, whether he be of the humblest in the social strata or among the mightiest in the financial world. Mr. Fischel's secretary has very positive orders that each visitor is to be received with courtesy and consideration and shown into his private office the very moment he is disengaged.

Although Mr. Fischel at once commands the respect that is due a man who has risen to a commanding place in the world by dint of his own ability and effort, there is nothing of austerity in his demeanor, no hint either in his manner or surroundings that he is anything but the warm-hearted, solicitous, unaffected gentleman which in truth, he undoubtedly is.

Mr. Fischel's modest tastes are further borne out by his dress. He wears no jewelry other than his watch and chain, though he will tell you he possesses thirteen matchless gems. These are his four daughters and nine grandchildren. For all his love of simplicity and modest personal requirements, Mr. Fischel does not believe in denying either his family or himself the really worthwhile things of life.

An afternoon spent in Mr. Fischel's office gives an illuminating insight into those characteristics which govern his life at all times. It is at once apparent that there is to be found system and method, without driving or waste, in short a harmonious, contented, efficient organization.

The furnishings of the office are dignified without being in any sense ostentatious, the quarters spacious and uncrowded. The clerks and stenographers proceed quietly and diligently with their work, each knowing what is expected of him and doing it, so that, although the volume of transactions both financial and philanthropic is very large, Mr. Fischel himself is seldom annoyed with details due to the fact that he has so efficiently organized his business that he has relieved himself of all but the major problems.

Practically all of Mr. Fischel's private fortune is invested in real estate. Mr. Fischel has never dealt in Wall Street nor has he ever owned speculative securities of any kind. Even to this day his surplus funds are invested only in United States government bonds, to which he turned during the war, purchasing Liberty bonds.

It is truthfully said that an accurate barometer of a man's disposition and character is to be found in what his employees and business associates think of him. That Mr. Fischel is a just, considerate, amiable employer, as well as partner, is best indicated by the fact that those to whom he has entrusted the chief responsibilities of his business have been continuously with him for many years as have most of his office assistants, who regard him not alone in the role of employer but that of friend.

In the matter of his correspondence Mr. Fischel is punctilious. It is the very first item to be attended to on his arrival at the office each day. Every letter, no matter from whom it comes or what its contents is answered personally and promptly by him in such a way as to make the recipient feel that Mr. Fischel has given to the matter under advisement his very best thought and judgment. If he is compelled to refuse a request, the declination is so considerately couched and the regret so evidently sincere as to disarm resentment.

Having finally disposed of his mail, Mr. Fischel is ready to receive the first of the many callers who invariably await him. It is inevitable that with Mr. Fischel's reputation for philanthropy and the general knowledge that he is by no means a poor man, a majority of those who seek him out should be in quest of financial assistance. Mr. Fischel seldom turns away any one whom he feels merits his aid and gives to each visitor that sympathetic attention which bespeaks genuine interest and solicitude in his welfare. For Mr. Fischel not alone has the broad understanding growing out of a lifetime of accumulated experience governing such problems as he is daily asked to solve but he has both the heart and the will to be of service.

Mention has been made of Mr. Fischel's private benefactions. Countless individuals, as well as whole families in this country, in Europe and in Palestine are partly or entirely maintained by stipends from his purse.

To this number must be added many others aided in like manner by Mrs. Fischel, to whom her husband has always opened his purse without limit. Mrs. Fischel even enjoys the privilege of drawing upon Mr. Fischel's bank account without consultation with him. At the Passover season, particularly, these private benefactions mount into a very large total.

Mr. Fischel's home and home life coincide entirely with what

people have been led to expect of him outside this intimate circle
as his devoted wife and fond children eloquently testify.   In his
youth a dutiful and loving son, Mr. Fischel has been an equally
loyal and affectionate husband and father.   His home has always
engaged his first interest next to that of his religion of which, of
course, the home is a most important part and he has given to
his wife and daughters every advantage and comfort consonant
with their welfare.

The content and happiness of his home is the best proof that
he has, during nearly forty years of married life, successfully
filled that most difficult of roles, that of a revered and loved husband and parent.   When his children were growing up, he was
never so busily engaged or had so important a conference on
hand that he did not have time first to consider them.   It was
his practice throughout their childhood to take each of his children to school every morning and in the evenings to assist them
with their lessons.

Even when they grew up and attended college and their studies
had advanced far beyond the point where his education ended,
he still continued to work with them, thus stimulating their interest and, at the same time broadening his own knowledge.   In
this manner Mr. Fischel came to be possessed of a vast store of
learning, acquired during his adult life, the opportunity to gain
that which was denied him in his youth.

Mr. Fischel's interest in his children has not ceased even with
their marriage and he holds himself at all times literally at their
beck and call, ready to help them with the problems which arise
in their lives and in connection with the upbringing of their families.   Due to his precept and example and constant instilling
of a love of religion in his children, while their minds were still
in a formative stage, Mr. Fischel has the satisfaction of knowing
that each is as true to the ideals of Judaism he set before them,
as is he himself, and that each is rearing her family with like
principles and aspirations.

Now that Mr. Fischel is permitted to abate somewhat the

strenuous labors of his earlier years, most of his evenings are spent at home with his wife, when they do not go together to visit one or the other of their children and grandchildren. The other evenings of the week are taken up with important board meetings of the institutions in which he is more than passively interested. Occasionally he takes in a movie. He also enjoys sitting by his hearthstone, a good book upon his knees and the radio supplying a fine concert or timely discussion of some current topic. Mr. Fischel has never played cards or other games, intended merely to pass the time, or indulged in any form of amusement not in some way connected with the advancement of his knowledge of the world or related to his physical well-being. For many years he had a team of horses. In recent years he has preferred an automobile for his airings.

When Mr. Fischel feels he requires a change of scene he goes to Atlantic City for a few days, there enjoying the sunshine of the boardwalk. Frequent short excursions to that resort have been his practice for a number of years and have constituted his principal outings. He still owns a country place in the Catskills to which he repairs at intervals in the Summer season. Here, however, his self-imposed duties in connection with the synagogue he established and in which he retains an active interest, renders his visits to the mountains not wholly a vacation. However, his greatest delight is when he can spend his vacation in the Holy Land. The anticipation and realization of doing good in the religious centre of his people and receiving afresh renewed vigor and inspiration, exalt and exult him.

Such, in brief, is a picture of Mr. Fischel as his family and host of personal friends know him.

CONCLUSION

FORTY YEARS OF STRUGGLE FOR A PRINCIPLE

THE title chosen by Mr. Fischel for his biography, namely "Forty years of struggle for a principle" epitomizes not only his entire purpose in life, but the sole motive which actuated him in supplying the data for this record of his most active and interesting career.

In conclusion, it is hoped and it is believed that this biography has demonstrated to the reader that the principle for which Mr. Fischel has so unremittingly striven is none other than the preservation of historic and traditional Judaism, as represented by Orthodox Jewish religious precepts and practices.

This is the religion which, throughout the centuries, has withstood the onslaught of inquisition and persecution, as well as the tests to which it has been subjected by philosophy and by science. It is the religion which was his grandparents' and his parents' and has, in turn, been practiced not alone by Mr. Fischel himself, but by his children and grandchildren as well.

Mr. Fischel has, during his life, encountered and triumphed over most severe trials and temptations which he was compelled to undergo in order that he might be able to observe the Sabbath and the Jewish Holidays in every detail and to scrupulously maintain the Jewish Dietary Laws.

This struggle was not confined to his own home, but was extended to the institutions for the care of the orphaned, the aged and the sick, as well as to the educational institutions to which he has devoted the major portion of his life.

Through his benefactions and his sincerity of purpose, Mr. Fischel has earned the respect and esteem not only of every faction of the Jews of America but of the Jews throughout the world, winning the regard and confidence of his gentile brothers as well.

It is Mr. Fischel's earnest prayer, at the conclusion of these forty years of struggle and effort, that the Almighty may grant him the opportunity of continuing his labors in behalf of religion, education and philanthropy, so that he may, at a later date, be able to record additional efforts in behalf of these same religious and humanitarian principles.

I fervently hope and pray that I may be privileged to edit the additional record of Mr. Fischel's noble and exemplary life.

INDEX

A

Abramowitz, Rabbi Duber, 298.
Abrams, Max, 239.
Adler, Dr. Cyrus, Committee of Five, 159.
Adler, Jacob P., 56.
Ahearn, John F., 32.
Allison, W. H., 235.
America, departure for, 9; arrival, 11.
American Hebrew—editorial on U. T. T. resignation, 113; on new Beth Israel Hospital, 279-80; on Yeshiva donations, 352-3; "Are Jews Losing Their Religion?" 365-9.
American Jewish Committee, formation, 62.
American Jewish Relief Committee, organized, appeal, 135sqq; executive committee, 137.
Amortization plan, 179-80.
Architectural knowledge, 5.
Associated Press, on mortgage problem, 175.
Astor Library building, to HIAS, 201sqq.
Auerbach, Rabbi Menahem, 303.

B

Balfour Declaration, 187.
Battle Creek, 337; 371.
Benderly, Dr. Samson, 93; 96; 106; 116.
Berlin, Rabbi Meyer, 153.
Bernheim, I. W., 122.
Bernstein, John L., HIAS, 203-5; 213; 231; letter of thanks, HIAS, 234-5.
Beth Israel Hospital, director, vice-president, 42; chairman, building committee, 45; cornerstone laid, 46.
Bijur, Justice Nathan, 78.
Bikur Holim Hospital, 291.
Billikopf, Jacob, relief letter, 154.
Blauner Brothers, 120.
Bloom, Congressman Sol, 382.
Blumenthal, George, 69.
Bone Bayit, 292.
Brandeis, Justice Louis D., 131; letter, Palestine Liberty Loan, 188.

Brass, Miss Jane (Mrs. Fischel), meeting with, 23.
Brass, Rubin, 24; 302.
Brass, Wolf, emissary to Palestine, 78.
Bureau of Education, of Kehillah, 93; letter on U. T. T. resignation, by Dr. Benderly, 115-6.
Business success, 31.

C

Cagan, Rabbi Israel Meyer (Chofetz Chaim), 307; 318.
Cantor, Jacob A., 58.
Catskills—colony at Hunter, 60.
Central Committee for the Relief of Jews Suffering through the War, 125; appeal, 126sqq; committee of 100, 129-30; men's and women's executive list, 151-3.
Central Jewish Institute, built, 184-5.
Chandler, Congressman, 212.
Charity, early days, 36.
Chicago, on tour, 168.
Children's synagogue, 94.
Citizenship, first application, 14.
Cobb, American consul, 301.
Cohen, Adolph, 70.
Cohen, Alfred M., 122.
Cohen, Harris, 43.
Cohen, Joseph H., letter on Palestine tour, 233.
Congregation Beth Hamedrash Hagodol; vice president of, 35.
Congregation Kehillath Jeshurun, 393.
Congregation Scharey Torah, 18.
Coolidge, President, letter on Yeshiva, 382.
Cooper Union, studies at, 21.
Copeland, Senator Royal S., 382.
Cornerstone (a publication), on Yeshiva building committee, 376-8.
Council of Y.M.H. and Kindred Associations, board of managers, 121.
Courtship and marriage, 25-7.
Cowen, Newman, employer, 30.

D

Davis, Secretary James P., 213.
Debrest, Harold, 113.

PRELIMINARY NOTES TO THE "CONTINUATION OF MY BIOGRAPHY"

Harry Fischel's full-length original autobiography, *Forty Years of Struggle for a Principle*, was published in 1928, having been edited by his son-in-law Rabbi Herbert S. Goldstein, and written in the third person. It is reproduced in full in the beginning of this volume. The Continuation, privately circulated in 1941 and basically limited to family members at that time, was written in the first person without any mention of the participation of Fischel's son-in-law or anyone else. It is likely that the Continuation was edited by Rabbi Goldstein, but lightly, with the intention of maintaining the language and the color of the colorful Mr. Fischel as much as possible. The Continuation was first circulated only in bound typewritten form. It has been edited further for this publication, but again very lightly, and again to continue to preserve the character and the writing style of the author. An effort was made to ascertain the correct spellings of names in particular, for the purposes of historical references and the Index. There had been no Index to the original Continuation. There is now an Index to the Continuation as currently published. This Index includes references to entries for all the other material, as well, that now supplements the original biography, as well as some material in the original book not included in the original Index.

It should be noted that *Forty Years of Struggle for a Principle* was published when Harry Fischel was a millionaire, even in pre-inflationary dollars, a year before the stock market crash. By contrast, most of the period covered by the Continuation was during the Great Depression that followed, and preceded the inflation that occurred since that time. The value of the dollar has increased by a factor of about 14 since 1919, when Harry Fischel signed the million-dollar check reproduced facing page 160, which would be worth about $14 million as this volume went to press, and by a factor of about 13 since the mid-1920s, which means that the

$160,000 that Harry Fischel contributed to Yeshiva University was the equivalent of about $2 million at the time of the publication of this edition, and the millions he owned in his prime would make him a multimillionaire quite a few times over in today's currency.

Additional minimal observations placing the Continuation in further context appear in the new Introduction to the current edition of the now supplemented biography beginning at page 14a.

AIR

Forty Years Sequel
CONTINUATION OF MY BIOGRAPHY
FORTY YEARS OF STRUGGLE FOR A PRINCIPLE
1928–1941
PREFACE

At the completion of the story of my life, known as *Forty Years of Struggle for a Principle*, I prayed to the Almighty to grant me the privilege of continuing the labors in behalf of religious education, religion and philanthropy, so that I may, at a later date, be able to record additional efforts in behalf of the same religious and humanitarian principles. Well, the Almighty answered my prayers and has given me the privilege of accomplishing several achievements which are beneficial, not only to our religious education, but to myself as well.

I was privileged to distribute large sums of money for religious education, such as Yeshivoth, *Talmud Torahs* in America, Palestine and all over Europe, as well as to many other philanthropic institutions.

I have given two large contributions, one to the Yeshiva, Rabbi Isaac Elchanan Theological Seminary and the Yeshiva College, adding up to the sum of $160,000, and the other to Beth Israel Hospital, in the sum of $75,000, as well as many smaller contributions to other institutions.

While this money was well invested and has given me great pleasure, I have done nothing to perpetuate the name of Harry Fischel, which would end with the present generation, because I have no sons to carry the name further. While the Almighty has blessed me with four daughters, four sons-in-law and ten grandchildren, all of whom are following in my footsteps, the fact remains that the name of Harry Fischel would be forgotten. This fact was always on my mind, and I was awaiting the time when the Almighty would help me solve that problem.

407

CHAPTER 1

INVESTMENT FOR AN ENDOWMENT FUND

The thought that the name Harry Fischel, which was familiar practically the world over in philanthropy, charity and religious education for more than two generations must disappear with the present generation has caused me many sleepless nights.

Many propositions traveled through my mind. Finally, in 1927 when I was in Palestine, I decided to perpetuate my name by erecting an institution for higher learning bearing the name of Harry Fischel. In order to assure the existence of such an institution, it first required the creation of an endowment fund to provide enough income to maintain such an institution as far as one can foresee.

For two years I waited for the opportunity to create such an endowment fund. Finally, I succeeded in purchasing a parcel of land in a first-class location in New York. This land was leased to a responsible tenant, a corporation, for eighty-five (85) years at an annual rental of $50,000.00 net. This corporation has invested over a million dollars in the erection of a twenty-six (26) story commercial building on this land.

It is impossible to describe the pleasure I enjoyed when I was assured with an annual income of $50,000 for an endowment fund. This made my plan half accomplished. But, with such a large income, I decided to elaborate on the plan of establishing such an institution. I had several plans in my mind. I consulted many scholars, such as Dr. Nathan Isaacs of Harvard University, the late Dr. Bernard Revel of the Yeshiva and Yeshiva College, also my own son-in-law, Rabbi Herbert S. Goldstein, and many others.

We finally decided to establish an institution in New York for research in Talmud to give post-graduate courses in Talmud, and to grant degrees of Master and Ph.D. on same.

I was advised that the first step to accomplish such a plan is to obtain a charter from the State of New York to grant such degrees.

CHAPTER 2

MEETING GOVERNOR FRANKLIN D. ROOSEVELT

I was privileged to have had the acquaintance of Franklin D. Roosevelt, then the Governor of the State of New York. I took advantage of this acquaintance and succeeded in having a one-hour conference with the Governor on September 15, 1929.

I laid my entire plan before the Governor, who was very much interested. He was so impressed that he gave me a letter of introduction to Commissioner Graves and letters to every member of the Board of Regents. He even called the Commissioner on the phone and asked him to do all in his power to help me obtain this charter. Before I left, the Governor suggested that should the Board of Regents find that such charter is impossible, in accordance with the present laws, then I should come to him next February and he would send a special message to the legislature to grant such a charter.

Having the financial problem assured and also the promised assurance from the Governor of the State for the granting of a charter, the next step was to build a building and provide the necessary material for such a school.

CHAPTER 3

REFERENCE TO *FORTY YEARS OF STRUGGLE* FOR A PRINCIPLE

I must refer to the first story of my life. This story ended with May 1, 1927, when I laid the cornerstone for the Yeshiva, Rabbi Isaac Elchanan Theological Seminary, and Yeshiva College, and left for Palestine.

As I was away from any thought of business, my entire mind was occupied with the thought of what to do in order to perpetuate the name of Harry Fischel. During the entire three months I spent in Jerusalem, I had many conferences with the late Chief Rabbi Abraham I. Kook on this subject. We then came to the conclusion that the best way of perpetuating my name is by establishing an institution which shall carry the name of Harry Fischel, and arrange an endowment fund to maintain such an institution [on three continents; see p. 411 and Ophir, in references, p. 485].

From the time I left Palestine, my only thought was how to carry out the idea of establishing such an institution.

The first step was to erect a building to house such a college. As it happened, some time ago I purchased a corner plot on Amsterdam Avenue and 185th Street, one block from the Yeshiva College. I made plans for a large building containing several lecture rooms, a large assembly hall and specially spacious library rooms required for such a college of research work.

CHAPTER 4

PURPOSE FOR WHICH THIS GROUND WAS BOUGHT

I believe it is of interest to note at this point the purpose for which this lot was purchased. When the new building of the Yeshiva, Rabbi Isaac Elchanan Theological Seminary, was opened, there were a large number of students, among them a number not suited either to be a rabbi, a teacher, or members of another other intellectual profession.

Then an idea came to me to establish a trade school in connection with the Yeshiva, so that those students desiring to learn a trade in connection with the Talmudical instruction could do so.

My plan included the erection of a six-story apartment house on the plot and to rent the apartments to the Yeshiva teachers at a low rental and use the income to maintain the trade school, to have the basement and first floor for the trade school, and five floors for apartments.

My plan was all completed, the money to erect the building without any mortgage was all provided for, but the Board of Directors of the Yeshiva felt that such a school would cheapen the Yeshiva, and refused my offer. Accordingly, my plan was dropped and the plot remained.

The next step was to provide the material required for such research work. To get the material here was impractical. I then came to the conclusion that such material could best be obtained in Palestine, Poland and Lithuania, where the talmudical colleges were then located, and where the talmudical students are spending all of their time at talmudical study, and are familiar with the Talmud in all its branches.

For this purpose I authorized the late Chief Rabbi of Palestine, Abraham I. Kook to select thirteen of the best talmudical scholars from all of Palestine, who would receive a good salary, and who were to give their entire time in the research of the Talmud. I transmitted the same order to the late Chief Rabbi of Poland, Chaim Ozer Grodzinski, and to the Chief Rabbi of Lithuania, Rabbi Avraham Shapiro. Each one was to select thirteen of the best scholars that could be found in their country.

My plan was that all of the three schools would be guided by a system established by the Chief Rabbi of Palestine, and would be followed by all the three schools.

The material obtained by these schools would be forwarded to the headquarters in New York regularly.

The plan was that when the building in New York was to be finished, this school would be opened free of any charge to students, and also to provide some scholarships to those who would be in need of maintenance.

All of the plans were ready and we were only waiting for the charter to be granted by the State Board of Education. However, this plan was not approved by the Almighty, for reasons best known to Him, and the panic of October 29, 1929 destroyed my elaborate plans. In one year the entire fortune invested in the property for the endowment fund had been lost.

My disappointment was indescribable when my life's ambition to establish an institution bearing my name entirely collapsed. However, I was thankful to the Almighty for losing this money before this gigantic plan was fully carried out, which saved me from the embarrassment of being compelled to stop the work after it was organized, and the large expense incurred.

However, my ambition to establish a school for research in Talmud was not shattered. [Fischel was indeed destined to establish graduate-level schools in Jewish Studies in Jerusalem (p. 410 sqq.) as well as in New York (pp. 408, 478–483)]. I decided to establish such a school in the city of Jerusalem, where only the best Talmudical scholars were found and the environment was more favorable.

At this time I decided to first provide a building to house this school. It seems that this plan had the approval of the Almighty because it met with great success right from the start.

CHAPTER 5

PURCHASE OF BUILDING IN JERUSALEM

We succeeded in purchasing a building in the city of Jerusalem suitable for a school, and after making extensive alterations we were ready to start to carry out my long-desired ambition to organize the school for research in Talmud.

During the time of the alteration, the late Chief Rabbi Abraham I. Kook gave out an order that only the outstanding scholars should apply, by submitting themselves to an extensive written and oral examination. This news spread throughout

Palestine like wildfire, with the result that 102 applicants applied for the written examination, and only 52 of them came back for the oral examination, which was before the Chief Rabbi and two other outstanding Rabbis. As a result, only 18 of the applicants passed the oral examination.

As stated before, my order was to select only 13 scholars, but the committee left the other five as alternates.

It is of interest that the purchasing of the house and the entire plan was accomplished by a committee in my absence, in accordance with orders given by me by mail and cables.

There was one thing on my mind, how to get the proper man to manage the institute in my absence, to look after the building and equipment, and also to act as Registrar when the Institution opened. This job required a man who was a great scholar and also to have had some practical experience to understand the physical part of a building, in addition to his scholarship.

As it happened, Rabbi Dove Kook, a brother of the Chief Rabbi, was in New York at that time. I sent for him and after a short conference I found in him all the qualifications required for this position. I engaged him and sent him to Palestine, and he was there before the school was opened. He took complete charge and thanks to the Almighty the right man was sent to me. He filled the position with great credit and with full respect from everybody. He occupied an apartment in the same building and managed the Institution to my entire satisfaction.

CHAPTER 6

OPENING OF THE HARRY FISCHEL INSTITUTE

It is impossible for me to describe my pleasure when on November 1, 1931 I received a cable that the building had opened, with 18 outstanding scholars, under the name of "Harry Fischel Institute for Research in Talmud"; also with many other activities, as the building was much larger than required for the 18 scholars.

There is a very interesting story attached to this building. In the year 1913 a wealthy Jew, Said Baruchow from Bucharia, part of Russia, came to Palestine. He decided to settle in Palestine and receive the Messiah, when the time will come for him to arrive. For this purpose, he bought a very large plot occupying a square block, with four streets around same. In a very high part of Jerusalem, he constructed an unusually fine building, suitable for this great prophet, the Messiah. He arranged unusually large rooms and very high ceilings. Any material he could not obtain in Palestine he had imported from the different parts of the world. However, his ambition was not fulfilled. Before the building was completed the great European war started. The Bolsheviks took away all his wealth and in order to complete the building, this man was compelled to borrow money from a bank in Jerusalem.

After 17 years of adding interest, which was not paid, the bank foreclosed the mortgage and this property was purchased for the Harry Fischel Institute for Research in Talmud, by the attorney, Dr. Eliash, at my request. So much for the story of the building.

CHAPTER 7

OBJECT OF THE HARRY FISCHEL INSTITUTE

I will now return to the Institute itself. The main object was to extract from the Talmud and other such publications, the science contained therein and to publish same for the benefit of the world.

A Board of Education was organized under the leadership of the late Chief Rabbi Kook, together with other Rabbis. Rabbi Kook was known the world over as a great scholar. He knew the Talmud, and many other great works, almost by heart. He, therefore, assigned the 13 scholars and the 5 alternates to the part in the

Talmud to which each one was fitted best.

Fortunately, I succeeded to have Rabbi Kook accept the position as the Dean of the Harry Fischel Institute for Research in Talmud. As such he delivered a lecture to the scholars every week. These lectures were attended by many outside scholars as well.

This building was much larger than required for the school of research; therefore, in planning the building, I fitted up a synagogue accommodating about 150 worshippers. In a short time the synagogue was full, not only on Saturdays but mornings and evenings as well.

CHAPTER 8

ESTABLISHING OF THE LIBRARY

I was informed that the Institute would need a large library. I, therefore, took advantage of the presence of Rabbi Dove Kook before he left for Palestine, in collecting all sorts of rare books which could be gotten in New York, and sent them to Palestine. Many books were ordered from Warsaw and Vienna, and the most were purchased in Jerusalem. Thus we fitted up one of the best libraries.

This library became very popular, and it was used to advantage by many students of the different *Yeshivoth*, also many *bal-habatim*, who enjoyed the building with its spacious accommodations, heated with steam in the winter (the only Yeshiva with central heating in Jerusalem).

The Synagogue became crowded by worshippers and especially by those who have taken advantage of the large supply of rare books in the library. A librarian was engaged to give out the books and to place them back in their proper places.

Today the entire building is being used practically twenty hours daily. It also became the place of study and worship by the many scholarly refugees who have settled in the neighborhood.

As stated before, the purchase of the property, the planning of the building and the entire organization were done by me in New York, because the financial depression in 1929 kept me home to look after our real estate and to save all we could from the destruction by the depression. However, I was eagerly hoping that the time would come soon when I would be able to leave my property in good hands and go to Palestine to enjoy the fruit of my labor in person.

Before realizing this hope there was a very important matter to be accomplished, namely: to bring the news of the whole project to my family, who did not know anything of the entire proposition. The only advisor I had was my personal friend, the late Rabbi M. S. Margolies.

CHAPTER 9

REPORT TO THE FAMILY

On one Saturday afternoon I called the family together and read this report to them:

"Report delivered by Mr. Harry Fischel to his family on July 18, 1931:

"The clock is moving steadily . The time is flying. Many years have passed and my desire, the dream of my life, and the hope of perpetuating the name of Harry Fischel has not as yet been realized. I have solved many difficult problems which required hard work and a great deal of thought and energy; nevertheless, my own problem and desire of creating an institution to bear the name of Harry Fischel has not as yet been solved.

"This thought has never escaped my mind, neither day nor night. I have been lying awake nights thinking, and also praying to the Almighty to give me vision and understanding as to how my wishes could be fulfilled and my dream of years realized; namely, to create an institution which shall serve the purpose of spreading Torah, for which I have spent the best part of my life; an institution which shall be recognized as a necessity in Jewish life.

"Well, dear family, I have fully decided not to postpone any longer, and start in a small way. If the real estate market would have lasted a couple of years longer, then my dream would have been realized by this time. However, since the Almighty saw fit to make this drastic change in the financial world, it is impossible to consider large plans at the present time, until the time will come when real estate returns to the position it occupied up to two years ago. One of the most prominent financiers has made the statement, 'Never put off for tomorrow, that which you can do today, as you do not know what tomorrow will bring.' The moral of this saying is especially worthy of my earnest thought and attention, considering my age and the desire for which I am praying daily; namely, that the Almighty shall grant me the privilege of carrying out my wishes during my lifetime and reap the benefit of my hard labor, and to enjoy this pleasure together with my entire family.

"On many occasions I have expressed to you my great desire to establish in America a college for research in Talmud, a college of this kind would require the right to grant the degree of Ph.D. Naturally, a state charter would be necessary for such purpose. I have succeeded in having a conference with his Excellency, Governor Franklin D. Roosevelt. I have explained to him that our Talmud contains a great deal of science in every field of knowledge, such as medicine, law, astronomy, psychology, and various other sciences; yet our Jewish people have never taken advantage of these sciences, with the result that up to this date the world has been deprived of the great benefit which the Talmud could bestow to the educational world. I explained to the Governor that during all our Jewish history and up to the present date, the Talmud has always been used by our people for religious purposes only, and the time has come, and I am thankful to the Almighty for having the opportunity to show the world of what benefit the Talmud could be, not alone to the Jewish people, but also to the world at large. The Governor was very much interested in this subject, and gave me a great deal of his time in discussing the proposition. He went so far as to address letters to every one of the Trustees of the Board of Regents of the State of New York, and has furnished me with copies of these letters. He has given me letters of introduction to each one of the Trustees, should I decide to call on them. In fact, he has instructed Dr. Horner, the Secretary of the State Board of Regents to call on me, which he did on two occasions, spending several hours in order to help me prepare the application for a charter. The Governor also stated that should I be unable, for any legal reasons, to obtain this charter, he would assist me by having a special bill passed by the Legislature for the purpose of granting me a charter for the college I had in mind; namely, a College for Research in Talmud.

"My plans were all complete. We have organized the Harry Fischel Foundation, and we have obtained a charter from the State. However, men make plans and the Almighty has the power to upset them; which is His wisdom. He saw fit to do so in my case. The investment that I made for this special purpose, which had shown a safe income of over $50,000 annually, has temporarily been discontinued, and from the present outlook, it will take many years until I will be able to depend upon the income from this investment. Therefore, since no one can tell what tomorrow will bring, and in order to prevent Satan from gaining his point; namely, to prevent me from carrying out my dream of years, I have decided at least to make a small beginning.

"It has always been my desire to create a permanent fund for the purpose of establishing and maintaining an institution of higher Talmudical learning in New York, with a branch in Palestine. In fact, provision for such project has been made in my will. Naturally, it was always my intention that the main expense should be allowed for the institution in New York, and a small portion should be set aside for the branch in Palestine. Since this large plan is impossible to be carried out at present, I have decided to begin from the other end; namely, to start in Palestine first.

"I will rather center all my efforts, and bestow my contributions for the benefit of the Torah, in one school of learning, under the name of the Harry Fischel Institute for Research in Talmud, with the hope of enlarging this school as time will progress and financial conditions will permit.

"For this purpose, I have succeeded in purchasing a house, with which I am very well acquainted, in a very nice section of Jerusalem, for a little over $10,000, which is probably less than 25% of the actual cost of the building only; besides, it has a large plot of ground covering an entire square block surrounded by four streets. This house is in first-class condition, and is just as if it were made-to-order for this purpose, since it has been occupied by an institution of learning for many years.

"I have authorized Chief Rabbi Abraham I. Kook, with the assistance of my brother-in-law, Rabbi Rubin Braz, to select from the entire land of Palestine, thirteen of the best known Talmudical scholars, who will spend all their time and effort in the Research of Talmud. They will be supported by the Harry Fischel Foundation with a monthly allowance of $25.00 each. The entire budget including the cost of maintaining the house will amount to about $10,000 annually. I am fully convinced that this is a step in the right direction, for which I am thankful to the Almighty.

"The first part of my life's desire to create an institution for the purpose of perpetuating my name will shortly be carried out. Although at present it will be on a very small scale, it is my intention to transfer most of my larger charitable contributions to this institution, with the hope that when the Almighty will see fit to improve the real estate conditions, it will enable me to enlarge the expenditures, so that this Institution will grow to a position where it will occupy a prominent place in the field of higher Jewish learning, which will be a pride to our entire family.

"I have given the best part of my life for the benefit of religious education. I have contributed large sums of money for this purpose, in America, Europe and Palestine. Nevertheless, I feel that all my activities up to the present date cannot be compared with the great benefit which we expect this institution to bring, especially through the purchase of this building, which has accommodations and space for a great deal more than required for the thirteen scholars at present.

"This institution will be known as the Harry Fischel Institute for Research in Talmud under the leadership of Chief Rabbi Abraham I. Kook, who is very enthusiastic about the Institute for Research in Talmud. He has promised to give his full and undivided attention to the organizing and supervision of this school for higher Talmudical learning. He will also deliver lectures on higher Talmudical learning on which his authority is recognized the world over. This will also draw to the Harry Fischel Institute a large number of Talmudical scholars, who will not require financial assistance.

"Our building will house the following activities:

1. A place of learning for these thirteen men who will be supported by the Harry Fischel Foundation.
2. A Synagogue with a capacity of nearly 150 seats, which will be used daily.
3. A lecture room for Talmudical scholars outside of those supported by the Harry Fischel Foundation. Many students from different Yeshivas, as well as many laymen, will come to listen to the lectures delivered by Rabbi Kook, as well as the daily lectures which will be given by the thirteen great Talmudical

scholars supported by the Harry Fischel Foundation.

"In addition thereto, there will be room for many of the Jewish activities, thereby making the Harry Fischel Institute Building the center of Jewish learning and communal activities, which will add no expense to the present budget. All we will give them is the use of the building.

"At this time, when my nerves are shattered daily from the great financial strain, the thought that the Almighty has helped me realize part of my life's ambition of creating the Harry Fischel Institute for Research in Talmud, is a great stimulant to me, and helps me carry through and solve the daily problems. I am fully convinced that if not for this great pleasure I would be unable to survive this great strain.

"My reason for starting with thirteen at the present time is that the symbol of Jewish life is connected mostly with thirteen.

"I am looking forward to the time when the Almighty will see fit to improve financial conditions so that my original plan may be fulfilled, which will produce men of the highest Talmudical knowledge with scientific accomplishments, and will radiate the 'light of the Torah' throughout the world, kindled by the Harry Fischel Foundation.

"I am fully convinced that I was sent down to this world to perform a certain duty; that is, to help spread the Torah among the Jewish people. There are two facts in my life's history which prove that my contention is right.

"First: I was born on the 17th day of Tamuz, the day when the Tablets of the Law were destroyed. I therefore, feel that it is my duty to try to restore the Torah among our Jewish people.

"Second: When a name was to be selected for me, my dear parents, Blessed be their Memory! must have had a vision from High, which made them name me Israel Aaron. According to our scriptures, we are told that it was the mission of Israel to keep the 'Light of the Torah' burning in the hearts of our people, and spread the knowledge of the Torah throughout our future generations. We are also told in the Bible that at the time of the dedication of the Tabernacle, it was Aaron who was ordered by the Almighty to kindle the light of the Menorah, which represents the 'Light of the Torah'. Therefore, in order to carry out the mandate given to me under that name, and in order to keep the 'Light of the Torah' from being extinguished from the present and future generations, I have decided to establish the Harry Fischel Institute for Research in Talmud in Palestine, in order to comply with the saying in the Scriptures, that 'From Zion shall come forth the Torah, and the words of G-d from Jerusalem'.

"There is also a selfish reason for my desire to create a college of this kind, and that is, in order to perpetuate the name of Harry Fischel in the same field of activities in which I have spent the best part of my life. While the Almighty has blessed me with four daughters, four sons-in-law, and wonderful grandchildren, all of whom are following in my footsteps by the strict observance of the 'Shulchan Aruch'; nevertheless, the fact is that I have no son who can carry my name to the next generation. Naturally, the name of Harry Fischel must cease with the present generation. Therefore, in order to perpetuate this name, which has always supported and fought for the Torah, I have decided to establish an institution for the study of the Torah, which shall carry the name of the Harry Fischel Institute for Research in Talmud.

"I pray to the Almighty that He shall grant us long life and happiness, so that all of us will be able to see with our own eyes, and together we will reap the benefit from the Harry Fischel Institute for Research in Talmud.

"Well, the Almighty has answered my prayers. With the house purchased and the thirteen best scholars of Palestine selected, my dream is practically fulfilled. I have received an answer from Chief Rabbi Abraham I. Kook as well as from Rabbi Rubin Braz, both of whom were very enthusiastic about the plan for Research in Talmud.

"Rabbi Kook, in his letter, stated that he is very happy to be in a position to carry out the dream of his life. It was always Rabbi Kook's desire to be able to find someone who would establish an institution for Research in Talmud. He has, therefore, agreed to organize and supervise this work, giving his name and all of the time necessary, without any remuneration.

"The next question was to find the proper man to act as supervisor of the Institution as well as of the building. It was suggested that Rabbi Dove Kook, a brother of Chief Rabbi Abraham I. Kook, who is now in New York, is the most suitable man for the position of Supervisor of this Institution. Rabbi Dove Kook, being in New York, I succeeded in engaging him as Supervisor. He is a man with a great reputation as a Talmudical scholar in Palestine and in America. He is also known to have business ability, and a straight mind. He is loved and admired by everyone who comes in contact with him, for his great knowledge and fine gentlemanly appearance.

"I was fortunate in having Rabbi Dove Kook accept the position as I feel that he is the proper man in the proper place. Having been in America twice on behalf of the Universal Yeshiva, he has met many people, and I believe that he has acquired enough business ability to enable him to manage the Harry Fischel Institute for Research in Talmud and also all the other activities in said building with great care and ability. He is leaving for Palestine this day. We prepared a complete set of rules and regulations for the guidance of the Harry Fischel Institute for Research in Talmud and all other activities.

"In addition thereto he is thoroughly familiar with all my views on this subject, and I am positive that he will guide the Institution so that it will be a credit to the Harry Fischel Foundation."

This report was a great surprise to everyone. They admitted that it is a great accomplishment and each one gave his approval, except they felt that I should have consulted them before I started this enterprise. My answer was that it took me many years to decide on this plan and even if they would have had objections, I would have carried out the plan in any event; and that would have been going against the will of my family, which I wanted to prevent.

When this was accomplished, I began planning the second and most important matter, namely: to provide sufficient funds to assure the perpetuation of this school with a budget between $10,000 and $15,000 annually, which would be largely increased by publishing the work prepared by our scholars.

I then came to the following conclusion, that my real estate holdings have large equities and still produced enough income for myself and for those of my family depending on me. I have before given to my children large sums of money. I felt that I am entitled to do something for myself to perpetuate the name of HARRY FISCHEL.

CHAPTER 10

ORGANIZING THE HARRY FISCHEL FOUNDATION

I then organized the Harry Fischel Foundation [later renamed the Harry and Jane Fischel Foundation]. I have assigned to this foundation practically all the liquid assets I possessed at that time, and by making careful investments the budget required for the Harry Fischel Institute could be easily provided for.

This foundation was organized on January 4th, 1932, with the full consent of the entire family. Everyone was made a trustee and each one signed the application for the charter.

With the creation of the Harry Fischel Institute for Research in Talmud in Jerusalem already functioning, and the Harry Fischel Foundation established to provide for the maintenance, I was the happiest man, seeing the dream of my life already materialized.

My mind was set on making provisions to go to Palestine and see with my own eyes, and reap the benefits of my accomplishments. However, conditions in the real estate became worse, and my time was required to look after same. I was compelled to delay going to Palestine until June 6th, 1933, when my late wife and I left for Palestine. [For more on the Foundation, see p. 16a and the web site at fischelfoundation.org.]

CHAPTER 11

MY ARRIVAL IN PALESTINE: FIFTH TIME

We arrived in Jerusalem on June 22, 1933. Words fail me to express my pleasure when we reached the house in Jerusalem and were welcomed by Rabbi Kook, accompanied by the 18 scholars , who were all lined up in the front of the building. The door was opened by Rabbi Kook, who led us into the Synagogue, and we were followed by all the scholars. There a prayer was offered for our safe arrival.

We then examined all the rooms and noted all the activities carried on, in the building. While I had pictured all of this in my mind, my surprise was with great pleasure, because I found everything better than I had expected, and for several days I enjoyed watching and getting acquainted with all the scholars, whom I considered as my own children, and have succeeded in getting them to feel the same way.

Then arrangements were made to celebrate my 68th birthday, which was on July 11th. This celebration took place on the outside piazza which was attended by 72 Rabbis and about 200 celebrities from different institutions. This celebration started at 2:00 P.M. and lasted until 11:00 P.M. Every one of the Rabbis made a speech, and in commemoration of this birthday, I accepted the five alternates as regular members of the scholars with the same salary as the others, and also gave an order to engage two more on the same basis, making altogether 20 regular scholars.

I had spent, at that time, seven weeks in the Institution which I consider the best time in my life.

CHAPTER 12

STARTED SUIT FOR POSSESSION OF BAYARA

In addition to the pleasure of the Institution (described above), I have gained a legal and moral victory in the Palestinian court, and came back with $30,000 in cash. The case was as follows:

In 1910 I brought to Palestine a brother of my late wife with a family of ten children. I then bought an orange grove partly producing fruit and partly vacant land. I supported the entire family for about ten years. During this time, the sons grew up. I sent them money during all this time for the purpose of planting the rest of the land. During all these years they enjoyed the benefit of the old grove as well as the new grove, which amounted to large sums some years. They never repaid one dollar to me, but they used the income to purchase other groves in their own names.

When I was in Palestine in 1927 there was a law declared in Palestine to allow owners of groves to register their holdings in the land registry, and receive a deed from the land courts, which was never entered before, as all land was purchased under a contract in Hebrew and handed over from one purchaser to the other. My contract was drawn up in the same way. Naturally, while being in Jerusalem at that time, I made an application to the court for a government deed to my name. It required publishing this application. To my great surprise, I found that the sons of my brother-in-law filed an injunction claiming that the property belonged to them by possession, in accordance with the old Turkish law. Naturally, the deed was stopped and I was compelled to bring suit.

I was compelled to prove that I was always in possession, because I have given the money to work the land. As I could not remain there to wait for the case to reach trial, I was compelled to leave it in the hands of an attorney and to try the case on taking evidence in New York, by the English consul. It took about six years for the case to reach trial and about two weeks before I came, in June 1933. Naturally, it was put off, and the shortest time for which my attorney could get an adjournment was for six months. Then, upon my arrival, my attorney made every effort to try to place the case on the calendar while I was in Palestine, but he did not succeed.

I then called on the American consul, explained my difficulties, and he gave me a letter of introduction to the English Judge, Sir Landay. I was very well received by him. The Judge explained that it was impossible to give preference in the court, but he offered to try the case on his own time after three o'clock, when the court adjourned. Naturally, I was very pleased, and in order to make sure I engaged a high-class attorney to try the case, because I found the other side had engaged the best-known attorney.

The case took six afternoons. The tables were full with law books, both sides quoting the law and the Judge taking every word down by hand, which is the custom in this court. I produced over $11,000. in checks which was claimed as presents to the family. I finally produced a check for $364.50 which I gave them to pay taxes for the land. This was also claimed to be given as a wedding present to one of the sons. I noticed that my attorney and the Judge were ready to pass this check also on the same basis. This was more than I could stand for. Then I requested the court to give me the privilege to question the attorney for the other side. The Judge granted me the privilege. Then I stated, "Mr. Horowitch, you are supposed to be a man of great reputation with worldly knowledge. I will ask you a question. Did you ever witness a case when the amount of $364.50 is given as a wedding present? You are trying to make the court believe that all the $11,000 checks were all presents, but you can't fool the court all the time." Then the Judge answered that in his experience he never saw a check for such an amount given as a wedding present. This was the climax of the case.

Then the Judge addressed himself and stated that he believed every word of my testimony and decided the case in my favor. He also rebuked the attorney for the other side, for all the falsehoods he was trying to make the court believe. Thereupon, the two sons of my brother-in-law offered me the sum of six thousand (6,000) pounds. Although I was offered much more from another party, however, I wanted to have the land remain in my late wife's family. So I accepted their offer of six thousand (6,000) pounds, and left for America with an order for thirty thousand ($30,000) dollars on the National City Bank, which I believe is the first large sum ever obtained by an American from Palestine.

As soon as we came back to America my mind was set on going back to Palestine at the first opportune time. However, conditions in real estate were getting worse, and it was impractical for me to leave my real estate holdings in strange hands. In one way I have benefited by the low real estate market because I bought a whole block of houses on the Grand Concourse, at a very low price as an investment for the Harry Fischel Foundation. This purchase was of great importance to me because the income from this property has shown to be of a substantial amount and the budget for the Harry Fischel Institute in Jerusalem was almost covered from the income of this property alone. The purchase of this property was also a great inducement to me in making plans to go to Palestine in the near future. However, the Almighty hastened my plans, as described in the next chapter.

CHAPTER 13

THE DEATH OF MY LATE WIFE

On January 3, 1935, about eighteen months after we came from Palestine, my late wife, to whom I was married over forty-seven years, passed away. I was left alone in the home. While all the children and grandchildren did their best to keep me company in order to make me forget my lonesomeness, being alone most of the time was more than I could stand.

I then sent for all the children, each one separately, and asked them to advise me what to do. Naturally each one, from the oldest to the youngest, suggested that I should give up the home and go to them. My answer was that each one of you have, thanks to the Almighty, a husband and children who need their time and attention. It is, therefore, impossible to divide their attention between their family and their father. They can't do both, and I have no right to interfere in their family life. It was too soon for me to make other plans because I had a very good housekeeper, an intelligent old woman, given to me by my daughter, Mrs. Goldstein. This woman was in her employ for several years, and was very reliable.

However, as time went on my lonesomeness increased, until one evening my granddaughter, Ann Esther Rafsky, the older daughter of Dr. & Mrs. Rafsky, only thirteen years old at that time, made the following statement: "Grandpa, I have been thinking that you must be very lonesome. It is true that we all come to see you for a short time, but you are alone twenty-four hours a day. I think you need a companion." The words of my little granddaughter started me thinking and after a great deal of consideration, I came to the conclusion to go to Palestine and maybe the Almighty will help me to get the right companion to spend the rest of my life.

I called the children together and informed them of my plan. I also told them that under any event I will not remarry before the year is over.

CHAPTER 14

PERPETUATING THE NAME OF MY LATE WIFE

I also told the children of my decision to perpetuate the name of their mother in the following way:

I exposed to them a complete plan which I had prepared for the purpose:

1. I gave them a check for $10,000 with which to establish the Jane Fischel Memorial Fund.

2. I purchased a Maternity Ward in the Hadassah Hospital in Jerusalem to be known as the Jane Fischel Maternity Ward.

3. I purchased a Maternity Ward in the Beth Israel Hospital also to be known as the Jane Fischel Maternity Ward.

4. I gave a sum of money to several colleges with an agreement that the income from such fund shall be used for the purpose of presenting prizes every year to a boy or girl who is to prepare an essay on Jewish Literature, and to be known as the Jane Fischel Memorial Prize.

5. The Harry Fischel Foundation passed a resolution to give to the Jane Fischel Memorial Fund every year on the "Yarzeit" of Jane Fischel, $500.00. This sum to be used for the purpose of paying annual dues to all societies, and also to give annual prizes in the educational institution to which Jane Fischel belonged before she died.

The news was greatly appreciated by all the children. They stated clearly that they had never expected such generosity on my part.

CHAPTER 15

DEDICATION OF LABORATORY IN
BETH ISRAEL HOSPITAL

I engaged passage on the steamer *Conte di Savoia* on May 11, 1935. This news spread among the institution, with the result that the Board of Directors of the Beth Israel Hospital arranged a reception for me on April 28th, and on this occasion they dedicated the chemical laboratory in my name.

In the presence of nearly 250 guests representing several of the institutions with whom I am connected, they also unveiled a bronze tablet, reading as follows: "This chemical laboratory was established and equipped in the old building at Jefferson and Cherry Streets in 1912 by Mr. Harry Fischel. It is dedicated in this new building in honor of Mr. Fischel's 70th Birthday, July 1935. Mr. Fischel is connected with the hospital as a director and officer since 1889."

I was very happy to be going to Palestine that year because it was always my desire to celebrate my 70th birthday in Jerusalem in my own institution.

Before leaving for Palestine I decided to share my fortune with my children, in case I decided to remain in Palestine for the rest of my life.

CHAPTER 16

DIVIDING THE STOCK AMONG THE CHILDREN

I have, therefore, distributed 40% of all the stock I held in all the real estate corporations, to my four daughters, equally divided.

While on the steamer away from everybody, my mind was set on the Harry Fischel Institute for Research in Talmud, and I forgot all about my personal future.

One day an idea came to my mind to pray to the Almighty that I should find my companion in Palestine. I reminded myself of the story in the Bible when Eliezer went to look for a wife for Isaac. He had made up his mind that if he found a woman who would answer certain questions which he had prepared, that she would be the one who was destined by the Almighty to be a wife for Isaac.

I therefore, also decided on similar lines. If a woman should come to my Institute, who could answer the qualifications which I feel would be required for a woman who is to be my companion, then I would try to arrange to marry her when the year is over.

CHAPTER 17

ARRIVING IN PALESTINE: SIXTH TIME

With this thought in mind I arrived in Palestine on May 23, 1935.

When I reached the Harry Fischel Institution building I found all the scholars lined up in front of the house, and with a greater welcome than in 1933, except that this time I was all alone. My late wife was no longer with me.

I entered my apartment alone, which was quite different than when I came to the same place two years earlier. I missed my late wife in every move I made. It took me some time acclimating myself to this condition.

It was only when I entered the study rooms listening to the voices of the *Talmidei Chachomim*, chanting and discussing the Torah, I was so overjoyed that I forgot about the whole world. I thanked the Almighty for the great privilege he has given to create this holy Institution, and for the privilege to be in Palestine again.

However, my entire pleasure was marred by the fact that the leader of my Institution was missing. The great scholar who was guiding the work was not there. Rabbi Abraham I. Kook, the Rosh Hayesheva was sick for some time, and the Institution was greatly disorganized. It took me several weeks to reorganize the work. I then came to the conclusion that we must find a man to continue the work left off by the great scholar Rabbi Kook. This was not so easy for two reasons; first, because we did not want to antagonize the sick sage by engaging someone without his knowledge and to consult him was not permitted by his doctors. Second, it was rather impossible to find the scholar who could replace this great *Talmid Chachom*. Many conferences were held by the family of Rabbi Kook and other rabbis, until we found the man who possessed all the necessary qualifications.

CHAPTER 18

THE ENGAGEMENT OF RABBI LIEBERMAN

This was Rabbi Saul Lieberman, and after several conferences with him, I succeeded to engage him as the Dean of the Harry Fischel Institute for Research in Talmud.

I well remember the first lecture he delivered. It made a great impression on all the scholars, and he was welcomed by everyone.

Rabbi Lieberman took full charge of the Institution and suggested to me that it is advisable to change the entire method of study and put it on a more scientific basis, in order to do real research work and publish the results, giving the benefit of the findings to the scholarly world. This was proven, for in less than two years the Harry Fischel Institute published a scholarly work of 600 pages. This book has been recognized the world over as a great useful work, and it was distributed to libraries, colleges and many individuals, free of charge.

While I was busy in the selection of the Dean and in reorganizing the work of the school, a committee was organized to arrange a celebration of my 70th birthday.

CHAPTER 19

CELEBRATION OF MY 70TH BIRTHDAY

On July 17th, 1935, this celebration was attended by over 300 people, most of the celebrities among professionals and laymen, were present. Speeches were made by Rabbis, leaders of the Institute and professors of the Hebrew University. Everyone praised the Harry Fischel Institute. I felt at that time that all the hardships I went through my whole life were worth the pleasure I derived at this time.

A book entitled the "Jubilee of 70" was published on this occasion by the scholars of the Institute, and was presented to each guest as a souvenir of this memorable occasion.

I almost decided to remain in Palestine and spend the rest of my life in watching the progress of my Institute. However, I reminded myself that the money required to maintain the Institute must come from New York, and on account of the depression in the real estate values, I would jeopardize the income of the real estate if I remained in Palestine. I therefore, decided to go back to America to look after the investments of the Harry Fischel Foundation and wait until the time would come when I could settle in Palestine, when the income required to maintain the Harry Fischel Institute for Research in Talmud would be safely provided for.

I will now return to my dream before arriving in Palestine, namely to find the proper companion who would fit into my life, to help me carry on the work in Palestine and in America. Thanks to the Almighty my dream came true.

CHAPTER 20

MEETING MY WIFE MIRIAM

On Sunday, June 23rd, 1935, while I was sitting in my study, I was informed that a Rabbi from England, together with his daughter, wished to see me in the reception room. I immediately came out and saw standing before me a man of a type like the prophets of old, and addressed himself to me with the following words: "Mr. Fischel, I am Rabbi Aaron Hyman. I heard all about your work in education and philanthropy. I heard also that you are looking for a companion. I brought you my daughter Miriam, the only woman who is suitable to help you in your life's work. Take her in your study, talk to her, and if you find that she will make you the right companion, then I will give you ten years of my life."

I then said to him: "Rabbi if she is the one sent to me by the Almighty, I want you to live a long life and to enjoy the pleasures from this union."

I took her into my study and conferred with her for one hour, and before she left I came to the conclusion that her father was right. She possessed all the qualities required to be my companion, to help me to continue my work. And in order to get better acquainted, I suggested to her that she might help me in my work at the Institute.

After I paid a visit at her home in Tel Aviv, she came to my study every day at 3:00 o'clock, and spent the rest of the day with me. I took her home to her brother in Jerusalem each evening. This lasted for three weeks. Each day I was more convinced that she was the proper woman to make my life happy, because she showed keen interest in my work.

When the day of the celebration of my 70th birthday came, I requested her to supervise the affair, which was done with great skill, never before witnessed in Jerusalem. It is a custom in Palestine that men and women are in separate rooms. In this case the men were seated on the large veranda. The women were all in the rooms adjoining with a clear view through the large window.

As soon as the last speech was finished, I left the men and entered the ladies room, and in the presence of every man and woman, I came over to my intended bride and kissed her in the presence of the guests. So our engagement was announced.

CHAPTER 21

ACCEPTED MIRIAM ON MY 70TH BIRTHDAY

I have accepted her as my future bride. We continued our friendship until July the 26th, when I left Palestine. Before I left we made arrangements that I would send for her at the end of January 1936.

I will never forget the scene when I called on the late Rabbi Kook at the hospital to bid him good-bye. While he was then already in a serious condition, he stated to me that he heard the news that I expected to marry Miriam Hyman, the daughter of Rabbi Hyman, a personal friend of his. He expressed his desire to see her and give us his blessing. The doctor at first refused to permit such an excitement, but this was his desire and I brought my bride to him. He had met her in her father's home in London. He took my hand and asked me to hold her hand and gave us the priestly blessing. This was the last time I was privileged to see this great sage of Israel, who was responsible for the organization of the Harry Fischel Institute for Research in Talmud.

When I arrived home I found that the children had received a cable from Palestine that their father had been married to an English woman. It took me some time to convince the children that I did not break my promise to wait until the year was over. I assured them that I had not married. However, I informed the children that before leaving Palestine arrangements were made for Miriam to join me in America at the end of January.

Miriam arrived in New York on January 28th, 1936, and we were happily married in Atlantic City at the home of the Rabbi on February 6th. Thanks to the Almighty we are as happy today as we were the day we were married.

Soon after our marriage we began to make plans to go to Palestine as soon as possible. As time marched on, the Harry Fischel Institute had increased its activities, and accordingly the expense of the Institute had also been increased. The problem was to provide more income. The Government bonds which are the safest investment produced between 2 and 3%. We, therefore, decided to take some chances and invest some money in good real estate. We succeeded in purchasing the property at 1100 Grand Concourse, Bronx, New York, an unusually fine property. This added a substantial income to the Harry Fischel Foundation . The purchase of this property has helped greatly to the preparation of our plan to go to Palestine, with the result that on February 27th , 1937 we left for Palestine.

During my six former visits to Palestine, each time the anticipation of visiting Palestine again was considered by me a great event. This seventh time was of greater consequence for the fact that I had additional interests, namely, the hope of seeing my father-in-law, the great and celebrated author, Rabbi Aaron Hyman. I was looking forward to the great pleasure of spending some time with him and giving him an opportunity to enjoy the happiness existing between my dear wife and myself. However, the Almighty saw fit to deprive me of this pleasure, because three weeks before we left for Palestine the sad news reached us that he had already passed away.

CHAPTER 22

ARRIVAL IN PALESTINE THE SEVENTH TIME

We arrived on March 11th in Lud, about ten miles from Jerusalem, where we met Rabbi Dove Kook, the Registrar of the Harry Fischel Institute, and Rabbi Saul Lieberman, the Dean of my Institute, who came to meet us. We arrived in our Institute and were taken into the Synagogue, where a prayer was offered by all the scholars, thanking the Almighty for our return to Palestine.

In the evening a reception was arranged by our scholars and the worshippers of our Synagogue. It lasted for several hours, and at the conclusion of the reception, a petition was presented to me by the gabai of my Synagogue requesting to enlarge the Synagogue, which could not accommodate the many refugee worshippers who had settled in this neighborhood. I lost no time in preparing plans, and in four weeks the alteration was completed, adding about 100 seats to the Synagogue, and the new decoration of the entire Synagogue.

CHAPTER 23

DEDICATION OF MY MAUSOLEUM ON MOUNT OF OLIVES

It has been the desire of every Jew, beginning with our father Abraham, to be buried in Palestine. The next mention in our Bible is that Jacob asked his son Joseph, the ruler of Egypt, that his remains shall be taken to Palestine. Then Joseph left a request with the Jewish people that when they would be redeemed from Egypt, that his remains shall be taken to Palestine. And as history tells us, since that time, it has been the desire of everyone, man or woman, to have the privilege to be buried in Palestine, especially on the Mount of Olives.

With this in mind I decided to take advantage of my stay in Jerusalem and build a mausoleum. For this purpose I purchased a large plot on the finest part of the Mount of Olives. I paid for same about the same price as our Father Abraham paid for the entire Me'oras Hamachpayla. I then prepared plans for the structure. I gave out contracts and have watched the construction with the same interest as I had in my large structures in New York, and probably more, considering that this is my future home. This building adds credit to the Mount of Olives.

When the building was finished, a dedication was held on June 8, 1937, attended by a large crowd, presided over by the Chief

Rabbi [Herzog]. The program consisted of first burying *shamos*, meaning the out-used (worn-out) religious books, which according to law must not be destroyed. Then speeches by the Chief Rabbi and many other Rabbis, prayers and psalms by a Cantor and a choir. Also music. Then Mincha was recited and the program was closed with buffet refreshments and drinks of all kinds. I was the recipient of a blessing from the Chief Rabbi that I shall have the privilege to visit this holy place for twenty-five years and always go back. To this everyone chanted, Amen, in such a voice, that I am confident that it reached Heaven. I am also sure that the blessing was accepted and so ordered.

There are many people who order in their will to be buried in Palestine. Some of these wishes are never carried out because of different reasons. Some are buried in their home temporarily and then transferred to Palestine. It is my wish, and I pray to the Almighty, that when my time comes to pass over to the better world, I shall then be in Palestine to be taken directly to the ohel which I have erected during the best time of my life.

This celebration was a sight which was never seen before. Automobiles were furnished by me for the entire crowd of more than 100.

CHAPTER 24

DECISION TO PUBLISH THE MISHNA

As I stated before, during the time from 1935, when I left Palestine, until our arrival in February 1937, the Harry Fischel Institute, under Rabbi Lieberman, had published a scholarly work. With this work completed, the question then came up, what will be the next work for the Harry Fischel Institute. For this purpose, my wife and I called on Dr. Joseph Klausner, one of the best-known scholars the world over. I called on him with my wife, because she has a great knowledge of literature; besides, she is the daughter of Rabbi Aaron Hyman, who is the author of several scholarly and useful books.

I told Dr. Klausner that the Harry Fischel Foundation, with its investments in New York, is maintaining the Harry Fischel Institute for Research work in Jerusalem, and is ready to finance a work of vital importance which should be used, not only by scholars, but should also be appreciated by a man with less knowledge. Whereupon Dr. Klausner suggested that he wanted a few days to think it over. He would also like to talk it over with Rabbi Lieberman, the Dean of the Institute. I lost no time, and on Sunday, July fourth, a conference was held and different works were suggested by both Dr. Klausner and Rabbi Lieberman.

Finally, Dr. Klausner suggested that the Institute should prepare and publish a new version of the six tracts of the Mishna. He stated that since print came into existence about 500 years ago, fourteen different versions have been printed in different places and in different generations. Many important subjects have been omitted on account of censorship, and many other matters have been added. Besides, there are many manuscripts hidden in the important libraries, such as the Vatican and in Oxford, which have never been printed. Dr. Klausner also suggested that all of these fourteen sets should be obtained, also copies of the unprinted manuscripts, and collaborate in one. This idea, while a very costly project, appealed to me, and without any hesitation, I consented.

The next question was, will Rabbi Lieberman undertake to carry out this gigantic work? With this idea in my mind, my wife and I were very happy. However, the next morning Rabbi Lieberman did not come to the Institute as usual and was absent for three consecutive days. He could not be reached at home or anywhere else. Naturally we were very much worried, fearing that something had happened to him, G-d forbid, or he might have left the Institution for fear of this great undertaking. Finally, three days later, early in the morning, Rabbi Lieberman entered our apartment, full of joy and contentment, and made the following statement, "Mr. and Mrs. Fischel, the suggestion of creating a new version of the Mishna is a colossal work and will cost an enormous amount of money. Before I was to undertake this work, I wanted to decide for myself whether I can undertake it. I have, therefore, closed myself in my library since I left you, and after I have given this matter due consideration, I am ready to undertake to prepare and publish a new version of the Mishna and also include a new commentary by our own scholars. Therefore, as far as we are concerned we are ready. Now are you ready to give us a free hand to buy all the necessary books, buy some manuscripts and obtain photostatic copies of hundreds of manuscripts in different libraries?" My wife and I were so pleased with the enthusiasm of Rabbi Lieberman, that we told him, "Rabbi, you have my full consent, and with the help of the Almighty, go on."

CHAPTER 25

APPROVAL BY RABBIS TO PUBLISH THE MISHNA

At the suggestion of Rabbi Lieberman, I called a conference of the most outstanding Rabbis, with the Chief Rabbi Dr. Herzog at the head. I declared to them that on behalf of the Harry Fischel Foundation, we agree to finance the publication of a new text of the six tracts of the Mishna, which is to be a popular edition containing the text and commentary by our own scholars. The text and the commentary is to be translated into English in order to give an opportunity to *bal habatim* in the English-speaking countries to study the Mishna.

At first the Rabonim suggested that the English translation should be published in the back of the volume. I proved to them that this would not answer the purpose, because in this way the

Hebrew would be entirely forgotten. I suggested that the translation shall be on the same page, right under the Hebrew text and after spending a whole evening, it was finally decided that we first publish this popular edition, consisting of the revised text of the Rav and a commentary by our own scholars. The text and commentary shall be translated into English; also a scholarly edition with many commentaries, including the translation of the Rambam from Arabic to Hebrew.

It was suggested that many thousands of the popular edition shall be printed. In fact there was a bid made by one of the Rabbis for the agency of this popular edition, to be sold in every English-speaking country. It was also decided that a scholarly edition should be published next and distributed to Yeshivas, libraries and outstanding Rabbis.

This meeting was attended by the Chief Rabbi Dr. Herzog, Rabbi Meltzer, Rabbi Charlop, Rabbi Hillman, Rabbi Berlin, Rabbi Dove Kook, Rabbi Lieberman, and myself. A resolution was drawn up and signed by everyone. This meeting has given me great spiritual pleasure, appreciating that the Almighty has granted me the great privilege of undertaking this most useful Jewish literature, the Holy Mishna. To this I was very much encouraged by the great leaders of our Jewish people, the most representative Rabbis of Palestine, with the Chief Rabbi Dr. Herzog at the head, and after receiving their blessings, I prayed to the Almighty to have the privilege to complete the entire six tracts of the Mishna during my life and residing in Palestine. To this they all said "Amen".

I am now looking forward to the time when the Almighty will bless the world with genuine peace, and that my wife and I shall have the privilege of going to Palestine and spending the rest of our lives in Jerusalem, watching and hoping to see the entire Mishna completed by the Harry Fischel Institute and published by the Harry Fischel Foundation.

CHAPTER 26

CHANGING OF SCHOLARS

I stated before that when the Institute was opened in November, 1931, we had engaged thirteen men for a term of five years. When I arrived in 1933 I engaged seven more. Some of them had left because they had obtained Rabbinical positions. Some have become *Rosh Hayeshivot*, and others obtained different positions, leaving only fifteen in 1937, but only ten were fit for the Mishna work. Then the problem arose as to how to dispose of the five others who were unfit for the Mishna work. There is a custom in Palestine that it is easy to engage men, but it is very hard to discharge them, especially married men with families.

I called the Rabbis together and organized an advisory board for the future to take care of matters which cannot be solved by Rabbi Dove Kook and Rabbi Lieberman alone. At the meeting the question of disposing of the five men was settled. Some of them received a year's notice with pay, and some received six months salary and this problem was solved.

Rabbi Lieberman declared that we need more men to work on the Mishna. He suggested that we engage young, unmarried men, who had no home responsibilities, who could devote all of their time to this work. I then authorized them to engage ten young men, from the ages of 19 to 25. This was no problem. In two days time fifty young men had applied for the examination. Ten were selected by Rabbi Dove Kook and Rabbi Lieberman.

When I left Palestine in August 1937, Rabbi Lieberman informed me that most of these young men were great scholars and fit for Mishna work and might be better than some of the older men. In fact the translations of the Rambam from Arabic to Hebrew were done by one of the young men. I was also informed by Rabbi Lieberman that the English translation is being accomplished by a son of Dr. Herzog, who is a great scholar, both in English and in Hebrew.

CHAPTER 27

MY SEVENTY-SECOND BIRTHDAY

During the time I was engaged in the organization of the different requirements to start the work on the Mishna, a committee was organized to celebrate my seventy-second birthday. The plan was even more elaborate than the plan to celebrate my seventieth birthday. When the plans were brought to me, I told the committee that it was unnecessary to celebrate my birthday every year. Five years apart was sufficient. I also told them that it is my hope to celebrate my seventy-fifth birthday in my own institution. The plans for an elaborate celebration were abandoned, and my seventy-second birthday was celebrated by our own scholars and a few Rabbis representing the Institution and some of the worshippers in our Synagogue.

We left Palestine July 28th, 1937 with great satisfaction because during the five months we were in Jerusalem we solved many important problems. We made all arrangements to fill a long-felt need by Jewish scholars to publish a new revised edition of the six tracts of the Mishna, a work never tried before. The Almighty blessed me with the privilege to undertake this holy work.

We arrived in New York August 24th with the hope and prayer to the Almighty that our real estate shall improve in order that we shall soon be able to go back to Palestine and watch the progress of the Mishna work. While conditions did not improve, however, eight months later, in April 1938, we reserved passage on the *Queen Victoria* to go again to Palestine, but we were compelled to cancel our passage on account of the preparations for war. During the two years since we left Palestine, the first tract of the Mishna, known as *Zeraim,* was completed, ready for print. However, printing was impossible on account of Italians trying to get near to Palestine. Everything in the printing line was disorganized. We were, therefore, compelled to abandon the printing until conditions improve in Palestine.

As it happened that our Dean Rabbi Lieberman received a call from the Jewish Theological Seminary in New York to come there as a visiting professor for one year. Rabbi Lieberman came here in October. We called a conference of the trustees of the Harry Fischel Foundation and decided that if conditions do not improve in Palestine, we may be compelled to print the first volume in New York. For this purpose we cabled to Palestine that copies of all the work should be made at once and sent to New York, to be print-ed, if necessary, under the direction of Rabbi Lieberman and Dr. Arthur Hyman, a brother of my wife, who is an expert in this work. We are now awaiting the first part of the work to be printed in New York, unless the Almighty will decide to bring peace soon, as we would rather print in Jerusalem, which is more preferable, since Rabbi Lieberman declared that he is waiting patiently to go back to Palestine and take charge of the work again.

A short time later, on January 27th, 1941, the Chief Rabbi of Palestine, Dr. Herzog, arrived in New York. Dr. Herzog is the President of the Harry Fischel Institute in Jerusalem and, as such, is thoroughly familiar with the progress of the Mishna work and also with conditions in Palestine. Naturally, I took advantage of the opportunity and had arranged a conference at my home between Dr. Herzog and Rabbi Lieberman, who is the Dean of the Harry Fischel Institute in Jerusalem, and after a great deal of discussion, we decided that as soon as Dr. Herzog will return to Palestine, and I hope very shortly, we will start printing the popular edition of the *Seder Zeraim* in Palestine.

The Chief Rabbi assured me that he will give his full coopera-tion to this work, as his son is the one who is translating the Mishna into English.

Rabbi Lieberman also reported that before he left Palestine, paper sufficient for this edition was purchased and is stored in our own building in Jerusalem.

CHAPTER 28

TEN YEARS OF ACCOMPLISHMENT

The ten years just past from 1930 to 1940 were the best in my life; while not financially, but spiritually, beneficially, and in self-preservation. Spiritually, because we succeeded in giving an opportunity to our scholars to increase their knowledge in the Talmudic studies; beneficially to twenty families who were provided with a living; self-preservation, because of the opportunity to perpetuate the name of Harry Fischel.

In the ten years the Almighty has given me the privilege to first establish the Harry Fischel Institute for Research in Talmud; second to establish the Harry Fischel Foundation, which made it possible to maintain this Institution; and third the perpetuation of the name Harry Fischel. Besides this, the Almighty has sent me my dear wife Miriam, at the time of my life when I needed a companion most, who has been of great assistance in my work from the first week I met her, through her ability, her cooperation, her influence and her inspiration. In spite of my adverse financial position, she urged me to continue this work as a labor of love to both of us.

The Almighty saw fit to prevent my celebrating my seventy-fifth birthday in Palestine. However, it is our intention to go to Palestine as soon as peace is declared, with the hope to remain there for the rest of our lives, in order to carry out the promise I made in 1923 at the dedication of the residence I built for the Chief Rabbi Abraham I. Kook and presented to the High Commissioner Herbert Samuel. On this occasion several Rabbis requested me to settle in Palestine. My answer was that now I can do more for Palestine by residing in

America at this time, but I expect to settle in Palestine when the Almighty will help me to reach the age of 80. I also promised that if the Messiah will come before, as we believe he will, and no doubt he must come to Palestine first, then the Chief Rabbi is to send me a cable and I will dispose of my real estate in New York and come to Palestine to help build the Temple, which is in my line of work. This was agreed by the Chief Rabbi, also by all those who were there. Everybody answered "Amen"!

Therefore, now at the age of seventy-five, as the time of my eightieth birthday is not far off, my wife and I are ready to make good my promise.

CHAPTER 29

MY WORK IN AMERICA

In my life's history, under the name of *Forty Years of Struggle for a Principle,* which was completed in 1927, the last chapter deals with laying the cornerstone for the Yeshiva Rabbi Isaac Elchanan Theological Seminary and leaving for Palestine. In this story, the continuation of my biography, I have recorded the additional work I have accomplished, thanks to the Almighty, during the ten years in Palestine, by creating and maintaining the Harry Fischel Institute for Research in Talmud.

I now take the privilege to record the work I have done at home in New York during the same time, especially for the Yeshiva and the Yeshiva College. For this purpose I must go back three years earlier from the time my late wife and I came back from Palestine in September 1927.

Upon our arrival I found that the construction of the Yeshiva building was progressing slowly. Then, as Chairman of the building committee, I took charge of the work of the building. In addition to this work, I was also compelled to take charge of the management of the entire Institution, because, to my great regret, I found that the President, Nathan Lamport, had passed away. I was then holding the position of First Vice President, so I was compelled to take the leadership. Having the additional responsibility, my time was occupied day and night, until the building was finished.

It took me some time to order and supervise the equipment of this large building, and for the dormitories. The next job was to prepare for a formal opening, which took place on December 9, 1928 in the presence of at least ten thousand (10,000) people. It would take a professional story writer to picture the opening of this, the finest Jewish institutional building in America, the pride of the American Jewish people.

I feel it my duty to record also in this narrative the financial problems which were also part of my duties to arrange for this great enterprise. The cost of the building and land including the equipment has reached the colossal sum of nearly two million five hundred thousand dollars ($2,500,000). A committee to raise the money required was appointed with Samuel Levy, Chairman. The committee arranged a dinner, and at this dinner over a million dollars was subscribed, from sums of $100 to $100,000. Two sums of $100,000 were subscribed, one by the late Nathan Lamport and one by myself.

Then, soon after the dinner a drive was made which resulted in getting subscriptions up to the amount of $3,000,000. The subscriptions of the larger amounts were to be paid in annual payments from five to ten years, in a legal form which was binding and negotiable. The largest majority of those subscriptions were made by real estate men who were very prosperous up to 1929, then as soon as the panic of October 1929 arrived the payments on this subscription stopped, except by a small number of us who have continued payments.

I want to record at this point, that before the building was finished I obtained a mortgage from the Title Guarantee and Trust

Company for $700,000, expecting to pay this mortgage from the monies to be collected from the subscription, but I was disappointed. We needed more money to pay the contractors, to pay for the equipment and other expenses, so I succeeded in borrowing $100,000 from the Chatham Phoenix Bank on the endorsement of sixteen directors, each one for $10,000. When this loan was due, only two of us, Samuel Levy and myself, paid the $10,000 each. Some paid part, and the rest have either filed legal excuses or were not responsible on account of the Depression. We also succeeded in borrowing $100,000 from the same bank on good pledges. We also owed Barth & Co. a balance of $90,000 on equipment. All the claims amounted to $232,000, and came into the possession of the Manufacturers Trust Co. We also borrowed from the Bank of the United States the sum of $100,000. On pledges, part of this amount was paid, leaving $68,000, for which they took judgments against the Yeshiva.

We also owed a balance of about $400,000 to the contractor. In addition thereto, the general income of the Yeshiva has been reduced on account of the Depression.

Therefore, as acting president and as chairman of the Building Committee, these financial troubles were more than I could carry myself. I called a meeting of the Board and asked them to relieve me from this great strain. My health was affected, but no one was willing to accept this responsibility. Then the late Rabbi M. S. Margolies, a personal friend of mine, decided to undertake the responsibility in order to relieve me. He stated that he felt as a Rabbi it was his duty, and he would maybe succeed in getting the cooperation of the directors. To my great regret, Rabbi Margolies was entirely disappointed. Those of the directors who had any responsibility had left the Institution.

Conditions went from bad to worse and the Institution was to close on July 15, 1932, with no chance to open in September.

CHAPTER 30

DESIRE TO OPEN THE YESHIVA

The happenings of this summer have made an indelible impression on my mind. As I was spending my vacation at Atlantic City, the late Dr. Bernard Revel and Rabbi Levinthal of Philadelphia called on me and informed me of the condition of the Yeshiva. I well remember their words. "Mr. Fischel, you have invested in this enterprise more than any man. You cannot afford to let the Yeshiva remain closed. We have tried every method and every one whom we thought we could interest, but we made no progress. You have carried the ship through all storms. It is your duty to open the Yeshiva on time to save our Jewish name."

It was a very hot summer; however, I went to New York immediately. On the way I was trying to prepare plans of how to begin. I decided to try to interest one who has not suffered in the Depression. The lot fell on the late Meyer Vessel, who, several times before, had spent the summer in Long Branch. I called on him, and I still remember our conversation. "Mr. Vessel, the lot fell on us to save the Yeshiva. It is a privilege that very few men can get in a lifetime. We need $100,000 to place the Yeshiva in a good position, but with $50,000 I can manage to open the building on time and keep it open. You and I will loan $25,000 each to the Institution." Mr. Vessel agreed and we both went to New York. We each deposited $25,000 with Samuel Levy, under an agreement that this money can only be available if we succeed in obtaining either loans or gifts of an additional sum of $50,000. With this understanding I went to the late Rabbi Margolies, the President, and we prepared a letter, reading as follows:

"Dear Sir:
It grieves me very much to inform you that the Yeshiva is closed

and I have done everything in my power to get people to come to our assistance, without any result.

Finally, a ray of sunshine has appeared. Mr. Harry Fischel and Mr. Meyer Vessel are willing to loan the Yeshiva $25,000 each, providing we will raise $50,000 additional.

If the Torah means anything to you, and if you have any respect for my old age, please come to our assistance in this time of distress, to save our Yeshiva, the only bulwark of our Jewish people in America."

This letter was signed by the Rabbi personally and was sent to every one of the directors and also to a number of the former subscribers, with the result that we waited two weeks and not a single dollar came in. I will never forget the disappointment of this great sage, seeing that the light of the Torah has been extinguished and no hope to rekindle it again. It was the Rabbi's expression of feeling that made me go on further.

In order to open the Yeshiva it required paying eight months interest on the mortgage, about $30,000, and eleven months salaries to the teachers at the rate of $5,000 per month.

I then went to the mortgagee and arranged to give them $10,000, for which they agreed to give us an extension for six months to pay the balance. I also agreed with the teachers to give each one three months pay, leaving the balance of eight months due for them for later. I decided to loan the $25,000 myself. However, I went to Mr. Vessel and offered him a partnership in this loan and to give him half of the *mitzvah*. Mr. Vessel accepted the offer. We both loaned $12,500 each for which we took notes to be paid at the rate of $1,000 per month; $2,500 of these notes were paid to each of us. The balance of $10,000 is still due to each of us. However, the Yeshiva was opened on time and the late Rabbi gave his blessing, and I had the great privilege to take off the stigma from our Jewish people in America.

Conditions commenced to improve from that time on, except that two years later in September 1934, the late Dr. Bernard Revel called on me with a sad story again, that he could not open the College in time because the professors had not been paid for several months. He needed $3,000. He had tried every which way to get a loan for this money, but he did not succeed. I was the only one on whom depended the opening the College. I gave him a check for $3,000 and the College was opened on time. It seems that this loan of mine was lucky, because since then conditions in the Institution have improved. Their income was sufficient to cover the expense. However, not a dollar could be saved for the reduction of the large obligations, with the result that judgments were taken against the Institution. The bank account was attached, a foreclosure notice was served by the mortgagee and the directors left the Institution one by one, fearing to be connected with a bankrupt institution.

As I stated before, my wife and I came home from Palestine in August 1937, with great satisfaction that the Harry Fischel Institute in Jerusalem had made great progress. While on the steamer, away from all thoughts of business, seeing G-d's creations around you, the mind is engrossed in nothing but the spiritual.

My wife and I decided that when we got home we would try to help our own Yeshiva, where I have put in years of hard labor. Besides, I had invested up to that time the large sum of $156,000. It also came to my mind the pleasure I enjoyed at the laying of the cornerstone, then watching the building going up, and above all, the opening of the building. Later on I had the privilege of making it possible to open the Yeshiva and the College when it was closed.

All this came to my mind. It made one feel that this institution is a part of my life. We then came to the conclusion that when we got home I would make every effort to try to relieve the institution of its colossal obligation. I lost no time.

As soon as we came, I made an investigation and found that the most urgent debt was to the contractors, amounting to about

$440,000, because they had started a foreclosure on a second mortgage they held on the Yeshiva property.

CHAPTER 31

CONTRACTORS' CLAIMS SETTLED

I well remember that several efforts were made before to settle this enormous amount of about $400,000, conferences being held without results. The best the contractors were ready to accept was not less than $100,000. However, on this occasion I was in a better position because the building was under a foreclosure by the first mortgagee, and after several conferences, I succeeded in buying the entire claims for $29,000. I gave them my own check of $5,0000 as a deposit. Then, with the assistance of Mendel Gottesman and Samuel Levy, we raised the balance, and the Yeshiva was released from the largest obligation. However, this claim was not discharged. We took an assignment in the name of the Yeshiva Endowment Fund, which I thought would help me to settle the other obligations.

CHAPTER 32

PURCHASE JUDGMENT FROM
THE BANK OF THE UNITED STATES

Next in line was the judgment held by the Bank of the United States, in liquidation for $68,000. For this purpose, I was compelled to make use of my acquaintance with the attorney for the bank in liquidation, also with the deputy of the bank examiner, to whom I was introduced by a man of high standing, which helped me considerably. I succeeded in settling this claim for the sum of $10,500. I had the contract drawn up by my attorney for the transfer of the judgment, and I gave them a deposit of my own money.

With this accomplished, I notified the temporary chairman of the Board of Directors, Hon. Samuel Levy.

A meeting was called and I reported my accomplishment, which was appreciated by everyone. I then suggested that this money should be subscribed by the board. I explained to them that with the removal of the obligation and judgment, every loan made to the Yeshiva is perfectly safe. However, no one was willing to make any loans. With my determination to relieve the Yeshiva from its obligations, I suggested to the board that the Harry Fischel Foundation would advance the money on condition that the Yeshiva shall assign to the Foundation some of the better subscriptions as security for the loan, and any additional loans which my Foundation would make. This suggestion was accepted by the board and a   resolution to this effect was passed by a unanimous vote, signed by those present.

Among these subscriptions was one from the late Nathan Lamport for the sum of $40,000. As soon as the assignment of the subscription was delivered to the Harry Fischel Foundation, I lost no time, paid the Bank of the United States the money and took the assignment of the judgment against the Yeshiva in the name of the Harry Fischel Foundation, thereby relieving the Yeshiva from the second large obligation.

I was thankful to the Almighty for this privilege of being able to carry out two-thirds of the plan I had prepared while on the steamer coming from Palestine. This was accomplished in a much shorter time than I ever expected, and for much less money than I anticipated, giving me more courage and a greater desire to continue the work to redeem the Yeshiva from all its obligations.

CHAPTER 33

PURCHASING CLAIM
FROM MANUFACTURERS TRUST CO.

The only claim left was to the Manufacturers Trust Co. for the sum of $232,000. I decided to handle this case differently from the way I had handled the other two cases, because in the case of the contractor I dealt with the chairman of the committee, who had worked for me for years. He himself was a real estate owner. He knew what the Depression had done to real estate. He also knew how much more the contractor had lost on other buildings.

In the case of the Bank of the United States it was a little harder, because it was in the hands of attorneys who had to get the approval of the court to the settlement.

In the case of Manufacturers Trust Co. I had to deal with a live institution and one of the largest banks in New York. I therefore decided to reach the head, the President, Mr. Gibson. It was not so easy to get an appointment with him. Fortunately, one of the Vice Presidents, Mr. Boyd, had known me for forty years. When he was manager of the Century Bank, which took over the Jefferson, I had dealings with him because I was the chairman of the Liquidation Committee of the Jefferson Bank. Since then we very often met, because I was a depositor in the Jefferson Bank. I went with the Jefferson Bank to the Century Bank, under the management of Mr. Boyd. Then the Century Bank was bought by the Chatham Phoenix Bank and I went with them. Eventually I came to the Manufacturers Trust Co., and having Mr. Boyd as my friend, I had no difficulty to get an appointment with Mr. Gibson.

CHAPTER 34

CONFERENCE WITH MR. GIBSON

I will never forget the reception extended to me by Mr. Gibson. I thought that half the battle was won, because once before I had such a reception by the President of the New York Central Railroad when I was introduced by the late Jacob H. Schiff. That reception brought great success. I therefore felt that in this case, too, the Almighty would guide me and lead me to success to clear the Yeshiva from this last obligation.

When our greetings were over, Mr. Gibson stated, "Mr. Fischel, I presume you came here not for your personal interest, because your reputation is well established in this bank, since you have paid up hundreds of thousands of dollars during the worst depression. Now, Mr. Fischel, what is your request, and before you state your case I will call in two of my associate officers, who I am sure will also be interested to hear your story." Then Mr. Gibson called in Mr. Van Elem and Mr. Faulkner.

I then proceeded, "Gentlemen, I am here on behalf of the Yeshiva Rabbi Isaac Elchanan [Theological Seminary] and the Yeshiva College. This institution is in existence for sixty years. Personally, I am connected with this institution for fifty-three years. During that period we have changed our buildings four times, in different locations in New York. In each instance, I had the privilege to be the Chairman of the Building Committee. Then in 1924, when the real estate men were prosperous, a few of us got together and decided to erect a large edifice with sufficient space to provide the need for future generations. For such an enterprise the estimate was to be about $3,000,000. As usual, such a campaign is started with a dinner. This dinner was an exception. We sold 1,000 plates at $1,000 each, making the sum of $1,000,000. Besides, subscriptions were obtained from $100 to $50,000. In a short time the subscriptions mounted up to nearly $3,000,000. Two of the subscriptions were for $100,000. each, one from the late Nathan Lamport and one from myself. Later on Mr. Lamport increased his to $200,000, and my own amounts to date [were increased] to $160,000, which is all paid, and most of the other large subscriptions were made in yearly installments, from five to ten years. Then came the 1929 Depression, and very few were able to meet the payments, with the result that we owe money to the contractors, interest on the mortgage, as we expected to pay off from the subscriptions. This mortgage is now being foreclosed. We owe your bank $232,000.

"I came to you, not as a Director of the Institution, but as the President of the Harry Fischel Foundation, [which] is willing to purchase this claim from you for the same price. We have just paid a claim of $68,000 from the Bank of the United States, in liquidation, namely at 12 1/2% percent, amounting in your case to about $30,000.

"I want to inform you that the Harry Fischel Foundation was established by me for charitable purposes only, and I have succeeded in having our Board of Trustees loan the amount necessary to give a deposit on the purchasing of the two bank claims, because we expect to collect the sum of $40,000 from the Lamport estate."

Well, my story and offer appealed very much to Mr. Gibson and his associates, especially when this offer came from me. However, Mr. Gibson stated that as an individual he sympathized with the Yeshiva, but as President of the bank he could not approve of this offer and make an exception to a Jewish institution, because there had been many such offers made by other institutions not Jewish, and it was the policy of the board not to entertain any settlements. He also told me that they had made one exception in the case of the Lafayette College, and that brought them lots of trouble, and the board had decided not to make any more exceptions, and if necessary they would rather lose the entire sum.

Then, while talking to them the Almighty came to my assistance with a new thought, and with great courage I made the following statement: "Gentlemen, the Harry Fischel Foundation is the owner of 1,000 shares of the Manufacturers Trust Company stock, and as a partner in the bank I feel it my duty, and take the liberty to warn you as officers, not to lose this offer of $30,000, because you will never see one dollar of this indebtedness, which also means a loss to my foundation. I beg of you to consider carefully before you turn down this offer."

This statement worked like magic. Their entire attitude was changed and Mr. Gibson asked me to increase the offer to $35,000, and he would advise the committee to accept and authorize their attorney to prepare the agreement. I asked them for one week's option, which they granted me.

Naturally, with such a victory I lost no time and ordered a meeting of the board. At this meeting I reported the entire episode. It took no time to convince the board of my accomplishment, and a resolution was passed unanimously, authorizing me to make the deal at $35,000. I then suggested that I was ready to give a deposit on behalf of the Harry Fischel Foundation. This offer was appreciated by the entire board, and was unanimously approved by the board.

I went to the attorney for the bank and told him that I was authorized to close the deal, and to my great surprise, the attorney informed me that my appeal to the board had made such a great impression, that they had decided to accept my offer of $30,000 instead of $35,000. The papers were drawn up, the bank agreeing to assign the claim of $232,000 to the Harry Fischel Foundation for the sum of $30,000. I gave the bank a check for $5,000 and agreed to pay the balance thirty days later, on January 10th, 1938.

The contract provided that if I fail to pay the $25,000 on that date, the deposit shall be deducted from the original sum of

$232,000. I signed the contract and gave a deposit of $5,000 as provided in the contract.

Words fail me to describe the pleasure I enjoyed when I left the office of the bank with the contract in my possession. This meant that my dream of clearing the Yeshiva from the last claim of $232,000 had come true, and especially since I had succeeded in making this purchase for such a small sum of $30,000, even $5,000 less than the amount approved by the board. However, my pleasure was marred when I found that the man who had made the promise to advance 50% of the amount required had backed out.

I tried hard to get someone, or a group, to invest the 50%, but without any success. If the Harry Fischel Foundation had the entire amount on hand, I would, no doubt, have induced the trustees to advance the entire amount. But since this was impossible, I was compelled to try other plans.

In the meantime, I succeeded in getting an adjournment for thirty days.

As I stated before, the claim against the Lamport Estate was assigned to the Harry Fischel Foundation for $40,000. As my next step, I went to the executors and to the attorney for the Lamport estate and suggested that they advance the $25,000 necessary to pay the bank. I offered to wait for the $4,000 advanced by the Harry Fischel Foundation for the deposit on the contract, also for the $10,500 advanced by the Harry Fischel Foundation too for the purchase of the judgment from the Bank of the United States in liquidation. This $15,500 deal could wait as long as they desired and without any interest.

I also went to the sons of Nathan Lamport and pleaded with them that their father had signed an agreement to pay this money. He had provided the money with which to pay. I said, "You are therefore in duty bound to carry out your father's desire."

The result was that one of the sons not only refused to grant my request, but stated that they would fight the claim in court, even if they had to pay the entire amount for legal expenses.

Realizing the position that we will never collect the $40,000 unless we take legal action, I decided that it was my duty, as the custodian of this claim, to start a legal action.

Accordingly, I engaged an attorney to bring suit against the executors, compelling them to file an accounting of the estate, which they should have done ten years earlier. The executors were served, and they then realized that they could not get away simply by refusing to pay. Then the attorney for the estate requested an extension of time in which to file the accounting. This extension was granted by us, from time to time, for a period of two years. We felt that we might get the money much sooner in this way, until we were convinced that they were playing for time. Then our attorney went to the judge of the Surrogate Court and explained the entire situation to him. The judge was very much impressed with the patience we have shown.

The judge sent for the attorney of the estate and advised him to pay the $40,000. Otherwise they would have to pay interest on this sum which was due several years ago.

The attorney saw that all these tactics would not work any longer, so he promised to produce the $40,000, providing the attorney for the Harry Fischel Foundation would agree to relieve the Lamport estate from any expenses whatsoever. This was promptly agreed upon by our attorney. The check was delivered to the judge, and the Harry Fischel Foundation contributed the sum of $2,400 for the legal expenses to Albert Wald, the attorney and trustee of the Harry Fischel Foundation, which was probably one-half of the amount which would have been charged by another attorney.

Once we were assured of the money, I lost no time and went to the attorney for the bank, Harry Kaufman, an old friend of the

Yeshiva and of mine, and informed him that the money was there, and that he should try to get the bank to accept the $25,000 in accordance with the original contract signed about two years earlier. To my great surprise the bank accepted the $25,000, omitting even the interest, to which they were entitled on the $25,000 for two years.

The matter was closed and the Yeshiva was freed from the large obligation of $232,000. While I was happy at the times I relieved the Yeshiva on the two former occasions, the settlement with the contractor and the Bank of the United States, there was no comparison with my happiness when I accomplished my entire job of clearing the Yeshiva from every obligation, except the mortgage on the property, which is expected to be settled shortly.

CHAPTER 35

REORGANIZING THE YESHIVA

With all the obligations of the Yeshiva removed, I decided that now was the time to reorganize the Institution, to get a new board of responsible men to undertake maintaining the Institution and to bring it to the high position which it should occupy in the educational field.

I reminded myself that some time ago my good son-in-law, Rabbi Herbert S. Goldstein, had prepared a complete plan to reorganize the Yeshiva, but the time was not ripe, because of the indebtedness. I had a conference with Rabbi Goldstein, in order to revive his plan.

Accordingly, in consultation with Mr. Sarr, we made a list of about thirty outstanding men. We invited them to a meeting at my home on October 9th, 1939. Twenty-one answered the call, and right then and there we organized a committee to elect a Board of Directors and the necessary officers. Rabbi Goldstein accepted the chairmanship of this committee.

I am proud to record that this committee, under the leadership of my son-in-law, Rabbi Goldstein, has succeeded in organizing an excellent Board of Directors, with outstanding men as officers. The existence of the Yeshiva is now assured.

I must confess that I am now taking a retired position, since the Institution is now out of obligation, and for this I am thankful to the Almighty that He gave me the privilege to accomplish this through the Harry Fischel Foundation. I therefore feel that at the age of 75, having given to the Yeshiva fifty years of active service, and having the privilege to subscribe and pay the sum of $160,000 according to the records of the Yeshiva during the last fifteen years only, I therefore feel that I am entitled to retire from active work. However, I am watching the work done by the new board, and I am ready to give my cooperation and advice based on my fifty years of experience.

I am happy to record that only about one month ago the Harry Fischel Foundation purchased $5,000 worth of bonds which helped to provide a majority of bonds for the mortgage on the Yeshiva building, thereby removing and discontinuing the foreclosure of the mortgage.

CHAPTER 36

THE DEATH OF DR. BERNARD REVEL

This record would not be complete if I failed to record the loss to the Yeshiva by the death of our leader, Dr. Bernard Revel, a prince in Israel, who passed away. The loss sustained by the Yeshiva and by its students is impossible to describe. His place can never be filled by any one man who could possess all the qualities of Dr. Revel.

I had the privilege of being in close touch with him during the twenty-five years that our Yeshiva was blessed with his leadership. Many times Dr. Revel disclosed to me his heartaches, his sufferings for the Yeshiva. Personally, I lost the best friend and adviser.

Only a short time ago Dr. Revel attended a meeting, at my home, as a member of the Advisory Board of the Harry Fischel Institute for Research in Talmud in Jerusalem. The Advisory Board will also miss him. His knowledge in the field of higher learning cannot be filled, and the institution will suffer this great loss.

As a friend I was closely acquainted with his family life. The attention given to him by his wife under adverse conditions is to be admired. She devoted all of her strength to bring him relief. She consoled him in all his grief, on account of the Yeshiva. I am very happy that I brought before the Board of Directors the necessity of providing a pension for Mrs. Revel, which is the best tribute the board could have paid to their leader, who died as a martyr to the cause of the Yeshiva.

CHAPTER 37

AS TREASURER OF THE HIAS

There are two more events which I feel should be included in this record. One began fifty years ago, but was celebrated last May. Namely, the HIAS, the Hebrew Immigrant Aid Society. I was elected Treasurer in 1890, and I was privileged by the Almighty to serve in this capacity for fifty consecutive years. Last March I was again re-elected for the fifty-first time.

Soon after election the President, Abraham Herman, called on me and presented to my wife and myself an elaborate plan for a public dinner commemorating my fiftieth anniversary of holding the position as Treasurer, also celebrating my 75th birthday. My wife and I decided that it was not advisable at this time to make such a public celebration. We told Mr. Herman that while we fully appreciated the honor and the good will of our directors, however, when our Jews all over the world were suffering, the expense of such a dinner could be used for a better purpose. Instead, we suggested to tender a dinner to the board in our own home. This offer was accepted by Mr. Herman, and this dinner was held on May 16th, 1940, and was attended by the entire board of the HIAS, also by my own family.

CHAPTER 38

AS PRESIDENT OF THE PILGRIM STATE HOSPITAL

The other event is of ten years duration. This event is probably not so important to the community, but it has given me lots of pleasure and contentment.

In September, 1930, Franklin D. Roosevelt, then Governor of the State of New York, sent for me and offered me the position as a member of the Board of Visitors of the Pilgrim State Hospital for the Insane, the largest such institution in the world, accommodating 12,000 patients. This institution had just been completed. The board consisted of four men and three women members.

Mr. Roosevelt informed me that he had appointed six members of other nationalities and myself, representing the Jewish people, who comprised about 15% of the patients. He also informed me that he had selected me on account of my connection with the Beth Israel Hospital. Soon thereafter I was requested by the State Commissioner of Mental Hygiene, Frederick W. Parsons, to call a meeting of the seven appointees for the purpose of electing a President and Secretary. I called a meeting at my office on October 20th. The Commissioner also came to this meeting. He introduced himself and informed us of our duties and privileges. Then, when it came to the election of a President, the Commissioner informed us that it was the desire of the Governor that Mr. Fischel be elected President. Naturally the election was unanimous. Up to this date I have never found out what was the motive of the Governor to have me as President, where there were three more men of very high rank.

When the year passed I was again elected President by a unanimous vote, which was repeated every year, and I am proud that I am still occupying the office of President, and in appreciation of my management, the board honored me with a portrait of myself, which is placed on the wall of the meeting room, with the portrait of Dr. Pilgrim, whose name the Institution carries, on one side, and on the other side is the portrait of Dr. Tiffany, the first superintendent, who is now occupying the position of Commissioner of the State.

The board meets every month. One meeting is held in the institution and one in my office. Our work is very constructive and interesting.

CHAPTER 39

PUBLICATION IN MEMORY OF JANE FISCHEL

The Harry Fischel Foundation in conjunction with the Jane Fischel Memorial Fund has just received from Palestine, a very important work, a book of ethics, written by the well-known sage, Reb Alexander Ziskind (ca. 1735–1794), 150 years ago, under the title *Yesod Veshoresh Hoavodo*. He was a great-great-grandfather of Jane Fischel. This book was published for the first time in 1790, then was republished in 1840, and again in 1875.

It is being used in the *Yeshivoth* practically the world over as the best book on ethics, and it is practically impossible to obtain in any bookstore. It was, therefore, decided by the Trustees of the Harry Fischel Foundation and the Jane Fischel Memorial Fund to republish this important work in a more elaborate form of printing and binding, with an English synopsis, which has been revised by Rabbi Dove Kook, the Registrar of the Harry Fischel Institute in Jerusalem. This book is now being distributed to *Yeshivas* and libraries, also to important Rabbis free of charge.

This book has been published in memory of the late Jane Fischel, my late wife, let her soul rest in peace.

CHAPTER 40

PURCHASE OF 987 FIFTH AVENUE

I mentioned before that I had purchased two parcels of real estate with money belonging to the Harry Fischel Foundation. Both of these purchases were in the best locations in the Bronx, on the best part of the Grand Concourse, promising an excellent future as far as anyone can foresee, but each one is subject to a bank mortgage at 4% interest . However, the Depression proved that no property is safe unless it is free and clear of any mortgage. Therefore, my last investment for the Harry Fischel Foundation has been the property at 987 Fifth Avenue, which is free and clear of any mortgage.

The history of 987 Fifth Avenue is unusual and it is worthwhile recording in this narrative. This building was a palatial residence, built by a famous New York millionaire, at a cost of over $300,000.00. There was a mortgage on this property held by the Franklin Savings Bank of $125,000.00. After the Depression, the bank foreclosed this mortgage and bought in the property. They held it about five years, paying taxes, without receiving any income from it. Then the property was sold to me for $40,000.00. When this purchase was recorded in the newspapers, comments were made that it was the cheapest property ever sold in New York, especially on the finest part of Fifth Avenue. I purchased this property for the Harry Fischel Foundation, and had the house reconstructed for thirteen families, at an expense of about $50,000. Adding this to the cost of purchase of $40,000, the property cost the Foundation about $90,000, and is free and clear of any mortgage. At this time the house is about 90% rented and produces a very fine income for the Harry Fischel Foundation.

CHAPTER 41

BEGAN STUDYING THE TALMUD AT 69

Our sages state that the best is always left for the last. In the paragraph entitled "TEN YEARS OF ACCOMPLISHMENT," I enumerated several of the achievements I was privileged by the Almighty to accomplish. However, I left for the last the most important accomplishment, namely, the beginning of my studies in Talmud at the age of 69.

There is, no doubt, many a man who has duplicated my work in philanthropy, and there are, no doubt, several competitors of mine who have spent large fortunes for religious education, and there is probably some man somewhere in the world who has created an institution for research work in Talmud. However, our Jewish history does not mention anyone who began studying the Talmud at the age of 69. However, history does tell us that one of our greatest sages, Rabbi Akiva, started his education at the age of 40. Therefore, in this accomplishment of starting to study the Talmud at 69, I stand alone, for which I am especially thankful to the Almighty for giving me the privilege to do so.

In my first biography, known as *Forty Years of Struggle for a Principle*, I have elaborated on my youth. However, in this narrative I will only mention one fact, and that is that I came to America at the age of 20, coming from a small town in Lithuania, and of poor parents. I had no opportunity to acquire very much Hebrew knowledge. I was, therefore, content with the knowledge of the Bible only. However, since I came to our free country of America, where knowledge can be acquired without any hardship and without any cost, I immediately took advantage of the opportunity and began the study of the Mishna. At first I received a few lessons at home. Then I took advantage of a *Chevra Mishnaoth* which was studying every morning after prayers. I could not take up any higher learning, for the reason that my mind and my time were immediately taken up with the responsibility of communal work at the very beginning of my life in New York, with religious education and philanthropy, and as mentioned previously, that I became Treasurer of the HIAS in 1890, four years after my arrival in America, besides the responsibility of raising a family. Also, some time was required for my real estate business.

As time marched on, the communal problems increased, leaving no time for me to continue any higher learning. I was therefore content with the knowledge of the Mishna, which I can happily state that I never failed to study every morning during the last fifty years.

Then in 1931, when the Almighty gave me the privilege to create the Harry Fischel Institute for Research in Talmud, the love for the Talmud developed in me greatly, and became part of my natural life. I then realized that it was absolutely necessary for me to have some Talmudical knowledge in order to appreciate the value of the research work being done in my Institute in Jerusalem, and also to participate in a Talmudical discussion whenever the opportunity would present itself.

On January 3rd, 1935, my late wife passed away, let her soul rest in peace, at which time I was 69 years old. I then decided to go to Palestine and probably settle there permanently. It was then that I decided that the time had come for me to begin my studying of the Talmud. I immediately started with a friend of mine, Joseph Adler, a good scholar of the Talmud. During the last six years we have studied together three sessions every week. It was rather hard at the beginning, but after a short time, I mastered the principles of the Talmud. Today, after six years of study, we have completed five volumes. I am now in a position to state that the Talmud has become part of my life, and is the best relaxation for the mind in times like these. I can safely state that it is the studying of the

Talmud that has broadened my mind, and has given me a clear vision and understanding of how to solve difficult problems.

I pray to the Almighty that He shall grant me the privilege of continuing to study the Talmud for many, many years to come.

CHAPTER 42

IN CONCLUSION

When I finished my life's history in 1927, I then prayed to the Almighty to have the privilege of continuing my labors on behalf of religious education and philanthropy, so that I might, at a later date, be able to record additional efforts on behalf of these same religious and humanitarian principles.

Well, the Almighty answered my prayers. I have had the privilege to record again some of my accomplishments during the thirteen years from 1927, to the present date, January 1, 1941.

At the time I completed the story of my life in 1927, I was worth millions in equities in real estate; also some liquid assets, which I put away for my old age. However, in 1929, the Almighty saw fit to bring the general Depression and washed away all real estate equities, and mine included. However, I am thankful to the Almighty that He gave me the vision and privilege to organize the Harry Fischel Foundation. I assigned to this Foundation the liquid assets which I had saved, otherwise this money would also have been lost, together with the real estate, and it is with this saving that I created the Harry Fischel Institute in Jerusalem, and provided a fund to take care of this work as far as any human mind can foresee. For this I am especially grateful to the Almighty.

I again fervently pray and hope that I may be privileged to record additional work, and that the Almighty will see fit to bring peace and happiness to the world, and especially in Palestine, so that the work of the scholars of the Harry Fischel Institute in Jerusalem will go on uninterrupted.

I especially pray that my wife and I be privileged to settle in Jerusalem and enjoy the pleasure of seeing the six tracts of the Mishna completed.

Epilogue

Harry Fischel's rags-to-riches story stands out in two ways. One is his service to the Jewish community, especially in the field of education, and the other is his dedication to public service in general, to the point where at various times while still in his prime, he dedicated more time to public service than to making money for himself. For the eight-year period from 1903 to 1911, he focused his energies almost exclusively on his philanthropic work, and again later as Chairman of the Building Committee of Yeshiva College in the 1920s, and, to a significant extent, in keeping Yeshiva College from going bankrupt and closing during the Great Depression in the 1930s. Many people lost their fortunes during the panic of 1907, but because Harry Fischel was devoted primarily to philanthropic work during that period, he was insulated from the catastrophic effects of the panic, and his fortune was preserved. While it was affected by the Great Depression, particularly as to equities, the story of his life and his achievements after 1929 show that, particularly with his preserved liquid assets, Fischel still managed to do far more good on behalf of far more people after the Great Depression began than most philanthropists did before it hit. Fischel did not waver in his faith in God, and was rewarded for this faith.

Harry Fischel decided to live out his last years in Israel, but in a manner unlike any other philanthropist. In America, he lived on Park Avenue in New York City, then and now one of the most prestigious neighborhoods in the world, in a custom-built apartment in a custom-built apartment house. He had built it to accommodate his own religious requirements of a low floor that did not require him to use an elevator, and with a room with a removable roof to enable him to celebrate the religious holiday of Sukkot with maximum convenience. This is described in the book, at page 370, with a photograph facing the page. In order to accomodate the removable roof, there was no line of apartments above his apartment, and in consequence he gave up the rent he

471

would have received from all the tenants who would otherwise have lived above him, as can still be seen at 910 Park Avenue on the southwest corner of 80th Street and Park Avenue, in New York City. He could have easily lived out his final years in such luxury, or in similar luxury anywhere else. He chose, rather, to donate most of his remaining money to a foundation to support the Harry Fischel Institute (the Machon), as well as other charitable entities he had established and future projects not yet initiated, and to live out his final years in a relatively Spartan apartment adjacent to the religious school he had built in Jerusalem, which was then not nearly as well developed as most other major cities at the time; Israel was not yet an independent country, and was on the brink of turning into a war zone. The reason for this decision? He wanted to bask in the sounds of the Jewish studies in his institution throughout the day, on the highest level, from his ground-floor apartment, from when he woke up in the morning until he went to sleep at night.

Even this was not enough of a sacrifice. When fuel was rationed, Fischel insisted on allocating his share to the students of the yeshiva he had built. Rabbi Yosef Cohen, Of Blessed Memory, who had been a leading religious court judge in Israel and the head of the program for training religious court judges at the Machon, recalls Harry Fischel's couching his sacrifice in Jewish literary almost poetic terms; Fischel declared that he wanted his share of the fuel to go "to the *Choshen Mishpat*," an allusion to the section of the *Shulchan Arukh*—the *Code of Jewish Law*—which deals with monetary matters. The students of the *Machon* were already known throughout the world to excel in this area of study, which lent itself to their future specialization as judges in the courts to be set up in the country that was about to be created.

This too was not enough of a sacrifice. Efficient and frugal until the end, Fischel was so focused on having every resource channeled into his beloved institution that he had the habit of turning off lights himself if he found any left on. When he eventually fell off a chair while doing so, his resulting injuries could not be overcome. The "lesson" he thereby "taught" was that we must all abhor waste; even the owner or sponsor of an institution should make sure that its resources are not wasted. The deeper lesson, of course, is that all of us are custodians of our bodies for only a limited period of time, and we should not waste the time we have in them or any other resource in serving our Creator, nor should we sit back and wait for our Creator to turn off our lights!

Even in death, Harry Fischel continued to serve his people well. During his lifetime, he had arranged for a mausoleum to be built on the historic Mount of Olives overlooking Jerusalem for his final resting place. When he passed away, on January 1, 1948, the fighting for an independent country of Israel was in full swing, and the remains of dozens, some say hundreds, of deceased persons who had burial plots on this most historic cemetery, were piled up in hospitals unable to be brought to their designated eternal resting place. Because of Harry Fischel's contacts, the fighting was interrupted in his honor, with the special passage of an armed convoy of the British army bearing his body to its final resting place on the Mount of Olives. Once the convoy was arranged, the remains of many of these other Jews were transported along with the remains of Harry Fischel. One of the young men who accompanied his remains part of the way on that day recalled his presence there at a ceremony that took place in the Machon the year this supplemented book went to press, more than six decades later. So Harry Fischel continued to serve his people even in his very first posthumous hours, and he has continued to do so ever since.

And now, through the many institutions that Harry Fischel created, supported, and maintained, including the three institutions that came into being after the original biography was published, and projects current and future, the influence of Harry Fischel continues, it is hoped, to make the world a better place, especially the Jewish world, not only for a limited number of years to come, but to eternity.

AIR

Harry Fischel Institute for Research in Jewish Law
Machon Harry Fischel

The Harry Fischel Institute for Research in Jewish Law, known in Hebrew as Machon Harry Fischel, was founded by Harry Fischel in 1931. It is located on the corner of Israel Aharon Fischel Street, in the Bukharian section of Jerusalem, near the neighborhoods of Geulah and Meah Shearim.

Fischel had originally planned a network of Talmudic institutes with branches in Israel, Eastern Europe, and New York (see Ophir in references). He even purchased real estate in a prime location in New York, intending to use the annual rental income to fund these institutions. However, when the Great Depression wiped out the huge fortune invested in this property, Harry Fischel decided to proceed with his plans on a smaller scale. He focused exclusively on the Jerusalem site, where the best Talmudic scholars were to be found.

Fischel established the Harry Fischel Foundation for the primary purpose of supporting the Machon. He had originally earmarked a sum of money, relatively small for a man of his means, to make use of in his old age. However, upon seeing how transient one's material possessions are in this world, and how a financial fortune can disappear so quickly, he decided to utilize this nest egg for an eternal project—a Torah institute to carry on his name and values.

The Harry Fischel Institute enlisted the greatest minds of the yeshiva world in Israel. These scholars pursued a unique and demanding course of study, applying Talmudic teachings and principles to reach a thorough understanding of *halacha* (Jewish law). Until his passing, Fischel maintained a close connection with the individual scholars at the institute and took a personal interest in their needs. His active involvement contributed to the Machon's atmosphere of intense scholarship and pursuit of excellence.

The tradition of excellence established in his lifetime has continued through the generations, and the Machon still attracts the top scholars of the yeshiva world. Since there are many applicants for each space that opens up, the Machon can pick the "cream of the crop." Machon alumni have served as *dayanim* (judges) in the Jewish court system in Israel, as well as in many other rabbinical positions throughout the world.

The Machon's *Dayanut* advanced study program, training scholars to serve as judges in the religious court system, was a trailblazer that later served as a model for other specialized high-level schools to train judges. The Machon was also a pioneer in the area of researched Torah publications. In the mid-1930s, the Machon spearheaded the field of publishing advanced works produced by scholars, at a time when such publications were almost nonexistent, especially in Israel. The Research and Publication Department of the Machon still continues this tradition today. Among its projects are:

(1) *Halacha Pesukah*—a comprehensive compilation of Jewish civil law based upon the works of hundreds of *poskim* (decisors) and responsa throughout the generations.

(2) *Tosafot HaShalem*—a comprehensive collection of commentaries on the Torah written by the Tosafists, the great scholars of the twelfth and thirteenth centuries.

(3) *Birkat Eliyahu*—a commentary on the Vilna Gaon's writings on *Choshen Mishpat*, the section of the Code of Jewish Law on civil matters.

(4) *Rishonim* and manuscripts—advanced research on the works of the *Rishonim,* the early commentaries on the Talmud, with comparative studies of various manuscripts.

An official statement by Israel's influential Government Advisory Committee, which assigns funding for Torah research institutes, notes that the Torah publications of the Machon "are of paramount significance." It states further that the Machon's "*Halachah Pesukah, Tosafot Ha'shalem* and *Birkat Eliyahu* projects [are] of particular national importance."

The Machon houses Harry Fischel's beautiful, historic synagogue, where communal prayers take place daily as well as on *Shabbos* and *Yom Tov*. Lectures are delivered there from time to time by prominent Torah scholars, attracting large audiences. In addition, the Machon supports public study programs, both in the mornings for retirees and in the evenings for lay people from the nearby neighborhoods. Years ago, the Machon *beis medrash* used to be unique in housing a number of full sets of *Shas* (Talmud), a rarity in Jerusalem of yore. It was also reputedly the only *beis medrash* to provide central heating! It is no wonder that the Machon *beis medrash* became a meeting place for scholars from all parts of the city. Though these "rare luxuries" are now commonplace, the Machon *beis medrash* still attracts many visiting scholars and neighbors at all hours of the day and night.

The Machon also sponsors a professional, economically self-sufficient book bindery, which serves the binding needs of the Machon, and provides employment for elderly as well as mildly disabled individuals.

Eighty years after its founding, the Machon continues to flourish as a direct, lasting result of the beneficence and foresight of Harry Fischel.

Rabbi Hillel M. Reichel
Director, Machon Harry Fischel

The Harry Fischel School for Higher Jewish Studies, of Yeshiva University

From its inception, in 1945, the Harry Fischel School for Higher Jewish Studies of Yeshiva University has added a critically important dimension to the Bernard Revel Graduate School.

The student body of the Bernard Revel Graduate School is made up of diverse elements. Among M.A. students, some attend full-time and wish to complete their degrees in a single year, sometimes because they have postponed their attendance in law school, medical school, or other professional school—and occasionally their direct entry into the workforce—in order to enrich their Jewish education. Such professionals constitute a major resource for the Jewish community as a whole. Others hope to continue as doctoral students and begin their work as expeditiously as possible. The M.A. degree at the Bernard Revel Graduate School requires ten courses. Even the most diligent student may well find a workload of five courses a semester unrealistic. The summer session offered by the Harry Fischel School enables such students to take eight courses during the regular academic year and complete the requirements of the Bernard Revel Graduate School by taking two summer courses at the Harry Fischel School.

Other M.A. students are simultaneously enrolled in the Rabbi Isaac Elchanan Theological Seminary or the Advanced Talmud Program for Women on the Beren campus and cannot realistically take more than two courses a semester in the Bernard Revel Graduate School. For these students as well, the summer program at the Harry Fischel School provides a precious opportunity to further their education in as expeditious a fashion as possible.

Doctoral students, who may be spending time during the regular school year taking a course in an allied non-Jewish field at another university (two such courses are generally required) or preparing for language examinations, take advantage of the summer program at the Harry Fischel School to complete their requirements.

478

In addition, the summer program enables Yeshiva University to offer a variety of courses taught by distinguished visitors from Israel and elsewhere that it cannot offer at the Bernard Revel Graduate School during the regular academic year. Such courses enrich the university's offerings immeasurably.

David Berger

Ruth and I. Lewis Gordon Professor of Jewish History and Dean, Bernard Revel Graduate School of Yeshiva University.

THE RABBI ISAAC ELCHANAN THEOLOGICAL SEMINARY
AND YESHIVA COLLEGE
AMSTERDAM AVENUE & 186TH STREET
NEW YORK

June 11th, 1945

OFFICE OF THE PRESIDENT

Mr. Harry Fischel, President
Harry Fischel Foundation
910 Park Avenue
New York 21, New York

Dear Mr. Fischel:

In connection with the Agreement signed this date, June 11th, 1945 between the Harry Fischel Foundation, and the Yeshiva Rabbi Isaac Elchanan Theological Seminary and Yeshiva College, I hereby agree as President of the Yeshiva:

1. Since the Agreement will not be in operation until September 1st, 1945, after the Summer Session, as stated in the letter attached to the Agreement. However, we agree to withhold any publicity until September when the Agreement shall begin, unless authorized by the President or Vice-President of the Foundation prior to that date.

2. It is also understood that should any one of the students take courses in both the Harry Fischel School for Higher Jewish Studies, and also in the regular Graduate School then in the event that the student should attend two Summer Sessions or more in the Harry Fischel School of Higher Jewish Studies then he shall be entitled to receive his higher degree only in the Harry Fischel School for Higher Jewish Studies.

3. Students who have attended our Summer Graduate School in 1944, and will continue with their work in 1945 will have their accumulated credits transferred to the Harry Fischel School for Higher Jewish Studies so that they may receive their degree from that School.

I am looking forward, with the help of the Almighty, that the Harry Fischel School for Higher Jewish Studies which will begin in July, 1946, will be a model School for higher Jewish learning which will enhance the spirit of traditional Judaism in America, and will give an opportunity to Rabbis, scholars, and teachers to equip themselves in even a more effective scholarly leadership in the spirit of our sacred traditions. I firmly believe that with the establishment of this School, a new chapter will be written in the Jewish History of America.

May the Almighty bless you with many years of good health, happiness, and joy from this School, as well as the Harry Fischel Institute for Talmudical Research, in our Holy Land, in Jerusalem.

With kindest personal regards, I remain

Sincerely yours,

Samuel Belkin

Samuel Belkin
President

sb;rs

THIS AGREEMENT made and entered into this *11* day of *June*, 1945, y and between "HARRY FISCHEL FOUNDATION", a body corporate, organized, created nd existing under and by virtue of the laws of the State of New York, hereinfter called the "Foundation", and "THE RABBI ISAAC ELCHANAN THEOLOGICAL SEMI-ARY AND YESHIVA COLLEGE, INC." a body corporate, organized, created and existng under and by virtue of the laws of the State of New York, hereinafter called he "Yeshiva",

W I T N E S S E T H:

WHEREAS, "Harry Fischel" established and is the moving spirit of the Foundation" and has spent the greater part of his life in sponsoring and upporting orthodox Jewish institutions and in propagating and enhancing orthoox Jewish ideals and education, and in that regard was one of the early founders nd liberal supporters of the "Yeshiva", and

WHEREAS, the "Foundation" is desirous of perpetuating the names both f its founder, "Harry Fischel", and of itself, and

WHEREAS, "Harry Fischel" and the "Foundation" have requested the Yeshiva" to establish the "Harry Fischel School for Higher Jewish Studies", and

WHEREAS, the "Yeshiva" is willing so to do upon the terms and condiions hereinafter stated,

NOW, THEREFORE, in consideration of the premises and the agreements erein contained and the sum of one ($1.00) dollar and other good and valuable onsiderations by each of the signatories hereto to the other in hand paid at r before the ensealing and delivery of these presents, the receipt whereof is ereby acknowledged, it is agreed as follows:

1. That the "Yeshiva" shall create a Graduate School to be known as he "Harry Fischel School for Higher Jewish Studies", which shall be associated cademically with the "Harry Fischel Institute for Research in Talmud in Jeru-alem".

2. That the purpose and object of such School shall be to train Yeshiva" graduates or any other Rabbis and scholars found eligible for admission y the faculty, to do original research in the field of Rabbinics and cognate ubjects.

3. That the said "Harry Fischel School for Higher Jewish Studies" hall require students to establish academic residence during the months of uly and August, and to continue their personal research work throughout the ear, wherever they may reside, under the direct guidance of the faculty of the aid School, who shall also assist them in the preparation of their theses.

4. That students who seek admission to said "Harry Fischel School for igher Jewish Studies" shall be required to have to their credit an academic egree of either Bachelor of Science or Bachelor of Arts from a recognized ollege, plus an accredited "Smicha". That the faculty shall have the right

to accept any other students who are in their opinion eligible to do research in the field for which said School is to be created as aforestated. Students of the "Harry Fischel Institute for Research in Talmud in Jerusalem", however, who shall be ordained Rabbis and who possess Palestinian State matriculation, shall be admitted to said "Harry Fischel School for Higher Jewish Studies" without a bachelor's degree.

5. That the subjects to be taught in said "Harry Fischel School for Higher Jewish Studies" are as follows: a) Rabbinical Codes; b) Jewish Philosophy; c) Jewish History; d) Cognate Subjects; e) Languages; f) Practical courses in community leadership; g) Courses in higher Jewish education and any other subjects that the faculty may see fit.

6. That the students who shall fulfil all residence requirements of said "Harry Fischel School for Higher Jewish Studies", and who shall write a thesis in Rabbinics or in a cognate subject which shall in the opinion of the faculty constitute a genuine contribution to scholarship, will receive the degree of Doctor of Hebrew Literature from said School, being part of the Yeshiva, or the future University as soon as charter will be granted.

7. That in order to induce the "Yeshiva" to found, maintain and bear the expenses of said "Harry Fischel School for Higher Jewish Studies", and in consideration thereof, the "Foundation" agrees to pay to the "Yeshiva" the sum of ten thousand ($10,000.00) dollars, annually, in equal quarter-annual payments of twenty-five hundred ($2500.00) dollars each during the months of August, November, February and May in each and every year, which said payments so to be received from the "Foundation" shall be deposited by the "Yeshiva" in a separate bank account in the "Yeshiva's" name and shall be used exclusively for the instruction only, and all other expenses be paid by the "Yeshiva" in running the said School, except that from said annual sum of ten thousand ($10,000.00) dollars, up to two thousand ($2,000.00) dollars thereof may be used for publications, the form, subject matter and scheme whereof shall be under the direction of the faculty of the "Yeshiva" but shall be published under the auspices of the said "Harry Fischel School for Higher Jewish Studies", it being agreed that any part of said two thousand ($2,000.00) dollars thereof may also be used for the purpose of publishing any other scholarly work in connection with and beneficial to the said School. No check shall be drawn against the aforementioned annual fund of ten thousand ($10,000.00) dollars without a voucher therefor approved in writing by the president of the "Yeshiva".

8. It is further mutually agreed that if the "Yeshiva" shall receive a charter granting to it the status of a University, then the said "Harry Fischel School for Higher Jewish Studies" shall become a part of the University and its graduates shall receive the degree of Master of Arts and/or the degree of Doctor of Philosophy, when and if entitled to the same, from the said University.

9. It is also mutually agreed that the said "Harry Fischel School for Higher Jewish Studies" shall always be conducted in accordance with the law and spirit of Orthodox Judaism.

10. This agreement shall be binding in perpetuity upon the signatories hereto and their respective successors and assigns.

IN WITNESS WHEREOF, this agreement has been duly executed by the parties hereto the day and year first above written.

HARRY FISCHEL FOUNDATION

By _Harry Fischel_
President

THE RABBI ISAAC ELCHANAN THEOLOGICAL SEMINARY AND YESHIVA COLLEGE, INC

By _____
Chairman,
Board of Directors

THE RABBI ISAAC ELCHANAN THEOLOGICAL SEMINARY AND YESHIVA COLLEGE, INC

By _Samuel Belkin_
President

Additional References to Harry Fischel

"Fischel, Harry." In *Encyclopaedia Judaica,* 1st ed. (New York: Macmillan, and Jerusalem: Keter, 1971), Vol. 6, cols. 1316–1317 (includes photograph).

"Fischel, Harry." In *Encyclopaedia Judaica,* 2nd ed. (Detroit: Thomas Gale and Thomson, Jerusalem: Keter, 2009), Vol. 7, cols. 51–52.

"Fischel, Harry." In *Universal Jewish Encyclopedia* (New York: Universal Jewish Encyclopedia, 1941), Vol. 4, p. 316.

Goren, Arthur A., *New York Jews and the Quest for Community: The Kehillah Experiment, 1908–1922* (New York: Columbia University Press, and Philadelphia: Jewish Publication Society, 1970).

Gurock, Jeffrey S., *The Men and Women of Yeshiva: Higher Education, Orthodoxy, and American Judaism* (New York: Columbia University Press, 1988).

Gurock, Jeffrey S., *When Harlem Was Jewish* (New York: Columbia University Press, 1979). Reviewed in Reichel, Aaron I., "When Harlem Was Jewish," *Tradition,* Winter 1980, pp. 374–375.

Klaperman, Gilbert, *The Story of Yeshiva University: The First Jewish University in America* (Toronto: Macmillan & Collier-Macmillan, 1969).

Levine, Yitzchok, "The Multimillionaire Who Remained True to Orthodoxy," *Jewish Press,* April 19, 2006 (front and back pages).

Levine, Yitzchok, "Harry Fischel (1865–1948) Orthodox Jewish Philanthropist— [Part] I," *Jewish Press,* May 3, 2006, p. 36.

Levine, Yitzchok, "Harry Fischel (1865–1948) "Orthodox Jewish Philanthropist Par Excellence—[Part] II," *Jewish Press*, June 1, 2006. p. 70.

Levine, Yitzchok, "The Founding of Yeshiva Etz Chaim," *Jewish Press*, May 2, 2008, pp. 48, 49.

Ophir (formerly Offenbacher), Natan, "Rav Kook and Dr. Revel: A Shared Vision for a Central Universal Yeshiva?" *Torah u-Madda Journal*, vol. 15, 2008–09, pp. 188–208.

Pfeffer, Jacob, ed. *Distinguished Jews of America: A Collection of Biograph-ical Sketches of Jews Who Have Made Their Mark in Business, The Professions, Politics, Science, etc.* (New York: America Publishing Co., 1917, 1918), pp. 126–130.

Rakeffet-Rothkoff, Aaron, *Bernard Revel: Builder of American Jewish Orthodoxy* (Jerusalem and New York: Feldheim, 1972, 1981).

Reichel, Aaron I., *The Maverick Rabbi* (Norfolk: Donning, 1984; 1986).

Reichel, Aaron I., "Pioneers of American Orthodoxy: Mr. Harry Fischel and Rabbi Herbert S. Goldstein," *The Commentator* (April 18, 2005). Significantly revised and supplemented in:

Reichel, Aaron I., "Pioneers of American Orthodoxy: Mr. Harry Fischel and Rabbi Herbert S. Goldstein," in *My Yeshiva College: 75 Years of Memories*, ed. Menachem Butler and Zev Nagel (Brooklyn: Yashar Books, 2006), pp. 114—117.

Sherman, Moshe D., *Orthodox Judaism in America: A Bibliographical Dictionary and Sourcebook* (Westport & London: Greenwood Press, 1996).

"Torah Supporters," *Olomeinu,* Torah Umesorah—National Society for Hebrew Day Schools, April–May, 1976, pp. 9, 18.

Weissman Joselit, *New York's Jewish Jews: The Orthodox Community in the Interwar Years* (Bloomington and Indianapolis: Indiana University Press, 1990). Reviewed in Reichel, Aaron I., "New York's Jewish Jews: The Orthodox Community in the Interwar Years," *Tradition,* Fall 1991, pp. 94–99.

Ziegelman, Jane, *97 Orchard—An Edible History of Five Immigrant Families in One New York Tenement* (New York: Smithsonian/Harper Collins, 2010).

Illustrations to Continuation

HARRY FISCHEL AS HE IS TODAY AT THE AGE OF 75.

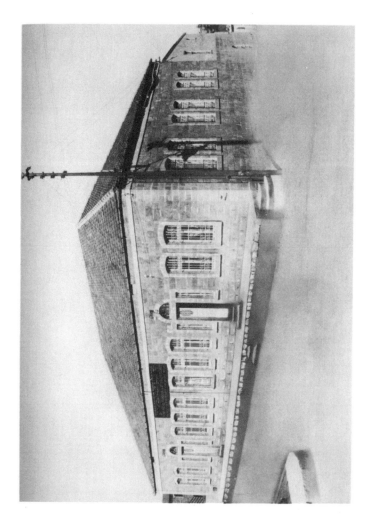

HARRY FISCHEL INSTITUTE BUILDING IN JERUSALEM.

*Original 20 scholars headed by the Chief Rabbi Abraham I. Kook,
his brother Dove Kook, the Registrar of the Harry Fischel Institute,
and Rabbi Braz, brother of my late wife.*

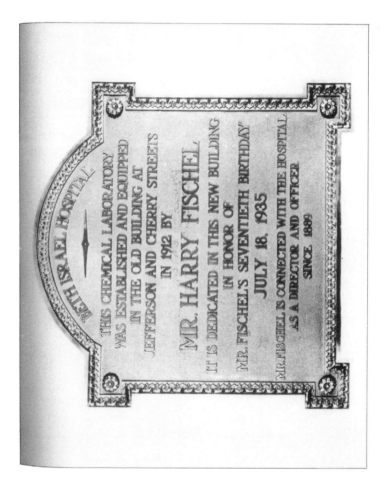

Medical laboratory dedicated to Harry Fischel in Beth Israel Hospital.

MY WIFE MIRIAM.

Interior of the Synagogue in the Harry Fischel Institute in Jerusalem.

MAUSOLEUM ERECTED ON MOUNT OF OLIVES IN JERUSALEM.

10 young scholars admitted in the Harry Fischel Institute on my visit in 1933.

*Opening of the Yeshiva Buildings on December 9b, 1928,
by the Building Committee, Harry Fischel, Chairman.*

*Portrait presented by the Board of the Pilgrim State Hospital
and placed in the Board Room.*

987 Fifth Avenue
Between 79th and 80th Streets

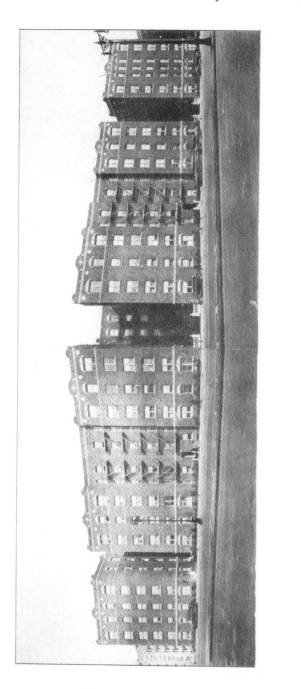

1454 to 1466 Grand Concourse
From 171st to 172nd Streets

1100 Grand Concourse
Northeast corner of 166th Street

Harry Fischel with his wife and all his grandchildren seated around the table in his succah room at 910 Park Avenue, in New York City, in the late 1930s. Left to right: Jean C. Rafsky, Ann E. Rafsky, Gabriel F. Goldstein, Simeon H. F. Goldstein, Josephine H. Goldstein, Harry Fischel, Miriam Fischel, Naomi Goldstein, Helen J. Kass, Babette Kass, Judy Wald, Neil Wald.

Supplemental Index

Note: This Index supplements the entries in the Index, at page 400, of the original volume, *Forty Years of Struggle for a Principle*, which is incorporated into the present book and also provides entries to all key names and words in the material published for the first time in this present book.

A

Aaron, 421.

Ackerman, Rochelle, 27a.

Adler, Joseph, 468.

Akiva, Rabbi, 467.

American Hebrew Symposium (Continued), "Are Jews Losing Their Religion?" 365–9.

American Jewish Relief Committee, Committee of Five, 131; 132; Committee of One Hundred, 132.

Amortization plan (Continued), 174–80.

Arab and Jewish harmony facilitated, 284; 332–3.

Architectural knowledge (Continued), Cooper Union, studies at, 21.

B

Bank of the United States, 449; 453; 454; 455; 459; 461.

Baruchow, Said, 414.

Bayara lawsuit, 426–8.

Beit Harav Kook, 16a; 23a; 238–41; completion of residence, 287; dedication of home and consecration of synagogue, 287–303; photo of ceremony opp, 302; organization of yeshiva, 361–2; photo on balcony with Chief Rabbi Kook, opp 390.

Belkin, Rabbi Dr. Samuel, 22a; 480; 483.

Bengal, Adam, 27a.

Berger, Dean David, 26a, 27a, 479.

Berlin, Rabbi, 442.

Bernard Revel Graduate School (affiliated with Harry Fischel School for Higher Jewish Studies), Yeshiva University, 16a; 20a; 478; 479.

Beth Hamedrash Hagadol, vice-president, xvi; 35.

Beth Israel Hospital (Continued), 42–6; further growth, 278–80; chairman, second building committee, 280; dedication, chemical laboratory, 280, 431; contributions to, 407; plaque, photo, 490.

Birkat Eliyahu, 476.

Birth, 2; 421.

Bnei Akiva, 23a.

Board of Education, Local School Board, elected secretary, 58.

Boyd, vice-president, 455.

Boyhood, 2–13.

Brandeis, Supreme Court Justice Louis D. (Continued), 252; 253; 270; 274; 276; 290; 305; used influence to secure letter from U.S. Sec. of State protecting H.F. on trip abroad, 288; gave credit to H.F. for initiating Palestine Building Loan and Savings Association, 331.

Brass (Americanized version of Braz). *See* Braz.